Speech and Language Therapy

The decision-making process when working with children

Second edition

Edited by Myra Kersner and
Jannet A. Wright

Routledge
Taylor & Francis Group

LONDON AND NEW YORK

First published 2001
This second edition published 2012
by Routledge
2 Park Square, Milton Park, Abingdon, Oxon OX14 4RN

Simultaneously published in the USA and Canada
by Routledge
711 Third Avenue, New York, NY 10017

Routledge is an imprint of the Taylor & Francis Group, an informa business

British Library Cataloguing in Publication Data
A catalogue record for this book is available from the British Library

Library of Congress Cataloging in Publication Data
  Kersner, Myra.
  Speech and language therapy : the decision making process when working
  with children / Myra Kersner, Jannet A. Wright. – 2nd ed.
    p. cm.
  Includes bibliographical references and index.
  1. Speech disorders in children. 2. Speech therapy for children. I. Wright,
  Jannet A. II. Title.
  RJ496.S7K42 2012
  618.92'855–dc23

                                                              2011036751

ISBN: 978-0-415-61407-8 (hbk)
ISBN: 978-0-415-61408-5 (pbk)
ISBN: 978-0-203-12559-5 (ebk)

Typeset in Garamond
by Wearset Ltd, Boldon, Tyne and Wear

Printed and bound in Great Britain by
TJ International Ltd, Padstow, Cornwall

Contents

Illustrations

Figures

Tables

Contributors

Carolyn Anderson is a senior lecturer at the University of Strathclyde and course director for the BSc (Hons) in Speech and Language Pathology. Her specialist areas are professional development, speech development and disorders, cerebral palsy and learning disabilities. She is co-author of *Speech and Language Therapy: issues in professional practice.*

Sally Bates is a Senior Lecturer at University College Plymouth St Mark and St John. Her specialist areas are clinical linguistics and phonetics and spoken and written language development. Sally co-edited the SLCN module within the government commissioned E-Learning for Health System, co-authoring sessions on typical development, SSI and SLI. She is also a co-author of the *Clinical Assessment of Vowels – English Systems (CAV-ES)*.

Sarah Beazley is a Senior Teaching Fellow at the University of Manchester and a Consultant Speech and Language Therapist working with deaf people for Liverpool Community Health NHS Trust. She lectures for CSD Consultants who train speech and language therapists working in the field of deafness. She was a Speech Therapy Advisor at the RNID. She is co-author of *Deaf Children, their Families and Professionals: dismantling barriers.*

Monica Bray is now retired from her post as Senior Lecturer at Leeds Metropolitan University, although she is still involved in some tutoring and teaching. She continues to work with children with special needs and their parents. She has contributed chapters on Down syndrome, on learning difficulties and on working with parents in a number of books and is the co-author of *Speech and Language Clinical Process and Practice.*

Michael Clarke is a Lecturer in speech and language sciences at University College London. As a speech and language therapist his work has primarily been with children with complex communication needs.

Mary Gale is a Senior Team Leader and speech and language therapist in the Community Child Health Partnership, North Bristol NHS Trust, Bristol.

Marie Gascoigne is a speech and language therapist. She worked with children with SLI in mainstream schools, lectured at City University, London then developed the Integrated Speech and Language Therapy Service for Children in Hackney and the City. She now works at a national level advising Local Authorities and Primary Care Trusts regarding commissioning and delivery of services for children with SLCN.

Judy Halden is a specialist speech and language therapist for deaf people, a teacher of deaf children and was a Speech Therapy Advisor at the RNID. She works as a specialist teacher for hearing impairment in Hertfordshire; and is an advisor/lecturer at the University of Hertfordshire's Teacher of the Deaf course. She also lectures for CSD Consultants and is an Honorary Research Associate at University College London.

Celia Harding is a Senior Lecturer and Clinical Tutor at City University, London. As a speech and language therapist she continues to practise at the Royal Free Hospital as part of the paediatric gastroenterology team. She teaches in the areas of learning disability, which includes augmentative and alternative communication and paediatric dysphagia both at pre-registration and post-registration level.

Anne Harding-Bell leads the specialist speech and language therapy team serving the East of England Cleft Lip and Palate Network based at Addenbrooke's Hospital, Cambridge. She also contributes to the Post Graduate Course in Cleft Palate Studies, at the University of Sheffield. Her many publications include a chapter in *Cleft Palate Speech: assessment and intervention.*

Sarah Hulme is the Head of Speech and Language Therapy in Whittington Health, London. Sarah's clinical speciality was working with pre-school children and their families in parent–child interaction therapy, a technique in which she has trained nationally, and has adapted for developing adult–child interaction techniques for nursery and children's centre staff.

Nicola Jolleff is a Principal Speech and Language Therapist at Guys and St Thomas' NHS Foundation Trust, London. Her clinical experience has focused on complex communication disorders in association with autism spectrum disorders, epilepsy and rare syndromes such as Angelman, Landau Kleffner and Worster Drought.

Myra Kersner has been a Senior Lecturer at University College London where for many years she focused on students' clinical and professional development. As a speech and language therapist and drama therapist she specialised in working with children and adults with severe learning disabilities. She won the Honours of RCSLT. She has co-written many articles and books with Jannet Wright including, *How to Manage Communication Problems in Young Children.*

Janet Lees is an Honorary Research Fellow at the Institute of Child Health, London and honorary lecturer at the University of Sheffield. She is an advisor to Friends of Landau-Kleffner Syndrome, and specialist Advisor to RCSLT. She is the author of *Children with Acquired Aphasias.*

Carolyn Letts is a Senior Lecturer at Newcastle University. Her research and teaching interests are in bilingualism, child language disorder and assessment. She collaborated with Susan Edwards and Indra Sinka to produce the *New Reynell Developmental Language Scales.*

Tom Loucas is a Lecturer in the School of Psychology and Clinical Language Sciences at the University of Reading. His clinical specialism and areas of research are in Autism Spectrum Disorders.

Helen Marks is a speech and language therapist and is the Clinical Lead for speech and language therapy at the Bristol Royal Hospital for Children.

Ruth Merritt (formerly Frost) is a speech and language therapist and freelance consultant specialising in working with deaf people. She co-ordinated the Advanced Clinical Studies Course in Speech and Language Therapy with Deaf People at City University, London and administrates and lectures for CSD Consultants. She worked for nine years on the Cochlear Implant Programme at Great Ormond Street Hospital, London.

Ann Parker has been a Senior Lecturer at University College London where she was responsible for clinical and professional development. Her specialist courses for supervising clinicians continue to run nationally and internationally. As a speech and language therapist she specialised in working with deaf people and is the author of *PETAL*.

Katie Price is a speech and language therapist at Great Ormond Street Hospital, London, working with children who have communication difficulties as a part of their neurodisabilities. She has a specialist interest in children with cerebral palsy, and how to support all aspects of their communication development, including consideration of assistive communication technology.

Kirsty Pullen has worked for many years within the Early Years Speech and Language Therapy Services across Camden and Islington, London, specialising in working with pre-school children with Specific Language Impairment. She currently manages the Early Years SLT Service in Islington and is an Early Language Consultant for *Every Child a Talker*.

Oonagh Reilly is a Senior Lecturer at Birmingham City University. Her research interests are learning and teaching in Higher Education and children's speech sound disorders. She also has an honorary contract with South Staffs PCT, working with children with speech sound disorders.

Deanne Rennie is a Clinical Lead for Speech and Language Therapy in Leicestershire Partnership Trust, Leicester, Leicestershire and Rutland. She has a specialist interest in developmental speech, language and communication difficulties.

Sue Roulstone is Underwood Trust Professor of Language and Communication Impairment at the University of the West of England, Bristol, and Clinical Director of the Speech and Language Therapy Research Unit, Frenchay Hospital, North Bristol NHS Trust.

Debbie Sell is Lead Speech and Language Therapist for the North Thames Regional Cleft Service, Joint Research Lead for Allied Health Professions, Honorary Senior Lecturer Institute of Child Health, University of London and Visiting Professor, City University. She has been a clinical researcher for over 25 years and has written extensively in the cleft palate field. She was awarded an OBE for services to the National Health Service.

Sarah Simpson is a Senior Teaching Fellow at University College London where her areas of interest are students' clinical and professional development and written language difficulties in children and adults.

Jocelynne Watson is a Senior Lecturer and Clinical Director in the Speech and Hearing Sciences Division at Queen Margaret University, Edinburgh. Her research interests include the effectiveness of computers in intervention, clinical vowel systems, the relationship between speech perception and production and the links between genetics and communication. She is a member of the SLI Consortium and is co-author of *CAV-ES*.

Alison Wintgens has worked for over 20 years in the Child and Adolescent Mental Health Service at St George's Hospital, London, seeing children who have both emotional/behavioural disorders and disorders of communication. She helped set up the RCSLT's SIG in Emotional and Behavioural Problems and has been an RCSLT advisor in child mental health. She has a special interest in selective mutism and is the co-author of *The Selective Mutism Resource Manual*.

Janet Wood is a Lecturer at University College London, where she is Programme Tutor for the MSc Speech and Language Sciences. Her areas of clinical and research interest are children with Specific Language Impairment and integrated service delivery.

Jannet A. Wright is Professor of Speech and Language Therapy and Head of the Speech and Language Therapy Division at De Montfort University, Leicester. She is a Fellow of the RCSLT. She has carried out extensive research into collaboration between speech and language therapists and educational practitioners. She has co-written many articles and books with Myra Kersner including, *A Career in Speech and Language Therapy*.

Louise Wright is a speech and language therapist working for the Cornwall Partnership NHS Foundation Trust. Her area of specialism is stammering in all ages and her area of research is outcome measurement. She is the author of several articles, an outcome measure for adults who stammer (WASSP) and the book *Stammering: advice for all ages*.

Terminology and abbreviations

Terminology

The term 'parent(s)' is used to cover parent, carer, guardian, significant other – anyone who takes on the care and responsibility for the children.

The terms 'treatment', 'therapy' and 'intervention' are used interchangeably throughout the book.

Children refers to children and young people.

Video is also used to refer to DVD and video and other technologies used for playback.

Abbreviations

Throughout the book there will be conventions and abbreviations used. The most common ones are listed below.

AAC	alternative and augmentative communication
ADHD	attention deficit hyperactivity disorder
ASD	autism spectrum disorder
ASLP	acquired speech and language problems
BSL	British Sign Language
CAMHS	child and adolescent mental health service
CDC	child development centre
CSAG	Clinical Standards Advisory Group
CV	consonant/vowel
DCSF	Department for Children, Schools and Families
DES	Department of Education and Science
DfEE	Department for Education and Employment
DfE	Department for Education
DfES	Department for Education and Skills
DH	Department of Health
EBD	emotional and behavioural difficulties
ENT	ear nose and throat
HPC	Health Professions Council
LA	Local Authority
LSA	learning support assistant
MLU	mean length of utterance
NQP	newly qualified practitioner

PCIT	parent–child interaction therapy
RCSLT	The Royal College of Speech and Language Therapists
SENCO	Special Educational Needs Coordinator
SLCN	speech, language and communication needs
SLD	severe learning disabilities
SLI	specific language impairment
SSI	specific speech impairment
TOM	therapy outcome measure
WHO	World Health Organisation
YDP	young deaf people (across the age range)

Introduction

This is the second edition of *Speech and Language Therapy: the decision-making process when working with children*. Following the success of the first edition it has been completely updated and revised to include current research and legislation and reflect current thinking. It will be relevant to speech and language therapy students and potential students, and therapists returning to the profession. It will also be of interest to newly qualified practitioners, specialist teachers, SENCOs and specialist teachers in training.

The focus of the book is on the decision-making process which underpins the management of children by speech and language therapists. The contributors all have expert knowledge in the subject on which they are writing. They have been drawn from speech and language therapy education establishments, specialist centres and specialist speech and language therapy services across the UK. Each author focuses on the decision-making process in relation to their given topic. They do not address intervention in detail but authors refer the reader to relevant texts where appropriate.

The book is divided into four parts. Each part has a brief introduction outlining the main focus of the chapters. Learning outcomes are given at the beginning of each chapter so that readers will know what to expect.

As this book will not necessarily be read in chronological order, there is cross referencing between the chapters to facilitate the reader in making links.

Chapter 1 provides a framework for the decision-making process. The skills required in order to make these decisions will be discussed in Chapter 2. This chapter also provides information about the knowledge and skills required to be a speech and language therapist and the learning process of the developing professional. Chapter 3 relates to newly qualified practitioners in their first job.

How the decision-making process varies within different settings in health and education, whether working with individual children or with groups, will be covered in Chapters 4–7.

Chapters 8 and 9 are concerned with different types of decisions which may confront therapists when working with others and the importance of collaboration is emphasised. The training role of speech and language therapists in relation to working with professionals and parents is also highlighted.

Chapters 10–22 include a wealth of information about a wide range of communication problems encountered in children and ways in which the decision-making process is made relevant to these specific client groups is considered.

Myra Kersner and Jannet A. Wright

Part I

Learning how to be a professional

In this part the decision-making process in speech and language therapy assessment and management is outlined and the skills required in order to work in professional practice are discussed. It is recommended that Chapters 1 and 2 are read together. The reader will be guided through the issues relating to professional development, the first job and the learning process of the developing speech and language therapist. A speech and language therapy manager highlights in Chapter 3 important areas of consideration when applying for a first job.

Chapter 1

The decision-making process in speech and language therapy

Myra Kersner

Learning outcomes

By the end of this chapter, the reader should:

- have knowledge of the speech and language therapy decision-making process when working with children;
- have knowledge of the choices available and how speech and language therapists make decisions in their work;
- have knowledge of the speech and language therapy management process.

Introduction

The management process in speech and language therapy begins as soon as children are referred and therapists need to make decisions about how to proceed. Initially these relate to the choice of assessment procedures and whether or not intervention is required. Then, choices will have to be made about the best approach to therapy. Further assessment decisions will be made, if appropriate, throughout the process resulting in options for review and discharge.

The management process can be divided into four major stages:

- forming working hypotheses;
- assessment, including information gathering, observing and interpreting behaviour;
- setting objectives for therapy;
- facilitating and evaluating change.

Any process comprises a series of actions occurring over time. Processes are organic, each aspect affecting and being affected by other aspects. Within the process there is fluidity of movement until an agreed end point and a desired outcome is eventually achieved. In speech and language therapy each decision within the process will affect, and be affected by other decisions as well as being influenced by the specific setting, the individual child and the context.

Figure 1.1 offers a framework in which the management process may be considered in terms of the decisions which need to be made. For different ways of representing the process see for example Bray and Todd (2005) and McAllister and Lincoln (2004). Although the decisions appear in linear order, it is in fact a cyclical process (see also Figure 2.1, Chapter 2) so that the sequence in which the decisions need to be made is not fixed. Some may be bypassed while others may need to be made simultaneously.

In this chapter there will be discussion about the types of decisions which need to be made within this framework, the overall choices available, the questions which need to be asked and the ways in which speech and language therapists approach the process as a whole. For specific decisions that relate to the nature of the setting in which the child is seen see Chapters 4–7; decisions made in relation to specific disorders will be discussed in Chapters 10–22.

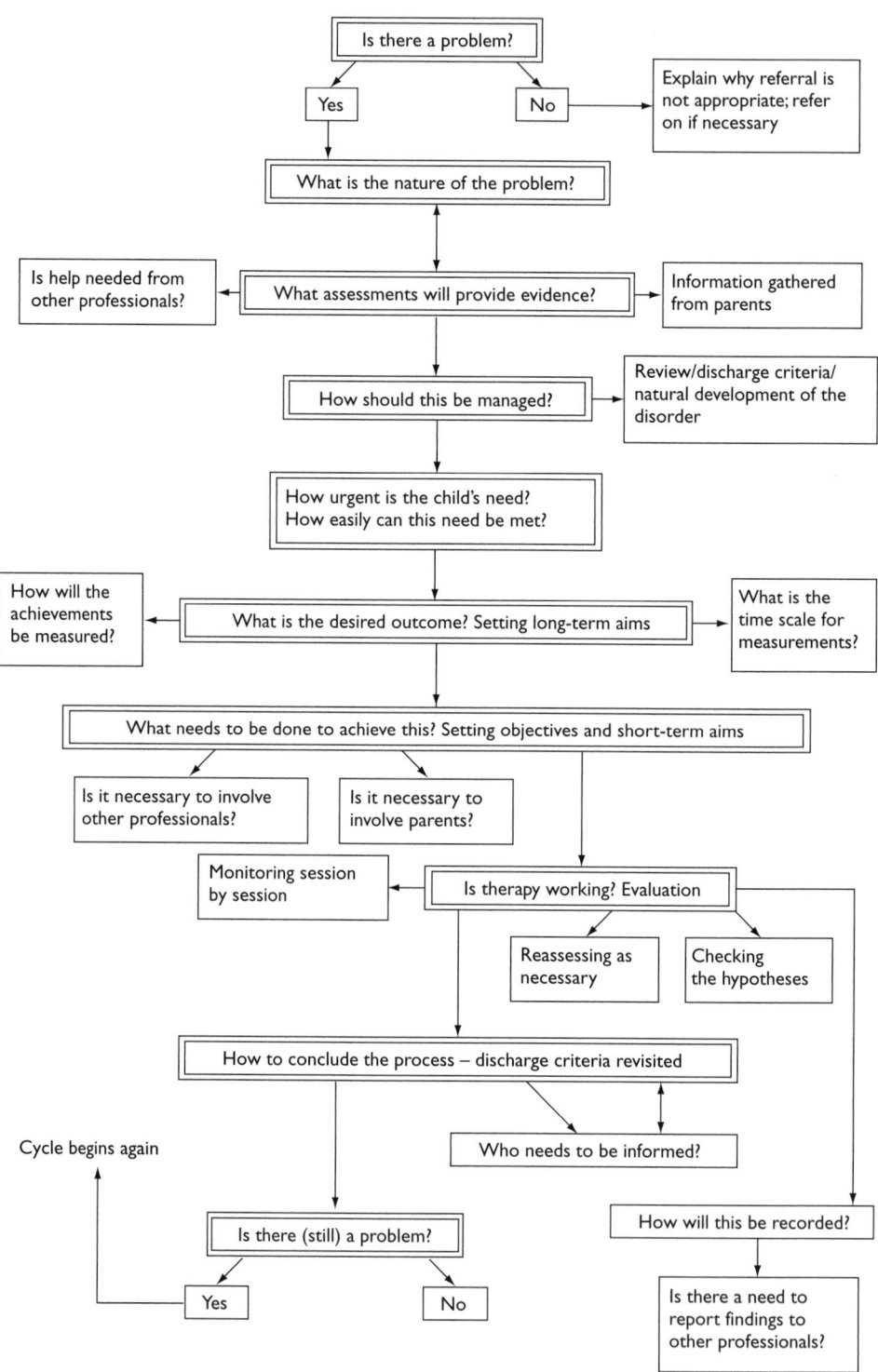

Figure 1.1 The decision-making process.

The decision-making process

The time period

The time in which individual decisions have to be made is normally governed by the context and the setting. In some instances, assessment and decision-making regarding future management may occur at the initial meeting. In a Child Development Centre, for example, the focus may be on multi-disciplinary assessment, and the children may only be seen once, or for a limited period, before being referred to other centres for therapy. However, when working with children in schools, the information may be gathered over a longer period and assessment-therapy reassessment may be part of an ongoing 'diagnostic therapy' process.

The length of time required for improvement or change to occur may vary greatly and, while some children will achieve their goals within a fixed-length block of therapy, others may require help and support over a protracted time.

A child is referred

Is there a problem?

DECISION: YES/NO

The management of a child with speech, language and communication needs (SLCN) begins on receipt of the referral. The therapist forms an initial working hypothesis about whether or not a problem exists, what might be the nature of the problem and what to do about it.

Case example: Sophie

Kate, a speech and language therapist, receives a referral letter from a nursery school teacher describing Sophie aged 3;2 as having 'unintelligible speech'. Kate will have to draw on her professional knowledge to help specify the nature of the problem, identify possible contributing factors and to establish whether such a problem may be dealt with appropriately by a speech and language therapist.

The first question to be asked is whether or not the problem actually exists. There are three reasons why this is important.

- The referral may have come from a concerned teacher, or a conscientious health visitor, but the parents may not consider there is a problem.
- The parents may believe their child has a communication problem but the teachers or medical personnel may not agree.
- The child may once have had a problem, but have improved spontaneously so that it no longer exists.

If Kate decides Sophie's communication does not require intervention, she will need to explain this, with her reasons, to the referrer.

It may not always be easy to discern whether or not a problem exists. For example, at initial interview some children may be unwilling to speak. Children often perform differently when faced with an unknown adult, than when interacting with a group of their peers. Some children have high level language difficulties which may not be apparent on first meeting. Or, a child who has been referred because of a stammering difficulty may speak fluently to the therapist at initial interview.

In order to make the decision about whether Sophie's problem exists, Kate must gather supporting evidence from a variety of sources, such as focused observations of Sophie's play and interactions with others, which can then be compared with the norms for her age and developmental stage. Kate will also ask Sophie's parents preliminary questions, talk to her nursery teacher and look at any previous records.

It may be that Kate's decision is 'no', this is not a problem for the speech and language therapist. She also needs to consider whether Sophie has a problem that would be more appropriately dealt with by someone else. For example, if she seems to be developing slowly in all areas she may need to be referred to a paediatrician or a psychologist, with an appropriate report.

If Kate's decision is 'yes', Sophie has a communication problem, then working hypotheses will need to be developed and tested.

What is the nature of the problem?

DECISION/QUESTION: WHAT ARE KATE'S WORKING HYPOTHESES?

In order to develop her hypotheses Kate will need to gather more detailed information. This will include assessing Sophie's comprehension of language, recording and transcribing a detailed speech sample and/or a language sample, using appropriate informal and formal assessment procedures (Lees and Urwin 1997). Kate will now ask more detailed and appropriately targeted questions of Sophie's parents and her nursery teacher to establish Sophie's communication patterns in a variety of contexts and settings. As Kate puts together pieces of the puzzle she will form new hypotheses which can be tested and accepted or rejected until she has an accurate, holistic picture of Sophie's communication skills. This should then indicate a possible approach to therapy.

What assessments will provide appropriate evidence to support or refute the hypotheses?

DECISION/QUESTION: WHAT ARE THE CRITERIA FOR CHOOSING OR REJECTING ASSESSMENTS?

What are the choices available? No child should routinely be subjected to a battery of tests without a clear rationale. Sophie, for example, is only 3;2 years of age and may well be upset by the use of formal tests. Kate must therefore decide which tests might provide the most detailed evidence to help support or refute her working hypotheses. Of course the specific tests will vary according to the nature of a child's problems. Details of different assessments are referred to in relation to specific areas of difficulty in Chapters 10–22. However, when choosing any formal assessment it is important to consider the following (Lees and Urwin 1997).

- It must be age appropriate.
- It should test what it purports to assess.
- It must be appropriate for the child socially and culturally.
- It must have been standardised on appropriate norms.
- The child must have adequate attention skills to be able to concentrate for the period of time required for testing.

Is help needed from other professionals to complement/aid assessment?

DECISION/QUESTION: YES/NO – WHICH PROFESSIONAL?

Speech and language therapists work alongside many other professionals such as audiologists, psychologists and different medical specialists all of whom may be involved in aspects of assessment. Additional input from such professionals may help the therapist to confirm or refute a hypothesis about the child's communication problems.

For example, Kate knows it will be important for an audiologist to establish whether Sophie has any hearing difficulties and to investigate whether there have been intermittent problems at a time that was critical to her speech and language development (Moorey and Mahon 2002). If appropriate, a paediatrician or a psychologist may help to establish Sophie's cognitive functioning levels.

When working with children with a cleft palate, a physical disability or children with severe learning disabilities, additional specialist input from members of a multi-disciplinary team may be essential for a more accurate diagnosis. (This is discussed in more detail in Chapters 10–22.)

How should the intervention with the child be managed?

DECISION: THE FREQUENCY OF THE INTERVENTION AND WHERE THIS WILL TAKE PLACE

Kate will share her findings with Sophie's parents and will work in partnership with them to agree a contract regarding possible intervention. They will discuss whether further assessment and/or a therapy programme is required or whether it would be better to put Sophie 'on review' to be called back to check any spontaneous progress at a later date. If they decide on therapy Kate will need to agree with the parents the number of sessions, where they will take place – whether in the nursery or a health centre – and the duration of each. This will be based on Sophie's attention span and ability to concentrate and engage in the process.

In order to make this decision Kate needs to understand the natural development of Sophie's type of problem. For example, therapy may be expected to take a longer period if Sophie is also found to have a significant hearing loss. Kate has to ask permission from the parents before she can see Sophie in nursery. This will also give her a chance to gather further information from them. After her session with Sophie, Kate will have a follow-up discussion with the parents about how she should proceed.

Several management options would be available to Kate at this stage.

If the assessment results indicate that Sophie could make spontaneous progress, Kate may suggest a 'wait and see' policy. The parents could then contact her at a later date if they are still concerned, or she could agree to send a review appointment to check Sophie's progress in several months' time.

If Sophie appears to have complex difficulties, further assessment may be required before a complete diagnosis can be made and Kate may embark on a period of 'diagnostic therapy', with ongoing in-depth assessment.

If Kate offers Sophie a period of therapy, she must agree with the parents whether to see her once a week individually, perhaps for a period of six weeks, or whether Sophie would benefit more from daily attendance at a language group within the nursery, possibly for a term. (See Chapter 7.)

How urgent is the child's need? How easily can this need be met?

DECISION: HOW TO PRIORITISE

Kate's decision regarding prioritisation will depend on:

- the child (Sophie);
- Kate's workload;
- local policies, professional standards and guidelines;
- the implications if no intervention/therapy is offered.

With regard to the child, it is important to establish the nature of Sophie's need within the context of her environment; to consider the severity of her problem in relation to her age, and to ascertain the extent to which her problem is affecting her ability to function socially and educationally.

Prioritisation decision case example: Jack

Kate has also been asked to see Jack who is 8 years old. He has expressive language difficulties which are interfering with his progress in school and he often refuses to attend.

If the prioritising decision is between offering therapy to Jack or Sophie, Kate may decide that Jack's needs are more suited to direct one-to-one intervention which should enable him to function more effectively in school. Kate may be able to help Sophie indirectly by supporting the classroom assistant or nursery teacher to work with her.

Kate will also have to consider her own workload. This includes the size and nature of her caseload, the needs of any other children on the waiting list, the commitment required by her administrative work and the resources available.

Kate is already aware of the professional standards and recommended guidelines of RCSLT (2005, 2006) and related legal requirements. In addition, she has to take into account the parents' wishes as well as her own Authority's/Trust's policies and guidelines regarding the allocation of therapy time for different types of problems and for children of different ages.

What is the desired outcome?

DECISION/QUESTION: WHAT SHOULD BE ACHIEVED BY THE TIME THE CHILD IS READY TO BE DISCHARGED

The long-term aim, that is the desired outcome at the point of discharge, has to be realistically set in relation to Sophie's problem. It may be difficult for students to consider an end point before therapy has begun but it is important for Kate to consider the criteria for discharge, even at the start of the intervention phase. So if Kate decides Sophie needs therapy, the long-term aim may be for her speech to be on a par with her peers.

What needs to be done to achieve this outcome?

DECISION/QUESTION: THE APPROACH REQUIRED IN ORDER TO HELP THE CHILD REACH THE DESIRED OUTCOME

Kate would need to identify the interim stages of the therapy. She will do this by setting short-term aims to be achieved within a specific time period. She would then write objectives for each session.

There are several approaches to intervention which she could consider.

- Working directly with Sophie either individually or in a group (see Chapter 7). She may benefit from a period of direct intervention, in which case Kate would need to decide whether to use a published programme or whether to devise an individual plan specifically for Sophie.
- Withdrawing Sophie from her class, or seeing her within the classroom.
- Working indirectly by training someone else such as a parent, teacher or assistant to work with Sophie. There are some parent–child interaction programmes, for example, which specialise in helping parents to work with their children (see Chapter 4).
- With some children it may be necessary to recommend a change in the child's environment in order for the outcomes to be achieved. So, for example, with Sophie, Kate may ask her teacher to support verbal instructions with gestures or with a visual timetable.
- Sometimes it may be necessary to involve other professionals. For example, specialist medical or orthodontic help and advice may be needed with a child with oro-facial abnormalities; or a psychologist may be able to help children with behaviour problems.

Is therapy working?

DECISION/QUESTION: HOW IS THE WORK TO BE MONITORED AND EVALUATED?

During therapy sessions, Kate will constantly monitor whether the tasks are appropriate for Sophie in terms of level of difficulty and interest, Sophie's motivation and attention, and whether the tasks are enabling her to make progress. Kate needs to be flexible so that she can make adjustments to the activities in response to feedback from Sophie's reactions, even while the session is in progress.

At the end of each session Kate will evaluate and review the effectiveness of the therapy and whether the objectives for that session have been achieved. She will keep records of progress to provide evidence.

When the number of agreed sessions have been completed, Kate will evaluate Sophie's progress to decide whether another period of therapy is required. This will take the form of re-testing, although if she has used any standardised tests there may be a specified period before they can be re-administered.

How to conclude the process

DECISION: WHETHER TO DISCHARGE, REVIEW OR CONTINUE THERAPY

When the original contract has expired Kate will need to discuss Sophie's progress with her parents so that she can make further decisions regarding future management. There are three major options available.

- To discharge Sophie if the long-term aims have been achieved. She would then send a report to any other professionals involved such as the nursery teacher or other referring agent, and include the parents in the distribution list.
- To put Sophie on a list for review within a specified period if it is felt that a plateau has been reached in therapy. Further improvement may occur spontaneously, or a break in therapy may enable Sophie to consolidate her newly acquired skills.
- To continue with therapy if the problem persists.

If therapy is to be continued then the cycle of decisions begins again.

The management process

Forming working hypotheses

Hypothesis-based investigation begins at referral. Therapists use working hypotheses to try to understand and explain a child's speech and language difficulties. Hypotheses are always tentative and by evidence testing, further investigation and constant revision it may be possible to understand the nature of the problem and to predict what intervention/therapy may possibly achieve (see also Bray and Todd 2005; McAllister and Lincoln 2004).

Case example: Emma

Speech and language therapist Suzanne receives a referral for Emma who is 4 years old and 'not talking yet'. Clearly, Suzanne may form several initial working hypotheses. These include the two extreme possibilities that Emma has severe communication difficulties, or that her language and speech development are normal and the referral is based on inaccurate evidence.

Suzanne must keep an open mind and consider a range of possible explanations. She cannot make an assumption and then seek supporting evidence. She must form several hypotheses and consider all confirming and refuting evidence for each.

If Emma's referral is accurate, there may be several initial hypotheses. For example:

- Emma has a hearing loss affecting her speech and language development;
- she has a specific language difficulty;
- she has a global cognitive delay affecting all her developmental milestones.

Suzanne will plan and structure her observations and assessments of Emma and will gather information from Emma's parents and other professionals to find evidence that will help her accept or discard these hypotheses, and form new ones if appropriate. Her knowledge of normal development of speech and language will then help her to interpret the evidence and decide on the next stage of action such as considering whether there is a need for intervention.

Assessment and information gathering

Continuing assessment: diagnostic therapy

Although assessment and intervention are often referred to as if they were two separate stages in the management process, in reality they overlap. Assessment is part of the first stage of the process but it does not necessarily end when therapy begins.

Assessment involves not only administering tests but gathering and collating additional information and then processing and interpreting the results, and reflecting on their implications. This can be time-consuming, depending also on the experience of the therapist. Often, beginning intervention enables the therapist to continue to develop and adjust the working hypotheses – diagnostic therapy – as new evidence affecting the understanding of the child's communication may emerge during the therapy process.

Information gathering

Information will normally be collated, for example, from taking a case history from the child's parents, checking existing records, ensuring that hearing is tested, receiving formal reports from other professionals or from informal conversations with educators and/or medical practitioners. It will also be gathered from interpretation of any assessment results, from a detailed linguistic analysis of speech and/or language samples from the child and through observation of the child's behaviour and interactions.

Observing behaviour

Observation in the therapy setting requires more active involvement than merely looking. Observations need to be structured, focused and related to the level of evidence required so that records of the observations can provide a basis for analysis.

Situations may be structured to facilitate observation, for example using specific toys to observe symbolic play. Selective samples of behaviour may then be observed during a set time period, for example, noting how many times a specific word is spoken or signed during a ten minute video sample. (For further discussion see Chapter 2.)

Interpreting behaviour: value judgements

When gathering data in this way it is important to record only the observed behaviour and to distinguish between that behaviour and any interpretation or explanation of what has been observed. There may be many different explanations for any behaviour and it is possible without verification to misinterpret what has been seen.

It is also important not to make value judgements, whether they involve a negative or positive attitude to the behaviour. Value judgements introduce a level of prejudiced certainty which may preclude the therapist from developing more appropriate alternative interpretations and they may lead to a false description of the original behaviour.

Case example: Dominic

Dominic, aged 6 years, has been referred by his mother. She is concerned that although his speech and language seem normal for his age he is not fluent and often 'gets stuck' on certain words. Therapist Tom assesses Dominic and observes and records that Dominic only produces single word utterances.

Given the obvious discrepancy between the mother's description and Tom's observation it is important that Tom does not try to interpret Dominic's observed behaviour without further carefully structured observations and investigations, for there may be several reasons for the behaviour. For example:

- the mother may have misreported and Dominic may be unable to produce utterances of more than one or two words;
- Dominic may be unable to understand longer sentences;
- the conversation concerned may not have elicited longer utterances because of the nature of the subject, material used or structure of the questions;
- Dominic may use longer utterances in other situations but have been inhibited by the assessment process.

Before trying to interpret Dominic's behaviour Tom must pay attention to all possible explanations. He will therefore have to structure new situations to test the different possibilities and must gather more information from Dominic, his mother and possibly his school in order to understand the nature of Dominic's problem.

It would also be inappropriate for Tom to decide that Dominic's limited output was because he was 'lazy', 'shy' or 'trying to be good'. Such value judgements may prevent Tom from accurately describing the original behaviour and considering the options of interpretations.

Case example: Connor

When 5 year old Connor, who had been referred for delayed speech and language, arrived in Tom's room at the Children's Centre he immediately disappeared under the table, shouting, 'Not coming out' and sat with his arms folded.

Interpreting Connor's behaviour as 'angry', 'wild' or 'determined to flout authority' may be inaccurate and lead to Tom taking inappropriate action. For it is possible that Connor's original intention was quite different from what he is now, intentionally or unconsciously, communicating. There are many possibilities for the behaviour to be misinterpreted when comparing Connor's intention with Tom's interpretation.

If Tom tries to consider the behaviour from the perspective of the child, it could be that Connor is tense, anxious or frightened. He may have had a previous bad experience at the Children's Centre, or he may just be playing a game. In each case Tom's approach would need to be different.

Value judgements such as Connor is 'bad' or 'naughty' which may then be extended to judgements regarding his parents and his upbringing have no place in professional assessment and it is important to describe only the behaviour that is being observed.

Facilitating change

After the initial assessment process has begun the therapist will decide whether specific intervention is needed in order to facilitate change in the child's communication.

The nature of change

Change may be achieved through:

- direct intervention – the therapist working with the child;
- indirect intervention – the therapist training others to work with the child;
- making changes in the child's communicative environment.

The expected level and rate of change will vary for each child as will the desired outcome, depending on the nature of the difficulty, whether there are additional medical or cognitive factors and the child's age. It is important to be realistic and to understand any possible limiting factors, while not imposing expectations which may limit the child's progress.

For example, the aim for children with minimal language delay may be for them to catch up with their peers following an 'episode of care'; whereas for a child with a significant hearing loss, bilingual language development in BSL and English may be the aim (see Chapter 13). For some children with cerebral palsy therapy may work towards helping them achieve a functional level of communication using electronic aids (see Chapter 21), while for older children who have residual language problems therapy may concentrate on the development of social skills and strategies to enable them to cope with the world they are about to move into.

Setting objectives for therapy

Long- and short-term goals are usually then set for the child by the therapist, often in conjunction with appropriate educators such as the SENCO or teacher, or medical practitioners.

Long-term aims usually reflect the desired end-of-therapy outcome. They may be written in general terms such as 'Sarah will be able to function within her environment', or 'Samir's speech and language will be age-appropriate', or for Alex who has a global delay and physical disabilities the long-term aim may be for him 'to reach his maximum potential with regard to functional communication'.

Short-term aims usually specify what might be achieved within a specific time period such as a six week therapy block or until the end of the school term. For example, 'By the end of term Charlie will be able to...'

SMART objectives (see Furnham 1997) are often used when therapists devise individual session plans within a block of therapy. The sessions will then be organised to enable these objectives to be met and the therapist will monitor and record whether or not this has occurred.

S: specific, relating to children's individual needs and the communicative and social environment.

M: measurable, specifying how they are to be measured.

A: achievable, given the time and resources available.

R: realistic, given the nature of the child and the difficulty.

T: time related, usually to be achieved by the end of the session.

An example of a SMART session objective: 'By the end of the session Rashid will have selected six familiar toys correctly from an array of eight toys in response to single-word requests.'

Evaluating change

Monitoring, reflection and evaluation are part of an ongoing process for the speech and language therapist. Sometimes progress may be due to natural development or, if illness or trauma were involved, may be due to spontaneous recovery.

Monitoring should take place during, as well as at the end of, each session, therapists constantly 'thinking on their feet' or as Schon (1983) classically calls it, 'on-line decision-making'. For if children are to make progress they need to be interested in the materials presented, yet be challenged by the activities and the therapist needs to ensure the demands of each task are at an appropriate level.

Monitoring questions during the session might include:

- Is the child engaged?
- Is the session enjoyable?
- Are the tasks and materials at an appropriate level?
- Is the communicative environment suitable?
- Are there too many distractions?
- Is the input at the appropriate level?

And at the end of the session:

- Have the specific objectives been met?
- If not, were they realistic and appropriate?
- Was the therapy appropriate?

Therapy then needs to be evaluated at the end of the specified period of intervention. This will involve re-assessment of the child to indicate the extent of any change and thus the effectiveness of therapy. It will also be important to explore the parents' and teachers' perceptions regarding change. This will enable the therapist to make decisions about possible review, discharge or the necessity for further intervention.

Summary

Within this chapter the speech and language therapy management process when working with children has been outlined and a framework presented in which to consider the decisions that need to be made from referral to discharge.

Chapter 2

Developing as a speech and language therapist

Myra Kersner and Ann Parker

Learning outcomes

By the end of this chapter readers should be able to:

- recognise some different learning models relevant to key skills in speech and language therapy;
- use professional feedback in the process of life-long learning;
- be aware of key skills required to be a competent speech and language therapist.

Introduction

This chapter is about the process of learning and professional development that enables speech and language therapists and therapists-in-training to make the decisions described in Chapter 1. The role of professional feedback in this process is discussed, as well as the skills and knowledge that are required in the workplace.

The learning process

The practice of speech and language therapy involves the use of specific skills – relatively complex actions which need to be learned and developed throughout the therapist's working life – combined with specialist knowledge and understanding, and appropriate attitudes to clients and their interactions. In the workplace this combination usually occurs at speed; the 'hot action' of real practice (Eraut 1994).

Theory and practice

The theory and knowledge underpinning speech and language therapy practice are drawn from several disciplines, including psychology, linguistics and anatomy (Wright and Kersner 2009), as well as from working experience.

A practical speech and language therapy education is gained as part of university course-based teaching and learning where opportunities are also provided for work-context experience on placement. Decision-making skills are developed through planned rehearsal; through the structured process of writing, planning, presenting and discussing proposed actions with peers, tutors and practice educators. The 'reflective practitioner', a well-known phrase from Schon (1983), constantly updates knowledge and self-monitors professional work and development. There are different approaches to professional learning and the relationship between theory and practice, and each involves different expectations of the learner in different contexts.

The Linear Technocratic Model

This model of learning involves a traditional linear structure, with what Eraut (1994) referred to as a 'front loading' of theory. There are instances when theory must precede practice; for example, prior knowledge of normal language development is required in order to understand the scoring systems of individual assessments and to explain the implications of a child's scores to parents. Similarly, knowledge of phonetics is required before a speech sample can be transcribed.

The Learning Cycle Model

There are many instances, however, where neither 'theory' nor 'practice' are necessarily the first point in the process. This is seen in the 'learning cycle' originally described by Kolb (1984: see the modified version in Figure 2.1) where learning may begin with any activity within the cycle. This concept also reflects the structure of speech and language therapy practice where therapists need to reflect on their actions once completed, as well as planning the process beforehand (see also Moon 2005). For example, with students, relevant theory, such as neurology or audiology, may be easier to learn after some practical experience with a particular client group, such as deaf children. Similarly, practising therapists will often need to reflect and gather new information after meeting a client for an initial assessment.

Speech and language therapy courses in the UK reflect both of these models. On some, students may experience a considerable amount of theoretical learning before starting practical work on placement. The first placement experiences may then require students mainly to observe their practice educator at work and may only begin their own supervised practice towards the end of the course (see Figure 2.2).

There is an increasing tendency, however, for students to be involved in 'real' practice from the start of their pre-registration training (Kersner and Parker 2004). In such instances initial placement experiences will involve therapists-in-training in active, experiential learning (Fry *et al.* 2009a) where they are responsible for working with clients from the beginning.

Problem-based learning

Some courses involve a particular type of structured experience, known as Problem Based Learning (PBL) (Boud and Feletti 1997; Clouston *et al.* 2010). Rather than providing a general theoretical introduction to speech and language therapy, such courses (or modules within them) begin with real cases or problems. Practice, and learning relevant theory, develop from

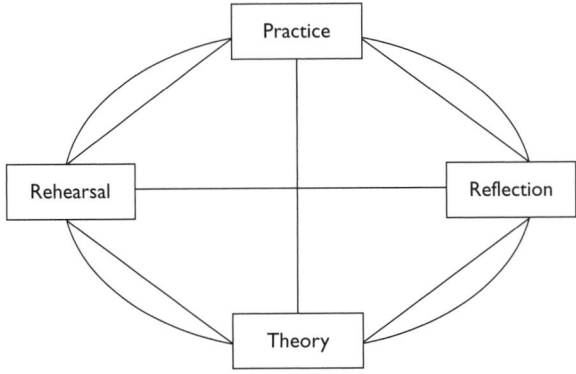

Figure 2.1 A professional learning cycle (source: modified from Kolb 1984).

Figure 2.2 A linear and technocratic model of professional learning.

students' inquiry, problem-solving and discussion. This process mirrors real practice, where practitioners are confronted with new problems on a daily basis. It is similar to the 'learning cycle' approach in that 'action' may be the first step in the process. Such active involvement in the early stages of professional development is seen as an advantage, providing more opportunities for students to develop problem-solving skills, and the creativity and innovation which will be a necessary part of their professional practice.

'Correct practice' or 'trial and adjustment'?

Having a direct, single route between a fixed starting and end point, as in the Linear Technocratic Model, suggests there is such a thing as 'correct practice'. This may be true with certain aspects of speech and language therapy practice. For example, decisions about children's speech development will be based on having made an accurate phonetic transcription and analysis.

However, it may be difficult to develop confident, creative problem-solving skills and to make decisions if there is an over-emphasis on 'correctness' and the avoidance of error. For in most situations therapists need to consider a range of hypotheses. They need to reflect and re-assess and sometimes to change their initial approach, having recognised that a different solution may be more helpful than the one originally tried (see Chapter 1). Morris (2001) suggests that such informed 'trial and adjustment', which involves a degree of risk-taking, more accurately reflects speech and language therapy practice.

The Navigation Model

Parker and Kersner (1998) suggested the importance of a Navigation Model for learning. Whilst acknowledging the fixed starting and end point, this model takes account of the need for adjustments to changing circumstances between these two points, such as may be used for example when piloting an aeroplane. They suggest that such adjustments are required in the professional learning process and the practice of speech and language therapy. This too is not an error-free approach but one in which risk is incorporated in the process and is carefully managed. Every decision to change direction is prompted by self-monitoring, evaluation and the professional use of feedback in what is sometimes referred to as 'reflection in action' (Schon 1983).

It is through such reflection, monitoring and feedback that therapists can also continue to hone, modify and develop their own professional skills as part of an ongoing learning process (McAllister and Lincoln 2004).

Professional feedback for learning

Feedback is crucial in the learning process (Irons 2007), for professionals in training as well as for practising therapists. It involves receiving information from others that reflects on performance, or it may come from self-reflection. If used positively, adjustments may be made where necessary that will improve or enhance future performance. Therapists need to learn how to self-monitor and reflect on their performance as well as to receive and give feedback in relation to individual children and their families. Therapists-in-training may need to learn how to ask for and make use of feedback from a variety of sources in order to improve their developing professional skills.

Figure 2.3 The Navigation Model.

Different sources of feedback

Feedback can come from a variety of sources. Situational feedback comes from the responses of clients – their engagement, their achievements relating to the activities, their interest in the materials – or from colleagues' interactions. Direct feedback may be deliberately elicited, for example through questionnaires to parents or educational staff, or by asking peers or senior colleagues. Both types of feedback are important for professional learning, and different levels of directness may be relevant at different stages of development.

Students may tend to focus on explicit feedback from 'experts' such as practice educators and tutors, or other professionals on their placement. However, as they move towards the transition from university to workplace and professional working life they must learn how to shift the emphasis from such dependency and to utilise implicit, situational feedback from the working situation itself. They need to learn how to utilise all possible sources of feedback and to hone their self-monitoring and reflection skills so that they can be used quickly and constantly within the workplace. This will impact on their decision-making skills so it is important that, as practising therapists, they can rely confidently on their own judgement. In pre-registration courses there is often an emphasis on peer feedback from other students, as a bridge between dependency on 'expert' supervisors and the relative autonomy of work as a therapist.

Experienced practitioners most often gauge their professional effectiveness by monitoring the progress of the children and the reactions of families and colleagues. Such feedback will not only indicate what changes may need to be considered but also what aspects of the therapy are working well. Direct feedback may be available for qualified staff, for example, through an appraisal process, a peer support group or individual peer support. However, the demands of everyday practice may mean that time for more frequent, formal, direct feedback for professional learning in the workplace has to be specifically arranged.

Giving and receiving feedback

Students and practitioners need to learn how to give and receive feedback. It is important that all feedback takes account of the distinction between objectively described behaviour and its possible interpretations (see Chapter 1). It should also be:

- balanced
- specific
- heard
- remembered
- used.

Achieving a balance

To counteract any tendency for givers or receivers of feedback to focus differentially on either positive or negative comments, it is important to aim for balanced feedback. This ensures that attention is paid to positive factors that should be continued, as well as to suggestions for change, with equal discussion of both aspects. Positive comments should be clearly separated from suggestions for change. Linking the two with words such as 'but' should be avoided to prevent negation of the positive aspects.

Being specific

Feedback does not have to include all the factors which have been observed, and will often be more useful if it is focused on specific skills, actions and clients' responses. If it is to be part of the learning process it also needs to be specific and the description of behaviour observed should be separated from its interpretation as discussed in Chapter 1.

For example, a comment that, 'The session was good', or even, 'The session was terrific', does not give any useful information about what worked in the session so that it should be repeated next time, or why the session was effective. It may be more helpful to say, 'The aims for the first activity were achieved because of the clear introduction and the games which were at an appropriate level.' Similarly, 'Can you think of three ways in which that activity might be improved next time...' is more helpful than a general, 'That didn't go well.'

Hearing feedback

It is rarely constructive to argue with feedback that has been given. Responses usually change on reflection and engaging in an emotional reaction is rarely helpful. The receiver of feedback should listen, make sure the feedback is understood, ask for clarification if necessary and then take time to reflect. Clarification is an important stage in any reflective professional discussion as it helps focus on underlying behaviours and activities, developing a deeper understanding of the positive interpretations or suggestions for change.

Remembering feedback

Writing down the main points of what is said can act as an aide-memoire. It enables the receiver to ask for any further points of clarification and can prevent only the negative aspects being remembered. It can also usefully provide evidence of progress over time.

Using feedback

It is usually helpful to end a feedback discussion and reflection with consideration of next actions, identifying what can be done to effect relevant future changes. The clarity with which behaviour and interpretation have been described will enable actions to be more easily identified and made specific. Therapists should monitor their work during as well as at the end of each session, to enable the continuous 'reflection-in-action' (Schon 1983) that enables practitioners to facilitate change in themselves as well as in their clients.

Structuring and managing the feedback process

The amount of structured feedback provided in placements will vary and the process should be reviewed regularly. If receiving feedback in order to support professional development is to be a positive experience, it is usually helpful to structure the process, and clear ground-rules about how to conduct the process need to be negotiated before the feedback session begins. For example, it is important to agree the level of confidentiality, so that participants can be clear about what will happen to any information which is exchanged.

Ground-rules for feedback

- Agree/negotiate the ground rules.
- Agree about confidentiality. (It may/may not be confidential. If it is, be clear about the level of confidentiality.)
- Agree roles (e.g. learner/facilitator/note-taker).
- Agree the scope and focus of the feedback (e.g. whole session? part of session? a particular aspect of the session?).
- Agree circumstances and status of the feedback (e.g. one-to-one or in a group; recorded by learner only for learning, or recorded for other purposes).
- Agree the structure of the conversation. (It is usually recommended that the learner comments first.)
- Ensure a balance of positive comments and suggestions for change.
- Use specific explanatory language (e.g. X went well *because of* Y).
- Include discussion about how agreed factors might change and how the learner can check whether the improvements have taken place.
- Focus on a specific limited number of behaviours/skills/client responses.
- Ensure a written record.

Knowledge and skills

Supporting knowledge

Much of a therapist's fundamental knowledge base such as speech and language pathology, psychology, phonetics and linguistics will be learned at university, although professional development is ongoing and qualified therapists need to constantly update and refresh their knowledge in the light of current research and theories. However, to be effective in their work, practitioners also need specific knowledge to enable them to make appropriate decisions and understand the available choices regarding assessment and intervention. For example, they need to know:

- how to interpret the results of assessment findings;
- different therapy approaches and techniques;
- tasks, games and activities for children of all ages that will enable the process of change;
- how to analyse the skills required at different levels of a task so that they may change the level – even during a session if required;
- how to set criteria for evaluating therapy;
- how to support the involvement of family and other professional input to the process.

Therapists need to understand about the development of a therapeutic relationship and to have an awareness of self; to understand about their own reactions to change, their own prejudices and attitudes if they are successfully to support change in others (Burnard 1997; Sanders 2002).

Required skills

To work effectively as a speech and language therapist, key skills are needed which can also be learned and improved upon as students and therapists continue their professional development. These may involve interviewing skills, or may be less obvious behaviours such as paying attention and actively listening. Most therapists-in-training have some level of key skills before they begin to study, but these will be developed for specialised application within the professional context.

Transferable skills

Many skills are transferable across professions such as basic communication, word processing or presentation skills. However, transferable skills are often used by different professionals in different ways. For example, listening skills are also used effectively by counsellors and teachers. But speech and language therapists need to hone their listening skills additionally so that they can not only comprehend the words and empathise with their client's situation, but can also linguistically analyse the words and the interaction at the same time.

Profession-specific skills

The ability to transcribe and analyse speech, language and communicative interactions is speech and language therapy profession-specific. So is the way in which some 'everyday' skills are developed and managed, usually simultaneously, in the professional context. For example, therapists are often required to listen, observe, record and transcribe whilst structuring and maintaining an enjoyable and seemingly relaxed interaction with the children. At the same time they will be considering working hypotheses about the problems being observed, deciding areas of priority for assessment, as well as offering reassurance and appropriate explanations to the parents.

The key skills

- interpersonal skills
- information gathering skills
- therapy skills
- problem-solving skills and decision-making
- organisational-management skills.

INTERPERSONAL SKILLS

These may be broadly classified into those needed to receive information, such as listening skills, those required for expression, whether spoken, non-vocal or written, and those that are required to work collaboratively with others. In practice, none of these skills is used in isolation. For example, when speaking there is normally a complex relationship between the explicit speech and the underlying activity of planning what to say. Overarching metalinguistic skills are needed to monitor what is heard and what is being said as part of the communication planning process (Hargie and Dickson 2004).

Communication tactics. Speech and language therapists need to understand clients whose speech patterns differ from the norm. They also need to be able to modify their own communication according to the needs of individual clients. For example, when working with deaf children in spoken English, therapists need to ensure that their speech is lip-readable. For sign language users they will need to learn BSL. When working with children who have difficulties understanding, such as children with severe learning disabilities, they need to simplify their input highlighting key words.

Receptive skills: active listening. The process of listening involves paying attention to verbal and non-verbal signals and therapists need to develop a more concentrated level of listening than is used in everyday conversation. They need to develop active listening skills, for example, when interviewing parents, so that they not only pay attention, but also convey the level of that attention to the speaker. This enables an empathic rapport to be established so encouraging fuller, honest and more open expression from the speaker (Hargie and Dickson 2004; Shewell 2009).

Ground-rules for active listening

- Provide speakers with a comfortable environment.
- Minimise external interruptions.
- Actively concentrate to a greater degree than in normal conversation.
- Be prepared to listen irrespective of personal feelings about the topic.
- Actively process the information heard.
- Provide opportunities for speakers to express themselves.
- Avoid interrupting unnecessarily.
- Overtly acknowledge that the speakers have been heard using verbal or non-verbal responses.
- Reflect back to the speaker what they have said to confirm that their message is being received correctly.
- Be objective but also empathic. Avoid selective responses which may be based on unsubstantiated pre-judgements.

Expressive skills. Receptive skills are also fundamental to the expressive process, for speakers need to listen to themselves to modify what they are saying and to listen to others so that they can plan what to say next.

Within a professional context, therapists are often required to structure and manage interactions for a specific purpose, for example, when greeting clients in a way that encourages a rapport to be established. They often need to give clear explanations such as describing activities; or provide information for parents or other professionals. Therapists may be asked to give a more formal presentation at a case review, or during a training session for parents or other professionals.

Expressive skills for professional practice include:

- oral skills used in everyday conversations adapted to suit the specific interactional purpose;
- specific oral skills which may be required when presenting to a larger audience;
- written language skills;
- non-vocal, verbal communication skills such as sign language, or AAC;
- non-verbal communication skills such as facial expression and gesture.

Ground-rules for explaining and presenting

- Explanations must be adapted to the needs of the listener and be compatible with the receiver's level of language.
- The language used should be clear and jargon should be avoided.
- Delivery should be well paced.
- Illustration by example is helpful as well as highlighting the key facts.
- Check that listeners have understood the information given.
- Plan the structure, content and even specific words and phrases.
- Rehearsal may improve the clarity of an explanation.
- To hold attention and interest when addressing a group, encourage members to participate.
- With larger groups and in specific contexts voice production and projection may be important.
- Audio-visual illustration and/or demonstration are particularly helpful when presenting to groups.

When explanations, presentations or reports need to be written, the language used must be appropriate for the receiver with the key points summarised and highlighted. Legal and ethical issues need to be considered in written records (see RCSLT 2006 and Bray and Todd 2005).

Collaborative skills. Speech and language therapists need to work together with different people in a range of settings such as with parents, teachers, assistants and medical colleagues (Wright and Kersner 2009). Often parents and colleagues may be supported or trained to continue therapy work in the absence of the therapist (see Chapter 9).

Ground-rules for collaborative working

- Arrange regular times to meet.
- Find out about setting-specific conventions and procedures which may differ, for example, between hospitals and schools.
- Consider the larger context – such as inclusion issues when working in the educational system or the effects of legislation on speech and language therapy services in the NHS.
- Clarify the nature of the therapist's role in relation to others.
- Be prepared to compromise and negotiate.

INFORMATION GATHERING SKILLS

These are very important in the decision-making process as they help to provide the evidence on which the decisions are based. They are a complex set of skills involving simultaneous actions and planning, analysis and interpretation. The subskills include,

- observation
- technical skills
- interviewing, questioning and researching
- assessment
- analysis and interpretation.

Observation. Long periods of inactive 'observation' may not be effective for students on placement. However, opportunities for periods of focused observation of a child's interaction or of an experienced practitioner during a therapy session may prove invaluable as part of their learning process. If the purpose of the observation is clear and appropriately structured, students' recordings should contribute towards the information gathering process and may help confirm or contest the working hypotheses.

In developing observation skills it is often helpful to vary the focus of any observations (Kersner and Parker 2004). The therapist-in-training may for example begin by observing the child's behaviour. Then the focus may shift to the therapist in order to observe and record his/her actions in the intervention process. They may then be asked to note aspects of the environment that helped engage or distract the child.

Ground-rules for observation

- Be clear about the purpose of the observation and the level of evidence needed to test a hypothesis.
- Have access to supporting knowledge, e.g. developmental norms.
- Decide the focus, the time frame and how to record the behaviour.
- Record whether the observer is detached or involved in the activity.
- Record the context as well as the focus of the observation.
- Avoid any value judgement.
- Record the exact behaviour observed to support any interpretation which may follow.

Technical skills. Three of the basic technical skills needed by speech and language therapists are:

- the ability to make a good audio recording;
- the ability to make a good video/DVD recording;
- the ability to transcribe and record speech and language as required into its phonetic, linguistic, non-verbal and interactional components.

Additional technical skills may be required in particular areas of specialism, for example, in using instrumentation related to voice work, or dysphagia, or knowledge of communication aids.

Interviewing, questioning and research. To gain a complete and holistic picture of any child referred for therapy, information needs to be gathered from a variety of sources, such as, the child, parents, educational staff and medical professionals, as well as researching existing records and reports.

Gathering information usually involves taking a full case history. It is important to be sensitive to parents' perceptions and feelings about their child's difficulties and the speech and language therapy process, and to offer empathic non-judgemental communication which supports them in their role. Particular types of questions may be more or less effective for different purposes. For example, closed questions which don't allow for expanded answers may provide specific information but will not necessarily help parents to feel relaxed and may even prevent free-flowing conversation. It is important to consider how questions may be interpreted as this may affect their response (see Hargie and Dickson 2004). Answers cannot be hurried and sometimes it will be important to leave a silence to allow time for reflection.

Ground-rules for compiling case history information

- Explain the purpose of the meeting when sending the appointment.
- If necessary arrange for an interpreter to be present.
- Prepare the environment.
- Begin with an explanation of the process.
- Know why the information is needed, how it may be used and only ask for information related to the speech and language therapist's role.
- Ask questions for clarification or that will help towards the acceptance or rejection of working hypotheses.
- Ask for relevant details regarding the child's social and educational context.
- Consider whether all questions need to be asked at the same time or could be left for future discussion.
- Be sensitive to whether questions may appear intrusive and may harm the relationship being established.
- Be observant about signs of distress and be prepared to stop.
- Have empathy with parents' feelings.
- Close the session with explanations, information and advice, as relevant.
- Check that parents understand the process and the information given.

Assessment. When carrying out an assessment the primary focus is on managing the interaction and the materials, while achieving the purpose of the assessment. At the same time, communication with the child and the parents needs to be managed sensitively.

Ground-rules for assessment

- Understand the different types of tests available and what the results might yield.
- Understand the implications of testing working hypotheses and how alternative hypotheses may be developed.
- Become familiar with the administration details of formal assessment materials.
- Construct activities for the specific purpose of focused informal assessment.
- Continue noting informal observations even during formal testing sessions.
- Record speech and language samples using phonetic and orthographic transcription.
- Pay attention to the details of the child's responses noting any verbal prompts given.
- Convey encouragement so the child does not feel judged.
- Help the child to feel positive about the assessment process.
- Remain objective but also empathic.
- Control non-verbal clues such as eye pointing, intonation or gestures.

Analysis and interpretation. The information and data from all sources then need to be collated, analysed and checked against the working hypotheses. The implications of the results will be considered so that decisions can be made regarding therapy and further management.

THERAPY SKILLS

The skills required for carrying out therapy are varied and complex and, as before, several skills will need to be employed simultaneously. They include being able to:

- work with individual clients;
- work with groups so that the therapy aims of individual children can be achieved as well as the group aims, while at the same time the children's behaviour is managed and their interest maintained (Chapter 7);
- work with parents and colleagues to facilitate children's communication;
- set appropriate aims and objectives;
- design and run appropriate activities in order to achieve the aims and objectives;
- monitor the appropriateness of the activities during the session and increase or decrease the levels of difficulty of the task;
- reflect on the overall therapy, evaluate its effectiveness and measure outcomes.

PROBLEM-SOLVING AND DECISION-MAKING SKILLS

As discussed above, speech and language therapy is not so much about 'correct practice' as informed 'trial and adjustment'. Practitioners need to develop creative problem-solving skills in order to clearly define their hypotheses, test them, interpret the results of their tests, consider all the implications and make decisions regarding therapy.

As outlined in Chapter 1 there are decisions to be made at many different points during the management process and the decision-making process is in itself a skill.

- Once the problem has been identified it may be helpful to consider a variety of possible solutions.
- They may be ranked in the order in which they might be tried.
- These can be reviewed for suitability and possible actions selected.
- Decisions then need to be made about how these may be implemented.

ORGANISATIONAL SKILLS

As students and as practising clinicians, speech and language therapists need organisational skills to manage themselves within the workplace. They need to manage:

- their time
- their overall workload
- requisite administrative tasks
- prioritisation tasks
- their caseload.

Summary

This chapter has been about approaches to speech and language therapists' learning and professional development. The skills that are needed by therapists to make some of their clinical decisions have been identified. A reflective model of practice was discussed in order to highlight the importance of feedback in the learning process and in therapists' continuing professional development.

Chapter 3

The first job

Bridging the gap

Deanne Rennie

Learning outcomes

By the end of this chapter the reader will be able to:

*   explain the key factors to consider when applying for and starting a first post in speech and language therapy;
*   understand the significance of personal and professional development and the specific needs of the newly qualified practitioner (NQP);
*   understand the structures and mechanisms to support safe and effective practice and their relevance for the NQP;
*   have an awareness of the importance of the health and well-being needs of the NQP.

Introduction

The NQP may feel a mixture of excitement and apprehension as they venture into their first post as a qualified speech and language therapist. The discipline of speech and language therapy offers a wealth of opportunities and can be stimulating and rewarding as well as demanding. At university, students will have been equipped with the theoretical knowledge, relevant frameworks and the basic professional and personal skills to enable them to commence practice. They have yet to acquire the range and breadth of experience which facilitates the application of this knowledge so that they can readily accomplish the complexities of clinical decision-making.

NQPs benefit from being supported and valued by the service in which they work. The professional body (RCSLT) and the regulatory body, the Health Professions Council (HPC), also help to provide the necessary elements to nurture, develop and protect the NQP. However, the newly qualified therapists themselves also play a vital part in this transition period. With a positive, 'can do' approach, reflection and questioning as well as good self-management, NQPs will facilitate their own development.

This chapter explores the issues faced by the NQP. It includes the first steps on the career pathway, personal and professional development, clinical effectiveness and also health and well-being. It provides an overview of the aspects which will help the NQP to bridge the gap to becoming a skilled and autonomous practitioner.

The first job

First decisions

Historically, most new graduates in speech and language therapy have found their first employment within the National Health Service. However, changes in health care policy have led to an increase in the number of providers of speech and language therapy services outside the

NHS (DH 2006). These range from independent, voluntary and charitable organisations and independent schools, to local authorities and private hospitals. As the number of different service providers increases so do the opportunities for the newly qualified practitioner to experience different work contexts. The NQP needs to evaluate the range and variety of choices available and decide which would best suit their personal and professional needs. There are a number of factors to consider, for example, location, clinical area, opportunities for professional development, levels of supervision as well as contractual issues such as pension opportunities, maternity/paternity provision and flexible working.

Additionally, the vision and values of the employing organisation may impact on the NQP's decision. Students considering working outside the NHS should contact the Association of Speech and Language Therapists in Independent Practice (ASLTIP) for further support and guidance. The NQP will find most posts for newly qualified speech and language therapists on NHS Jobs Online and the RCSLT Bulletin. However, different providers may advertise independently through other sources such as newspapers or internet adverts. The new graduate will need to research potential employment widely. Competition for posts can be varied and affected by the political context, therefore the new graduate who is able to be flexible and open minded about their job preference will naturally have more options.

Career progression and diversity of roles

The range of career opportunities for therapists are broad and diverse as the skills of speech and language therapists have become increasingly recognised. In addition to traditional clinical roles, therapists find themselves contributing more widely to the health, education and social care of the universal population as well as to those who have more specialist needs. Thus, new and innovative roles have been developed in preventative work, social care, training and for those working within the criminal justice system. In 2005 the NHS introduced Agenda for Change which aimed to provide a national structure for grading and pay in the NHS across England and Wales (DH 2005). At the time of writing, most new graduates start on a Band 5 or pay equivalent if outside the NHS and are unlikely to find themselves working in highly specialist clinical areas during their first two years. As their career progresses they may have opportunities to specialise within a clinical area or develop management, leadership or research skills.

Most services offer an appraisal system which provides an opportunity for practitioners and managers to share feedback on performance and opportunities to discuss career aspirations. For many, the appraisal system will relate to the Knowledge and Skills Framework (KSF) (DH 2004) which complements Agenda for Change. The KSF details the key competencies expected at each pay band and provides a pathway for progression. One factor for the NQP to consider is their area of clinical interest. Some new graduates may be clear about their choice of clinical area and career pathway; however, others may not be. There may be some areas that still have opportunities to work across adult and children's services. However, there may be a reduction in these opportunities because of recognition of the need to consolidate clinical knowledge and skills within a given area as well as grasping the differing governance and policy demands. The NQP should not be concerned if they are unsure of their chosen career pathway. They should focus on finding a post they will enjoy, that offers good support and provides a range of opportunities for further development.

The NQP as an HPC registrant

On completing their qualifying degree the speech and language therapy graduate will need to apply to be admitted to the HPC register. In the UK all practising speech and language therapists must be registered with the HPC. This is a regulatory body whose primary function is to protect the public by ensuring no one can practise without the necessary qualifications. The HPC also provides guidance for practitioners and protects the use of the professional title of 'Speech and Language Therapist'. New graduates will have demonstrated the knowledge, skills and competence set out in the Standards of Proficiency (HPC 2007). A speech and language therapist must maintain their Standards of Proficiency and adhere to the HPC Standards of Conduct, Performance and Ethics (HPC 2008) throughout their working life. They do this through maintaining their Continuing Professional Development (CPD) which may be audited by the HPC. Further information on the role of the HPC and the expectations of practitioners as registrants can be found on the HPC website. Employers must check the registration status of applicants and the NQP should expect to provide evidence of registration at recruitment and at intervals throughout ongoing employment.

The wider context

As an NQP it is essential to understand the issues and challenges faced by services. This knowledge is important for the application and interview process but will also help the NQP understand how their role relates to the wider context. The political and economic climate is constantly changing and impacts on public and independent services directly. When applying for posts initially and throughout their career, the speech and language therapist needs to be aware of the national and local policies affecting services.

There are several sources that can provide the NQP with the most up-to-date and relevant information. The RCSLT regularly publish information on policies and Position Papers which state the views of the professional body to ensure consistency and quality standards across the profession. The RCSLT's professional magazine, *Bulletin*, is an excellent source of information on current clinical and professional issues. Government websites such as the Department of Health and the Department of Education are also useful sources to find information on the latest policies and consultation documents. Developing an awareness of whole service issues at an early stage in the NQP's career will help contribute to the wider picture of the organisation. Additionally, the RCSLT have increasingly recognised the significance of political influence in protecting and developing the profession. Thus, the NQP will need to be aware of and contribute to service and professional agenda where relevant.

Applying for an NQP post

The recruitment process provides the employer with information about the skills, experience and personal attributes of the NQP, therefore they should use the opportunity well and present themselves positively. Brumfitt *et al.* (2005) found that managers perceived the 'ideal therapist' as somebody who is a good communicator, practitioner, administrator and a person with integrity and honesty. Employers want the best candidate for the post and the NQP should try to determine whether the post and employer is suitable for them. It is often advisable to contact the service by telephone for an informal chat before completing the application form and, where possible, visit the service. Many posts will have an online application process and care should be taken in completing and submitting the relevant sections. Where available the person specification and job description should be used to help select and structure the content of the application, in particular paying attention to the quality of the personal statement section. It is important to keep a copy of the application form as this will help prepare for the interview.

On receipt of the applications those candidates considered most suitable for the post will be shortlisted for interview. The application form provides a snapshot of the candidates' qualifications, skills and experience and should be well presented and relevant to the post applied for. Interviews are likely to vary in formality, content and length depending on the context of the service. Interviewees may be asked to complete an activity, for example, case discussion, and prioritisation exercise in addition to the interview. However, prior notice of this should be given before the interview in case the interviewee has any specific needs.

The interview is an opportunity to demonstrate knowledge and skills and highlight relevant experience for the post. NQPs should try to use their learning gained from clinical placements as well as other experiences, from employment or relevant interests, to support their answers. It is also recommended that the applicant should research the service and local context prior to the interview. Most services have websites to help with this and there may be additional reports available, for example, published articles and OFSTED reports. This helps to ensure the interview answers are tailored to resonate with the local service needs. The NQP should use the application process to find out as much information as possible about the post and ask relevant, pertinent questions at interview. Important areas to explore include the availability and type of supervision provided and opportunities for ongoing professional development.

Starting a new post

On being selected for a post the NQP must undergo relevant recruitment checks. This includes providing references, information for a Criminal Record Bureau Check, qualification certificates, declaration of health status and identification documents. On starting a new post it is considered good practice for services to provide a full induction for their new staff (RCSLT 2006). Within some organisations there may be a generic organisational induction which should be accompanied by a more service- and job-specific induction. Induction topics are likely to cover relevant introductions to important personnel, a tour of the settings where the NQP will be working and signposts to relevant policies and procedures. The amount of information covered during the induction can be vast and potentially daunting which is why close supervision and mentorship is crucial during the first few weeks of work so that the NQP does not feel overwhelmed.

On commencing a new post, the NQP should be introduced to their line manager. A line manager is the person who will have direct management responsibility for the NQP and who is likely to be responsible for aspects of the NQP's work such as health and well-being at work, appraisals and day-to-day operational issues. In addition to a line manager the NQP may be assigned a supervisor or mentor, though in smaller services these roles may be combined. The supervisor or mentor will support the NQP in developing their competencies as well as offering more general support.

The NQP will become aware that in addition to working directly with service users and their carers there are a variety of further activities essential to their role. This may vary according to the context; however, core tasks are likely to include recording and maintaining accurate records, report writing, contributing their views to service-wide issues and audit, providing statistical information such as caseload size or waiting times, and completing travel and expenses forms. Other activities are likely to include attending and contributing to meetings, participating in training sessions and liaising with colleagues and other professionals. Many of these tasks are learnt within the workplace (Brumfitt *et al.* 2005), thus, the NQP will need time to acquire these skills.

Working with others

The field of speech and language therapy provides a plethora of interesting opportunities to work with other professionals, which the NQP will find crucial if they are to develop a holistic approach to their work. Inter-professional education is an important component of many speech and language therapy programmes and the concept of working within a multi-disciplinary team will not be new to the NQP. The reality of collaborative practice is that it can be both rewarding and highly beneficial to the service user, but also challenging. The NQP will need to develop knowledge of local services and build up a bank of contacts to help them engage in multi-professional working. Often information about relevant local services is provided during induction; however, the internet can be a useful source of information on services such as children's centres, schools, local authorities and hospitals. To achieve true collaborative practice the NQP will need to learn to apply the skills and concepts of partnership working through good reflective practice. See Chapter 9 for further discussion.

The NQP and service users

Working directly with children and families is stimulating and is the part of the work that many therapists find enjoyable and motivating. As a student there will have been opportunities to work with service users and their families and carers. This will have enabled the NQP to begin to develop the interpersonal skills needed for the role. The NHS has placed an increased emphasis on ensuring that service users are at the heart of all decision-making, service delivery and improvement (DH 2010a). The NQP will have an important role to play as a frontline clinician as partnership working and joint decision-making will be essential to their success in providing effective therapeutic intervention. Thus, the NQP will need to further develop their communication skills as they extend their range of clinical interactions.

Personal and professional development

The NQP has the opportunity to apply their new learning and lay the foundations to becoming a competent and innovative clinician. Ongoing personal and professional development is essential to ensure safe and effective practitioners who deliver a quality service. It is recognised that the NQP will need careful supervision and mentoring during the first year to 18 months on commencing a new post to achieve the competencies. RCSLT has developed a specific framework to help with this transition (RCSLT 2007). CPD is an ongoing, essential component of practice for all practitioners throughout their career to facilitate learning and comply with requirements of professional registration.

NQP competencies and support

Speech and language therapists are considered to be safe, autonomous practitioners who are accountable for their own decision-making (RCSLT 2006). However, there is also recognition that initially the NQP will need additional support to consolidate the skills developed as a student and apply theory to practice. During the transition period there should be a focus on embedding and nurturing the competencies of an NQP to develop their confidence in their clinical decision-making and to ensure they are equipped to deal with the complexities of professional practice. It is acknowledged that, 'Practitioners who manage the transition successfully are able to provide effective care more quickly, feel better about their role and are more likely to remain in the profession' (DH 2010b, p. 4) Thus, quality of support provided is crucial to enable practitioners to flourish, enjoy their work and withstand the rigours of professional life.

The Speech and Language Therapy Competency Framework (RCSLT 2007) aims to provide employers and the NQP with a structure for supporting the transition period following graduation. The framework uses competency statements which the NQP works towards, gathering evidence to show they have achieved the standard of practice described. The framework may be implemented using different levels of supervision and mentorship and further guidance on the recommended type and level of support is detailed in the document. It is stipulated by RCSLT that supervision in any NQP post should be carried out by an HPC-registered speech and language therapist. RCSLT will not verify any framework that has not been countersigned by an RCSLT registered member.

Brumfitt *et al.* (2005) report that NQPs found it challenging to bridge the gap between theoretical study and clinical application. However, they also reported that opportunities for observed clinical practice and feedback helped significantly. Completion of the NQP Competencies enables the practitioner to transfer from a supervised RCSLT membership to fully certified practitioner. The use of the NQP Framework is now common practice amongst services and indeed results from the RCSLT Q-SET Survey found over 95 per cent of services reported its use (see RCSLT website). At interview this would be a useful aspect for the interviewee to explore to ensure they will be provided with the support needed to complete their competencies.

Continuing Professional Development

CPD has been defined by the HPC as, 'a range of learning activities through which health professionals maintain and develop throughout their career to ensure that they retain their capacity to practise safely, effectively and legally within their evolving scope of practice' (RCSLT 2006, p. 119). The aims of CPD are to ensure ongoing career development for practitioners so that they may progress or change their career pathways, and to ensure quality service delivery for service users.

The NQP will need to be aware that CPD can and should take a variety of forms including reflection on day-to-day practice, self-directed learning, attending formal taught courses and voluntary related activities. With all these forms it is important that the practitioner reflects on the impact of their learning and adapts their practice. Bray and Todd (2005) emphasise the significance of work-placed learning for the NQP stating that this is where most professional development occurs. It is through careful reflection and questioning that the NQP will begin to enhance their clinical decision-making skills and develop their practice. The RCSLT has developed an online diary to facilitate the recording of CPD activities and all NQPs will be able to use this to keep an up-to-date record. There is a variety of resources to help practitioners in maintaining and recording effective CPD including the RCSLT Toolkit for CPD and E-learning Reflective writing.

Clinical safety and effectiveness

Within the speech and language therapy profession there is a need for therapists to practise independently and safely whilst delivering effective and timely therapy. This is increasingly pertinent given the changing demands of providing quality health care in a fluctuating political and economic climate. Clinical effectiveness and safety have been recurring themes within government health policy. Speech and language therapy students will have learnt many of the legal and professional duties expected of practitioners. Indeed, while on clinical placement it is likely that practice educators may have discussed the importance of confidentiality and consent with their student. Most services will provide access to relevant training and should direct new employees to the relevant policies.

For many health service organisations a programme of continuous mandatory training is in place to ensure the ongoing maintenance of current knowledge and skills. The number of policies can be numerous and change in relation to national or local policy directives therefore maintaining up-to-date knowledge of these will become embedded in work life. Whilst many guidelines and procedures exist to facilitate clinical safety and effectiveness many of these fall within the areas of Clinical Governance, Information Governance and safeguarding of vulnerable people and clinical supervision. At first glance the NQP may find these concepts less inspiring than the direct clinical work of assessment and intervention. However, it is worth noting that such processes exist to ensure safe practice for service users and are the principles on which speech and language therapy practice is based.

Clinical Governance

Clinical Governance first came to prominence in the NHS in 1997 (DH 1997) in order that health organisations carried accountability for safe and effective clinical practice. It encompasses the need to deliver evidence-based practice, capture outcomes for therapy, reduce risk and implement clinical audit and guidelines. An NQP will be contributing to this by ensuring they have the relevant skills and knowledge for the post and maintaining these through CPD. Participating in clinical supervision and relevant service-wide audits may also be part of the NQP role. Measuring outcomes is not new to the field of speech and language therapy; however, recent policy has increased the emphasis on services capturing and reporting on the impact of service delivery (DH 2010a). The NQP may therefore have a role in measuring the effectiveness of their therapy through service-wide systems and collecting service user feedback. Care pathways are frequently used within services and an NQP would be expected to implement these pathways to provide quality, effectiveness and evidence-based practice for their service users.

Information Governance

Information Governance relates to the legal, safe and effective management of information held about patients and employees. Acts relating to Information Governance include the Data Protection Act (1998) and the Freedom of Information Act (2000). The NQP should be provided with relevant training at induction about where to record and store relevant records to ensure data protection and confidentiality. Many NHS-based services use Electronic Patient Records instead of, or in addition to, paper records. Therefore access to relevant IT equipment and training will be essential. Most organisations will have policies on standards for recording and maintaining records and there is also additional information on professional standards in RCSLT Communicating Quality 3 (2006).

Safeguarding

All services have a statutory responsibility to safeguard vulnerable adults and children (Children Act 2004; Safeguarding Vulnerable Groups Act 2006). Health, social care and education services require all employees to undertake relevant safeguarding training appropriate to their role. This is likely to be provided at induction. An NQP would have responsibility to contribute to this statutory agenda by attending training, reading relevant policies and procedures and where necessary take action to promote safeguarding, for example, referring to social services. This is a sensitive and difficult area for even the most experienced practitioner; therefore it would be expected that the NQP would receive support from management and/or specialist named professionals with specific roles in safeguarding. Some services offer supervision in this for practitioners who have had to attend case conferences or make referrals to social services. While this is a challenging part of the professional role, at all times the needs of the child or vulnerable adult should be prioritised and the NQP must seek support.

Clinical supervision

Speech and language therapists face many new situations and challenges throughout their career. Clinical supervision provides a structured opportunity for therapists to reflect on these aspects of working life and consider changes to their working practice to improve future service delivery. Supervision is closely aligned with the Clinical Governance agenda and aims to promote critical and reflective practice (RCSLT 2006). Clinical supervision is distinct from managerial and safeguarding supervision. Although all these processes should complement each other, in some cases they may overlap. Clinical supervision aims to improve practice through providing protected, designated time for reflection within a confidential and facilitative context. For many NHS service providers clinical supervision is mandatory (RCSLT 2010). The RCSLT expect all practising speech and language therapists to engage in clinical supervision as it is recognised that this improves patient care and supports the health and well-being of practitioners (RCSLT 2006). It is considered good practice for the NQP to record the outcomes from clinical supervision for their own records. Within some organisations these may be collated across the service to contribute to the wider clinical governance agenda and to identify future training needs for staff.

Health and well-being

Working as a speech and language therapist is stimulating and challenging and thus requires practitioners to manage themselves and their workload effectively to maintain their own health and well-being. The novice practitioner will rapidly have to apply many learnt skills and face many situations which may be cognitively and emotionally demanding. This has the potential to be stressful for the new clinician unless they develop good self-management strategies. As a student on clinical placement it is likely that their workload has been managed by clinicians and they may have limited experience of coping with the varied demands of caseload management and competing workload priorities. Establishing a healthy work–life balance from the outset is essential. As a student it may have been necessary to work into the evenings and weekends to complete assignments and plan for placement; however, this is not recommended on starting work. While the workload can be demanding it is important to meet regularly with a supervisor and/or line manager to ensure that effective organisation, workload and time management skills are developed from the start. Caseload sizes are variable and developing good caseload management skills will be essential. Furthermore, the ability to prioritise tasks and good time management skills will be needed. Many organisations recognise the health and well-being of employees as fundamental to the productivity and effectiveness of service delivery. Some organisations provide access to counselling and occupational health services in addition to clinical supervision programmes. Regular contact with colleagues for ad hoc support is also beneficial alongside more formal management and clinical supervision meetings.

Summary

The NQP is embarking on an exciting and rewarding career path in an innovative, constantly evolving professional field. As a student the NQP will have been given a set of tools consisting of theoretical knowledge and frameworks, and practical skills. It is through experience, reflection and supervision that the NQP will learn how to use these tools effectively and safely. The NQP should be supported from within the service and professional body; however, they also must take responsibility for their own learning and development needs. Whilst finding it challenging, the NQP should enjoy the opportunity to work with a range of people in a variety of different contexts. Through support, reflection and CPD the NQP can have a fulfilling career and strive to contribute to improving outcomes for children and their families.

Part II

Management in different settings

This part addresses the different ways in which speech and language therapy may be delivered including how services may differ in specific settings such as Health Centres, Children's Centres, Child Development Centres and hospitals. Chapter 6 includes factors that affect the educational context within which speech and language therapists work.

Chapter 4

Managing pre-school children in community settings

Kirsty Pullen and Sarah Hulme

Learning outcomes

By the end of this chapter readers should be able to:

- identify who refers pre-school children;
- understand why it is important to intervene in the pre-school years;
- understand why certain children may be considered a priority;
- identify effective packages of care;
- understand why parent–child interaction intervention might be used.

Introduction

This chapter focuses on the management of pre-school children with language and communication needs in community settings, including health centres and children's centres. The information is based on the London borough where the authors are based. The emphasis is on collaborative working with parents/carers and other key professionals. The value of focusing on parent–child interaction as part of initial assessment will be highlighted and how this informs clinical decision-making will be shown.

Referral process

Community Clinics and children's centres are usually geographically close to the child's home. Community Clinics may be part of a GP surgery. Often there is an open referral system, which means that anyone may refer a child for therapy, with parental consent. The majority of the referrals of children in the pre-school years are from health visitors, GPs, paediatricians, nursery staff and parents themselves. Referrals may follow routine health surveillance checks carried out by GPs and health visitors or concerns may arise once a child starts at a nursery or children's centre. Children who are referred to an Early Years Speech and Language Therapy service may have delayed or disordered language which may be specific to communication or be associated with a more general delay in learning. These children are likely to have difficulties in one or all of the following areas:

a   attention and listening skills
b   symbolic and social play
c   verbal comprehension
d   expressive language
e   speech development
f   pragmatics
g   fluency.

Typically, a child aged 2 years would be referred if there were parental concerns, if the child had less than 50 recognisable words and/or no two-word combinations, if the child demonstrated limited play skills and/or if the child was not asking for things with gestures or words. A 3 year old child might be referred if there were parental concern, if speech were unclear to familiar adults and the child had reduced interest in talking and communicating or used only single words or two-word utterances. If a child is from a multi-cultural environment, the therapist will need to identify whether the child's difficulties relate to developing language itself or whether they are specific to learning English as an additional language (see Chapter 14).

However, not everyone is familiar with the remit of a speech and language therapist, nor do they know the developmental milestones of all the aspects of communication. People would probably have more confidence in identifying speech difficulties than language difficulties. Problems with understanding can be masked by a child's use of context, routine and other visual cues that help them follow spoken language. It is, therefore, vital for the speech and language therapist to become involved in the planning process of local Health Monitoring programmes and ensure referrers have access to guidelines about which children to refer and when. Increasingly speech and language therapists are becoming involved in interdisciplinary preventative and capacity-building work within a setting to support children, through government initiatives, for example, *Every Child a Talker* (DCSF 2009).

Justification for early intervention

Speech, language and communication needs are common amongst pre-school children. Approximately 10 per cent of children present with significant and/or persistent needs and upwards of 50 per cent of children present with 'impoverished' language abilities at school-entry age (Hartshorne 2006). Such problems are among the most common developmental difficulties in childhood and, left unaddressed, have been linked with difficulties with later learning (Cain 2010; Catts *et al.* 2006) as well as exclusion from school, placement in pupil referral units and youth offending (Cross 2007).

About 60 per cent of language difficulties may resolve without treatment between the ages of 2 and 3 years. The multi-layered nature of language and communication development makes clinical decision-making an uncertain process (Law *et al.* 2000).

Research studies such as van Balkom *et al.* (2010) show that parents do not cause their children's communication difficulties. However, in response to their child's difficulties, parents appear to adapt their interaction, for instance by using the more 'confrontational' interaction of clarifications, requests and interruptions. That is to say they may develop a less facilitative conversational style over time.

The rationale then for early intervention is to prevent these 'confrontational' interactive patterns developing and becoming entrenched. An approach focusing on positive parent–child interaction, as well as developing communication-friendly environments by building staff capacity to support children within children's centres, is likely to be effective in helping to redress the interactive balance.

Parent–child interaction

Different intervention packages (Kelman and Schneider 1994; Kelman and Nicholas 2008) have been developed from the Interactive Model of Language Impairment (Girolametto *et al.* 1999). One of these is described below.

Video Parent–Child Interaction therapy (VPCI)

VPCI was developed in a speech and language therapy service in North London and was based on the original work by Kelman and Schneider (1994). The basic philosophy of VPCI is partnership between the therapist and the parent(s): the parent providing the expertise about the child, and the therapist providing appropriate knowledge about language acquisition. Such collaboration combines parents' insight and experience with the therapist's knowledge and observations, enabling strategies to be developed which may increase the child's rate of language development.

VPCI offers self-learning and video for self-reflection. In this model, a video is made of the parent playing with the child. The therapist and parent then watch the video together, analysing the interaction and identifying the communicative strengths in relation to the child's needs. The therapist enables the parent to identify the strategies which are supporting the child's communication and the therapist and parent then discuss ways in which these positive strategies can be used more often within regular 'special times' at home.

Assessment

One of the ways of dealing with a high referral rate of pre-school children to speech and language therapy services is to operate a two-stage system for initial appointments. This system provides a time-effective way of managing non-attendance at initial appointments, allows the therapist to prioritise children with more significant needs and gives the opportunity for multi-agency liaison prior to the full assessment.

An initial interview, lasting up to 30 minutes, is offered first. This allows the therapist to meet and observe the child, to understand the parents' perceptions of their child's difficulties and carry out a case history, and to explain the assessment process. For the parents, the appointment provides an opportunity to meet the therapist and ask initial questions, while the child has the chance to become familiar with the environment. A full assessment appointment can then be arranged according to the child's needs. For example, an appointment may be made immediately for a child with a potential language disorder, while assessment of a child with a mild phonological delay may be scheduled several weeks later. This encourages the speech and language therapist to make decisions about prioritisation from an early stage.

During the assessment process the therapist will use formal and informal assessments to provide a profile of the child as there is no single screening tool which can be applied universally (Law *et al.* 1998). Information about any changes which may have occurred in the child's communication skills in the preceding weeks or months are a useful prognostic indicator. This is particularly relevant for children between the ages of 2;0 and 2;6 as this is often a period of rapid spontaneous change.

Assessment of pre-school children usually commences informally. The therapist will observe the child on the way into the therapy room. Materials may then be presented in order to observe the child's responses. The toys chosen need to put the child at ease, and will have been specifically selected to provide the therapist with information relating to the child's symbolic play level and developmental stage (Lewis and Boucher 1997).

When using the VPCI approach an assessment session may start with the parents and therapist talking whilst the child is at play, with the therapist and child playing or with the parents and child playing together whilst the therapist observes the interaction, ideally through a video link in an adjoining room. The use of a video link can put the child at ease and allows the therapist to make initial observations of the child's spontaneous use of language. It also provides information about the parent and child's current interaction style; for this reason the play is usually filmed so the video can be watched later in the session with the parent.

Having observed the child's play, attention and concentration span, the therapist may join in the play to facilitate further investigation. Particular attention will be paid to the child's turn-taking abilities and responses as the therapist mirrors the child's actions and extends the child's play through non-verbal modelling. At this point there is no specific focus on talking.

If the child does not have the attention level required for formal assessment, an informal assessment based on the *Derbyshire Language Scheme* (Knowles and Masidlover 1982) may provide a baseline profile of the child's comprehension and expressive skills. This will complement the therapist's observations of the child's attention abilities and play skills, and may provide an elicited language sample to add to the spontaneous language already recorded on video. Observations of the child's non-verbal communication skills are also made.

It is as important to consider what supports the child's communication as it is to understand where their difficulties lay. Within a dynamic assessment the therapist will look carefully at how easy it is to stimulate the child, the child's response to adapted interaction style, how the child benefits from different support strategies (for instance visual cueing, the use of Makaton and repetition of instructions) and the child's ability to learn (for example new vocabulary) as a predictor of change.

The therapist will then talk through the child's assessment profile with the parent, highlighting strengths and areas for development. The video is then watched by the therapist and parent. The therapist supports the parent to identify a positive strategy already being used which they can utilise more during play at home. Any aims need to be realistic, attainable and clear so that they can be implemented immediately and successfully. The philosophy of VPCI is that the parent identifies a strategy that works for them, one that is meaningful and relevant to them, and this increases the likelihood it will be confidently used and successfully maintained.

Case example

Philip aged 3 is slow in his speech and language development. The family have been offered VPCI by the speech and language therapist.

Having watched the video, Philip's mother comments that she's doing most of the talking. She feels it would be helpful to wait more often for Philip to talk. She plays with Philip again, with this in mind, and then watches the video with the therapist. Philip's mother is encouraged to reflect on what she has achieved and she notes the impact of her new approach on Philip's communication. She is asked to use this strategy at home during 'special times' throughout the week. That is, to set aside five minutes of uninterrupted time on a few occasions to play with Philip and to modify the way she interacts with him.

The decision-making process

The therapist's role is to differentiate those children whose difficulties are likely to resolve, either spontaneously or with the support of others, from those children whose difficulties are more persistent and who will need speech and language therapy input in order to make progress. Key clinical criteria which may be used to identify those children most at risk of ongoing language difficulties appear to be:

- hearing – fluctuating glue ear
- positive family history
- reduced use of gesture
- reduced CV babble
- reduced range of consonants
- paucity of verbs.

Other potential risk factors include:

- children who are 'looked after' as they can often move across and between boroughs before accessing or completing intervention;
- family history of speech/language, communication and literacy difficulties;

- lack of parental engagement with services;
- limited opportunities for interaction and communication;
- parental anxiety.

It is important to consider both 'risk' and 'resilience' factors together with the clinical information from initial assessment when making decisions about further management. The therapist needs to draw together the information gained from the parents and other professionals as well as the clinical observations and assessment findings in order to make decisions about the most appropriate intervention.

Providing specific labels at an initial assessment is not necessarily appropriate, particularly with young children whose profile is likely to change over time. A description of the child's strengths and any areas of difficulty will provide a more relevant and useful summary for the parents at this stage. A written report, which includes the strategies discussed during the session as well as additional suggestions for the nursery/children's centre, is given to the parents. It is then, with their consent, distributed to the key professionals involved. Referrals may be made to other professionals, with parental consent, for example, to a clinical psychologist for support with behaviour difficulties or a paediatrician for an assessment of general development.

It is helpful if written information about language development is given to parents and nursery staff at this time. The therapist can then make reference to this when explaining the stage at which the child is currently functioning. Where a child's difficulties are of particular concern, close liaison with the nursery and other key professionals will be necessary to ensure the right support is in place. The emphasis should be on multi-agency collaboration, with professionals liaising as closely as possible and working as a team around the child.

Throughout the process of intervention, review appointments are paramount. Where there is a gap between initial assessment and start of therapy, a child's abilities should be reviewed before therapy is started to gauge progress and ensure the most appropriate package of care is offered. At this point it is often easier to make a more informed decision about the child's prognosis based on the amount of change seen in the child's language abilities, and in the parents' interaction style. The child who has made large gains in language development with the help of the parents' adapted interaction style is likely to continue to make spontaneous progress and may be discharged from the service or reviewed again following a further consolidation period.

After any therapy package, which should always include a consolidation period to allow the child chance to embed and generalise new skills, the therapist should arrange a review appointment in order to monitor progress, consider the efficacy of the intervention and to inform further decision-making.

Therapy packages of care

It is important that within a speech and language therapy service there is a range of direct intervention packages available which can be matched to the wide range of individual children's needs and that there is built-in capacity to prioritise children with more significant needs. Thus a child with a more persistent, severe difficulty should be able to receive therapy as swiftly as possible.

Children considered a priority are those who present with:

a   disordered or severely delayed language development;
b   difficulties that persist in the context of limited parental change;
c   difficulties that persist, despite the parents having effected change in their own interaction style;
d   disordered or severely delayed speech development or dyspraxia;

e   social communication difficulties, including pragmatic language impairment;
f   selective mutism;
g   children with associated/additional behaviour issues which are impacting on other areas of
     learning and development.

Four week course of video parent–child interaction therapy

This therapy package (Cummins and Hulme 1997) builds on the video interaction work introduced in the initial assessment and consists of four individual weekly parent and child sessions. It is generally offered as the first package of care to families. As described above, a video is made of the child and parent at play and this video is watched by the therapist and parent. The parent is encouraged to reflect on their interaction style and the strategies that best support their child's communication, sometimes using a written self-rating scale to guide the discussion.

Through discussion, and always relating adult interaction to the needs of the child, the therapist supports the parent to identify one area to focus on in their 'special times' during the coming week. As always, the therapist does not instruct the parent, suggest areas to work on or model strategies for the parent to copy. The therapist's role is one of facilitator, supporting the parent through the process of self-reflection and it is the parent who chooses the interaction strategy that is most meaningful and important to them.

In families where English is an additional language, the sessions are structured in exactly the same way but with the support of an interpreter or bilingual co-worker.

Sessions two to four build on the developments of the previous week, with the pace and focus being set by the parent. At the end of the four weeks there is a consolidation period of approximately six weeks. The parent is asked to continue with the special times at home, consolidating the new patterns of interaction. The parent and child then return for a review session to evaluate progress and make further decisions about intervention. The child's speech and language skills are fully re-assessed and the new profile compared with the initial assessment profile. The therapist's decision about future intervention is based primarily on whether the discrepancy between the child's abilities and that of his/her peers is reducing and how quickly this may be occurring (Cummins and Hulme 1997).

It is important to stress this style of intervention cannot be achieved without the use of a video camera, since the key to change is in the opportunity provided to the parent to self-reflect and make their own decisions.

Language groups

Language groups may be weekly or run more intensively over a shorter period. Each group is run by two therapists with a maximum of six children per group. Groups may last between 30 and 60 minutes depending on the attention/listening skills and ages of the children. There may be several groups running throughout the day so children can be offered a group at the appropriate level for their language and communication needs.

Parents are expected to be involved in the language groups, either by joining the children in the room to support their attention/listening and participation and reinforce vocabulary, or by observing the sessions through a viewing mirror or via a video link system. Parents should be given a clear plan of each session, with information about the aims behind each activity and for their individual child.

It is vital for the parents to have the opportunity to discuss their child's progress with the therapists at regular intervals throughout the groups, whether this is a five minute discussion at the end of a group, a telephone discussion at the end of the day or a separate meeting. Parents may also be invited to attend a workshop. These workshops seek to combine parents' mutual support with information about the therapist's aims and objectives, general information about communication development, and strategies for consolidating and facilitating change at home.

If the child is attending a playgroup, nursery or children's centre, but the speech and language therapy service is being offered within a clinical centre, the child's key-worker or teacher is encouraged to observe at least one of the language group sessions. This provides an opportunity for the therapist to share information and suggestions with key-workers whilst demonstrating additional strategies with the child in the group. Ideally, the key-worker will be in a position to carry out an agreed activity on a regular basis in their own setting. For the child, this provides helpful carry-over into nursery while offering the key-worker pre-planned activities with specific targets. This may also be helpful to other children with similar needs within the setting.

Some children may need to attend more than one course of language groups according to the nature of their difficulties.

Intensive therapy courses

An intensive six-week parent–child interaction therapy course (Kelman and Schneider 1994) is considered for children who have accessed support and therapy in their local Community Clinic but who continue to present with significant and ongoing language difficulties. It consists of 18 sessions of therapy over six weeks. The three sessions each week consist of a VPCI session, a language group and a parent workshop. The focus is on working together with parents by sharing information, knowledge and skills as well as through direct intervention.

The other option for intensive therapy is the pre-school language unit. Children attend a language group three times each week over a period, typically ten weeks. Parents are encouraged to observe groups regularly and to meet with the therapist at regular intervals during intervention to discuss progress, ongoing needs and useful strategies/activities. Key-workers of children attending the unit are also offered training around adult–child interaction so that the support strategies used with the child are consistent across all communication environments. Most children access two of these intensive ten week courses and for the majority their progress is accelerated during the second course.

Children with communication difficulties seem to benefit greatly if they are offered such intensive help prior to school entry and this may then preclude the necessity for additional support at school age.

Evidence is gathered using parental feedback and comments which are included in the clinical notes.

Training for practitioners/capacity building

Ideally, the therapist will visit a child's nursery or children's centre in order to observe the child, discuss aspects of the child's communication with the staff and offer advice about relevant activities and strategies. In practice, however, this is not always possible. Three further packages of care may be offered to nursery staff or key-workers that are aimed at building the staff capacity to provide an appropriate environment for the child and therefore maximise the potential progress.

The first is similar to the four week VPCI therapy package. In order to develop the child's abilities and the key-worker's interaction with the child, a video course is offered to the key-worker who is invited to attend the local clinic with the child once a week for four weeks.

The second package is ACT! (Hulme 2005) which is a one-and-a-half day training course for groups of practitioners. All participants are required to bring a video of themselves playing and interacting with a child in their setting. The first day starts with background and theory around language development and adult–child interaction. During the second part of the day, in small groups, practitioners watch their videos and reflect on their interactions. They analyse their interaction using a tally sheet, where they record how many times they ask questions, direct the child, praise/repeat/copy the child and comment on the child's play. Unlike VPCI it isn't necessary for the therapist to take on the role of facilitator because the tally-counting system gives practitioners the structure they need to reflect on their interaction style with their colleagues. Each practitioner selects an interaction aim to focus on during regular five minute 'special times' in their setting.

Practitioners then bring a new film clip to the second part of the ACT! training which is usually scheduled for four weeks later. Again in small groups, practitioners reflect on their interactions, noting any changes and the impact of these changes on the child's communication and, with the therapist's support, identify further interaction goals.

A third package has a pre-emptive function, focusing on children who are considered to be 'at risk' of having future difficulties with their language development or children who would benefit from developing their communicative confidence. A four week language enrichment programme is offered within a nursery setting as described by Parker and Cummins (1998). Here, the students screened the language and communication skills of all the children in the setting and, with the staff, identified children to access daily groups. In addition, students worked with one child on an individual basis, videoing themselves in play and analysing their interaction to develop a facilitative interaction style.

Some children will be discharged after attending a course of VPCI or language groups. Others will need more sustained support and may go on to attend one or both of the intensive therapy courses.

Summary

Although there are different ways of working with pre-school children with language difficulties, focusing on parent–child interaction has been shown to be particularly useful as part of initial assessment, to inform clinical decision-making and as a therapeutic package of care.

Chapter 5

The roles of speech and language therapists working in community clinics, child development centres and hospitals

Sue Roulstone, Mary Gale and Helen Marks

Learning outcomes

By the end of the chapter the reader should:

- be aware of the range of children seen in each setting;
- be aware of the unique aspects of the therapists' role in each setting;
- understand some of the key issues for speech and language therapists;
- be aware of strategies for evaluation.

Introduction

In this chapter the aim is to examine the work of speech and language therapists who are based in community health centres and clinics, in child development centres (CDCs) or who work with children in hospitals. Although there are commonalities shared by therapists across work settings, some aspects of the work are particular to a diagnostic group or to the specific function of that setting.

For example, the identification of risk is a common issue. In order to establish whether or not a child is at risk for long-term speech, language or communication difficulties, therapists must investigate features of a child's history as well as the presenting symptoms. A family history of speech difficulties or a history of birth trauma might alert a therapist to the potential for long-term difficulties for a child. Additionally, within each diagnostic or clinical setting, there will be particular clues to be found. For example, when dealing with pervasive developmental disorders, aspects of joint attention will be crucial.

Community clinics

Background

Over recent years, the way that the NHS is organised has changed a number of times and there is now much more variation in how services are commissioned and delivered. However, community clinics and health centres are still commonly the base from which speech and language therapists working with children operate, although therapists typically work with children in the context of most relevance to that child.

Following the recommendations of the Field Report (2010, p. 7), children's centres are set to become 'a hub of the local community' and are therefore likely to take on increasing prominence in the community therapist's role.

Centres including clinics, health centres and children's centres are the focus of primary health care for local communities, and referrals to therapists working within such centres may cover the full range of speech and language difficulties. The speech and language difficulties seen in local health and community centres will depend on the availability of other specialist services, the structure of the speech and language therapy service and the geographical location. For example, therapists working in rural areas may see children with a larger range of difficulties than therapists working within urban contexts where specialist clinics are available, or where initial assessments are dealt with on a centralised or specialised basis.

Open referral is the norm, so referrals are accepted from parents, early years' practitioners, nursery nurses and teachers as well as community paediatricians and GPs. Referrals from health visitors are set to increase again with the emphasis on early intervention and the role of the health visitor (Allen 2011). Although a local community speech and language therapist may still receive direct referrals, it is now common for referrals to be channelled through a 'single point of entry', that is, referrals to speech and language therapy are received by a central office, checked and then allocated by a senior therapist to a particular location or therapist. In some services, this initial checking will include an assessment as part of a triage process that prioritises those children considered to be most urgent, or who will most benefit from intervention. Despite this central processing of referrals, therapists' regular contact with those making the referral is invaluable for developing appropriate referrals and for accessing additional information and support.

The role of speech and language therapists in community clinics

Being based close to the primary health carers in this way puts the community speech and language therapist 'in the front line' – responding to concerns raised in the community by parents about children's speech, language and communication development. Depending on the location and size of the speech and language therapy service, the therapist may be part of a team of speech and language therapists serving a local area, or they may be the only one for miles around. Whichever the case, the therapist's response to others' concerns should be part of an agreed role, structured as part of the speech and language therapy service response.

There are four key aspects to the speech and language therapist's role.

Health promotion and information giving

An important role for therapists working at the 'coal face' is to provide information to parents and primary care workers, including nursery staff and school nurses about normal language development and appropriate referral processes.

Evidence about screening and early intervention for children with speech and language difficulties has not supported the introduction of universal screening for these problems (Law *et al.* 1998). However, recommendations about early identification and intervention (Allen 2011; Field 2011) are likely to lead to new initiatives in screening and surveillance. Speech and language therapy services can support these initiatives through the provision of training and literature as well as by supporting decisions about appropriate evidence-based screening or surveillance packages.

Selection and prioritisation

Speech and language therapists working in community clinics may be the first recipients of a referral into the service and therefore play a crucial part in making the decision about whether or not a child will gain access to the service. This is not simply about determining the presence or absence of difficulty, but should also take into account the family's needs and wishes as well as the service's ability to deliver an effective package of care. Not all parents wish to bring their young child for a regular appointment; some may prefer to receive information about the nature of their child's difficulties and an opportunity to make contact at a later date (Glogowska and Campbell 2000).

With younger children, there is the added complication of distinguishing between a speech and language delay that is in the process of being resolved and a long-term difficulty. There is some research to suggest that children with comprehension difficulties are particularly at risk for having ongoing problems and that the difficulties of those with purely expressive delays are more likely to resolve spontaneously (see Law *et al.* 1998 for a review).

There is a range of flow charts available in the literature to support therapists through the initial assessment process (Roulstone 1997; Whitehurst and Fischel 1994; see also Chapter 1) and local services commonly have guidance and evidence-based care pathways to support therapists. However, the application of these general principles to particular cases still requires professional judgement in making complex decisions, and it is important that the therapist allocates an appropriate amount of time for this. If an appointment is planned to cover initial selection and allocation to a care pathway, there needs to be time available to provide opportunities for exploration of the difficulty with parents, to liaise with other people in the child's life such as family workers or nursery staff, to discuss options for intervention and to write up case notes and reports. Exploration of the family's goals and preferred outcomes should also be a part of the discussion to ensure that intervention pathways are relevant to the family's goals and motivations.

The therapist's investigation must culminate in a decision which confirms whether or not the child's current communication context – the context currently provided by the child's family, and/or nursery – is sufficient for the child's level of need (Roulstone 1997). For example, a child with a relatively major delay may not require an intensive level of intervention if the family are relaxed and supportive, can handle the child's behaviour constructively, are able to adjust their own levels of communication, can provide appropriate activities and there is access to nursery attendance.

By comparison, a child with a mild to moderate delay may need a different level of intervention if the parents are anxious and isolated, if they have few ideas about the most appropriate toys, games or activities for their child, and if they find the child's behaviour puzzling and difficult to manage. The first child might benefit from access to periodic advice spread over a long-term period; for the second, relatively short-term therapy which is specifically targeted and intensive may be preferable.

Finally, decisions about intervention have to be matched with relevant evidence-based care pathways which are linked to intended outcomes. If children are prioritised, do they get fast access? Do they receive more therapy? Or, do they have therapy for longer? Ideally, general principles for these decisions should be established at a service level and allow for interpretation for individual children.

Onward referral

A community therapist must also decide whether or not the child's problem is a relatively contained and manageable one or whether further referral and investigation is appropriate. Decisions about when, and to whom, to refer will depend on the speech and language therapist's own expertise and on the range of specialist services available, but typically will include the community paediatrician; so community clinic therapists should always acquaint themselves with the structure of services in their locality. This process may be guided by the Common Assessment Framework (CWDC 2009). This framework is shared across the children's workforce with the aim of coordinating early assessment and identification of children's needs.

The most common type of onward referral will be to the paediatrician or to the CDC for a multi-disciplinary assessment for children who may have other developmental difficulties. Referral for hearing assessment may have been initiated already but, if not, this should always be considered. Other investigations might be appropriate for children who are observed with 'absences' which might be construed as epileptic in origin; a neurological investigation might be appropriate in this case. A referral to social services might be necessary if a family is in need of support. In some cases, it will be more appropriate for the referral to be made by the GP since they will be able to give a child's full medical history. However, a therapist's observations about the speech, language and communication as well as other more general observations about the child's behaviour will be invaluable to members of other disciplines and should be part of the onward referral.

Any further referral should, of course, always be discussed with the family first. This can be a difficult process where child safeguarding issues are involved (DCSF 2010). Therapists working with children may be involved in child safeguarding procedures where the physical or emotional well-being and safety of a child are considered to be at risk.

Ongoing intervention

Decisions about the most appropriate therapy regime need to integrate existing knowledge from the literature about the efficacy of particular regimes and their effectiveness in clinical contexts with the speech and language therapist's knowledge of a particular child. Most speech and language therapy services now specify the interventions available within a service through evidence-based care pathways.

It will often fall to a local community therapist to provide ongoing care for a child. Specialist assessments may take place, but regular intervention is usually needed as close to home as possible. For unusual or complex cases, therapists will require support from their specialist colleagues and may need to set up joint sessions to access their expertise in areas such as acquired language problems or autistic spectrum disorders (see Chapter 20).

Issues for the community clinic therapist

Large diverse workloads and caseloads

There is no doubt that therapists working in community clinics face major issues relating to controlling their workload in order to remain effective. The range of communication impairments is often diverse, challenging the therapist's knowledge and expertise. Therapists need to balance the number of children and the number of sites in order to maintain effective practice. There are no national accepted standards for caseload size and although recommendations have emerged from research, these are not necessarily accepted in local services (Law *et al.* 2000). Caseload sizes and waiting times are now often specified through service agreements. Therapists responding to the pressures around them to see children need to remember to allocate time to conduct thorough assessments, complete reports and case notes, to plan therapy and prepare materials and to think through cases thoroughly. This is particularly important where the impairment range is diverse and the therapist must draw on knowledge about multiple assessment and intervention procedures.

Working in children's contexts

Some therapists are fortunate enough to have a purpose-built base, designed to provide a child-centred environment with access to the child's family so that an understanding of the child's context can be developed from the start. An important decision is whether or not to provide intervention in the clinic or whether to move to more child and family-friendly environments, such as children's centres, nurseries, playgroups or indeed the child's home.

In practice, most therapists arrive at a decision which is a compromise between what is feasible and what is ideal. Where there are several children in one nursery, the establishment of good working relationships with nursery staff may provide the opportunity to have an impact on the child's broader communication environment and offer additional insights into a child's needs and difficulties.

Child development centres

Children are referred to CDCs primarily for in-depth assessment and diagnosis, and management of complex and multiple disabilities. Referrals to the centres come from a range of sources such as neonatal units and locality teams including speech and language therapists. Typical referrals would include children with cerebral palsy, learning difficulties, autistic spectrum disorders as well as relatively rare syndromes. Children are usually seen initially during their pre-school years but may be followed up throughout their childhood. The increasing complexity of these disabilities means that there is a higher number of children with feeding and swallowing problems coming to a CDC for assessment and this initially often takes priority over the child's communication difficulties as concerns regarding nutrition and aspiration risk are raised.

The speech and language therapist works as a member of the multi-disciplinary team which could include a paediatrician, psychologist, physiotherapist, occupational therapist and social worker. The team might also include play workers or nursery staff. Typically speech and language therapists working in this context will have had more than five years' experience but in some services, junior therapists will work under the supervision of a more experienced colleague.

The role of the CDC therapist

The therapist within a CDC has two particular roles.

Detailed and coordinated diagnostic assessment

Therapists in this context need to be able not only to make detailed observations of a child's speech, language and communication behaviour but also to interpret them diagnostically in discussion with the team. For example, differences in a child's social communication and pragmatic skills can be instrumental in differentiating between autistic spectrum disorders and severe language delays.

As assessment information is acquired, a mechanism is needed whereby the therapist regularly feeds information into and receives reports from the rest of the team so that a coherent and inclusive picture develops. Changes needed to the assessment process will have to be negotiated as emerging data lead to new hypotheses about the child's needs and difficulties.

With so many professionals involved, there is the potential to 'flood' children and parents with repetitive questioning and tasks. Having a collaborative plan for the assessment process is therefore vital for effective working. Ideally, this would be discussed with the family by a key-worker who is a member of the team.

Liaison and support

As inclusive policies have become predominant in education it has become more usual for ongoing intervention to be provided by local therapists rather than continuing at the CDC, although this varies according to the distribution of expertise and supervision within a local service. A management plan needs to be negotiated with the local therapist and should specify the level of support required. This might include joint sessions for demonstrating particular strategies, training for local nursery staff, for example in the use of Makaton, or the acquisition of particular equipment such as symbol boards (see Chapter 21).

As children return to the CDC for family support and planning meetings, the CDC therapist will need to liaise with local speech and language therapists to obtain up-to-date information on the child's progress and on the current issues requiring investigation or support.

Issues for therapists working in CDCs

Dealing with parents' grief

For many families, the CDC assessment process may bring them to the point of diagnosis, to be faced with the prospect of their child having a long-term disabling condition. The therapist may therefore have to work with families who are coming to terms with this knowledge, and to deal with their denial, their anger and their distress. Knowing the typical stages of the grieving process (Kubler-Ross 1997) and being able to recognise one's own limitations in dealing with these is important. A therapist should be able to help the family in accessing other support mechanisms, either from voluntary groups such as Afasic, a charity supporting families with children with speech and language difficulties, or Mencap, the main charity for people with learning disabilities, or through appropriate staff within the NHS and social services. This responsibility may well be passed to the local community therapist as more of the everyday management of these children passes to the locality team.

Knowledge of rare conditions

As the survival rate for infants improves, the range of conditions presenting within the CDC increases. Therapists working within this context will therefore need to be aware of relatively rare conditions, such as Fragile X syndrome or Rett syndrome, and their likely impact upon a child's developing speech and language and feeding and swallowing skills.

Working in hospitals

Background

Speech and language therapists working in hospitals are usually attached to medical specialities, for example, ENT, neonatology, gastroenterology and neurology. Their role is a responsive one, attending to whatever communication and feeding and swallowing difficulties arise from the medical conditions. For example, therapists may be working with children who have a tracheostomy, who have had head injuries or children who have been admitted due to failure to thrive or with a history of nasogastric tube feeding (see Chapter 22). Referral of children with feeding and swallowing difficulties, particularly in the neonatal period, has been increasing in recent years and now constitutes a significant demand on therapy services in hospitals.

As members of the multi-disciplinary team, speech and language therapists' co-workers will include paediatricians, surgeons, physiotherapists, dieticians, occupational therapists, clinical psychologists, social workers and, if the child is in hospital for a long time, the hospital teaching service provided by the local authority. Typically, therapists working in children's hospital contexts are experienced therapists with specialist training in dysphagia.

The role of the hospital therapist

Constraints of medical and surgical interventions

Uniquely, the nature and organisation of speech and language therapists' interventions will be structured and constrained by the timing and location of the medical and surgical interventions.

For example, when working with children presenting with a cleft palate, the therapist may meet the family soon after the child is born, have recurring contact as the child undergoes surgery and follow-up until the child reaches adulthood. With the development of regional centres for cleft surgery, the specialist therapist has become the provider of ongoing assessment, of diagnostic or intensive therapy. Liaison with the child's local therapist will also be important since children will be seen in their home town for ongoing therapy (see Chapter 17).

On the other hand, for children who are recovering from a traumatic head injury which has affected their speech and language, short sessions on a daily basis for the period of their stay in hospital might be appropriate. The therapist's role would be to monitor their progress and, through ongoing assessment, to support the child, the family and the ward staff to establish effective and supportive communication strategies.

In this responsive mode, a therapist may be responding to an acute condition and therefore have to make a rapid response to referrals but be involved for relatively short time periods.

Informing medical and surgical interventions

Information about a child's oromotor functioning and progress in speech and language development can be crucial in determining the timing of medical and surgical interventions. For example, subtle changes, progress and deterioration in a child's speech or language noted by the speech and language therapist might be an important indicator of changes in a child's medical condition which may alert a doctor to the need for action. For example, in children who have had tracheo-oesophageal repairs and associated narrowing of the oesophagus, a slight decrease in toleration of oral feeding and swallowing ability and an increase in secretions may indicate the need for a surgical review to see whether further management of the stricture is necessary.

In the same way, information about the safety of a child's swallow may enable a decision to be made about when the child may be discharged from hospital, and whether nasogastric feeding needs to be considered. If a therapist is to provide timely input to such decisions, regular involvement in medical rounds and specialist clinics will be an important feature of the therapist's working week.

Issues for the hospital therapist

Families in distress

Admission of children to hospital is, in most cases, in response either to an acute episode or to a serious medical problem. Families are, therefore, often in considerable distress. They will almost certainly be tired from the constant demands of supporting a child in hospital, from heightened levels of anxiety and, if they are staying in the hospital, from disturbed sleep. They will frequently have been exposed to a number of different professionals and may well have supported their child through a number of invasive procedures. Speech and language therapists working in this context have to take account of this when discussing management strategies with families, considering, for example, the amount of new information provided at any one time, and the need for repetition and explanation.

Rapid change

While conditions such as cleft palate now have quite a predictable history, many of the children seen in a hospital context will be in a period of rapid change and children can make progress that is at times quite astonishing. Times arranged for seeing children may be disrupted by other medical procedures or the child may be asleep or too ill when the therapist arrives on the ward. An ability to respond appropriately and flexibly to such changes is acquired through experience, although even the most experienced therapist can be surprised. Caution and good record keeping is vital in these circumstances.

Evaluation

Different aspects of a therapist's work will require different monitoring and evaluative approaches to ensure that the management and therapy offered to each child and family is appropriate and effective.

Evaluating training and the referral process

The effectiveness and appropriateness of any training offered and the appropriateness of referrals received from primary care may be evaluated using questionnaires (van der Gaag *et al.* 1999) or the use of vignettes (Wren 2003). These sources provide ways of gaining feedback on the value of training, for examining referral processes and for the interpretation of the results of an audit.

Selection and prioritisation

The decisions about the selection of children for therapy and about prioritisation in relation to existing caseloads and waiting lists will be made by several different therapists in any Trust. It is important, therefore, to ensure that equity of access is maintained. Analysis of routine data collection can provide important information about the level of severity of children who are offered care. For example, if all therapists collect a similar measure for children with speech deficits, such as the percentage of consonants correct, these data can be analysed at a service level to monitor the decisions made by therapists. Use of an outcome measure such as the Therapy Outcome Measure (Enderby *et al.* 2006) could provide a similar routine measure in order to monitor therapists' intake decisions.

Periodic peer review is also useful. An example of how this might be used to discuss consensus within a department is given below.

Peer review of initial assessment

- One speech and language therapist videotapes an initial assessment session (with the parents' permission).
- The therapist then watches the videotape and identifies key decision points – that is, where one activity was terminated by the therapist and another begun. For example, the therapist decides that enough case history information has been collected and moves on to ask parents to engage in play with their child.
- Following this, the therapist selects approximately four decision sections to show to peers.
- The therapist provides referral information for peers plus information gained during the session up to the first decision section to be shown.
- Peers and the therapist view the first decision section.
- At the end, peers are asked to write down their conclusions about the child's condition so far, and what they would do next.
- Peers and the therapist then discuss. Writing views down prior to the discussion helps to anchor views and provides evidence as to where and how their judgements coincide.

At the end of this process, the therapist may provide another piece of information and video section and the whole process may be repeated.

Onward referral

When evaluating the appropriateness of onward referral, there are various questions which need to be asked, for example about the relevance of the detail and complexity of any reports written by the therapist and whether the parents are happy with the process.

The process of peer review described above, together with feedback reports from the specialist provision, can provide insight into whether each child has been referred on to the appropriate professional. It would also be good practice to confirm with parents at each stage that they understand and support the process.

Ongoing intervention

Even where programmes have proven efficacy through research trials, it is still imperative that therapists monitor the effect of that intervention as applied to an individual child.

If therapy is well structured and goal related, then therapists can assess the child's progress against previously specified goals negotiated and agreed with a parent. For example, there may have been a specific and measurable objective set such as: 'by the end of the episode of care, a child will be able to use two word utterances'. At the end of the specified time, if the child has not achieved that goal, the reasons for this can be explored. It may have been, for example, that inappropriate tasks were set; or that there was insufficient input, or too high expectations; or that other underlying skills were insufficiently established. This sort of process has been formalised within procedures such as the *Goal Attainment Scaling* (Kiresuk *et al.* 1994).

Primary or secondary outcomes can be the focus of the evaluation. Primary outcomes will be those directly involved with changes in the child's communication, for example, their level of understanding, or their intelligibility. Secondary outcomes are those which measure related aspects but not the communication behaviour of the child directly, such as the observed changes in the parents' interactions with the child (see Chapter 4).

Commissioners of services require evidence of impact from a parent's perspective, so therapists need to ask parents to complete questionnaires and feedback forms or encourage parents to keep diaries of progress so that at the end of a period of intervention, they can summarise the parents' perspective.

The assessment process

It is important to establish whether the assessment process has been effective. Consensus amongst the team, parent satisfaction with the process and outcome, the provision of timely and complete reports and a clear management plan should all be part of such an evaluation. Multi-disciplinary audits will be appropriate in this context and might include the use of parental questionnaires and the involvement of parents in user groups.

Team support structures

Speech and language therapists working in teams, for example in a CDC, can evaluate whether the support was structured in the most productive way, for example by asking for feedback from local therapists. Although this could be done by questionnaire, periodic meetings to review the process, for example once a year, might be more productive. Topics for discussion might include the effectiveness and efficiency of the joint sessions, the training offered, the reports provided and the resources available.

In well-established teams, children's progress in speech, language and communication and the therapist's input may be part of an ongoing clinical audit of the team's performances. Speech and language therapists in these contexts, for example in a hospital, might be expected to suggest appropriate measures for the audit process and subsequently provide data for the team. These data would be used to evaluate the team as a whole as well as the medical or surgical interventions.

Summary

All of the contexts considered here have their specialist aspects. Therapists working in community clinics, CDCs and hospitals will carry out many similar functions and share common skills, but the demands of each will enable the development of an expertise that is particular to the context.

Chapter 6

Working with children with speech, language and communication needs in school settings

Marie Gascoigne

Learning outcomes

By the end of this chapter the reader should:

- have an understanding of the factors influencing the clinical decision-making process in school settings;
- have an understanding of the national and local commissioning processes in England, and the extent to which they influence models of service delivery;
- have an understanding of the educational context in which speech and language therapists work;
- be aware of the role of the speech and language therapist as part of the wider children's workforce.

Introduction

In this chapter the decisions will be explored which underlie the speech and language therapy support provided for children in school settings, including mainstream schools, mainstream schools with specific resourced facilities and special schools. The emphasis will be on the factors which influence the model of support offered by the speech and language therapist.

Increasingly, in both health care and education, decisions as to what interventions should be funded, whether directly or via a commissioning process, are taken by non-specialists who rely on evidence-based data, set against the identified need of the population for which they are responsible. The engagement of the speech and language therapist with the decision-making process will vary according to their role within the system.

The RCSLT position paper (Gascoigne 2006), together with Communicating Quality 3 (RCSLT 2006), provide the professional view regarding how speech and language therapists should work with children. In 2011 the RCSLT released a report commissioned to investigate the economic case for speech and language therapy across four conditions (Marsh *et al.* 2010). One of the findings was that for every £1 spent on speech and language therapy, £6.40 was saved in long-term benefit to the economy.

In this chapter the research evidence for the different models of service delivery in schools will be considered and the decision-making process around the individual child will be reviewed.

Figure 6.1 shows the levels of decision-making which impact on the support for individual children and also groups of children, such as a school roll, or population of a local area.

The figure also identifies key blocks of knowledge and specific documents, the production of which are part of the overall process of translating a budget for a given population into a speech and language therapy package for an individual child. These blocks provide a framework through which to consider the decision-making process as a whole.

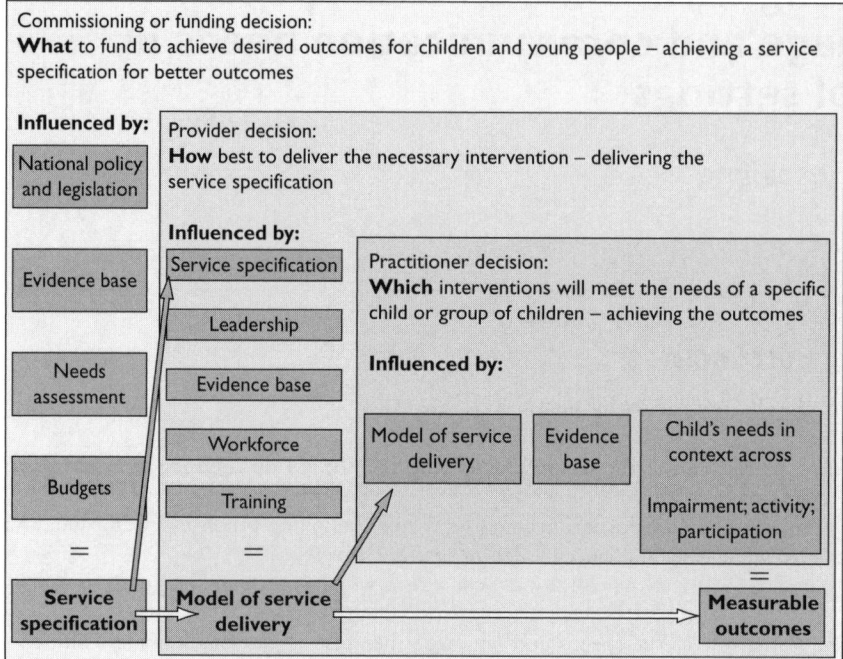

Figure 6.1 Decision-making for service delivery.

The commissioning or funding decision

In the current legislative framework, commissioners are specific to England. Since the devolution of powers to the Scottish Parliament, Welsh and Northern Ireland Assemblies, the devolved administrations have not adopted the same degree of separation between those who make the funding decisions and those who are engaged to provide the services. The term 'commissioning' will be used in this chapter; however, those outside English jurisdiction can draw useful conclusions from the decision-making process by thinking of 'funding' as the key parameter.

Commissioners of services need to develop a service specification that sets out clearly what the outcomes are which they have prioritised for children and which they expect to see achieved. In order to achieve a robust service specification, commissioners need to understand:

- the policy and legislative framework;
- the population they are responsible for;
- the range of provision and support infrastructure which exists within their area;
- the evidence base for the given area;
- what they can expect to achieve with their available budget.

The legislative and policy context

The commissioning process in England is complex. It illustrates the extent to which the locus of control for clinical decision-making is held at the level of the therapist, as opposed to the level of the 'system'. It highlights the potential tension between 'clinical autonomy' and 'service specification'. In a well-commissioned service, this tension should be minimal provided the service specification has been based on a sound needs assessment and evidence base and developed in conjunction with stakeholders. However, the commissioning processes are in themselves evolving and it is worthy of note that the Bercow Report (Bercow 2008) highlighted the need for a commissioning framework for children with speech, language and communication needs (SLCN).

In England, the Health and Social Care Bill (DH 2011), Education Bill (DfE 2011a) and the Special Educational Needs (SEN) Green Paper (DfE 2011b) together introduced a transformation of the governance and administration of public services, with the removal of many of the national and regional bodies that had previously been responsible for ensuring implementation of policy and supporting practitioners. The most recent legislation is considered in the context of its precursors in order to provide a comprehensive overview.

Health legislation and policy

The Health and Social Care Bill (DH 2011) set out legislation to disband strategic health authorities and primary care trusts, devolving the commissioning of health services to consortia of GPs with a National Commissioning Board overseeing the commissioning of low incidence complex needs. This extends the principles previously introduced that a provider must be able to evidence their claims regarding provision and effectiveness, and that there should be a choice of providers. The 2011 legislation created space for providers to become greater in number and variety. With this comes an implicit challenge regarding the traditional employment of speech and language therapists within the statutory health sector as services will move to other organisations such as hospital or foundation trusts, social enterprise organisations, or to private or voluntary sector providers.

Education and children's services legislation and policy

The Every Child Matters (DfES 2003) outcomes of children's entitlement to be healthy, stay safe, enjoy and achieve, make a positive contribution and achieve economic well-being, were adopted with local interpretations across the UK and therefore provide a useful backdrop to understanding the move towards integrated services for children.

In order to achieve these outcomes, all services for children within a Local Authority (LA) area were required to work in an integrated way. The concepts of universal, targeted and specialist tiers of service were introduced as part of this policy agenda with a view to identifying a continuum of services for children. This included universal services which anyone could expect to make use of such as a school or a GP, targeted provision, which was available for those who are vulnerable, and specialist provision for those with specific needs.

Other core elements included an emphasis on supporting parents, early intervention and prevention, localising of provision and encouraging information sharing between professionals. This prompted the emphasis on the need for training for all professionals around core competencies in order to work effectively with children.

Special education needs policy and legislation was increasingly interpreted through the concept of integrated children's services. Starting from a premise that inclusive education was a desirable and achievable concept (DfES 2004), the integrated children's services approach introduced the possibility of moving towards a system where the child and its family were placed at the centre of planning. For children with complex needs, the Aiming High for Disabled Children initiative (DCSF 2008a) provided a cohesive strategy bringing together elements from education, health and social care. The revised Code of Practice for Special Educational Needs (DfES 2001) outlines the school-based stages of support, School Action and School Action Plus, as well as the process for moving through Statutory Assessment and possibly having a Statement of Special Educational Needs. The Code views educational provision on a continuum. This is from mainstream schools to resourced schools, where a mainstream school develops a specific expertise in an area of SEN with specialist support staff, to special schools where the whole environment and curriculum is adapted to take account of the children's special educational needs. The placement of an individual takes into account the views of the parents and if possible the young person themselves.

Speech and language therapy support for children has been the subject of case law and judicial review (R v. *Lancashire County Council* 1989; R v. *London Borough of Harrow* 1996) regarding the educational nature of SLCN and the responsibility for providing speech and language therapy. The 2001 Code of Practice sets out a range of activities relevant to the support of children with SLCN.

There is explicit recognition that speech and language therapy support can be more than one-to-one therapy. The Code also made explicit the responsibility for ensuring the provision is made available to an individual child, placing the primary responsibility with the health service but ultimately with the LA if the health service is unable to provide the required support.

The SEN Green Paper (DfE 2011b) will precipitate a further revision of the Code of Practice for SEN. The proposals within the Green Paper include a move to replace Statements of SEN with an Education, Health and Care Plan which is described as a multi-agency document with the same statutory force as a Statement of SEN but applicable to all parties and not just the LA. However, the NHS remains a resource-limited service to which there is no absolute right. The Green Paper also asserts that children are over-identified as having SEN and proposes to have one school-based stage instead of two, with a higher threshold of need to qualify. There are two obvious areas of risk.

*   the commissioning of speech and language therapists will be limited to those with Education, Health and Care Plans;
*   schools may be reluctant to recognise the significant needs of children who might be at a targeted level of need for speech and language therapy.

The Green Paper should be seen in the wider context of the Education Bill (DfE 2011a) which focuses on the establishment of academies and free schools. The Green Paper also paves the way for special schools to become academies or free schools. As schools become more autonomous so LA control and influence decreases. The implications for therapists working in schools include the impact of this increased autonomy and the increase in the commissioning power of head teachers. Speech and language therapists providing support in schools will need to take account of the outcomes desired by the school for all the children on roll as well as the specific-child outcomes.

Policy documents relating to SLCN

The RCSLT position paper (Gascoigne 2006) interpreted the core principles of Every Child Matters as they might specifically apply to working with children with SLCN.

There were a number of key concepts which speech and language therapists were asked to consider in their decision-making for children. Attention was drawn to the *International Classification of Disability* (WHO 2001) taxonomy of impairment, activity and participation. In making clinical decisions regarding therapy, the suggestion is that there should be a balance between all three in order to ensure that intervention takes account of:

*   functionality;
*   the impact on activity and participation of the individual's difficulties;
*   the therapeutic intervention offered.

This is not to say that impairment-focused interventions are undesirable, but rather to make explicit the link to functional impact as the ultimate purpose of intervention.

The position paper sets out some core principles which speech and language therapists should consider in planning and delivering services. These include:

- children should be able to access speech and language therapy in the setting most appropriate for their needs;
- speech and language therapists should always work with others who are involved in a child's care;
- speech and language therapists should not only work on core speech or language difficulty but also spend time helping to transfer strategies into everyday activities;
- speech and language therapists have a key role in planning and delivering services across the spectrum of all children;
- training parents, support staff and other professionals is a part of the role of a speech and language therapist;
- speech and language therapists working with other professionals should plan together a 'joined up' programme for the child and their family with different team members leading on the direct support of the child as appropriate.

The Bercow Report (2008) has five key themes.

- Communication is crucial.
- Early identification and intervention are essential.
- A continuum of services designed around the family is needed.
- Joint working is critical.
- The current system is characterised by high variability and a lack of equity.

The Better Communication Action Plan (BCAP) (DCSF 2008b) was the government response to the Bercow review. It included a number of initiatives to address the majority of the recommendations within the review. These included the appointment of a Communication Champion to provide a focus for the issue at a national level and to co-ordinate 'Hello', a national year of speech, language and communication, in 2011 and the development of a suite of commissioning tools to support commissioners (CSP 2011). The BCAP also included funding for a research programme into the effectiveness and efficacy of interventions for SLCN.

What to commission?

Commissioners for children of school age need to decide whether they are able to commission across the tiers of universal, targeted or specialist services, or whether they have to prioritise one element of the whole system over another. In times of financial pressure, the temptation is to commission only for the most severe and specific needs. However, this approach often leads to waiting lists and many pressures.

A universal service within schools includes supporting the school to be a communication friendly environment, contributing to the development of school policies on communication and access, and providing whole staff training around identification of SLCN and strategies to support communication. The level of input will vary from school to school according to need. For example, a mainstream school with little experience of children with SLCN may need a significant amount of initial support. A special school familiar with supporting communication may have well-developed universal systems and require less from the speech and language therapist at that level.

Upward of 50 per cent of children entering school in areas of high socio-economic deprivation may have delayed speech, language and communication skills (Locke *et al.* 2002). Not all of these will require direct intervention from a therapist; however, the priority given to prevention of longer term need through provision of good universal and targeted support may be greater in areas of deprivation than in more affluent areas. The links between deprivation and delayed language acquisition are not simple. Indeed, not all children from deprived environments will have language delay whilst children with relatively affluent environments might still be 'deprived' of stimulating early experience (Law and Harris 2006). The impact of not providing support at the universal and targeted levels for those who are disadvantaged can been seen later when language and behaviour difficulties become enmeshed and potentially in extreme cases can result in contact with the criminal justice system (Stringer and Clegg 2006).

The targeted and specialist levels within school are on a continuum. Targeted interventions might include language groups jointly run by a speech and language therapist and a member of school staff with the dual purpose of delivering intervention and providing training for the staff in order that they continue similar group interventions independently. Some individual children might be seen at the targeted level, but always in conjunction with school staff. Here the differentiation with a specialist intervention will be the level of complexity of the case – the targeted child will either be subject to certain vulnerabilities for speech, language and communication difficulties, or will have needs where the response to intervention is relatively predictable and the delegation of intervention to a colleague from the wider workforce for the majority of the child's programme is appropriate.

Specialist level interventions can also be group or individual and should continue to involve members of school staff. The key factors distinguishing these from targeted interventions will be the complexity and predicted rate of change for the child. A child who has a specific speech or language impairment, who is likely to require a highly skilled practitioner to interpret subtleties of responses, is more likely to require specialist intervention. Conversely, a child with complex needs may have their SLCN adequately supported with targeted interventions delivered predominantly by school staff. This is especially true of special schools where the environment and the workforce is already enhanced, and yet it is often assumed that special school provisions require more speech and language therapist's time than mainstream schools.

The commissioner will need to make informed decisions and translate these into a service specification which sets out the outcomes to be achieved and some of the core parameters of the service they wish to see in place to deliver these outcomes.

The provider decision: how to deliver?

Historically, providers have decided which model of intervention they favour and commissioners have usually accepted this so long as outcomes have been met. Increasingly providers are being asked to respond to a commissioner-led service specification. Individual speech and language therapists need to consider that those within their organisation who are agreeing the model of service delivery may not come from a speech and language therapy background. So, evidence base and external reference points are key to influencing the provision received by children.

Service specification

There is increasing evidence focusing on the model of service delivery as opposed to the specific interventions themselves (Topping *et al.* 1998; Lindsay *et al.* 2010). Traditionally special schools have had an amount of speech and language therapy time allocated on the assumption that the need is significant as defined by the nature of the school. Inclusive education, parental choice to include children with complex needs in mainstream schools and the increased understanding of the contribution made by the universal and targeted tiers of provision, have provoked the need to consider all schools and their pupils on a continuum.

A series of randomised controlled trials conducted in Scotland to examine both the clinical effectiveness and cost effectiveness of different modes of intervention in schools have concluded that there is no significant difference in terms of child-based outcome between therapy delivered by a therapist and therapy delivered by a speech and language therapy assistant following a therapy manual. The results relate to children with language difficulties and are not generalised for those with severe phonological or speech difficulties (Boyle *et al.* 2009). A follow-up study investigated the effectiveness of school-based staff delivering the ongoing therapy programme as opposed to speech and language therapy assistants. The findings showed the children receiving therapy via school staff did not make the same gains as those receiving it from speech and language therapy assistants or speech and language therapists (McCartney *et al.* 2011). The conclusion was that the results were most likely due to compliance issues. The speech and language therapy assistants' delivery of the therapy activities was more consistent than that of the school-based staff. This has important implications for service providers in terms of securing collaboration and commitment from school staff in the delivery of therapy.

Bringing together the policy context and evidence base, the following principles apply to a robust service model for schools. All schools should have the following.

- A named link therapist who is the primary link between the school and the speech and language therapy service as well as being the 'default' therapist in the first instance for all children within the school.
- Access to specialist speech and language therapists who use their skills not only to work with small numbers of children for limited periods but to enhance the capacity of the link therapists to manage the children appropriately
- A speech and language therapy presence in schools so that the schools become the main venue for the delivery of speech and language therapy – this may involve moving resources from traditional 'health' venues
- An allocated amount of speech and language therapy time based on a transparent formula. This will include a range of parameters such as the size of the school, attainment levels, number and complexity of needs of children already known to the speech and language therapy service, information about the infrastructure within the school to support special needs in general and SLCN in particular. These factors will interact to enable schools to be grouped into different levels of need.
- Regular opportunities for parents to meet with therapists.

The speech and language therapy provision to a given school could potentially be delivered by a local health provider, a social enterprise or alternative provider, an independent practitioner contracted directly by the school or a voluntary sector organisation. For the purposes of this chapter, and given the differences across the countries of the UK, the assumption will be made that speech and language therapy is provided by speech and language therapists who work for a local health provider.

In responding to the service specification, the provider has to consider how best to meet the outcomes which have been specified, within the budget available. They have to demonstrate that they can provide high quality provision within the overall philosophy of the specification.

Outcome measurement

Evaluating outcomes is a crucial element of the decision-making process. The increased focus on outcomes as opposed to inputs has led to a debate about the nature of the outcomes most appropriately measured and the methodology for capturing and reporting the data.

The commissioning tool Evaluating Outcomes (CSP 2011) provides a useful overview for the provider and practitioner. It presents child level and group or population level outcomes as a guide for users with SLCN. The use of population-based outcomes is less familiar to speech and language therapists but increasingly important to those funding services.

A number of outcome measurement systems have been developed to help set in context the multi-factorial profile of clients for therapy at the individual level (Malcomess 2005; Enderby *et al.* 2006; Johnson and Elias 2010).

Therapy Outcome Measures (TOMs) (Enderby *et al.* 2006), use a four strand system for profiling the client at a point 'a' which can then be revisited at a point 'b'. The strands link to the *International Classification of Functioning* (ICF) (WHO 2001) and therefore provide a robust profiling tool.

TOMs provide scaled descriptors for severity across the parameters of impairment, activity, participation and well-being/distress. The scaled descriptors provide reference outlines for the therapist for each of the points on the scale. Using a tool such as TOMs will allow a structured classification of the information gathered at initial assessment to provide not only an evaluation of the degree of severity of the child's communication difficulties but also a baseline for measurement of efficacy of any intervention provided.

The practitioner decision: intervention to deliver outcomes

The systems level decisions considered up to this point will have influenced whether or not a child is eligible to receive support from the speech and language therapy service. On the assumption that they are, the therapist will make three key clinical decisions:

- assessment
- intervention
- evaluation.

In order to consider these decisions in context, three case studies will be used. Table 6.1 provides a brief overview of these children.

Assessment

This may be initial assessment or a subsequent re-evaluation of the child's needs. It needs to be clear that there is a clinical purpose to the assessment. For example, a child new to the service or presenting with a complex and disordered profile may require ongoing detailed assessment, whereas a child well known to the service and moving between therapists may be able to move directly to an intervention.

Assuming an assessment is indicated, it should include a range of tools which will allow a profile of need to be developed which goes beyond the language impairment and also takes into account the impact on activity and participation in both the learning and social environment of school. Information gathered from school staff, including copies of any individual education plans, will provide invaluable information and a joint framework for discussion between the staff and a therapist.

A concern of many school-based services is the potential loss of contact with parents. A range of strategies might be employed to ensure adequate parental involvement. The school may prove an appropriate venue for the therapist to meet with the parents particularly if they already have a relationship with the school. Schools where there is a speech and language therapy service presence across universal, targeted and specialist tiers have provided regular informal opportunities for parents to meet therapists in school, for example, coffee mornings including discussions on a topic around language and communication. Such events could take place 'pre-referral' when parents have the opportunity to raise concerns and may receive general advice which prevents the necessity for a formal referral to the service.

Whether a formal assessment process has been necessary or not, before planning intervention the speech and language therapist should have a comprehensive profile of the child's communication and the information necessary to set goals and outcomes measures.

Table 6.1 Case examples

	Michael	Anita	David
Overview	• 6 years old • Attends local primary school • LA has moderate to high levels of deprivation • Has a Statement of SEN • School receives additional funds which equate to 2 hours per week with an individual support teacher or 10 hours per week with an LSA • Part 3 of the Statement specifies Michael will require a programme of activities devised by and monitored by a therapist carried out by school staff • Three hours per term have been identified as the appropriate amount of therapy time	• 6 years old • Is in the same class as Michael • Does not have a Statement of SEN • Being supported in school at School Action Plus • Referred to speech and language therapy service by SENCO, who has concerns regarding her speech intelligibility and the impact this seems to be having on her ability to acquire reading and writing skills using the phonic approach that the school favours	• 10 years old • Attends a special school • Has a Statement of SEN which specifies placement in the special school with an adapted curriculum • Delayed speech and language skills are outlined in the statement but not specific requirement for speech and language therapy • Known to speech and language therapy service in the past – when last assessed language and communication skills were in line with other abilities
Assessment	• Comprehension standard score = 75 • Expressive standard score = 80 • No speech sound difficulties identified • Functionally able to follow simple instructions with the support of peers and LSA • Able to take part in group activities with some success • Socially isolated in the playground	• Comprehension standard score = 110 • Expressive standard score = 80 • Unintelligible to unfamiliar adults when speaking out of context • Evidence of speech sound difficulties which need further investigation • Evidence of frustration • Non-verbal abilities felt to be age appropriate • Generally included in peer group	• Comprehension standard score = 70 • Expressive standard score = 70 • No speech sound difficulties identified • Responds well to modified curriculum with visual timetable • Participates in group activities with adult support • Well integrated with peers in the playground
Ratings using TOMs			
Impairment	3	1	2
Activity	3	2	3
Participation	3	4	4
Well-being	4	4	4
Intervention			
Speech and language therapy intervention	Language activities within school led by school staff devised and monitored by therapist	Periods of direct intervention with therapist in conjunction with school staff and parents plus additional activities for school staff and parents	No active intervention at present – David is discussed at termly meeting and therapist can become involved at any point should his needs change.
Intervention tier	Targeted	Specialist	Universal (within special school setting)

Intervention

The action taken following assessment will be influenced by the systems level decisions outlined above combined with the clinical interpretation made by the speech and language therapist. For example, Michael could be supported at the targeted level with collaborative working between the therapist and the school.

Anita is likely to need periods of direct intervention from a therapist with additional activities carried out in school and at home to support her therapy. The therapy should be integrated into the education plan. There should be coordinated support from the literacy specialist in the school so as to maximise the impact of both interventions. Anita will therefore need some support at the specialist level, but this does not preclude her benefiting from targeted interventions during the same period.

David attends a special school where the curriculum is modified to meet his needs and the school staff have received training and are experienced at supporting children with his profile of SLCN. Speech and language therapy intervention is not indicated at this time.

Where a 'whole school' approach is taken, a child can simultaneously access a number of interventions placed at different levels of the universal, targeted and specialist continuum which focus on different elements of impairment, activity, participation and well-being.

Some services experience capacity and demand issues resulting in waiting lists for access to speech and language therapy interventions. One of the benefits of a systems level set of decisions, to include the full range of universal, targeted and specialist provisions, is that there may be appropriate interventions not led by a speech and language therapist which are more immediately accessible to the child. These may address an element of overall need – perhaps at the participation level.

Evidence on the importance of effective collaboration between the speech and language therapy service and the wider workforce (McCartney *et al.* 2011; Martin 2008; Dunsmuir *et al.* 2006; Hartas 2004) means that the speech and language therapist must proactively seek the integration of their goals for a specific child with the school-based goals identified through the education plan.

Evaluation

The outcome measurement tools mentioned above offer systematic ways of evaluating measurable change. If the service model allows for delivery in discrete 'packages' or units of intervention, then for each child there will be a number of outcomes to consider at this stage.

When evaluating the outcome, the decision is whether to continue with the same interventions, whether to adapt or change some of them, or whether to stop intervention. Placing a child on 'review' where an open duty of care is maintained without any intervention should be viewed with extreme caution in an efficient model of service delivery. Of course, some children will have long-term complex needs and can expect to have periods where their speech and language therapy needs will become more evident, for example during a period of transition. If the system is operating efficiently, it should be possible to confidently 'cease contact' with these children at the point where perhaps their pace of change is stable and they are well supported within their environment. If the context changes or the child's needs change, they can be immediately redirected to appropriate intervention.

Summary

The reader should now have an understanding of the complex layers of decision-making which result in an individual child accessing the appropriate intervention to meet their SLCN. Much of the decision-making is beyond the level of the individual therapist–client relationship but there is a drive to achieve greater consistency for children. There is a need for every speech and language therapist to contribute to the evidence base and to ensure that commissioners of services and managers within provider organisations are well informed as to best practice.

Chapter 7

Managing children individually or in groups

Oonagh Reilly

Learning outcomes

By the end of this chapter, the reader should be able to:

- discuss the current evidence base in support of group or individual therapy;
- identify the advantages and disadvantages of group and individual therapy;
- identify the decisions to be made when planning group or individual therapy;
- identify sources of problems and conflict within groups and provide possible solutions.

Introduction

In this chapter, the complex process of group therapy will be explored. The initial focus will be on the decisions surrounding whether children should be seen individually or in groups.

The management process

As discussed in Chapters 1 and 2, although the speech and language therapy management process, like the students' learning process, may appear to be linear, it may be considered as cyclical, as assessment is ongoing throughout intervention (see Figure 7.1).

Assessment and intervention

At any point in the assessment process the clinician may make a diagnosis or provide a description of the child's needs, but this can change as the child's needs change, and as further evidence is gathered.

In Figure 7.1, intervention is shown as an integrated sub-process, because the therapist will move between assessment and intervention as necessary and, as discussed in Chapter 1, many therapists use diagnostic therapy to help elucidate the underlying nature of the child's speech, language and communication needs.

Important decisions need to be taken regarding the form and nature of the intervention. Each of these decisions may interact with or be determined by the others, as will be seen in the rest of this chapter, as the specific decisions surrounding group or individual intervention are considered.

Direct or indirect therapy

The therapist needs to decide whether to provide direct therapy for the child or indirect therapy as this will affect 'who' works with the child. In indirect therapy the therapist works with the child's parents or other professionals such as teachers, teaching assistants or early years workers.

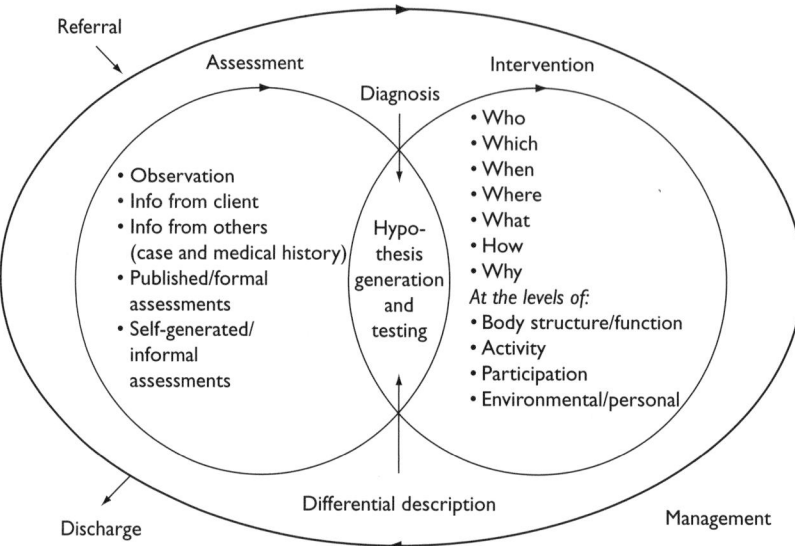

Figure 7.1 Management process framework.

Both direct and indirect therapy may be provided in a group, for example, a parental-based interaction group, or individually. Reilly *et al.* (2004) found moderate evidence to support the Hanen model of parent-based intervention, and Gibbard *et al.* (2004) found a significant increase in language outcomes for children receiving such intervention versus advice on a review basis. The choice between direct and indirect therapy will depend on several factors including the child's communication needs, the theoretical rationale underlying the intervention approach, its evidence base, resources and child/parent values. Direct and indirect therapy approaches are not mutually exclusive, and the decision to use one over the other may change during the course of therapy as the child's and parents' needs change.

Still, part of the 'who' decision is whether to provide therapy for children in a group or individually. Although this decision should not be made solely on the basis of resources, the availability of resources must be considered. Group therapy should not be seen merely as a way of reducing waiting lists for intervention.

Group versus individual therapy: the evidence base

Meta-analyses and systematic reviews of the literature (Law *et al.* 2004; Cirrin *et al.* 2010) reveal mixed results both for group and individual therapy. There are many variables in each study to be considered such as the type of communication need, who delivers the intervention and how, when and where the intervention is delivered. Cirrin *et al.* recommend that until more evidence becomes available, the therapist must prioritise internal (therapist's personal experience and judgement) and client factors over external (published) evidence.

Internal factors to be considered

- What is the therapist's preferred theoretical approach? Does it lend itself more to one type of intervention than the other? Although some approaches have traditionally been considered more appropriate for individual therapy such as the psycholinguistic approach or computer-based interventions they can be utilised successfully in groups (Stackhouse and Pascoe 2010; Wren *et al.* 2010).

- Is the intervention approach relevant to a particular setting, e.g. teaching vocabulary in the classroom with collaboration between the therapist and teacher? Throneburg *et al.* (2000) found this to be more effective than direct individual speech and language therapy.
- Who will deliver the therapy and what training have they received?
- Cost analyses are also a factor to consider and cost-effective studies are becoming more popular. For example, whilst Boyle *et al.* (2007) found no significant differences between direct and indirect and group and individual modes of service delivery on a variety of language measures, Dickson *et al.* (2009) in a cost analysis of the same study found that indirect group therapy was the least costly and direct individual therapy the most costly.

Client factors to be considered

- Whether the client will benefit from individual or group therapy, and which method will maximise their participation (see Fry *et al.* 2009b).
- How the parents will be involved to maximise outcomes not only at the level of impairment, but also at the level of activity and participation. These are domains in the *International Classification of Functioning, Disability and Health for Children and Youth* (WHO 2007), which include body structure and function, activity and participation, environmental and personal factors. For example, the therapist can devise and carry out activities in a community clinic that target the child's impairment in body function, e.g. phonological impairment, stammering or receptive language delay. However, it is the parents and other adults in the child's life who can carry through the targets into different contexts, enabling the child to participate in conversations, group activities in school, or social and community activities outside school. Some parents will require a great deal of training and support to enable them to do parent-based intervention.
- Logistical aspects such as child's age and location and whether they meet the criteria for the group.

Advantages and disadvantages of group and individual intervention

The rationale for providing intervention for a particular child will be based upon the balance between the advantages and disadvantages of each approach in relation to the child's needs.

Opportunities for interaction with others may be better provided through group therapy.

Some of these are based on the work of Fawcus (1992), Andersen-Wood and Smith (1997) and Rustin and Kuhr (1999).

Table 7.1 Questions for the decision-making process regarding intervention

Who:	will be involved in the intervention?
Which:	aspects of communication will the intervention address (e.g. speech, pragmatics, receptive language)?
When:	will the intervention take place and for how long?
Where:	will the intervention take place?
What:	will the intervention be (e.g. 'psycholinguistic'; 'The Lidcombe Program'; 'meaningful minimal contrast therapy')?
How:	will the intervention approach be presented (specific activities)?
Why?	rationales should be provided for each decision made.

Table 7.2 Advantages and disadvantages of individual therapy

Advantages of individual therapy	Disadvantages of individual therapy
The child's individual needs can be targeted with greater ease.	It creates an artificial communication environment.
The pace of therapy can be matched to the individual child.	Parents do not meet with other parents who have children with communication needs.
Children who are lacking in confidence may be less intimidated: a safe and secure environment for both parent and child is provided.	The total attention of one adult may be threatening or overwhelming for some children.
All of the therapist's time is dedicated to the individual.	Fewer children can be seen within the same time period.
Appointments may be more flexible.	It can be more costly than group or indirect interventions.
It is easier to monitor progress and make notes.	Generalisation may not occur automatically.
Distractions can be minimised so children with attention difficulties can be focused more easily.	

In individual therapy, the dynamics between the therapist and child can ensure a focused response to the child's strengths and needs so the child is sufficiently challenged to effect change and therefore gain success. This is an interactive process, related to the theoretical construct of Dynamic Assessment (see Hasson and Joffe 2007). The therapist can scaffold the child's responses and model appropriate techniques for parents to carry over into other settings.

However, a skilled therapist can also accomplish this within a group. The difference is that the explanations and discussion about techniques can only occur after the session and time may need to be allocated for this.

Case example

Oscar is 5;3 years of age. He was referred for therapy when he was aged 4;0. Since then, he has had two blocks of individual therapy for his phonological impairment. Progress has been slow, with little consolidation between the therapy blocks. Oscar continues to use the phonological processes of stopping, cluster reduction and gliding of liquids. His hearing is within the normal range and there are no known causal factors that may account for his phonological impairment. He has been at school for six months in a class where there is a high ratio of children to adults and a large number of children with specific needs. Oscar is able to recognise a few written words, but cannot identify phonemes and his phonological awareness is delayed.

The therapist, in negotiation with Oscar's mother, has made the following decisions about his intervention:

- *Who will be involved?*
  Oscar will receive direct intervention in a group with his mother observing.
  Rationale: other children with similar speech needs are available to make the group viable; Oscar is judged to be demotivated, but a group would offer a greater variety of activities, greater opportunities for generalisation of skills and so may be more motivating. Parents can observe through a two-way mirror and be shown facilitatory techniques (Bowen 2009).
- *Which aspects of communication will the intervention address?*
  Oscar needs to increase the use of meaningful contrasts in his speech.

Table 7.3 Advantages and disadvantages of group therapy

Advantages of group therapy	Disadvantages of group therapy
Provides a more natural communication environment.	Not all clients learn best this way – some may be too shy or inhibited.
Helps to encourage awareness that others also have communication needs.	There will be less time focused on the individual.
Children may learn from each other as each has different strengths and resources.	There may be personality clashes within the group.
Offers a range of different communication models.	Children with disruptive behaviour may inhibit the group achieving its aims.
Competition may lead to greater motivation.	Some children's attention difficulties may be exacerbated by the group situation.
Increases the possible range of activities and the opportunities for interacting with others.	Parents may worry that children will learn 'bad' habits from each other.
Fosters the generalisation of skills taught in individual sessions.	Absence of members may alter the group dynamics in a negative way.
More suitable for those who find the intensity and attention in individual therapy threatening.	The initial setting up of groups requires time for planning, organisation and other resources, e.g. rooms, training.
Multiple skills may be focused on.	Confidentiality may be more difficult to maintain.
May provide a support network for parents and for children when groups are run in schools.	It may be easier for children to opt out.
Self-monitoring behaviours may be established through peer feedback.	Parents may be daunted by group involvement.
Offers a greater variety of child–child interactions, e.g. child-led clarification requests and repair.	Parents may feel upset if their child is functioning at a lower level than others.
Can be part of the classroom activity and so may help the child not to feel singled out for therapy.	Specific resources will be needed to enable the parents to observe, e.g. video link, two-way mirror, larger room.
Group work may be a more cost-effective method of service delivery.	The therapist and helper must be skilled in group facilitation and may require additional training or experience.
	It is often difficult to find enough suitable participants to make the group viable.

Rationale: this should increase intelligibility, and Oscar has no other communication needs.

- *When will it take place and for how long?*
  The group will start as soon as possible and last for six weeks.
  Rationale: Oscar is aware of his difficulties and his participation in different settings may be affected. Also, he is learning to read and will need to improve his phoneme awareness and grapheme knowledge if he is to sound out written words. There is currently no specific evidence to support six week blocks of therapy, but this is the provision available in Oscar's local clinic.
- *Where will the intervention take place?*
  In the community clinic.
  Rationale: other potential participants attend different schools, so a school-based group is not feasible at this time. Adjacent rooms with a two-way mirror are available at the clinic.
- *What will the intervention be?*
  Meaningful Minimal Contrast Therapy (Baker 2010).
  Rationale: this is the preferred approach of the therapist and is appropriate for Oscar's type of speech impairment.
  Metaphonological therapy.
  Rationale: intervention which includes phonological awareness and grapheme knowledge is likely to improve speech and support the development of literacy (Hesketh 2010).
- *How will the intervention be presented?*
  Homophony confrontation utilising minimal pairs of fricative versus plosive contrasts.
  Rationale: this is taking a phonological approach to a phonological impairment. The metaphonological components will involve reflecting upon and manipulating the properties of the fricatives and plosives and their position within words.

Group planning

When planning any group, decisions must be made with regard to:

- function of the group;
- criteria for entry, group composition and size;
- aims of the group;
- structure of the sessions;
- learning opportunities and strategies for generalisation;
- group leadership.

Function

Goldberg (1997) suggests that speech and language therapy groups may have four functions:

- teaching of new behaviours;
- generalisation of behaviours;
- gathering of data by further assessment;
- discussion group for support or training.

In Oscar's case, the group will primarily have two functions – the teaching of new behaviours and their generalisation.

Criteria for entry, group composition and size

The more the members are matched in age, needs and interests, the more harmonious the group is likely to be. However, group harmony (a high level of comfort or ease within the group) should not be mistaken for group cohesion in which members of the group are actively engaged, supportive and accepting of each other. For example, in certain groups with older children when conflict arises it needs to be addressed openly and the group can then learn different strategies for dealing with it. This can only happen with the support of a cohesive group. However, the children do not need to be strictly matched. Yalom (2005), describing psychotherapy groups states: 'Time and energy spent on delicately recasting and rebalancing a group cannot be justified given the current state of our knowledge' (p. 280) and this must certainly apply to speech and language therapy groups. It is helpful to combine a mix of abilities to balance the group so that children can learn from each other and provide different models (Lees and Urwin 1997).

Limiting group size, or running small, interactional groups within the larger group, perhaps in pairs, may help to prevent group sessions becoming mini individual sessions. Choosing activities which involve turn-taking, but in which everyone contributes in a different way, can also help.

Other factors to be considered in group composition are the gender and culture of group members. Smith and Inder (1993) found that groups of boys tended to be more boisterous than groups of girls, and that mixed groups functioned more like boys' groups than girls' groups. This has implications for the activities chosen, but given that boys are at higher risk of speech, language and communication problems than girls a balance can be difficult to achieve.

It may be culturally inappropriate for some children to speak without permission from an adult. Likewise, lack of eye contact may be considered a sign of respect. The therapist needs to be aware of these cultural differences and to avoid activities in which these behaviours are challenged. It may be necessary to discuss such issues within the group if they are relevant to some of the group members such as in a social interaction group. Culture and religious beliefs must also be considered when choosing vocabulary and resources.

Additionally, behavioural factors such as hyperactivity, impulsivity, inattention and sensitivity must be taken into account when considering group composition. One disruptive member may negatively impact upon the group dynamics.

The communication needs of potential group participants must be considered, and, in the case of Oscar, it would be helpful if all children in the proposed group had a phonological impairment and age-appropriate comprehension. Ideally the children would all be in the same year at school.

Finally, group size must be considered. This will depend on the logistical aspects such as room size or staffing, but small groups often have better outcomes than large groups. In a group of three, members may be more engaged and the intervention better targeted. A group of eight children is the maximum, as anything above would require breaking into sub-groups for most activities.

Aims

These are determined by the needs of the individuals in the group. In the case of Oscar, the aims for the group would be:

- to improve phonological awareness skills at both large unit level (syllables; rimes) and small unit level (phonemes);
- to eliminate the use of inappropriate phonological processes, initially, stopping of fricatives;
- to generalise the use of new sounds in short phrases, sentences and spontaneous speech.

There will also be aims for the individual members and specific measurable objectives for each session.

Learning opportunities and strategies for generalisation

These must be considered carefully when planning any group so that the structure of the tasks is not just a list of activities. Rather, the learning and teaching methods must be considered so that each member's learning style can be accommodated and deeper learning can take place (Kolb 1984). This would involve giving members opportunities for reflective observation of their own and others' performance, abstract conceptualisation where they identify or describe patterns or rules, and active experimentation where they practise in a restricted way. Experience allows group members to practise new skills in a real life situation and this may therefore involve trips outside the setting, if resources allow.

Structure

It is important to maintain the structure of each session to ensure aims are met and all members know what to expect. Different types of groups require different structures. A possible structure for Oscar's group during a 45 minute session is suggested below.

1   Welcome/orientation.
2   Introduce target sound(s) (*abstract conceptualisation*).
3   Listening activity – phonological awareness (*reflection*).
4   Production activities (*active experimentation*).
5   Minimal pair activities (*active experimentation; reflection*).
6   Listening activity – more phonological awareness (*abstract conceptualisation; reflection*).
7   Farewell, homework and discussion with parents.

Group dynamics and group process

In order to run groups effectively, therapists should be aware of what is happening within the group aside from the content. They also need to be aware of the group process or life cycle and the skills required by group leaders to facilitate the group (Yalom 2005).

Group dynamics are dependent on group composition, but need to be considered in the context of the group process. Tuckman (1965) described the group process in adults as comprising four phases: forming, storming, norming and performing. These phases can also be applied to children's groups although they are probably less overt in young children's groups and apply more to discussion groups such as social interaction or specific language groups for older students in secondary school settings.

During the first phase, 'forming', the group comes together for the first time and members are discovering their roles within the group as well as what will be expected of them. The second phase, 'storming', may be a time of conflict as members begin to stamp their personalities on the group. There may also be tensions between individuals' needs and the needs of the group. Out of this storming develops the 'norming' phase, when the members come to terms with the nature of the group and their role within it. By now members know each other better, and usually a more secure and trusting atmosphere has begun to develop. The most productive phase in the group's life cycle is the 'performing' phase, where the group has achieved a collective identity and the members work cohesively together.

It is important to establish ground rules at the start of any group. The number and type of rules will depend upon the purpose of the group, the composition and the ability of the members to remember the rules. It is useful to encourage members to determine the rules themselves, as then they are more likely to own them and respond to them. Such rules could be selected and adapted, for example, from those suggested by Andersen-Wood and Smith (1997).

1   Be supportive of each other.
2   No teasing or laughing at others.
3   Take responsibility for yourself (no excuses or telling tales).
4   Keep hands and legs under control (no poking or kicking).
5   Listen to the person who is talking.
6   Participate in role-plays.
7   Address positive feedback to the group member, not the therapist.
8   Complete homework between meetings.
9   Allow others to have a turn at talking.
10 Talk one at a time.

Rules for pre-school groups are less likely to be negotiated with the members at the beginning, but introduced in a simple way such as those used in the Social Use of Language programme – 'good listening', 'good looking' and 'good sitting' (Rinaldi 1992).

Leadership

Group intervention is not the equivalent of simultaneous individual intervention with a larger number of clients. The therapist therefore needs specific skills to handle the group dynamics, to work with colleagues acting as helpers and to ensure that the group and individual aims are being met.

Skills and qualities

*   Flexibility to adapt to changes within the group and to alter targets as and when necessary for individual group members;
*   ability to develop strategies to maintain group cohesion and interest;
*   ability to model techniques;
*   ability to deal with behavioural problems quickly and effectively;
*   ability to guide members so that all may participate equally;
*   sensitivity to interpersonal issues;
*   ability to train co-therapists or helpers;
*   ability to deal with problems and conflict.

(adapted from Rustin and Kuhr 1999)

A further decision is what style the therapist should adopt – leader or facilitator.

Burnard (1997) proposes six dimensions of facilitatory style. Whilst these are based on work in the field of counselling, these dimensions may be transferred to the facilitation of groups of older students. Three of the dimensions will be discussed here that may help the therapist decide upon style.

Planning dimension: setting up the group
1   Therapist sets the aims/objectives for the group prior to setting it up.
2   Therapist negotiates the aims/objectives with the group once set up.
3   Therapist encourages the group to set their own aims/objectives.

Meaning dimension: helping to make sense of the group
1   Therapist offers explanations, theory or models to enable the group to make sense of what is happening.
2   Therapist sometimes listens and sometimes offers explanations.
3   Therapist encourages group members to verbalise their own ideas about what is happening.

Confronting dimension: how individuals and the group as a whole are challenged

1   Therapist challenges them directly to encourage all members to confront others.
2   Therapist encourages an atmosphere in which people feel safe enough to challenge each other by establishing clear rules of communication.
3   Therapist does not challenge at all – though the group may become stuck.

The therapist can lead or facilitate, moving from greatest control to the least. Experience and confidence are needed to relinquish control yet still run effective groups, so it may be best to start with a leader style and gain experience and confidence in running groups prior to adopting a more facilitatory style in which group members are active in the running of the group.

Challenges and conflict within groups

There are many sources of problems and conflict within group work; a selection is considered next, together with some possible solutions (see also Rustin and Kuhr 1999).

One member does not participate

There may be many reasons for this. It is possible that the individual's abilities are different from those of the rest of the group members, having been placed in the group inappropriately. In this case, if possible, it may be best to remove the individual and to try to find a group more suitable to the child's needs.

Assuming the child has been placed appropriately and the activities are at an appropriate level, there are several strategies that may be employed. First, the child should be encouraged to participate, for example, by choosing a topic or activity known to be of particular interest. Second, it may be possible to pair the child with another supportive group member, or with a helper. If the child has appropriate language skills, it may be helpful to talk outside the group to try to discover the reasons for the lack of participation.

One member constantly disrupts the group

Behaviour within the group should be clearly defined from the start, so that all members understand what is acceptable. Disruptive behaviour may occur if a child has been inappropriately placed. The tasks and activities of the group may not be at an appropriate level for each member's attention level and concentration span. It could also be that the child finds the work of the group to be challenging, exposing weaknesses so the behaviour becomes a form of sabotage. It may be necessary to ensure the tasks chosen highlight the individuals' strengths. Possible strategies for dealing with the behaviour may include: strict reinforcement of the rules agreed at the beginning of the group, with temporary exclusion if necessary; open discussion within the group of the impact of the behaviour; encouragement of other members to become more active; to ignore the disruptive behaviour and praise appropriate behaviour; or, discussion of the problem with the individual outside the group.

With younger children or those whose difficulties make reflection on behaviour impossible, it is important for the therapist to identify the triggers of the behaviour, with a view to avoiding them.

Two members constantly talk amongst themselves

There are times when talking in sub-groups is to be encouraged but this is not appropriate when the group as a whole come together to listen to other members or during a listening activity.

Burnard (1997) refers to two members consistently talking amongst themselves as 'pairing', and suggests it can arise as a result of insecurity of one or both of the pair, as a result of boredom or even as a means of testing the group leader. With older children a possible solution could be to talk to each individual separately, explaining the disruptive nature of the behaviour and encouraging them to propose a solution. This may involve changing the pace of the sessions and ensuring their roles become more active. If a group member is having difficulty speaking in front of the whole group, preferring to talk to one other member, the leader – and possibly group members – will need to encourage that member to share the comments with the rest of the group.

With pre-school children, distraction could be non-verbal and may be eliminated by changing the activities to include movement, enlisting the support of helpers, ensuring that the distractions within the room have been eliminated and reminding all the group of the ground rules in order to keep them focused on the task, possibly with the use of picture cue cards.

Helper unintentionally sabotages the group

This may happen in many different ways, and usually stems from the helper misunderstanding the aims for the group or individuals within it. These must be made explicit to the helper and any specific strategies must be demonstrated. For example, in the case of Oscar, the therapist might say to the helper, 'Oscar needs time to reflect – he may be slow to answer, but if given time he will get there.' The helper should be advised to avoid jumping in and asking if anyone else knows the answer, because periods of silence are acceptable.

When working with a helper it can take time to learn how to work well together and to appreciate each other's methods. Time set aside for note-taking and reflection after the session by the therapist and helper is, therefore, important and may speed up their process of learning how to work together efficiently. Additionally, specific reflection and feedback on each other's role and performance may help to develop the working relationship.

Summary

The decision to provide group or individual intervention is multi-factorial, based on child's and parents' needs and values, resources and the skills of the therapist. Both have advantages and disadvantages, and the current evidence base to support either decision is still in its infancy.

Part III

Working with others

The two chapters in this part highlight the breadth of the role of speech and language therapists who increasingly work together with parents and other practitioners. Information is provided about models of working, how approaches to training may change when working with different groups and factors to consider when planning training.

Chapter 8

Working with parents

Monica Bray

Learning outcomes

By the end of the chapter the reader should:

- understand the philosophies and models that guide our work with parents;
- reflect on personal values and attitudes;
- have a critical awareness of some parent-based approaches.

Introduction

In recent years there has been a major shift in thinking about the relationship between professional and parent and the parental role in the therapeutic context. In the UK, health authorities and schools are now legally bound to involve users (the patient or client and/or the family) in decision-making around policy and practice (DH 2006; DCSF 2009). Partnership with parents and person-centred planning must therefore be central to all work with children in need of speech and language therapy.

Philosophies behind working with parents

Psychological models (Corey 2004)

Our interactions with other people are shaped by our value systems, our attitudes to others and our hypotheses about what affects our own behaviour and that of others. There are numerous psychological models which may be used when coming into contact with clients, whether they be the children or their parents, but those listed below are probably the most commonly used within the speech and language therapy field.

a   A *behaviourist perspective* sees the behaviour of parents or children as being shaped by the consequences/rewards of their actions. Children or parents can therefore be taught to modify their behaviour through a process of analysis of the factors initiating and reinforcing that behaviour, a process of modification of the environment and/or rewarding wanted behaviours and ignoring unwanted ones.

b   A *client-centred perspective* means that the therapist takes the lead from the child or parent. The therapist encourages open discussion, decision-making and change from the parent or child, based on the belief that the individual has within himself or herself the ability to make positive changes in the direction of self-actualisation or betterment.

c   A *cognitive perspective* takes account of the children's or parents' belief systems and the ways in which they think about and make sense of themselves. These attitudes may be influential in the way in which issues are dealt with. The cognitive cycle suggests that anticipation of difficulty within a context leads to negative thoughts and reactions which then influence the behaviour within this context. The therapist needs to challenge negative attitudes and engage with the parent and/or child in jointly challenging and modifying habitual patterns of response. Behaviourism and cognitive approaches are commonly used together as in *cognitive-behavioural therapy* and therapists will encourage clients to challenge their own ways of looking at the world by setting up 'mini-experiments' to test these. Many therapists use *solution focused therapy* (Burns 2005) which stems from a combination of client-centred and cognitive theories. Clients are supported in looking positively towards solutions and encouraged not to dwell on negative problems.

d   A *constructivist and narrative view* sees people within particular social communities as being influenced by the values of that community and by their own experiences and histories. Our own life stories influence the way in which we deal with the world. Therapists will help clients understand their own life views or stories and reconstruct these or construct more positive ways forward (Freeman *et al.* 1997).

Models of health care

The requirement to have parents in a central role in therapy is based on a shift from a medical model of health care to a social model. Social models are person centred and assume that the experience and knowledge of the person closest to the 'issue' should drive the planning and decision-making about how and when change can be brought about. Medical models are 'expert' based and involve diagnosis and treatment of disorders by the professional. Consider the situation of a child of 3 years who is having difficulty in talking. Who is the most knowledgeable about the child's behaviour and needs? The speech and language therapist may have 'expert' knowledge based on study and training in the area of developmental difficulties, but the parents live every day with the child and are the most influential people in the child's life. They organise and guide their child's learning and they interact with their child based on their own philosophy of child development and child rearing. A person-centred approach to this 3 year old would require the therapist to get to know the parents' attitudes to the child's learning and the activities of daily life which are 'normal' in this family and to agree with the family how best to tailor therapy.

Case example

Tracey is 4 years old. She has been slow in developing language but her parents have not been particularly worried. They both have a history of slow language development. Tracey is due to start school. She still has difficulty making others understand her, although her parents can interpret what she says. The nursery, with the parents' permission, refer Tracey to a speech and language therapist who assesses Tracey's language and finds that she has a delay in both comprehension and expressive language and may need help in developing these abilities. Mrs F, Tracey's mother, is very upset as she had assumed that Tracey would soon grow out of the speech difficulty and she now feels that she has been negligent in not identifying a problem. Mr F, Tracey's father, is very angry. He feels that either the therapist is wrong or some other professional should have noticed this problem earlier. The parents cannot agree on what to do next. Mr F wants Tracey to have therapy daily if necessary to get Tracey's speech 'up to par' before she starts school. Mrs F is worrying that she did something wrong. Now she feels it is too late and she is to blame. She is aware that Tracey may need therapy, but she also wants someone to talk to about how she feels.

How is the speech and language therapist to proceed? All members of the family need to agree about goals for Tracey but the emotional involvement of both parents must also be accommodated. If Tracey is seen for a half-hour weekly session based on language development activities and the sessions are therapist led, is this sufficient? Possibly not – Mr F's anger and his unrealistic expectations of therapy, and Mrs F's guilt and desire to understand 'what has gone wrong' will need to be addressed in some way in order for therapy to be successful.

Family systems approach (Barker 2007)

The family is a system in which each part is dependent on the other parts for its efficient functioning. A speech and language problem needs to be considered in relation to the effect it has, not only on the child, but also on the other members of the family, on the extended family, on friends and others. The actions and reactions of each of these have an effect on the 'identified symptom bearer', in this case the child with the speech and language difficulty.

So, in Tracey's case, her lack of language development is having an effect on her mother's levels of guilt and her father's anger. Every time she is misunderstood by another person, these feelings emerge. It is more comfortable for the family to be insular and self-sufficient. But, Tracey is about to start school and the boundaries around the family will broaden and merge with other systems – the school, the wider community and so on. The speech and language therapist will need to ask each member of the family what is hoped for, what is realistically possible, who will be involved in helping to achieve these outcomes and who needs to be informed and enlisted in supporting the family to help Tracey in her speech and language development. If the family does not feel engaged in the therapy process, then, according to systems theory, they may well undermine the process as change is uncomfortable and there may be an unconscious need to return to the status quo.

Transtheoretical model of change

All therapy is directed at changes of behaviour. In speech and language therapy there is an attempt to change, or accelerate development, in the language domain but there is also recognition of the importance of change in the whole system (see above). Prochaska and Di Clemente (1986) proposed that change could be conceptualised in stages, processes and levels. This model calls on an understanding of a number of psychotherapeutic ideas, hence 'transtheoretical' model, and is often applied within the health care field, although it has been criticised for not achieving the hoped-for outcomes in a number of non-speech and language therapeutic programmes (Bridie *et al.* 2005). However, as a model it helps therapists to conceptualise their role within the therapeutic relationship and thus is useful in directing the focus of their work. The model suggests that the therapist should be sensitive to whether the client is in the early stages of thinking about the problem (*pre-contemplation and contemplation*), or whether s/he has moved to a more active stage of wanting to do something to engender change. The model recognises that change can be circular with relapse a common aspect of the process. The therapist needs to provide ideas or support strategies that are specific to the stage of change of the client. Levels of change may be behavioural, cognitive, interpersonal, systems or intrapersonal giving the therapist possibilities for directing intervention at one or more of these levels.

Case example

John, at 5 years of age has a noticeable stammer. He has already begun to show an awareness of his difficulties and will stop talking when he is having particular difficulty, especially at school. John has a very talkative 7 year old sister and a 3 year old brother. Both his parents work and he lives in a very busy environment where 'getting a word in edgeways' requires a lot of tenacity. John's parents have brought him for a consultation as they are concerned that he is finding speaking more difficult and that their family life may not be helping him. The parents are both in the *contemplative-action stage*. They need to talk about John and the family and what is happening within the home and at school but they also want some action – a programme that they can follow to help John. John is aware that something is not right so is on the cusp between *pre-contemplation*, where he is not at all aware, and *contemplation*. He himself is not considering any action, or direct change of how he speaks. John's older sister is aware that he doesn't speak as well as she does and often tries to get him to 'say things better'. His young brother is at the stage where his needs must be fulfilled immediately to keep him happy. The speech and language therapist needs to take into account that all the family are at different stages when planning intervention and must engage at each of the levels of change:

1   the behavioural level by helping the family analyse what events may be affecting John and looking at possibilities for changing these;
2   the cognitive level by identifying each member of the family's attitudes to the stammer and how these may affect their reactions to it;
3   the systems level by helping the family look at how each member affects each other member, and finding ways in which family interactions may be positively shifted;
4   the intrapersonal level by helping John and other family members look at the positive aspects of their lives and interactions in order to increase self-esteem.

Ways of working with parents

In order to work closely together and to make joint decisions about goals and techniques of therapy, the therapist and the parents need to understand each other's perspectives and needs. Partnership with parents is a worthy goal but how can this be achieved?

What do parents need?

Asking parents what they hope for in therapy is often neglected in the drive to assess and set a behavioural programme of change for the child. This is particularly true when children are of school age and parents are not regularly present. When parents were asked by this author what they found helpful and unhelpful when relating to the speech and language therapists they had had contact with, they provided feedback which could be grouped in the following ways:

a   intrapersonal factors (enthusiasm, genuine interest, patience, openness and honesty);
b   cognitive factors (knowledgeable, shares information, gives feedback);
c   interpersonal factors (relates well to child, likes and respects children, has good communication);
d   behavioural skills (good at holding child's attention, gives child time to respond, gives clear models of behaviour, uses praise, is imaginative).

Parents wanted to work in partnership with therapists, they wanted to be given a range of options and to discuss therapy approaches. Parents found it difficult to relate to the therapist and the therapy if their concerns were not listened to.

A study by Marshall *et al.* (2007) showed that parents and speech and language therapists had different ways of explaining and understanding the children's language delay and/or interventions to enhance language development. Parents in both studies saw themselves as experts in relation to their child and his/her needs and wanted this to be acknowledged in the relationship with the therapist. Consequently, if the therapist adopts the 'expert' role and does not acknowledge the parents' contributions, therapy for the child is likely to be undermined by a lack of parental involvement and support for the language activities.

What do speech and language therapists offer?

In 2008, Pappas *et al.* surveyed speech and language therapists in Australia to find out how they were responding to the shift in ideology from 'expert' to family-centred models of working. They found that, while parents were being asked to participate in goal setting, very few were making final decisions about the nature of therapy for their child. Also, while the majority of parents in clinic-based therapy sat in the room during therapy, few of them were asked to participate directly. The authors concluded that a gap still existed between stated beliefs and actual practice which continued to be primarily therapist-led. Parent-centred therapy was being undermined by factors such as therapist confidence in this way of working, inflexible forms of service delivery and parents' own beliefs and attitudes.

In the UK, many speech and language therapists have been involved in Sure Start provision. Sure Start was set up in 1998 in order to address issues of child poverty and exclusion (MacNeill 2009). The basic assumptions underlying Sure Start were that context and poverty influence cognitive and social development, and that early positive experiences are critical for healthy development (Fuller 2010). Involving and empowering parents was seen as crucial for long-term gains. Fuller explored the way in which speech and language therapists worked within Sure Start Local Programmes and found that there was a shift to more flexible/open referral patterns, and more flexible access policies with therapists working more in family homes and outside normal office hours. Therapists were also involved in the wider community through training of others and were offering a range of preventative and facilitative approaches, such as parent-and-baby groups involving singing, nursery rhymes and talking to your child. However, there was still a need for a realignment of power in the therapist–family relationship. MacNeill (2009) suggests that therapists continue to use a passive 'consumer' model where parents are invited into decision-making sessions but given a minor role and expected to conform to the structures and procedures set by the professionals, instead of a 'democratic' model where parents are true partners. Professionals are still unwilling to let go of power and to really understand the needs of the communities they are supposedly trying to help.

Parent programmes and working practice

There are a number of approaches within the speech and language therapy field which involve parents. Some of these will be discussed below. Their effectiveness and the way in which they are delivered will be explored. The programmes are based on different philosophies and models of working and it is important that speech and language therapists understand these and feel comfortable with the approach they are using with parents.

The Hanen parent programme

The Hanen programme was developed in Canada in the 1970s and has become very popular as a model of working in the UK. It is based on social-interactionist models of communication between parent and child and tries to enable parents to use everyday situations as settings for encouraging language development in their children. Parents are taught in groups to be responsive to their children's communicative attempts by giving immediate and positive responses. They are encouraged to observe, watch and listen to the child rather than taking control of the interaction (Pepper and Weitzman 2004). The philosophy behind Hanen's parent–child interaction is primarily client centred but parents are instructed in useful skills through a cognitive-behavioural approach. Parents video-record themselves at home and use this as the basis for discussion with the therapist on how they might change their interactive style towards a less directive language approach. Speech and language therapists therefore take a teaching and a collaborative role.

Case example

Mary is 4 years old and has cerebral palsy. Because it is difficult for her to engage in communication, her parents have become used to anticipating her needs and to 'talking for her' when she is with others. Mary is becoming more upset and angry and her parents enrolled on a Hanen course to try to get some help in how to manage her. They learn to observe her carefully and to identify a number of movements of her eyes and limbs that seem to be communicative. They see how they talk to her all the time but give her very little opportunity to engage in any 'give-and-take'. It is difficult for them to change as waiting for Mary to respond requires a lot of patience and time so they need regular support from a sensitive and understanding therapist. The therapist must be very client centred which includes acceptance of the parents' views and respect for their values and attitudes. S/he must have skills in transcription and coding of communicative interaction as well as sound knowledge of speech and language development and cerebral palsy and must understand how adults learn in order for the programme to be successful. This seems like a tall order but it is what is expected of speech and language therapists on a daily basis.

Does the Hanen programme improve children's speech and language? This is a difficult question to answer because there are so many facets of speech and/or language and parent–child interaction that are individual, and each set of parents will respond to the approach differently. There is also a tendency for parents to adapt programmes to suit their own needs and situations, thus reducing the fidelity of the programme (Williams 2006). A study by Pennington *et al.* (2009) showed that children with cerebral palsy initiated more in communicative exchanges after Hanen training although parents still tended to dominate. This is a positive finding as initiation of communication is a vital starting point for language development and is often problematic for children with special needs. Baxendale and Hesketh (2003) compared Hanen and direct clinic therapy and found equal outcomes for both approaches. Their qualitative data showed that certain families were better suited for Hanen which is twice as intensive as traditional clinic therapy. As mentioned above, therapists need to be sensitive to the professional–parent balance of power and be prepared to offer parents choice from a number of different types of approaches. For some parents Hanen may not fit with their current life situation.

Every Child a Talker (DCSF 2009)

This strategy came into use as part of the National Strategies Early Years initiative. Like Sure Start, it aimed to provide the best start in life for children. The philosophy is child centred and social-interactionist and based on the belief that children learn best through a stimulating, supportive environment where they can be challenged to try out new things in a safe setting. Language is the primary focus and the 'Early Language Consultant' may be a speech and language therapist. Parents are seen as the most essential people in supporting the child's development. Speech and language therapists working in early years' settings are likely to work alongside other professionals to provide support to parents, early years staff and other community workers. They will encourage talking and reading to babies and young children, telling stories, singing and playing in quiet, comfortable environments. The speech and language therapist needs to have an understanding of the family systems and the working relationships between the different agencies and the parents. S/he needs excellent grounding in early communication and language development and in the concepts of 'scaffolding' of language through step-by-step support (as suggested by Bruner in the 1950s). The speech and language therapist must also have good collaborative skills and know how to engage a wide range of different people with different backgrounds and must develop ways of thinking about decision-making in language learning.

Case example

Afreen is currently at an early years centre three times a week. Her mother speaks very little English but is keen that her daughter should be given a good start in the language. The therapist, who visits the centre on a regular but infrequent basis, needs to assure early years workers that mother-and-daughter shared talking time in Punjabi is just as important for the little girl's development as are the English nursery rhymes that they are both learning to sing. Knowledge of bilingual language acquisition is needed as well as an understanding of family systems theory. An awareness of the effects of this family's social constructs and life narratives on their behaviour and expectations of their child are helpful in giving the therapist confidence in this working environment. The therapist has developed innovative ways of encouraging the parents to be involved such as 'Walking and Talking'. This interaction between therapist and parents, and parents and children, takes place outside traditional environments and parents are invited to walk across the park and have a drink at the café, for example, while engaging in discussion about using words and signs for the trees, flowers and squirrels as they are seen (DCSF 2009, p. 20).

How effective are early intervention programmes? Because long-term outcomes are notoriously difficult both to specify and measure, the quantitative measures of these types of programmes have been disappointing (Fuller 2010). However, an evaluation of the qualitative changes seen so far in the Every Child a Talker project suggests that practitioners improved in their ability 'to respect and trust children as creators of their own learning and development' (DCSF 2009, p. 47) that is, they became more client centred. Parents were more engaged with their children's communication development in the home and wider environment, and all were more aware of the concept of working together.

Behavioural therapy

Speech and language therapists are trained in behavioural techniques. They learn to observe behaviour carefully, to identify the sequence of steps in learning a task and to help children move through these steps to reach the goal. Ideas based on work by Lovaas (1987) in the 1980s have emerged as Applied Behavioral Analysis (ABA), a structured learning programme which can take place in either the school or the home. It is used with children with special needs, especially autism. It is based on the theory of behaviourism and uses operant conditioning (contingent rewarding of wanted behaviours) to support learning (Riddall-Leech 2003). The therapist will observe the child in an environment and identify the specific behaviour that is to be learned or unlearned, the stimuli in the environment that initiate the behaviour and the rewards that maintain the behaviour. The therapist acts as expert in the setting of goals, although parents will choose specific problem behaviours to work on with their children. Parents will work, under the instruction of the therapist, on a specified programme with very detailed plans and clear goals. The child will be expected to produce the required behaviour consistently before moving on to something new.

Case example

Philip has been identified as a child with autistic spectrum disorder. At 7 years of age he is showing a number of challenging behaviours which seem to be associated with his lack of understanding of what others are saying to him. His parents ask the speech and language therapist to help set up some form of communication system that may help Philip. Using a behavioural analysis approach, the therapist and parents observe Philip in a number of settings and record his strategies for obtaining a chosen item. The antecedents to the behaviour and the consequences of it are also noted. The therapist feels that Philip can be trained to give an object. This approach is known as Objects of Reference so that, for example, Philip gives an item such as a shoe when he wants to go outside to play (Park 2002). The parents keep a chart of Philip's responses to their introduction of this system and are taught to be consistent in the way in which they respond to/reward his attempts to use it. The therapist needs to have a good understanding of operant conditioning and behaviour analysis. S/he needs to support the parents in carrying out the programme with regularity and consistency.

Behavioural programmes are more easily measured than client-centred ones as the task analysis has clearly set out the steps that need to be achieved. A meta-analysis of studies on children with autism using ABA conducted by Virues-Ortega (2010) showed that this approach, used long term, had positive outcomes on the receptive and expressive language scores of the pre-school children. However, in a British study (Reed *et al.* 2007) changes in adaptive behavioural functioning were limited despite some positive changes in educational progress. This suggests that generalisation of skills to everyday life continues to be poor.

Parent–child interaction therapy

A number of approaches now use parents as agents of change in therapy and there is evidence that the involvement of parents makes a difference to the child's language skills. It also helps parents to feel more empowered and skilled in managing their children's speech and language difficulties. The therapists at the Michael Palin Centre for Stammering Children use parent–child interaction therapy in their work with families who have a child who stammers. Millard *et al.* (2009) have shown that a combination of clinic-based (six sessions) and home-based therapy (six weeks of regular 'special time' interactions where the child leads and the parent modifies his/her own input) has positive outcomes on the children's fluency, on the impact of stammering on both the children and the families, and on the parents' knowledge and confidence in dealing with their children's stammering. Long term follow-up ensures that the process continues. The philosophy behind the approach is child centred and social-interactionist similar to that of the Hanen programme but deals with each family on an individual basis.

Integrated intervention

Van Bysterveldt *et al.* (2010) report on a programme of integrated intervention focusing on speech and phonological awareness in children with Down syndrome. The children receive clinic-based individual and group therapy and follow a home programme. The parents are trained to use a specific therapist-initiated joint storybook/letter-referencing approach which the parents carry out regularly throughout the 18 week intervention period. Changes in the children's speech and phonological awareness were identified, although in a study like this it is hard to isolate the main factors leading to change. The authors do not discuss the monitoring of the parent programme so it is difficult to know how well they followed the instructions given them by the therapist.

Summary

Working with parents is no longer a peripheral therapy decision, it has moved centre stage. Programmes involving parents have proved to be beneficial to parents' well-being and their interaction with their children. However, working in this way presents a number of challenges to the speech and language therapist in order to be successful. Challenges include enhanced personal development, embracing new ways of working, flexibility of working patterns and skilled time management.

Chapter 9

Working with other practitioners

Jannet A. Wright

Learning outcomes

By the end of this chapter the reader will:

- understand the benefits of working with other practitioners;
- be aware of the challenges involved in working with others;
- understand speech and language therapists' involvement in the training of other practitioners;
- appreciate what needs to be considered when planning training sessions.

Introduction

Children with speech, language and communication needs (SLCN) do not exist in isolation. They have parents and families and, depending on their age, will be part of the education system at some level. If they have more complex needs they may also be involved with additional carers and other professionals such as occupational- and physiotherapists. Speech and language therapists need to take all of these factors into account when planning their own intervention. They must ensure that any speech and language therapy extends beyond the therapy sessions and can be integrated into children's lives.

Readers are directed to Chapter 8 for information about how speech and language therapists can work with parents so that, wherever possible, therapy may be continued and generalised in the home setting. The focus of this chapter is on how speech and language therapists may interact and work with other practitioners who may be involved in the care and education of children with SLCN, so that the effects of therapy can be generalised into all settings. This interaction may occur through formal meetings but it may also be the result of specially targeted collaborative working practices and/or specifically designed training sessions. Speech and language therapists will aim to share their knowledge and expertise with all practitioners with whom they work while endeavouring to learn from others at the same time.

Collaborative working practices

Why work with others?

It is crucial that any therapy is incorporated into children's lives in order for it to be effective. Meaningful change in a child's communication is more likely to occur if the therapy is continued and integrated into the rest of the child's activities so that s/he can understand its relevance to daily life and realise that it is not something that is only undertaken for a short period of time with a therapist on a weekly or even on a daily basis. In order to achieve this integrated approach speech and language therapists need to work with other practitioners so that what is offered to children and their families is a holistic approach with consistent management strategies.

Working with others can also help speech and language therapists become more reflective in their own practice, particularly if they receive constructive feedback on any sessions they have run jointly (see Chapter 2). As Tollerfield (2003) observed, 'shared successes appear to fuel the enthusiasm for further joint practice'. New knowledge and ideas can be gained from working together. In studies by Wright, educational practitioners and therapists highlighted the 'cognitive gain' they felt resulted from working together as they learned new information and gained ideas from each other (Wright 1996; Wright et al. 2006).

In the late 1990s the Sure Start initiative brought together practitioners from education and health providing a unique opportunity for them to collaborate to help children at risk of language difficulties in the early years. In some areas of the UK it has been found that 40 to 50 per cent of children enter school with delayed language skills (Locke et al. 2002). This means they are not ready to adapt to the learning environment or to benefit from the teaching they receive. Spoken language skills are known to underpin reading and writing abilities (Snowling and Stackhouse 2006). However, if therapists and Early Years practitioners are able to work together to improve such children's communication skills before they enter school then it may be possible to minimise the risk of those children having literacy difficulties. In the long term, children with SLCN are also at risk of developing the kind of behaviour that can lead to truancy and consequent exclusion from school. It may also lead to other kinds of problems as research shows that over 60 per cent of offenders have significant communication disabilities and 35 per cent of offenders have speaking and listening skills below Level 1 of the National Curriculum (Davies et al. 2004).

The Government has for many years been urging professionals to work together to provide a 'seamless service' (DfES 2001) even stating that 'joint working is critical' (Bercow 2008). The value to speech and language therapists of trans-disciplinary working practice has been highlighted by Gascoigne (2006) and the need for therapists to work in partnership has been further endorsed by the RCSLT standards and guidelines (2006). However, if working together to support children with SLCN were easy then successive governments and the professional body (RCSLT) would not have needed to issue statements about the desirability of joint working, it would have happened automatically. There are many different factors that can make it difficult for speech and language therapists to work with others.

Factors affecting joint working practice

Different employers

In the workplace, the different types of practitioners who work with children with SLCN are often employed by different agencies, such as health, education, social services or even private agencies. All are therefore likely to have different terms and conditions of employment. They may not have the same hours of work or entitlement to holiday leave and the continuing professional development requirements for each might be different. In addition each of these agencies will have different ways of delivering their services and different priorities. City, borough and county boundaries may also contribute to differences in the ways in which services are organised. Not all children will access the services in the same way. It is mandatory that education is provided for all children but not all necessarily have access to health services. Different professional groups may find there are different expectations of their service delivery depending on where – and how – they work. For example, some practitioners such as teachers, or teaching assistants, will be based in one place whereas speech and language therapists may be peripatetic, moving from setting to setting.

All of these factors will influence the time available for meetings and the opportunities to work together. They will also affect the ways in which each of the practitioners prioritises collaborative working and the efforts they are prepared to make for it to be successful.

Different terminology

Profession-specific terminology can cause barriers to working effectively with others. For example, for practitioners working in the NHS such terms as 'prognosis', 'caseloads' and 'presenting symptoms' are part of their everyday vocabulary, whereas in the education system phrases such as 'Key Stages', 'attainment targets' and 'education plans' will be in regular use.

Professional terminology is usually acquired early in training and becomes a shorthand used between colleagues, indicating membership of a particular group. Such terminology is quickly internalised and embedded in life at work. But it is important to remember that some of the words and phrases used by one group of professionals are not necessarily understood by others. When practitioners come from different training backgrounds they need to bear in mind that when working together they may have to explain the more 'technical' vocabulary they use without thought, and that it is acceptable to ask for clarification of the meaning of specific terms or phrases used by others in order to avoid misunderstanding.

Professional boundaries

For some practitioners, being asked to carry out a task, or to comment on something they perceive as not directly related to their area of expertise, can make them feel uncertain and vulnerable; for example, physiotherapists being asked to consider communication issues as part of a holistic approach. Their response to approaches to working together may therefore be negative and they can appear inflexible. This could make it difficult for the speech and language therapists trying to work with them. This apparent inflexibility, however, may be because they feel as though they are being asked to do another person's job. Or, it could be that they feel threatened by another professional's interest in their area of work. It would be important therefore for the speech and language therapist to approach such situations with sensitivity.

Also during times of reorganisation it is usual for staff in individual services to pay particular attention to their 'core business' as their managers may be showing some concern about those who appear to be involved in a wider range of activities such as collaboration with others. It will be important to demonstrate that working together is related to the core business of helping children with SLCN.

Time

Time is needed to develop working relationships and practitioners therefore need to recognise the importance of allocating time for any method of working together. It takes time to understand the roles of other practitioner colleagues and to appreciate what each person brings to their work with a particular child. Time is needed to meet and discuss strategies and plan interventions. There are now a variety of ways available for maintaining contact besides face-to-face meetings, such as mobile phones, emails and text messages, all of which are helpful for those striving to collaborate. The process of working together and keeping in contact with each other, however, does take time.

An 'additional burden'

For some practitioners even arranging to meet can feel like an additional burden, as though it is 'just one more thing to do'. If this is so, then the benefits of working together will be missed, for without appropriate planning and opportunities to talk to each other collaborative work is unsustainable. In order to work successfully with other people, therefore, there is a need to allo-cate time to meet together and it is crucial that collaborating is seen as valuable by the practi-tioners involved and their managers so that it can be appropriately prioritised.

Learning to work together

All therapists-in-training need opportunities to learn to work with others while they are still students. Such opportunities may occur through specific Inter-Professional Education events which bring together students from a number of professional courses to work together on set tasks. Or there may be opportunities, for example for speech and language therapy students on placement, or teachers-in-training on teaching practice, to gain experience of working with other students and qualified colleagues as well as members of other professions.

During their education and training students gain the knowledge and skills that will enable them to begin their working life and a part of that will be observing and hearing about the appropriate attitudes that facilitate the ways in which practitioners work together. Speech and language therapy students on placement need to see how qualified therapists use their skills to work with others. They also need to take advantage of any opportunities involving working with others. There is a risk that students will think that working together is best left to their supervising clinicians (Kersner and Wright 2002) but unless they take the opportunity to work on this themselves while in a safe setting they will not acquire the appropriate skills and knowledge needed to work collaboratively with others. Effective professional communication skills are not only central to speech and language therapy students' education but should be seen as linking with partnership working. If students can maintain their central focus on their clients this will help them to understand the need to work with others for the children's sake. And as they work with other practitioners they will endeavour to develop a mutual respect.

Deciding who to work with

Sometimes the decision for a speech and language therapist about whom to work with is not really a decision at all. It will be the practitioners who are based in the same place as the thera-pist, such as at an Early Years Centre, a unit or a hospital ward. Real decisions have to be made when there are larger pools of people who are in contact with the child with whom the thera-pist is working, as for example in a school. The therapist may decide to work closely with the SENCO who will then pass information on to others in the school, or it may be that the thera-pist decides to work with one or more of the teachers, or with some of the teaching assistants. Sometimes the decision about whom to work with is based on the school structure and how it is managed, or on the school's philosophy. Sometimes it may depend on whether the other person has previous experience of working with a speech and language therapist. Or, the thera-pist may choose to work with the colleague who has shown the most interest in speech, lan-guage and communication issues. Some people may volunteer to work with the speech and language therapist, whilst the therapist may need to persuade others if it is seen as being in the best interests of the child.

It is a misconception that practitioners who work in the same place will be more likely to work effectively together because they will have more opportunities to meet and exchange information, even informally. Wright *et al.* (2008) acknowledge that even when people share the same base, they are not always available at the same time during the day and are therefore not always able to utilise the potential opportunities for informal collaboration.

Once the decision is made and the working relationship begins to develop it will be important to set a date for review. This will provide both parties with an opportunity to discuss whether the partnership is functioning well and to agree any changes that may need to be made in order for the working relationship to work as effectively as possible in the best interests of the child.

Training

Training offers an opportunity for all practitioners to learn from each other and, for many speech and language therapists, providing training opportunities for other practitioners has become a significant part of their workload.

Training and facilitating others

If working together with colleagues can provide a more holistic service for children with communication needs, then increasing the knowledge and skills of the other practitioners in relation to speech, language and communication can only facilitate collaborative working. Training may be offered by speech and language therapists for a number of reasons: to raise awareness of SLCN, to provide knowledge and information that may help other practitioners recognise children's early difficulties and possibly to prevent more severe problems arising in the future. At a more specific level, training can enable others to carry out therapy so that the therapist does not always have to be present, and may help other practitioners to integrate therapy into other areas of the child's life.

The crucial points that will shape the content of any training session are:

- to identify the purpose of the session – the goals;
- to identify what participants will take away from the session – the learning outcomes.

Raising awareness

It is recognised that there is a need to raise the awareness of all who come into contact with children with SLCN so that they may have a better understanding of the children's communication problems and extend their communicative environment. It will also provide more understanding for the families. Training may be available for practitioners with a variety of educational backgrounds ranging from specialists in other fields to drivers of the school or hospital transport, administrative staff in the Local Authority or hospital, school staff, health care staff, librarians and staff employed in social services. Some will have short periods of contact with particular children whilst others will have regular, daily, possibly more protracted, contact. Some may already have an understanding of the children's problems and may even have attended previous training sessions, while others will not. All will have to be accommodated by the therapist running the session. However, one of the most challenging issues therapists face when offering this type of training is that the people attending may not have chosen to come to the session. On a mandatory training course the challenge for the person carrying out the training is to make it as relevant and interesting as possible to those attending and to enable them to see the relevance of improving their communication and hence their relationship with the children in their care.

Pre-emptive training

Training may be provided with the aim of preventing some 'at risk' children from developing severe communication problems, for example, the adult–child interaction work with young children and their parents described in Chapter 4. If this can be introduced to early years practitioners in the same way it may help them develop their skills so that they can modify their interaction patterns when working with children whose language development is delayed. This type of training will enhance the work carried out by practitioners in early years centres who support children with SLCN.

Increasing knowledge

Through training, speech and language therapists can provide other practitioners with specific knowledge about communication problems to assist early identification and appropriate referral to a speech and language therapy service. Therapists may also provide training which offers specific information for those who have daily contact with children with SLCN as, for example, in a school. Here the therapist may be involved in the introduction of a signing system or a communication aid not only to the child or children but also to the staff. In such situations therapists also have the opportunity to explain and demystify some of the speech and language therapy 'jargon' which staff employed by education services can find difficult to understand.

In some settings the therapist may not work directly with a child who has SLCN. After some training, the intervention work may be carried out, at least some of the time, by another practitioner such as an assistant. The aim of such an approach is to facilitate the generalisation of specific speech and language work across different activities, contexts and settings and to ensure that the child has more regular therapy than the therapist alone could offer. This will occur most appropriately after some joint planning and goal setting, then classroom assistants, teaching assistants and learning support assistants will be able to work with the children who have SLCN.

Therapists may provide training on a one-to-one basis or they may be involved in training all assistants in a particular school or across a group of schools. Some professionals may already have knowledge about communication problems but, through training, therapists may be able to extend that knowledge in relation to particular children. It may be an issue for staff development that individual training is not award bearing and it may be a concern that staff do not receive a certificate to acknowledge how much they have learnt. However, there are other advantages to being offered individual or 'bespoke' training sessions. Therapists will often explain what they are aiming to do and demonstrate the activities to be carried out with a particular child so that the assistant can observe and then carry out the activities themselves. They will then receive individualised constructive feedback from the therapist and be encouraged to reflect on and evaluate what they have learned.

Feedback

Any practitioner who has been trained to carry out specific activities with a child with SLCN needs to know whether they are presenting and carrying out these activities with the child in an acceptable and appropriate way. It is helpful for them to receive feedback from the person who has trained them and to reflect with that trainer on their own performance. They need to know which aspects of the activity they are carrying out appropriately and which aspects of their presentation could be improved.

There are other ways of gaining feedback too. For example, if a practitioner is carrying out an activity with a child which has been set by the speech and language therapist, and the child responds well and is successful in carrying out the activity, then the practitioner has immediate, positive feedback about his/her presentation from the degree of the child's success. However, the child may not be able to do the task and/or may become upset with the activity. The practitioner then needs to have enough understanding of the task to be able to modify it appropriately, or to move to another activity. In order to make such decisions the practitioner needs constructive and specific feedback from the person who set the task so that they can understand how to develop their own skills to improve the child's chances of success. Some practitioners are instinctively good at carrying out certain activities without being aware of exactly what they are doing. Appropriate feedback will help them to understand their actions when carrying out activities so that they can reflect and continue to advance their own learning. See Chapter 2 for a more detailed discussion of feedback.

Developing more 'specialist' knowledge

In educational settings where the emphasis is on providing a specialist service for children with SLCN, practitioners will need specific training in order to increase their knowledge of language and communication. This type of training may be part of an in-service programme arranged for staff in the school. This would be seen as good practice as training more than one person in any setting makes it more likely that useful, new approaches can then be introduced which may benefit a range of children, not only those with SLCN. Training may need to be offered on a regular basis to accommodate staff changes within a school setting so that new staff can be trained as they begin work. In specialist settings there will be an expectation that teachers and assistants will automatically be involved in joint goal-setting with speech and language therapists so that it would be helpful for them to have knowledge of a number of different types of interventions.

Where does training take place?

Training can take place almost anywhere that participants can travel to but it is important when offering training to a multi-professional group that there are discussions with all the managers about accessibility of the training to their staff. This will prevent difficulties arising before the training session actually starts. It is also important that trainers are aware that the choice of venue will convey a subtle message about ownership of a training course. So, when bringing together course participants from health, education and social services it will be helpful to find a mutually acceptable site. It is important to bear in mind that some sessions have certain requirements regarding the actual space. For example, would it be suitable for the trainer to deliver a lecture, if that is what is required? Or is there adequate space so that the room can be used flexibly for small group work? Individual training with a parent or an assistant could take place in a classroom or even in the parent's home.

Multi- or uni-professional training

When training is provided to groups of practitioners it may be offered on a multi- or uni-professional basis. To some extent this will depend on the purpose of the training although in recent years there has been an emphasis, especially in the Health Service, on multi-professional training. When running such a course it will be important for the trainer to ensure that individuals from the different professional groups mix with each other right from the start and do not remain only talking to the people with whom they work. This requires careful management and readers are referred to Wright et al. (2008) for further discussion of how to manage this and other issues when planning multi-professional training sessions. The trainer also needs to bear in mind the different professional backgrounds of the participants and their differing levels of knowledge and expertise relating to children with SLCN.

Types of training

Training offered by therapists may be 'on-the-job' as when working with assistants, or it may take the form of a course which is delivered over a half day, a whole day or spread over several days. Courses running for a term or more, however, are likely to be 'award bearing' with assessments to be completed. These courses are frequently offered by higher education institutions, although therapists may be involved in running some award-bearing courses within a school. Even on courses that are not award bearing it is important for participants to reflect on their learning and to ensure they have achieved the learning outcomes.

It may be that such award-bearing courses are run 'face-to-face' but the course, or some components of it, may be offered as a distance-learning or technology-enhanced course. In that case the tutor/trainer will maintain contact with students by email, telephone and video links. It is also possible to use distance-learning courses and web links for a number of staff in a school at the same time. This approach is particularly useful when schools are geographically spread, as in rural areas and travelling to a central point to receive training would be costly as well as time-consuming.

Evaluation

Evaluation of training

It is important for all courses or in-service training to be evaluated. Questionnaires have traditionally been used to elicit the perceptions of those attending the courses, although continued attendance at a course is probably the best way of knowing whether participants appreciated what was taught. Questionnaires are used to find out what people felt about a course, what aspects were felt to be successful (or not) and whether it met the participants' expectations.

However, the UN Convention on the Rights of the Child in 1989 highlighted the importance of gathering children's views as part of any evaluation process, as they are service users. The Code of Practice (DfES 2001) also stressed that practitioners working with children in schools need to obtain the children's views. Children's perceptions about changes in their own learning have to be the ultimate measure of the success of staff training as Crosskey and Vance (2011) reported on the use of questionnaires with pupils to find out whether training offered to teachers had been successful.

Evaluation of working together

There are several factors that need to be considered when evaluating and reflecting on collaborative working practice; factors such as the heterogeneity of the children who have SLCN, the variation in the amount of contact that children have with specialised professionals, the different levels of children's maturation and the ways in which educational settings are organised. Although it is often easier to recall attempts at working with other practitioners which have proved difficult or may even have failed, it is important to reflect on positive experiences and identify the factors that contributed to making working together a success. But it is also helpful to ask others about their perceptions of working together. The use of questionnaires and interview schedules provide an opportunity to explore everyone's expectations of collaborative working: what they have learnt from the process and whether they think that the service offered to the children has improved through the practitioners working together more closely. Questions can be asked of the parents to find out whether they agree that there is now a 'seamless service' being offered by practitioners working together in closer cooperation.

Summary

In this chapter the benefits of working collaboratively to help children with SLCN have been outlined, together with some of the challenges practitioners face when they work together. Consideration has also been given to training, an aspect of work that for speech and language therapists is becoming increasingly important. Multi-disciplinary training sessions offer opportunities for people to acquire knowledge from each other, to understand how others function when working with children and to think about ways in which practitioners from different backgrounds can work together to support children with communication needs.

Part IV

Assessing and managing children with communication problems

In this part, the focus is on children with a wide range of communication problems, demonstrating the decision-making process involved in assessment and management. The chapters are discrete and may be read in any order and the titles reflect the client groups discussed. All the authors are specialists in their field. There are suggestions for further reading regarding intervention and information about the efficacy of intervention is provided where available.

Chapter 10

Working with children with specific speech impairment

Sally Bates and Jocelynne Watson

Learning outcomes

By the end of this chapter, the reader should:

*   be aware that children with speech intelligibility problems form a heterogeneous group;
*   understand why detailed transcription and analysis of the child's speech output at regular intervals is fundamental to the clinical decision-making process;
*   recognise why management needs to be driven by an understanding of the child's speech perception (input) as well as their speech production (output) skills.

Introduction

Children who have difficulty producing age-appropriate, intelligible speech form a diverse group in terms of the presenting characteristics and the underlying reasons for their difficulty. For some children, difficulties occur as a secondary consequence of primary conditions such as hearing impairment, anatomical abnormalities (e.g. cleft palate), motor deficits (e.g. cerebral palsy), developmental syndromes (e.g. Down Syndrome or Autism Spectrum Disorder) or general learning difficulties. For the majority of children, however, difficulties occur in the absence of any overt organic cause. These children are described as having specific speech impairment (SSI) and will be the focus of this chapter.

Children with SSI account for the highest rate of referral to paediatric speech and language therapy services. Prevalence rates are notoriously difficult to establish but are believed to be in the region of 10–15 per cent of pre-schoolers and 6 per cent of school-age children (Williams *et al.* 2010).

In some cases, SSI may resolve spontaneously. However, for many children, difficulties persist and can significantly impact on their social-emotional and/or academic development. Children who still have difficulty making themselves understood at school entry are at greater risk of peer rejection and social isolation than their intelligible peers. They are also likely to experience difficulties learning to read and spell since phonological processing skills underpin both clear speech and early literacy development (Gillon 2004). Fortunately, there is a substantial and growing evidence base that appropriately targeted intervention for this clinical group is highly effective (Gierut 1998; Law *et al.* 2004).

Defining SSI: presenting features and classifications

Children with SSI vary widely in terms of the nature and extent of the speech errors they show and in their underlying phonological processing strengths and weaknesses. For this reason, classification has been problematic and a range of terms, both historical and current, has been used to describe this clinical group. Another umbrella term commonly used is Speech Sound Disorders and the following may also be employed generically or to describe sub-groups:

- phonological disorder
- phonological delay
- childhood apraxia of speech (CAS)
- developmental verbal dyspraxia (DVD)
- functional articulation disorder
- articulation disorder
- phonetic disorder
- speech intelligibility impairment.

Three broad sub-classifications which are widely used, although not always consistently, and which will be used here are: phonological impairment, articulation disorder and CAS.

Phonological impairment

Phonological impairment (PI) which is the largest sub-group, refers to speech which is characterised by systematic error patterns or 'phonological processes' which affect the structure of words or the pronunciation of groups of sounds which share phonetic features such as voicing, place of articulation and/or manner of articulation.

Examples of error patterns affecting word structure include:

- deletion of unstressed syllables (e.g. [nɑnə] for /bənɑnə/, [putə] for /kəmpjutə/);
- deletion of final or initial consonants (e.g. [bʌ] for /bʌs/, [ip] for /ʃip/);
- consonant cluster reduction (e.g. [pun] for /spun/, [tein] for /trein/);
- addition of consonants or vowels (e.g. [napəl] for /apəl/, [gəlʌv] for /glʌv/);
- diphthong reduction (e.g. [tam] for /taim/, [has] for /haus/);
- diphthongisation (e.g. [ðaim] for /ðɛm/).

Examples of error patterns affecting natural classes of sounds include:

- velar fronting (e.g. [tɑ] for /kɑ/, [dɜl] for /gɜl/, [wɪn] for /wɪŋ/);
- stopping of fricatives (e.g. [ti] for /si/, [pɔ] for /fɔ/, [tu] for /ʃu/);
- voicing or de-voicing (e.g. [bi] for /pi/, [gɑ] for /kɑ/, [glʌf] for /glʌv/);
- lowering of mid-low vowels (e.g. [bad] for /bɛd/, [bag] for /bʌg/).

In these cases, the error patterns reflect difficulty achieving a particular phonetic contrast, for example, between velar and alveolar or between fricative and oral stop consonants rather than difficulty with a particular sound. Such difficulties result in a loss of *phonological* contrast, that is, reduced ability to signal meaning differences between words. For example, the child who produces alveolar consonants in place of velar consonants will be unable to make their meaning clear in word pairs such as: 'tea ~ key', both pronounced as [ti], 'bad ~ bag', both pronounced as [bad] and 'thin ~ thing', both pronounced as [θin]. Words that are pronounced in the same way are called 'homonyms'. Generally, the more homonymy there is in a child's speech, the greater the impact on intelligibility.

Many of these processes are heard in the speech of younger children when they first start to talk and so are thought to reflect immature speech perception (input processing) and/or speech motor (output processing) skills (Stackhouse and Pascoe 2010; Stoel-Gammon and Vogel Sosa 2010). Children are diagnosed as having a phonological impairment when they show an unusually high number of processes occurring simultaneously in their speech or when processes persist beyond the time that they are typically expected to resolve. For example, velar fronting typically resolves by 3;6 yrs (Grunwell 1987) but in phonologically impaired children can still be present at school age and beyond.

Phonologically impaired children are often further classified as having phonological delay or phonological disorder depending, respectively, on whether they show processes commonly found in the speech of younger, typically developing children (e.g. velar fronting or stopping) or, more unusual, atypical patterns such as alveolar backing and gliding of fricatives. A child's system may also show delayed and less typical patterns in parallel. It is important to note that the terms delay and disorder here are used purely descriptively. There is currently no evidence to suggest an unequivocal relationship between disordered patterns and degree of unintelligibility, or reduced response to intervention. Degree of unintelligibility and speed of process resolution depend more on the number, range and consistency of error patterns operating in any one system and on the individual child's particular speech processing profile.

Individual PI children vary greatly in terms of the number and type of processes operating within their system and also in the number of sounds within a class that are affected. It is important to remember that their productions change over time as speech processing skills emerge and the rate of this development can also vary greatly between individuals. Consequently, at the time of assessment, a given process may already have started to resolve and the child will be able to say the problem sound/s correctly in certain words but not in others. Variability might also be due to the influence of word position or phonetic context. For example, a child may find it easier to produce velars when they occur in word-final position, than in word-initial or medial position. In such a case, correct production might be achieved in words like 'fork' and 'bag' but not in words like 'car' [tɑ], 'goat' [dəʊt] or 'singer' [sɪnə]. Another child may only have difficulty producing velars in the context of a following front vowel such that 'key' and 'gate' are pronounced as [ti] and [dɛit] but words like 'car', 'caught' and 'goat' are produced correctly, where /k/ and /g/ precede back vowels, which share a similar place of articulation.

PI children also present with different profiles in terms of their underlying phonological processing skills. These refer to:

- speech perception or 'input' processing skills: hearing, auditory discrimination, phoneme classification;
- memory and pattern recognition processing skills: storage and retrieval;
- speech production or 'output' processing skills: motor programming and planning.

Difficulties in any one of these areas will have implications not only for the child's ability to produce intelligible speech but also the development of phonological awareness and early literacy skills (Stackhouse and Wells 1997; Gillon 2004).

Articulation disorder

Articulation disorder is most commonly used to describe a condition where a child is producing one or a few sounds in a non-standard way, for example, /s/ as [ş] or [θ] or the lateral fricative [ɬ] – all different types of pronunciation commonly called 'lisps'. Production is consistent as the problem sound is typically always pronounced in the same way and, for this reason, although the speech may sound unusual, intelligibility is usually comparatively intact.

Childhood apraxia of speech

There are currently no definitive diagnostic criteria for CAS (Shriberg and Campbell 2002) which explains why the descriptor preferred by the American Speech-Language-Hearing

Association (ASHA) is 'suspected Childhood Apraxia of Speech' (sCAS). One of the major difficulties is that children with CAS may show many of the same speech characteristics as children with a moderate-to-severe PI (see Bowen 2009 for a full review).

Despite the lack of any speech characteristics that are unique to CAS, there are some which are considered more representative or indicative than others. These include:

- prosodic difficulties, most typically excessive or equal stress placement;
- unusual resonance and/or poor voicing control;
- sequencing errors, for example, 'umbrella' pronounced [bʌmrɛlə], also referred to as 'transposition of consonants' or 'metathesis';
- consonant insertion, for example, 'shark' [ʃɑk] pronounced as [ʃɑts];
- higher incidence of vowel errors.

It is important to note here that, as with consonant errors, most vowel errors reflect the application of systematic phonological processes. Phonetic variations in vowel quality (i.e. vowel distortions) may, however, also arise in conjunction with the 'groping behaviour' associated with CAS (see Ozanne 2005).

Another key feature of CAS is inconsistent production although, again, this is a characteristic that may be shared with some PI children. Inconsistency is perhaps best defined as the variable production of the same word across different repetitions, for example:

- 'helicopter' [hɛdipɒptə], [hɛðipɒptə], [hɛdɪkɒtə];
- 'umbrella' [bʌnɹɛlə], [mʌnɹɛlə], [bʌmɹɛlə].

It is very important to distinguish this from other types of variability which can indicate progression within the child's system. For example, realisation of some word-final consonants as [ʔ] may represent an intermediate step between pervasive final consonant deletion and process resolution. Similarly, the change in attempts to pronounce 'Sam' as initially [pam] and then [fam] can be taken as a positive signal that the child has recognised the fricative quality of the initial /s/. Progressive variability is also obviously indicated by the presence of correct as well as incorrect productions of a given sound.

With CAS, difficulties also tend to be more noticeable in multi-syllabic as compared with mono-syllabic words and in spontaneous conversation as compared with single word naming. Poorer performance with increased task demands is one of the reasons CAS is primarily associated with online motor-programming/planning deficits. The child knows what they want to say but is unable, under real-time constraints, to achieve appropriate timing and coordination of the articulators. However, children with CAS may also show input processing deficits. It has been suggested that their speech difficulties may reflect arrested development at the whole word phase, an early stage in phonological development during which stored phonological representations for words are, as yet, incompletely specified (Stackhouse and Wells 1997).

Differential diagnosis

The initial hypothesis regarding diagnosis (and prognosis) guides decisions regarding the long-term aim of therapy and discharge criteria. In the case of phonological impairment where there is no obvious physical, physiological or neurological cause, the ultimate goal of therapy is age-appropriate phonology and a limitation of any impact on early literacy development. In the case of articulation disorder, the long-term goal is normal articulation unless the errors are a secondary consequence of low-level processing deficits such as hearing impairment, or subclinical structural anomalies or muscle weakness. In the latter case and in the case of children with CAS where prognosis is generally poorer, long-term aims tend to be specified in terms of intelligibility gains. For some children with CAS an augmentative or alternative communication system may be required in the long term or as an interim measure to relieve frustration in communication.

Within each clinical sub-group children may also present with language difficulties and these should be duly considered when prioritising therapy goals.

The variation observed within sub-groups and the potential for over-identification of CAS, especially in the pre-school population, highlights the importance of appropriate, detailed evaluation of the child's speech and, in all cases, treatment which focuses on the symptoms rather than the label (Flahive 2009).

Assessment

Two complementary approaches are routinely taken in the assessment of children with SSI: linguistic and psycholinguistic.

Linguistic

This approach aims, through phonetic transcription and regular, systematic analysis of speech error patterns, to provide the speech and language therapist with a detailed description of the child's sound repertoire and system. Phonetic transcription crucially helps the therapist infer how the child is using their articulators (i.e. the interplay between movements of the tongue, lips, jaw, vocal cords and velum and breath support) and how this deviates from typical use. Each phonetic symbol infers the place, manner, voicing and nasality status of the sound being transcribed, e.g. /p/ is typically produced with lip closure and release, without voicing and without nasality.

This information currently provides the basis of all further management decisions. There are specific instrumental techniques which can directly examine how articulators work dynamically together such as laryngography (vocal cord movement), nasometry (oral and nasal airflow), electropalatography (tongue palate contact patterns) and ultrasound (tongue configuration) but these techniques are not at present routinely available within speech and language therapy services.

Psycholinguistic

This approach aims to identify the areas of weakness in the child's speech processing system that give rise to the errors (Stackhouse and Wells 1997). This information informs all aspects of session planning including short-term therapy goals, selection of activities and stimuli design (Rees 2002a). The process of hypothesis formulation and testing regarding a child's speech processing profile takes time and is arguably best managed through a process of 'diagnostic therapy'. This is where the therapist can carefully monitor the child's performance across different therapy tasks, for example, in real word repetition compared with picture naming and in response to different stimuli, for example, real or non-words. This provides insight into whether the child's errors reflect input and/or output processing difficulties and whether the difficulties are ongoing or result from inaccurately stored information for words (Stackhouse and Pascoe 2010).

In the majority of cases children's speech processing skills are not static. They typically change over time and in response to appropriately targeted intervention. Change, positive or otherwise, can only be monitored through repeated transcription and analysis of the child's speech at regular intervals. Careful monitoring of the child's performance is also integral to evaluating the effectiveness of any intervention (Gierut 2008).

Assessment battery

The assessment battery for children with SSI typically includes:

- case history
- phonological analysis
- phonetic inventory.

A hearing screening may be included if recent or current hearing status is unknown and an oro-motor examination where structural and/or motor deficits are suspected. Information regarding processing strengths and weaknesses, including phonological awareness, is typically collected following initial assessment and diagnosis.

The case history allows the therapist to gather relevant background information about the child's medical history, attainment of developmental milestones and social and educational context. It also provides the therapist with the opportunity to explore the parents' understanding of the difficulty, their level of anxiety and the extent to which they are able to support the child at home. This information can be helpful in making decisions regarding prioritising a child for therapy.

A phonological analysis provides insight into a child's sound system, that is, the extent to which the child uses sounds appropriately in words. A phonetic inventory lists the sounds a child can physically articulate. This is an important difference since a child may be able to articulate sounds that they do not use in their speech or which they use in place of other target phonemes, for example, 'sea' mispronounced as [ti] but 's' used in [si] for 'she'.

A phonological analysis of the child's speech output is necessary to identify:

- which sounds are present in the child's system and which sounds are absent;
- which sounds are pronounced incorrectly;
- how they are pronounced;
- the phonological processes (i.e. error patterns) in operation;
- the range of syllable and word structures a child can produce (this is particularly important where structural processes such as weak syllable and final or initial consonant deletion are present);
- evidence of process resolution in different word positions (i.e. word initially, medially and finally) and/or in different phonetic contexts;
- variable incorrect realisation of target phonemes, for example, /s/ produced variably as [t, d, ʃ] or deleted.

The phonological analysis can also form the basis of the phonetic inventory but will need to be supplemented in the case of any sounds not yet observed to be present in the child's system. This can be done by the therapist asking the child to repeat sounds in imitation. Information about the stimulability of sounds is particularly important in the case of children presenting with a severely limited system of contrasts.

The amount of information obtained from the analysis is directly dependent on the size and range of the speech sample analysed. Typically, the therapist starts by screening the child's system using a formal procedure such as the South Tyneside Assessment of Phonology (STAP) (Armstrong and Ainley 2007) or by analysing a speech sample collected informally.

Formal procedures provide pictorial stimuli that are designed to elicit a representative selection of consonants in word-initial, word-medial and word-final position. These more structured approaches, where the therapist knows the intended target, are especially helpful in cases where the child is severely unintelligible. In principle, however, the therapist can use any stimuli such as objects in the environment, body parts or counting to encourage speech and can also transcribe spontaneous utterances produced during play or conversation. Analysis of connected speech data can give the therapist a better idea of the child's functional speech and a comparison of the child's performance across sampling situations can provide important diagnostic insights.

The results of the screen give an initial indication of the child's difficulties and a pointer to what further data collection and analysis is required. Depending on the nature and severity of the difficulty, the therapist may choose to perform a standardised assessment such as the Diagnostic Evaluation of Articulation and Phonology (DEAP) (Dodd *et al.* 2003) or design their own stimuli to target specific processes and/or phonemes in different word positions and phonetic contexts. At least three, and ideally five, examples of each 'problem' sound in each word position are required in order to look at patterns of variability across word positions and phonetic contexts and so gauge the extent to which a given process may be resolving.

Standardised assessments allow the therapist to compare the child's performance against scores obtained by other children in their peer group. There are, however, other sources which give information on developmental norms (McLeod 2007a). These vary in terms of the precise age at which processes are said to resolve and consequently the order of acquisition of phonemes. It is, however, possible to distinguish three groups of early, middle and late acquired phonemes (Shriberg 1993 cited in Bowen 2009).

In cases of moderate-to-severe impairment, it is often necessary to assess the consistency of a child's production. This is minimally achieved by comparing a child's production of the same word across three repetitions. An oro-motor assessment can help distinguish children with CAS from PI children who also show inconsistent errors (Dodd *et al.* 2003).

A fully comprehensive analysis is not required for every child. A systematic, principled analysis is, however, necessary in all cases since it forms an integral part of the clinical decision-making process. For example, where a child is presenting with one or two residual processes, it is not necessary to collect multiple tokens for the full range of consonants in all word positions. However, even in cases of mild impairment, it is important to collect sufficient data to confirm observations made during the initial screen and/or to assess the extent of the process application. Repeated assessment at regular intervals should also be carried out, targeting specific processes/phonemes to monitor change as a result of therapy.

Is intervention warranted?

The decision about whether or not to intervene is based on a holistic appreciation of the child. This includes consideration of the nature and severity of the child's speech difficulties and the extent to which these may be having a detrimental impact on the child's participation in activities at home and in nursery or school as well as other environmental and personal factors (McLeod 2007b).

Intervention is warranted if the child presents with speech errors or phonological processes that are developmentally inappropriate. This is indicated by any one or a combination of the following:

- a higher number of processes in operation than typically would be expected for the child's age;
- a more pervasive application of processes, i.e. affecting a greater number of phonemes, or syllable structures;
- the application of atypical or idiosyncratic processes;
- a high level of non-progressive variability, i.e. variable realisation of the same sound across different words which cannot be explained in terms of positional or contextual constraints;
- inconsistent production of the same word across repetitions;
- persistence of processes beyond the expected time of resolution.

Intelligibility will be more or less affected depending on each child's particular pattern of difficulties. It is also important to bear in mind the potential impact of the speech difficulties on other areas of the child's language and literacy development. For example, problems occurring at the ends of words, e.g. word final consonant deletion, word final cluster reduction or stopping of fricatives word-finally will affect the child's ability to mark plurality, possession or third person agreement using '-s' or the regular past tense using '-ed'.

Extensive operation of structural processes can also constrain a child's use of multi-syllabic words and multi-word phrases and sentences. For some children, avoidance of longer words and sentences is a deliberate strategy to maximise intelligibility. In the case of older children, ongoing perceptual deficits and poor phonological awareness skills may also impede progress in early reading and spelling.

Priority for treatment is typically given in cases where there is evidence that the child's difficulties are causing them frustration or otherwise impacting on their confidence and self-esteem, possibly leading to aggressive or withdrawn behaviour and/or a high level of parental anxiety.

Service delivery model

Individual service providers often have a preferred model of delivery. For example, many services are currently operating a consultancy model. However, where there is flexibility in the system, the following factors should guide decision-making:

- nature and severity of the child's speech difficulties;
- child's age;
- available home and/or school support.

Direct one-to-one intervention is usually indicated for older children and/or in cases where specific error patterns need targeting and careful assessment and monitoring of progress is required. The frequency and format of sessions will vary depending on the specific therapy approach adopted and as dictated by the child's needs, but also, realistically, by the size of the therapist's caseload and any prioritisation constraints within which the therapist is operating. An indirect approach may be appropriate in the case of children with a mild impairment and for whom a suitable level of informed external support is available. Very young or mildly impaired children may sometimes benefit from participating in a group. The venue for therapy, clinic, home and/or educational setting, will vary according to mode of delivery as determined by each of these factors.

Therapy approach

Selection of the therapy approach and the timing and frequency of intervention is made on the basis of:

- the child's speech profile;
- ongoing developments in the child's speech system;
- possible prognosis and long-term goals;
- medical factors (e.g. intermittent otitis media);
- social factors (e.g. sources of additional support) in the child's environment.

Service delivery patterns and constraints will also be influential.

There is a wide range of intervention approaches each with its own evidence base. These differ in terms of factors including the therapy aim, primary focus, goal attack strategy and criteria for target selection and stimuli design.

The number of intervention approaches available and the subtle ways in which these can differ may appear bewildering for the speech and language therapy student or newly qualified therapist. Generally, a 'broad brush' distinction may be made between phonetic and phonological approaches.

A phonetic approach is taken in the case of articulation disorder. Here, the aim is to help the child lay down new 'motor' patterns for the sound/s they are producing incorrectly, primarily through speech production activities which incorporate articulatory drills. Typically, sound production is first encouraged in isolation and then in syllable structures of increasing complexity and, finally, to encourage generalisation of the newly formed motor patterns, within words produced within phrases, e.g. 'k', 'key', 'blue key', 'very blue key', 'Mummy's very blue key'.

A different contrastive approach is recommended in the case of phonological impairment. This approach works primarily at the word level where minimal pairs or sets (e.g. 'pea, bee, tea, key, sea') are used to promote system-wide change through the establishment of phonological contrasts. Thus, several sounds or processes may be worked on simultaneously. The aim here is to improve the rate of phonological acquisition by targeting underlying phonological processing skills and improving the child's ability to self-monitor and self-correct.

Activities are designed to raise the child's awareness of how sounds are used to make meaning differences. For example, in production tasks the child may be encouraged to name one of two pictures illustrating minimal pair items such as 'tea' and 'key'. Successful communication relies on the child producing the sound sufficiently clearly for the therapist to understand their meaning and select the appropriate picture. If the wrong picture is selected, the child is directly confronted by the communicative consequences of not making the contrast sufficiently clear and can, therefore, actively seek to repair breakdown by changing production.

Auditory discrimination activities incorporating minimal pairs enable the child to focus attention on the relevant acoustic information that distinguishes a pair of phonemes along a given phonetic dimension, i.e. voicing, place or manner of articulation. Phonetically similar sounds like /p/ and /b/ which differ in only one feature are more difficult to discriminate, particularly in connected speech, than sounds which have several feature differences (e.g. /p/ and /z/). Repeated, focused experience of the relevant acoustic contrast/s can help a child develop perceptual skills and/or update inaccurately stored phonological representations.

Auditory bombardment provides more intense exposure through multiple repetitions of the sound targets in a range of different words (Lancaster 2009). This is particularly useful for developing a child's phoneme classification skills. For example, the ability to recognise that the [k]s in 'car', 'key', 'back', 'bank account' are all examples of /k/ despite subtle variations in their acoustic properties as a function of context.

Inclusion of both a perception and production component allows the child to experience simultaneous auditory and tactile/kinaesthetic feedback which can help them monitor their own speech online and amend accordingly. For this reason, role reversal tasks are particularly relevant. These provide multiple opportunities for the therapist to model the sound target/s as well as for the child to practise producing them and therefore afford the child an immediate comparison of their own attempts against the adult model.

For children with CAS, treatment can incorporate both articulatory and phonological principles (Williams and Stevens 2010). It can also involve sequencing different approaches, for example, taking a core vocabulary approach initially to establish consistency of production, followed by a contrastive approach (Dodd *et al.* 2010).

In practice, an eclectic approach in which the therapist carefully selects and orchestrates elements from different approaches is frequently also taken for PI. In all cases, it is essential to:

- make the activities motivating and fun for the child;
- ensure through careful modification of stimuli and tasks that the child can experience and build on success;
- provide appropriate scaffolding through use of visual cues or shared meta-language (Rees 2002b);
- provide appropriate praise and specific, targeted feedback (Gardner 2006a).

Evaluation of therapy approaches

There are several studies which support the efficacy/effectiveness of individual therapeutic approaches. The reader is referred to Williams *et al.* (2010) for an overview where each chapter looks at a particular approach including its evidence base.

Summary

It will be clear from this chapter that the management of children with SSI requires a systematic and theoretically principled approach. Each stage of the clinical decision-making process should be informed by the therapist's knowledge of phonetics and phonological development as well as a detailed understanding of the client's individual speech profile.

Chapter 11

Children with autism spectrum disorders

Tom Loucas

Learning outcomes

By the end of this chapter the reader should be able to:

- list the diagnostic features of autism spectrum disorders (ASD);
- list alerting signs for identifying children at risk of ASD;
- explain the need for a multi-disciplinary team approach to managing children with ASD;
- describe the role of the speech and language therapist within the multi-disciplinary team;
- describe the features of language and communication assessment in ASD;
- describe evidence-based approaches to intervention.

Introduction

Autism spectrum disorders affect over 1 per cent of children (Baird *et al.* 2006) and potentially represent a significant part of the paediatric speech and language therapist's caseload. Whether the child with ASD becomes a part of that caseload depends on identification and diagnosis. However, many children who meet diagnostic criteria for ASD remain undiagnosed. The Special Needs and Autism Project (SNAP) (Baird *et al.* 2006) reported that only 58 per cent of children with autism and 23 per cent of those with milder forms of ASD had an ASD diagnosis recorded by local services. Identification was more likely if a parent had completed secondary education and less likely in children with an IQ less than 70. In order to ensure consistency in services for children with ASD, the National Autism Plan for Children (NAPC) (NIASA 2003) was produced to identify and disseminate best practice. What follows will draw on these guidelines and more recent evidence to address issues of identification, diagnosis and management of children with autism spectrum disorders, situating the role of the speech and language therapist within a multi-disciplinary team (MDT) approach.

Definition

ASD are a group of strongly genetic neurodevelopmental conditions characterised by a triad of impairments in reciprocal social interaction and communication and by restricted and repetitive behaviours and interests. Children with ASD show wide variation in the severity of autistic symptoms, intellectual functioning and language ability. This range of ability in different aspects of development can exacerbate the problem of identification and diagnosis.

The constellation of behaviours that define ASD are agreed internationally (WHO 1993b). At least half of the children with ASD have intellectual disability (that is IQ below 70). In the sample of SNAP (Baird *et al.* 2006) 55 per cent of 9 to 14 year olds with ASD had an intellectual disability and 28 per cent had an IQ in the average range (115 > IQ > 85) (Charman *et al.*

2011). Language presentation is notable for its variability, ranging from those with Asperger's syndrome who show normal language milestones to the 10 per cent of individuals with ASD who are non-verbal (Hus *et al.* 2007).

Identification

Before management can begin children with ASD need to be identified. One approach would be to screen all children for ASD, but the evidence does not support the use of available screening tools (NIASA 2003). The Checklist for Autism in Toddlers (CHAT) (Baron-Cohen *et al.* 2000) is a short screen, combining 'yes/no' questions to parents and direct observation, for use by health visitors or GPs to identify 18 month olds at risk of ASD. Key items focus on play and joint attention. In a study involving 16,000 children, the CHAT was used to identify nearly all of infants who were at low risk of ASD, that is, those who did not go on to receive an ASD diagnosis at follow-up. However, the screen only identified about one-fifth of children at high risk of an ASD who then went on to receive an ASD diagnosis in early childhood. NIASA (2003) argued that rather than relying on screening tools, such as CHAT, that identification is carried out through surveillance. All professionals involved with young children should receive training in 'alerting' signals of ASD at pre-school and school age. For further details see 'Alerting signals for autism' in the *National Autism Plan for Children* (NIASA 2003).

Professionals also need regular opportunities to discuss a child's development with parents as part of surveillance to detect and respond rapidly to any developmental concerns. Within a surveillance context CHAT may be of value because its high specificity means that it could identify cases before they had come to attention by other means (Baird *et al.* 2001). In older children, screening instruments, such as the short parental report Social Communication Questionnaire (Rutter *et al.* 2003a), may have a role in high-risk children, such as those who have been identified with concerns about development.

Among the alerting signals, loss of skills, in particular loss of language, reduced social interaction and responsiveness, and an increase in repetitive play behaviour in the second year of life can be considered a 'red flag' for ASD. When comparing young children with ASD and developmental language disorder, Lord *et al.* (2004) found loss of language is unique to children with ASD. In the SNAP sample, loss of language was reported in 30 per cent with autism, 8 per cent with broader ASD, and regression was associated with higher rates of autistic symptoms in late childhood (Baird *et al.* 2008).

Language regression represents a clear difference in development in some children with ASD, but recent research has uncovered less dramatic indicators of ASD in the early years. Increasingly research with infants and young children at high risk of ASD (i.e. those with an older sibling with the condition) is sharpening the ability to identify 'at risk' children before 2 years of age (Zwaigenbaum *et al.* 2009). Between 12 and 18 months infants who go on to develop ASD can be distinguished from typically developing children in a number of areas. In visual skills they may show atypical visual tracking and fixation on objects. In motor skills they may show decreased activity levels, and delayed fine and gross motor development. Atypical play may include delayed development of motor imitation, limited toy play and repetitive actions with toys. Social communication may include atypical eye gaze, orienting to name, imitation, social smiling, reactivity, social interest and affect, and reduced expression of positive emotion. Language may show a delay in babbling (especially to-and-fro social babbling), receptive and expressive language, and gesture. General cognitive development may be slower as evidenced by declining scores on standardised assessments. A number of early atypical behaviours also distinguish between infants who go on to develop ASD and those with other developmental delays, including language delay. They include atypical exploration of toys, repetitive motor behaviours, and reduced social communication and shared positive emotion.

Assessment and diagnosis

The complex presentation in ASD means that a multi-disciplinary team is essential for effective management at all stages of the clinical process. The NIASA framework recommends that assessment and diagnosis of ASD can be seen as a three-stage process: a general developmental assessment followed by a multi-agency assessment and possible referral to tertiary services. In practice both assessments may be collapsed into a single appointment.

After initial identification the child should be referred to a child development service for a general developmental assessment as for any child with a possible developmental problem. The aims of this stage of assessment are a clear identification of concerns, a developmental history and a full examination and appropriate further tests. Routine use of autism specific screening tests was not recommended as at the time of writing there was a lack of evidence in the UK for the utility of screening tests, although some tests may help identify children who need a further multi-agency assessment. There has been evidence for the use of the Social Communication Questionnaire as a screening test, at least with older children (Chandler *et al.* 2007). At the developmental assessment the family should be informed of assessment outcomes immediately and given an opportunity to discuss the assessment fully. A key outcome of this stage of assessment is that a plan for appropriate provision should start at this point where possible, and the Local Authority should be notified if special educational needs are suspected.

The main feature of the multi-agency assessment is that it provides an ASD-specific assessment, in contrast to the more general assessment. It is essential that existing information is gathered from all settings. An ASD-specific developmental and family history needs to be taken by an experienced team member with ASD training. The history needs to take account of the strongly genetic aetiology of ASD, the broader ASD phenotype, as well as the association between ASD and other neurodevelopmental disorders such as specific language impairment (Bailey *et al.* 1995, 1998). Essentially, the history taker needs to probe systematically for information about current and past behaviour in all three areas of impairment diagnostic of ASD. Through asking open questions, detailed descriptions of behaviours need to be elicited and these behaviours judged against the child's developmental level so that a clear chronology and pattern of development can be established. NIASA provides guidance on the content of an informal ASD-specific history but several standardised interviews are available: the Autism Diagnostic Interview – Revised (Rutter *et al.* 2003b), Diagnostic Interview for Social and Communication Disorders (Wing and Gould 2011) and Developmental, Dimensional and Diagnostic Interview (Skuse *et al.* 2004). The Autism Diagnostic Interview – Revised is seen as a 'gold-standard instrument for diagnosis' along with its complementary observational assessment, the Autism Diagnostic Observation Schedule (Lord *et al.* 2001).

To complement the ASD-specific history, an observational assessment is also recommended. Focused observations need to be made across several settings, including in school for school-aged children. As in the ASD-specific history, observational assessment needs to address the child's reciprocal social interaction, communication, and restricted and repetitive behaviours and interests. In the clinic, focused observations can be made using the semi-structured assessment, the Autism Diagnostic Observation Schedule.

The paediatrician will conduct a full physical examination, including appropriate medical tests. The examination will take account of the increased risk of medical conditions such as Fragile X syndrome and epilepsy in children with ASD (Fombonne 2003). The child's mental health and behaviour also needs to be investigated because children with ASD are at an increased risk of mental health problems. In the SNAP cohort, 70 per cent of children had at least one co-existing disorder and 41 per cent had two or more (Simonoff *et al.* 2008). The most common diagnoses were social anxiety disorder, attention-deficit/hyperactivity disorder and oppositional defiant disorder. Cognitive assessment is another key component of a multi-agency assessment. NIASA recommends an assessment in an appropriate setting by either a clinical or educational psychologist with ASD training. It identifies several areas of potential difficulty, including attention, processing speed, working memory and writing difficulties, especially in more able children. Establishing the child's overall level of intellectual functioning is important as over 50 per cent have an intellectual disability and outcomes for children with ASD are related to IQ (Howlin *et al.* 2004). Motor skills assessment carried out by an occupational therapist is a likely component of the multi-agency assessment because movement impairments are common in children with ASD. NIASA also recommend communication assessment by a speech and language therapist with ASD training.

Language and communication assessment

Within the multi-agency assessment, the speech and language therapist has a central role. Impairments in language and communication are core features of ASD. There is remarkable heterogeneity in the language abilities of children with ASD, ranging from those who are non-verbal to those with above average verbal skills, and even in children who do not have impaired language, use of language for communication is impaired (Loucas *et al.* 2008). RCSLT Clinical Guidelines (RCSLT 2005) recommend that assessment takes account of the triad of impairments and gives specific consideration of the following areas: joint attention, readiness to shift attention, social interaction, communicative strategies, play skills and interests, learning potential and preferred learning style, and mental health.

Assessment in the early years

Zwaigenbaum *et al.* (2009) identify current best practice in the assessment of communication in toddlers with suspected ASD as the use of standardised tests, such as the Pre-school Language Scales (Zimmerman *et al.* 2009), observational measures such as Communication Symbolic Behaviour Scales Developmental Profile (Wetherby and Prizant 2002) and parental report measures such as the MacArthur-Bates-Communicative Development Inventories (Fenson *et al.* 2003) to assess communication skills. Luyster *et al.* (2008) found good agreement among direct and parent report measures. Gestures and non-verbal cognitive ability were significant predictors of receptive and expressive language. Additionally response to joint attention significantly predicted receptive language and imitation predicted expressive language abilities.

Careful, informal observational assessment can provide an important source about whether early communication is deviating from a typical pattern. Paul and Wilson (2008) recommend the speech and language therapist's observation should include assessment of frequency, functions and means of communication, and responsiveness to communication. The rate of communicative acts in typically developing children is two acts per minute at 12 months and seven per minute at 24 months; in young children with ASD it is lower. Thus the therapist may count the frequency of initiations the child uses, such as gaze, touch, gesture and vocalisation. By 18 months children use proto-imperatives to regulate others' behaviour and proto-declaratives to share attention and interest. At 18–24 months children extend their repertoire of communicative functions to include requests for information, acknowledgements and answers. Young children with ASD show a more limited range of communicative functions, using more that have a regulatory function (requests and protests) and fewer that are for social interaction, commenting and establishing joint attention. Children with ASD may use non-conventional means of communication, for example using another's hand as a tool, pulling it to the object s/he wants rather than pointing. While by 12 months typically developing children will respond if their name is called and understand approximately 50 words, children with ASD are less likely to respond to their name and show a delay in verbal comprehension. The child's responsiveness to verbal and gestural bids for attention and interaction should be assessed in a variety of contexts that aim to tempt a child to communicate, for example, social routines such as peek-a-boo, withholding play materials or action to elicit requests.

Spoken language assessment

Understanding spoken language is a particular area of difficulty for children with ASD compared to children with SLI (Loucas *et al.* 2008). In young children, at least, expressive language may be stronger than receptive language (Luyster *et al.* 2008). This underlines the need for a standardised assessment of receptive language.

Tager-Flusberg *et al.* (2009) offer evidence-based benchmarks of expressive language in children with ASD with a view to providing a framework for assessment and describing language progress during intervention. They recommend gathering data from multiple sources to avoid sampling effects, including language samples, parent report measures and direct standardised assessment. Language samples should be at least 30 minutes long to provide sufficient time to collect a representative number and range of utterances and ideally in different communicative contexts. A language sample will provide a rich source of data about phonology, the lexicon, grammar and pragmatics. If the Autism Diagnostic Observation Schedule was used as part of a diagnostic assessment, it can provide a range of contexts for collecting a language sample. Tager-Flusberg *et al.* (2009) use a developmental framework to divide early language into five phases with approximate age ranges. Within each phase they define the minimum criteria for deciding if the child's language level falls within that phase. For example, in the first words phase (12–18 months) the minimum criteria for phonology are CV combinations and an inventory of four consonants; for vocabulary, five different words used referentially are expected in a 20 minute observation; for pragmatics, comments and one other communicative function are expected. By the sentence phase (30–48 months), the minimum criterion for phonology is 75 per cent intelligibility; for vocabulary, 95 different words used in 65 utterances; for grammar, an MLU = 3.0; for pragmatics, one narrative in a language sample and two full turns on the same topic following an adult utterance in conversation.

Paul and Wilson (2008) argue that observational assessment needs to address the communication patterns typical of children with ASD. The child's responsiveness should be evaluated; for example, a record made of the number of times the child does not respond to the therapist's overture as a proportion of overtures made. Children with ASD may have unusual prosody (e.g. very flat, 'sing-song' or otherwise poorly modulated intonation) and so note should be made of the prosodic features of the child's speech, including unusual volume, rate, rhythm, fluency and/or intonation. Children with ASD tend to show more use of stereotyped and idiosyncratic language than children with other developmental difficulties. Stereotyped language may take the form of over-used chunks of memorised language, such as phrases taken from a favourite television programme. Idiosyncratic language includes neologisms, making up words, such as 'fire-cake' for birthday cake or using words in an idiosyncratic way (e.g. using girls' names for colours). Pronoun reversal may be observed, where children use second or third person in place of first person pronouns (e.g. the child says 'You want a drink' when they mean 'I want a drink').

Pragmatics is impaired regardless of the level of language achieved and a detailed assessment is required. The Children's Communication Checklist (Bishop 2003a) can be completed by a parent or teacher and provides a standardised measure of pragmatic skills. Direct observation of the child's social communication is essential. It may be the case that a child's social communication skills are stronger when they are interacting with an adult than with their peers, and so information from several settings is recommended. Observation of pragmatics should include assessment of communicative functions, conversation and non-verbal communication.

Intervention and evaluation

Rogers (2006) identifies three approaches which have been used to support the development of language and communication in children with ASD. These are behavioural, didactic and naturalistic, and developmental approaches. Behavioural interventions can be used for all aspects of difficulties associated with ASD including language and communication. The Picture Exchange Communication System (PECS) (Bondy and Frost 1994) is a behavioural approach to communication using symbols. Its focus is on teaching functional communication behaviour without regard to developmental considerations. PECS is highly structured and uses careful shaping techniques to teach the child to communicate with pictures. Training is divided into six phases which must be followed in the prescribed order. Requesting is learnt at phase 1 where the child is taught to exchange a picture for a desired object with prompting. In phase 2 the distance between the child and the communicative partner is increased and prompts are faded. The child is taught to choose the appropriate picture from a selection in a communication book or board at phase 3. At phase 4 the child learns to combine a set phrase (e.g. 'I want') with a picture to construct a short phrase. At phase 5 the child learns to respond to questions (e.g. 'What do you want?') with pictures and/or verbalisation. In the final phase, the child is taught to comment by responding to questions such as 'What do you see?' and 'What is it?' with pictures and/or verbalisation.

A recent systematic review into the effectiveness of PECS by Preston and Carter (2009) identified 27 studies and concluded there was evidence that PECS was learnt easily by children and provided a means of communication for those with little or no functional speech. There were also some limited data that PECS had a positive impact on both social-communication and challenging behaviour. However, it was uncertain if the approach facilitates the development of spoken language. The authors also noted that there were few well-conducted randomised controlled trials, which are considered the gold standard in evidence-based practice.

More comprehensive interventions, addressing the broad range of difficulties experienced by children with ASD have also adopted behavioural approaches. A randomised controlled trial of one such intervention, the Early Start Denver Model, suggests that early intensive behavioural intervention for pre-school aged children with ASD is effective (Dawson *et al.* 2010). The Early Start Denver Model is delivered by therapists trained in the approach and parents who implement a programme individualised to the needs of the child based on a range of techniques. The Early Start Denver Model integrates applied behaviour analysis with developmental and relationship-based approaches, such as those used in the Hanen programme. In Dawson and colleagues' efficacy study, 24 children aged between 18 and 30 months at the start of the study were followed over two years and compared with a control group who received standard management in the community. The Early Start Denver Model group showed significantly more gains in intellectual functioning and language and a reduction in autistic symptoms compared to the control group. More children in the Early Start Denver Model group moved from an autism diagnosis to a milder, broad ASD diagnosis. It is important to bear in mind that these gains were made with a very high level of intervention. Trained therapists offered on average 15 hours of input each week and the parents reported offering an additional 16 hours per week over the two years of the programme.

Pre-school Autism Communication Therapy (Green *et al.* 2010) uses a developmental pragmatics approach based on interventions that have been shown to be effective for children with specific speech and language delays, such as the Hanen programme (Girolametto *et al.* 1996). Pre-school Autism Communication Therapy has a developmental orientation, focuses on naturalistic interactions and collaborative work with parents. It targets core impairments in shared attention, understanding and intentional communication through a parent training programme that focuses on changing the interaction of the parent–child dyad in order to enhance child communication.

The approach was evaluated by Green and colleagues (2010), who compared Pre-school Autism Communication Therapy with therapy as usual in a large group of pre-schoolers with ASD. Parent training was achieved through bi-weekly, two-hour clinic sessions for six months followed by monthly booster sessions for six months (36 hours over 18 sessions in total). Between sessions, families were also asked to do 30 minutes of daily home practice. Pre-school Autism Communication Therapy was effective in enabling parents to provide well-timed responses to their children, increasing the frequency of initiations made by the child, and the amount of parent–child shared attention. Thus, the intervention had clear effects on those aspects of behaviour directly targeted by the intervention. However, the degree to which the intervention generalised beyond the parent–child interaction was less certain. No improvement was seen in the child's interaction with another adult, the person assessing post intervention or on the child's functioning in school, as measured by a teacher interview.

For older children, Adams and colleagues (2005) offer an intervention framework aimed specifically at pragmatic impairments. Three broad areas are targeted through direct intervention and advice on strategies to parents and teaching staff. The techniques used included modelling and individual practice, role play, practising specific pragmatic skills in conversations, meta-pragmatic therapy, promoting self-monitoring and coping strategies, and rule flouting exercises.

The first area is the communication environment. It is important to establish the language and communication level of the child to ensure that demands do not exceed the child's competence as this may lead to greater impairment in pragmatic functioning and contribute to avoidance and communication failure. Parents and teaching staff may adopt an overly directive approach to interaction because of the child's limited initiation, lack of reciprocal responsiveness or their over-estimation of the child's language ability, particularly if the child is apparently fluent. Advice to parents and teaching staff on how to adapt their interaction can increase the child's experience of successful communication. Access to the curriculum can be improved by matching classroom demands to the child's communicative competence. For example, reducing language demands by having a teaching assistant (TA) to translate language into short meaningful utterances with visual demonstration; matching written language to the child's level of spoken language comprehension. TAs also need training to support the generalisation of individual intervention approaches into the classroom.

The second area of intervention focuses on social cognition and flexibility. This includes understanding emotions. Scenarios from the child's everyday life in school and with peers can be visualised using cartoons and used to help the child identify and label the emotions they experience. The cartoon stories also offer a way of depersonalising the experience and emotion and relating it to another story character with the aim of increasing insight into other people's emotions and what influences them. The intervention aims to increase the child's flexibility by regularly adding one small change to routines s/he might have. Forewarning the child about anticipated changes will help him or her anticipate and understand the change. Social and verbal inferences are targeted using cartoon stories about typical social scenarios which can be used to support the child to make a deduction of the likely meaning from the social context. Generalisation of understanding of non-literal language can be supported by the TA interpreting complex language within social and classroom situations on a daily basis.

Language pragmatics therapy aims to reduce the child's verbosity and to improve coherence and quantity of information offered in conversation. Key areas targeted are exchange structure, turn-taking, topic management and conversational skills, building sequences in narrative, referencing in discourse, cohesion and coherence. Explicit teaching, for example, asking the child to identify what makes a good listener or speaker, can be used to work on language pragmatics targets, as well as advice to teaching staff about supporting the child in the classroom.

Initial evidence from case studies suggests that the intervention may lead to positive changes in targeted skills with three 60 minute sessions per week over eight weeks (i.e. 24 hours of therapy) from a specialist speech and language therapist (Adams *et al.* 2005; Adams *et al.* 2006).

Summary

ASD is a common developmental condition characterised by a triad of impairments in reciprocal social interaction, communication and by restricted and repetitive behaviours and interests.

Communication impairments are a hallmark of ASD and make the speech and language therapist a key professional in managing the condition. There is no screening test for ASD that has proven effective in identifying children at risk of the condition. Best-practice guidelines recommend that professionals who work with children should be trained to recognise the alerting signals which may indicate a possible ASD. The pervasive nature of the disorder and the risk of other medical and developmental conditions associated with the diagnosis, means that management needs to be by a multi-disciplinary team, which should include a speech and language therapist. The recommendation from best-practice guidelines is for diagnosis to be made in an ASD-specific assessment by ASD specialists. In addition to a broad, general language and communication assessment, the therapist will need to make focused observations based on knowledge of language and communication features in ASD. The evidence base provides support for a range of interventions, including clinician based and parent based, and the use of symbols for non-verbal children, if the therapy input is sufficiently high.

Chapter 12

Working with children with language delay and specific language impairment

Janet Wood

Learning outcomes

By the end of this chapter, the reader should be able to:

- explain the factors to be considered when identifying children with language delay and specific language impairment (SLI);
- briefly describe the nature of SLI;
- plan an assessment for a child with primary language impairment;
- describe possible intervention techniques;
- describe the existing evidence relating to the efficacy of intervention techniques.

Introduction

Children may fail to develop language typically for a variety of reasons. In some cases, the cause is attributable to difficulties such as hearing impairment or autistic spectrum disorder, while in other cases the difficulties are related primarily to language development. This chapter focuses on the latter of these groups. A number of terms are used to describe children for whom language is the primary area of concern. These include language delay, primary language delay, SLI and developmental language disorder. The range of terms that are used can be confusing, especially as they are used inconsistently within the literature. It is therefore important to check an author's definition before making comparisons between statements.

Identifying children with language delay and SLI

Early language delay is typically defined as the use of fewer than 50 words and/or no two word combinations at 2;00 years. This equates to approximately 10 per cent of the population (Fenson *et al.* 2003). Some of these children will be 'late talkers' who catch up without intervention, some of them will catch up with support and a third group will go on to have persisting primary language difficulties. This latter group are those that are likely to have a diagnosis of SLI.

For toddlers with purely expressive language delays, it seems that about 60 per cent catch up without intervention by the age of 3 years (Law *et al.* 1998). However, the outcome appears less favourable for those with mixed receptive-expressive delays (Roulstone *et al.* 2003) and it is also important to consider the 40 per cent with expressive delays that do not make spontaneous progress. Language impairment that persists to school age is relatively common: a large epidemiological study in the United States estimated the prevalence of SLI to be approximately 7 per cent in the population of 5–6 year old children (Tomblin *et al.* 1997).

A number of researchers have attempted to identify a means of predicting which children with early language delay will have persistent difficulties. The findings from different studies are not all in agreement but a review of the literature (Olswang *et al.* 1998) identified a number of likely 'risk factors'. These are limited use of verbs, few spontaneous imitations, poor verbal comprehension, a limited range of consonants and a family history of language difficulties. This list is clinically useful and also makes sense in light of current theories regarding the nature of SLI.

Children with SLI are a heterogeneous group, so it is not possible to describe a 'typical' case. However, some areas of difficulty occur frequently within this group. Schwartz (2009) provides a detailed discussion of the common linguistic deficits which are:

- difficulty with the use of verbs and verb argument structure;
- difficulty with word learning and word finding;
- difficulty with understanding and using verb morphology;
- difficulty with understanding and using complex sentence structures;
- difficulty with producing cohesive narratives.

These difficulties can persist into adolescence (Stothard *et al.* 1998) and adulthood (Mawhood *et al.* 2000). It is also the case that young adults with a history of language impairment are at risk for poor outcomes in terms of academic achievement, social participation and self-esteem (Tomblin 2008).

What is SLI?

The two diagnostic systems that are commonly used are the ICD-10 (WHO 1993a) and DSM-IV (American Psychiatric Association 1994). In each of these, SLI is defined using exclusionary criteria, that is, language impairment that is not attributable to neurological, sensory or physical impairment, or to a pervasive developmental disorder. There is also a requirement that language skills are significantly impaired in relation to non-verbal IQ. In the ICD-10, this is defined as language skills that are at least two standard deviations below the mean and at least one standard deviation below non-verbal (or performance) IQ. The DSM-IV criteria also require that the language impairment interferes with academic or occupational achievement, or social interaction.

Although these definitions are still commonly used, the degree to which SLI is specific to language has been increasingly questioned, as has the validity of using discrepancy criteria, that is, a discrepancy between verbal and performance IQ. It seems that such criteria may be neither valid nor clinically useful. The size of the discrepancy is partly arbitrary, considering that both verbal and performance tests are liable to measurement error. The discrepancy size is also dependent on exactly which aspects of language and non-verbal ability are tested (Bishop 1997, 2004). Furthermore, the profiles for individual children are not stable over time: children can move in and out of a group defined by discrepancy criteria at different points of testing and, overall, IQ scores have been shown to decline with age for children initially diagnosed with SLI (Botting 2005). It is also notable that, while language impairment has been shown to be highly heritable, this finding does not hold up if strict discrepancy criteria are used (Bishop *et al.* 1995). Finally, it seems that a discrepancy between verbal and performance IQ is not a good predictor of adolescent outcomes for children diagnosed with language difficulties at 5 years (Tomblin 2008). In view of these findings, researchers may use the term 'language impairment' rather than 'specific language impairment' and include children with learning ability in the low-average range within this group (i.e. IQ scores of 70 or above). This has significant implications for speech and language therapists, who may need to prioritise intervention across a caseload, according to diagnostic categories.

A second issue that relates to the specificity of SLI is the fact that there are high rates of co-morbidity between SLI and other disorders, including dyslexia and motor coordination disorder (Hulme and Snowling 2009). Additionally, as our understanding of the underlying nature of SLI improves, it seems that the observable language difficulties might be caused by more general cognitive deficits in, for example, processing or memory. Developing an understanding of the underlying nature of SLI has implications for both assessment and intervention with this population (Schwartz 2009).

Theories of SLI

Theories of SLI fit broadly into two categories, linguistic and cognitive. The key points are highlighted and the reader is referred to two overviews of relevant research: Schwartz (2009) and Hulme and Snowling (2009).

Linguistic theories of SLI explain the disorder in terms of an underlying deficit in the ability to learn or apply morpho-syntactic rules. They make the assumption that linguistic knowledge is independent of other cognitive functions and that linguistic rule-learning explains normal development. These assumptions are controversial. Furthermore, problems arise because linguistic theories can only explain the morpho-syntactic deficits seen in SLI and also because the explanations do not all hold up well in cross-linguistic studies. There is not yet a linguistic theory that adequately explains the overall nature of SLI (Schwartz 2009).

Cognitive theories explain SLI in relation to deficits in cognitive processes, which may be domain general processes or those that are specific to language processing. A wide range of theories has been presented, with deficits proposed in auditory perception, working memory, speed of processing, processing capacity and central executive functions. It is evident from the research that most children with SLI do have deficits in these areas. What remains to be proven, however, is how these deficits interact with each other and how they relate to the specific language difficulties that are seen in SLI (Schwartz 2009). There are some theories that attempt to address these questions, such as the Surface Hypothesis (Leonard 1998) and the Procedural Deficit Hypothesis (Ullman and Pierpont 2005). One of the possible outcomes of research in this area is the identification of a clinical marker for SLI. Non-word repetition is a potential candidate for this, as it appears to discriminate children with language impairment from their peers, across the age range (Schwartz 2009). However, more research is needed before this can be used diagnostically.

Aetiology of SLI

The aetiology of SLI is likely to be multi-factorial, associated with the interaction between many different genes and various environmental factors (Hulme and Snowling 2009). There is now good evidence from twin studies that SLI is highly heritable (Tomblin and Buckwalter 1998) and that genetic influences are stronger for deficits in grammar than for deficits in vocabulary (Kovas et al. 2005). Four chromosomal regions have been identified as being associated with SLI and it seems that some of the heterogeneity in language profiles may be reflected at the genetic level (SLI consortium 2002, 2004). This is, undoubtedly, an area that will be subject to further research.

Another area that is beginning to be understood is the neurobiology of SLI. The use of electrophysiology (ERP) and functional magnetic resonance imaging (fMRI) has revealed both structural and functional differences between the brains of children with SLI and those of children who are developing typically (Schwartz 2009). Again, however, in order to understand the relationship between these differences and the language difficulties that appear to be caused by them further research is needed.

Initial clinical decisions: planning an assessment

During assessment, the speech and language therapist will need to ascertain:

- whether the child really does have a language impairment;
- whether language is the primary area of difficulty;
- the severity and nature of this impairment;
- the likelihood of the impairment persisting (for a toddler with early language delay);
- the impact of the difficulties on the child's activity and participation.

Assessment information will need to be gathered from a range of sources, including referral information, a case history, observation of the child, formal and/or informal assessment and verbal or written information from other professionals. Naturally, the therapist will also assess other aspects of communication, such as speech and social interaction skills, in order to rule out alternative diagnoses.

Does the child have a language impairment?

This is relatively easy to answer for a toddler, as it is usually possible to ascertain a young child's language profile from referral information, a case history and observation of the child. This profile can then be compared to developmental norms. The therapist would want to find out, for example, whether the child:

- is using any words and, if so, approximately how many;
- is combining words;
- is able to select objects on request, without the aid of contextual cues;
- is able to follow simple instructions.

In order to get full information, it might be useful to ask the parent or carer to complete an early language checklist, such as the MacArthur Communicative Development Inventories (Fenson *et al.* 2003). Observation would ideally be carried out when the child is playing with the parent or carer, as this should produce a representative sample of language. This type of observation would also provide an opportunity for the therapist to note the manner of parent–child interaction; information that may prove useful when planning intervention.

For an older child, it is likely that some form of formal or informal assessment will be required in order to ascertain if the child does have a language impairment.

Is language the primary area of difficulty?

This can be achieved via case history information and input from other professionals. Information can be gathered about any sensory impairment, such as deafness, structural abnormalities, such as cleft palate, neurological disorders, such as epilepsy, and pervasive developmental disorders, such as autism spectrum disorder. For some children, it will be clear that language is the primary area of difficulty, as there are no other relevant diagnoses. In other cases, however, it will be necessary to make a clinical judgement about whether additional areas of difficulty are causing or merely contributing to the language impairment. In the case of a child with fluctuating, conductive hearing loss, for example, it would be necessary to compare the child's language level to that expected of a child with this impairment before considering a diagnosis of SLI. This is, of course, partly subjective and it may be that relevant clinical hypotheses can only be evaluated over a period of time. This is particularly true when there are several potential contributing factors.

It is also useful to gauge the child's level of cognitive development by considering progress made with, for example, self-help skills or skills such as counting. Results of IQ tests may also be available if the child has previously been referred to a psychologist. Information about general learning ability is useful in order to gain a holistic view of the child's functioning but this may not be as important in relation to a diagnosis of SLI as has previously been thought.

Finally, it is important to gather information about the child's environment, including the nature of language input to the child and the opportunities provided for communication. If lack of language stimulation is the main causal factor, any language impairment is likely to be transient. As has been discussed above, however, environmental factors may also influence outcomes for children who are genetically at risk for persistent language difficulties.

What is the severity and nature of the impairment?

When presented with a child with language impairment, the speech and language therapist will need to assess the understanding and use of vocabulary, morphology, syntax and, if appropriate, narrative. Formal and informal assessments can be used, and then information combined in order to test clinical hypotheses. There is likely to be more emphasis on informal assessment with a younger child but information from this source remains important at all ages.

Informal assessment of a language impaired child may include:

* observation of the child in a natural setting (such as home, nursery or school);
* structured play (in order to obtain a language sample and gauge response to questions and instructions);
* picture naming and/or description;
* story telling and/or recall (from a picture book or series of pictures);
* discussion of a story or of real events that the child has experienced.

Formal assessment will frequently include an assessment battery. Assessment batteries contain subtests which assess different aspects of receptive and expressive language, so that scores can be compared across domains. Some that are used commonly in the UK are:

* Clinical Evaluation of Language Fundamentals – Preschool 2 UK (CELF – Preschool 2 UK) (Secord et al. 2006): age range 3–6 years;
* Clinical Evaluation of Language Fundamentals – 4th Edition UK (CELF – 4 UK) (Wiig and Semel 2006): age range 5–16 years;
* Assessment of Comprehension and Expression 6–11 (ACE) (Adams et al. 2001): age range 6–11 years.

In addition, there are numerous standardised assessments that can be used to assess specific aspects of vocabulary, syntax or narrative, for children in different age brackets. These may be useful if the therapist wishes to obtain detailed information in order to form baselines for therapy outcome measures.

Is this likely to be a transient or persistent language impairment?

In order to address this question, it is useful to consider the risk factors for persistent language impairment, as presented above, and also information regarding the nature of SLI. As SLI is known to be highly heritable, one of the first things to ascertain is whether there is any close family history of language impairment. It also seems sensible to take note of family members who were late talkers but who did catch up, as the relationship between genetic and environmental factors is still not understood. Children with mixed receptive-expressive delays are known to have a poorer outcome, as are children who have speech, as well as language, difficulties (Roulstone *et al.* 2003). It is therefore important to note the pervasiveness of the communication difficulties when conducting an assessment.

Another risk factor is limited use of verbs. Typically, children who are at risk of SLI have no verbs in their early vocabularies. Then, later on in development, they over-use non-specific verbs, such as 'having' and 'doing'; creating sentences such as 'doing the letter' instead of 'posting the letter'. Children with SLI may have particular difficulty with verbs because of the impact of broader syntactic difficulties (Leonard 1998). It is relatively simple to judge the extent of a child's use of verbs from a language sample or from picture description.

The final risk factor for persisting difficulties is a lack of spontaneous imitations in early development. One of the cognitive theories of SLI is that of a phonological working memory deficit. This deficit results in a child being unable to retain the phonology of a new word adequately, leading to difficulties with non-word repetition tasks and, more functionally, with word learning (see Schwartz (2009) for a review of this research). This deficit may also explain the observable symptom of few spontaneous imitations in early development. If appropriate, the therapist may wish to conduct a non-word repetition test as part of the assessment, to test hypotheses regarding the likely persistence of the language impairment. Alternatively, for a younger child, it may be sufficient to ask parents or carers about the frequency with which the child spontaneously imitates new words.

The symptom of SLI that appears to be most resistant to intervention is that of difficulty with using verb morphology (Conti-Ramsden *et al.* 2001). It may therefore be interesting to note whether or not a child has made progress in this area during therapy, when attempting to predict long term outcomes.

What is the impact of the language impairment on activity and participation?

The *International Classification of Functioning, Disability and Health* (ICF) (WHO 2001) describes health status in terms of impairment, activity and participation. The latter two of these concepts relate, respectively, to the extent to which the child is able to (a) carry out tasks and activities, and (b) participate in life situations. Activity and participation may be limited by either personal or environmental factors. Washington (2007) explains how the ICF framework can be applied to children with language impairments. There is also a 'children and youth' version of the ICF framework (ICF-CY: WHO 2007), which is relevant for this population.

In order to assess the impact of a language impairment on activity and participation, the therapist should observe the child in everyday settings and also gather information from those that spend time with the child on a regular basis. This is likely to include parents or carers and also nursery or school staff.

Examples of limitations in activity include, being unable to:

- formulate a question;
- learn new vocabulary;
- follow instructions.

These limitations may, in turn, lead to restrictions in participation, such as being unable to:

- ask for desired objects;
- participate in a classroom discussion;
- participate in a new playground game.

It is also important to find out about the factors that either support or hinder the child in overcoming these limitations and restrictions. These might include:

- the child's willingness to ask for help;
- the level of background noise in the home or school environment;
- the understanding that others have of the child's needs;
- the availability of adult support in the classroom.

The next stage of decision-making: planning intervention

The nature of speech and language therapy intervention for children with language impairment will, of course, depend on the age of the child and the outcome of assessment. The following intervention options are organised in relation to the child's age, the severity of the language impairment and the degree of perceived risk for persisting difficulties. The list of options is intended as a guide to decision-making rather than an exhaustive list.

Management of a late-talking toddler

A toddler under the age of about 3 years, who is presenting with expressive language delay and no evidence of risk factors for persisting difficulties, is unlikely to require active intervention. In fact, Paul (1996) suggests that early intervention can have negative consequences for late-talking children who are likely to catch up spontaneously. The final decision regarding management is likely to depend on the level of concern expressed by parents and the presence of any negative environmental factors. Possible options include any or all of:

- offering an 'open door' for self re-referral, if concerns continue;
- providing information about services that are available on a open access basis, such as drop-in clinics and parenting skills workshops (so-called 'universal services');
- offering advice on general language facilitation techniques.

Intervention for a pre-school child with mild to moderate language impairment

Intervention is most likely to involve language facilitation techniques, at least in the first instance. These techniques are designed to enhance the language input that the child receives, in order to support development. Intervention may be provided directly to the child, either individually or in a group, or else may be conducted via parents (see Chapter 8).

There are several language facilitation techniques, two of which are recasting and focused stimulation. There are also published parent-focused programmes that include a range of facilitation techniques, such as the Hanen Parent Programme (Pepper and Weitzman 2004). Recasting involves responding to a child's utterance with an utterance that is more complete or accurate in terms of semantics or syntax. Particular structures are focused on, according to the child's needs (Camarata and Nelson 2006). In focused stimulation, the child is exposed to multiple examples of a particular word, morpheme or structure. This occurs within a meaningful communicative context but without expectation of the child responding to or using the target. In all these techniques, the principle is that particular aspects of language are presented more frequently and/or in a more salient form than they would be in normal conversation. This takes account of the processing difficulties that are likely to underlie language impairment.

Ebbels (2008) reviews the evidence regarding the efficacy of language facilitation techniques for pre-school children with difficulties with grammar. Overall, there is good evidence that these techniques are beneficial, although particular techniques may be more suited to some children and to some language targets than others. It is also possible that, for children with expressive language delay, indirect therapy using these techniques is equally as effective as direct therapy (Law *et al.* 2004).

Intervention for a pre-school child at risk of persistent language impairment

A young child who has severe or pervasive language impairment, or who otherwise appears to be at risk of persistent difficulties, should be a priority for speech and language therapy intervention. The language facilitation techniques described above continue to be appropriate, although it is likely that more explicit teaching of targets will also be required. There has been little research into the effectiveness of intervention for children with severe receptive and expressive language impairment but one study (Gallagher and Chiat 2009) indicates that intensive therapy is required in order to facilitate change in receptive language skills in this population. This study compared a once weekly, four hour direct therapy session, provided within a group setting, with a more consultative approach, delivered within the child's nursery and also a 'no treatment' control. Only children in the first of these groups demonstrated progress with receptive language targets.

Children with severe language impairment are sometimes offered specialist nursery provision, where language input is optimised throughout the nursery day and where language development can be supported by signing and other visual support techniques. This is regarded as good practice but there is not any research evidence to support the effectiveness of this approach in comparison to others.

Intervention for a primary school aged child with language impairment

Once a language impaired child is of school age, it should be possible to include a meta-cognitive approach to intervention within the management plan. That is, an approach in which the child is required to consciously reflect on specific aspects of language. Examples include making judgements about word meanings and colour coding sentences according to their semantic or syntactic structure. Ebbels (2007) argues that this more explicit form of intervention is necessary for children with persistent difficulties, who have not managed to acquire language from general facilitation techniques alone.

Meta-cognitive therapy techniques for word learning and word finding, typically involve:

* the use of 'word webs' for target words, to support the formation of more detailed and accurate lexical representations, both in terms of phonological and semantic information;
* teaching the child strategies that can be used to support retrieval of these words.

Progress with lexical skills has frequently been demonstrated in intervention studies, although much of the evidence comes from single case and small group studies, with no or limited experimental controls. Relevant studies include those of Parsons *et al.* (2005) and Zens *et al.* (2009).

As has already been stated, one of the most persistent areas of difficulty for children with SLI is that of grammatical difficulties, especially difficulty with verb morphology and complex syntax. Colourful semantics is a meta-cognitive technique for improving grammatical ability that is suitable for primary school aged children (Bryan 1997). This technique uses colour coding of the thematic roles of words within sentences, to support children in the development of argument structure. Children in a number of case studies have been shown to make improvements following this form of intervention but none of the studies have included experimental controls and so the findings need to be interpreted with this in mind (Ebbels 2008).

As well as meta-cognitive approaches to developing vocabulary and grammar, school age children are likely to require support with both producing and understanding narratives. Intervention for producing coherent narratives typically involves teaching the child to use a 'story grammar', or structure for the narrative, using story planners and cue cards. There are a number of resources that are available for supporting this type of work but there has been little research into the effectiveness of intervention.

Finally, as well as providing intervention that focuses on aspects of the impairment, it is important to teach school age children strategies that will help them to reduce the impact of their difficulties. These strategies include asking for repetitions and clarification, visualising language, self-monitoring errors and using personal prompt cards.

Intervention for adolescents

Young people of secondary school age often receive lower levels of speech and language therapy intervention than do younger children. The reasons for this include younger children being prioritised to avoid academic and social disadvantage, and the attitude that it is, by that stage, 'too late to make a difference' (Lindsay *et al.* 2002). However, recent studies have indicated that language intervention with this population can be effective in improving vocabulary, narrative and social skills, with positive outcomes being demonstrated via improved test scores and also reports from teachers and the young people themselves (Joffe 2006; Stringer and Clegg 2006).

A meta-cognitive technique called shape coding (Ebbels 2007) has been shown to be effective with a range of secondary aged pupils with SLI, who have persistent difficulties with grammar. Shape coding uses a written system of shapes, colours and arrows to support work on phrase and sentence structure and verb morphology. The level of research evidence for this technique is strong, as one of the studies was a randomised control trial. However, its use has yet to be investigated with anyone other than the author delivering the therapy.

Summary

This chapter has described the nature of language delay and specific language impairment. The reader will be aware that some children have a language delay that will resolve, either spontaneously or with intervention, whereas others have difficulties that can persist throughout childhood and beyond. Persistent difficulties are likely to be a result of processing difficulties that are caused by an interaction between many genetic and environmental factors. Assessment of a language impaired child should take account of the underlying nature of language difficulties and should aim to identify the level of impairment and any restriction in activity and participation. Possible intervention techniques are many and varied and their selection will depend on the age of the child and the severity of the impairment. Overall, intervention that is targeted appropriately can be effective with this population.

Chapter 13

Working with deaf children

Sarah Beazley, Ruth Merritt and Judy Halden

Learning outcomes

By the end of this chapter the reader should be able to:

- recognise possible barriers to the development of effective communication for young deaf people of all ages (YDP);
- consider the role of the speech and language therapist in decreasing such barriers;
- reflect on factors that may impact on the decisions around assessment for YDP and their families;
- identify the decisions around the provision of direct or indirect speech and language therapy support for YDP and their families;
- understand the processes involved in planning therapy with YDP and their families.

Introduction

In this chapter the decision-making processes that a speech and language therapist employs in working with YDP are examined using a two stage approach. First, the focus is on environmental factors that might create barriers to inclusion for YDP and which influence the therapist in making decisions about the need for therapy, its timing and location and the people to involve. The second stage relates to the communication processes surrounding YDP and how these influence planning decisions. A series of questions will be posed after each section to enable the reader to reflect on how the issues raised might be of direct relevance to his/her own contexts.

Throughout the chapter the term 'deaf' is used as in the Early Support Programme (DfES 2006) which refers to children and young people with 'all levels of hearing loss'.

The influence of environmental factors on the decision-making process

When a referral to see a young deaf person reaches a speech and language therapist, s/he has first to consider whether therapy is appropriate and if so how it is best delivered, by whom, where and when. The influences on the initial decision-making process are outlined in Figure 13.1.

Influences of YDP's close community

Language environment

There may be a combination of different languages used in the young deaf person's home, school and other contexts which could include a sign language, such as British Sign Language (BSL). Such information will influence how the therapist might assess communication and whether a co-worker, who is a skilled user of another language, is needed (see Chapter 14).

Figure 13.1 The influence of potential enabling/disabling factors in a young deaf person's environment on speech and language therapy provision.

YDP need to discover their preferred language for themselves. This might be spoken or signed language and might or might not be the majority language of the dominant culture in which they develop their communication (Marschark and Spencer 2010). Those involved with the child such as teachers and speech and language therapists, need to consider the language that is going to provide the greatest likelihood of equal access to information.

- What spoken and signed languages are used in a young deaf person's regular environments?
- What is the preferred language of significant family members?
- What is the young deaf person's preferred language?
- Are family members learning sign language?
- How effectively are the spoken and/or signed languages used by significant family members?

Attitudes of others to deafness and different language choices

The choice of whether to use only a spoken language, a signed language or both with YDP, has been an ongoing debate for generations (Marschark and Spencer 2010). Research has confirmed the role of speech reading (Woodhouse *et al.* 2009) in typical language development and also the brain's use of multimodal input in language acquisition (Woll 2010). This indicates that both auditory and visual processing need to be taken into account in considering not only which language to use but also the means by which it is conveyed. Such decisions remain both complex and emotional. For example, some families and professionals might be fearful that YDP would be excluded by using BSL. Others may feel anxious about the use of speech as the only medium for language acquisition and communication. Speech and language therapists need to be sensitive to how the mixed and sometimes conflicting messages around these issues can be difficult for families (Young *et al.* 2006).

Gaining an understanding of the family's wider experiences and goals is also important. Many parents, for example, may never have met a deaf person before and in the early years might be anxious to seek answers to questions such as 'Will my child talk like hearing children and go to mainstream school?' The therapist and other team members will need to spend time with the family sharing information and discussing expectations.

- What are the attitudes of others towards signed or spoken languages?
- What are the family's goals for their young deaf person?
- What is the family's experience of deafness, of other YDP or adults who are deaf?

The speech and language therapist

A therapist hoping to work regularly with YDP will need specialist post-qualification training, whereas a therapist who rarely meets YDP could refer to a clinical specialist for support as needed.

Attitudes to deafness and language choices

A therapist's attitude towards deafness, disablement, the place of spoken/signed languages and technology will have a strong bearing on decision-making (Young *et al.* 2006). It is helpful therefore for therapists to examine their own position and share this with the families with whom they are working whilst remaining supportive as parents make informed choices for their deaf child (DfES 2006).

- What are my feelings about the place of spoken and sign language in society?
- How might that influence my decision-making about therapy for YDP?
- Have I met a deaf person?
- Why did I decide to become a speech and language therapist?
- Where can I discuss my feelings further?
- How would I talk to families about my attitudes?

Knowledge for working with deaf children

Speech and language therapists can draw effectively on existing understanding of language and communication for making decisions, especially if referring to other professionals or specialist therapists for specific support. However, for more informed and independent decision-making, speech and language therapists need to acquire knowledge about the following areas:

- the context for working with deaf children alongside other professionals (BATOD/RCSLT 2007);
- language development in YDP (Meadow-Orlans *et al.* 2004);
- current research in the area of deafness including cochlear implantation (Nicholas and Geers 2007);
- the evidence base for evaluating intervention for YDP (Geers and Brenner 2003);
- the debates relating to communication practices (Marschark and Spencer 2010);
- the range of amplification devices available (Madell and Flexer 2008).

Skills for working with YDP

In order for speech and language therapists to work with YDP they need to be able to:

- identify specific adaptations needed for the communication environment;
- adjust language levels and mode of communication whether signed or spoken;
- alter their own communication to make it fully accessible – this includes being lip-readable;
- transcribe speech, using detailed narrow transcription including vowels and non-segmental features (Teoh and Chin 2009);
- apply acoustic phonetics in the development of comprehensive auditory training programmes;
- trouble-shoot a range of listening devices.

It is essential that the therapist should continually reflect upon his/her ability to carry out these skills (Skeat and Roddam 2010).

Educational context and other influences

As soon as young people are diagnosed as having a hearing loss they may be referred to speech and language therapy and are usually also seen by a teacher of deaf children. The team (see below) around the YDP need to work in close collaboration with families (DfES 2006) to support establishment and acceptance of personal and educational listening devices as well as checking how listening skills are progressing. In addition, parents may need advice on methods of communication, and support in monitoring the development of speech and language skills. The various professionals around the YDP and their families need to find the best ways to work effectively together for each case (BATOD/RCSLT 2007). Often, the teacher of deaf children will have an influential role in any local procedures around educational provision for the YDP with the speech and language therapist providing a contribution to the complex team decisions around appropriate placement. For pre-school children, teachers may make regular home visits and the complementary and overlapping of roles of the therapist can be very effective. YDP with less significant and perhaps fluctuating hearing loss might not be supported by a teacher of deaf children, and the therapist may refer to a specialist teacher and/or work closely with the class and head teacher.

- Is a teacher of deaf children involved with the child and the family and how does his/her input complement that of the speech and language therapist?
- How effective is the communication between members of the team and is the family being kept central to the process?
- What type of educational provision does the therapist and others, including the family, feel may be needed once the child reaches school age?
- What is the Local Authority's provision for deaf children?
- What communication contexts are available locally?
- Is there a discrepancy between the professionals and/or parents concerning the communication mode/method believed to be suitable for this child?
- If so, whom should the therapist consult so that the child's communication needs in education are met? This may be, for example, a speech and language therapy manager, or a specialist therapist for a second opinion.

Other agencies

There are often representatives from a range of agencies working with YDP and their families and the team around the YDP may include a specialist speech and language therapist for deaf people, health visitor, social worker, deaf support worker and/or communicator, members of a cochlear implant team and medical officers as well as professionals from audiology services. The speech and language therapist will need to find out about the teams, services and their policies in the area. It is important for the therapist to identify and contribute to how any team works, particularly its success at interdisciplinary communication.

Technology

Speech and language therapists need to keep well informed of technological developments including the constantly expanding range of devices available for YDP. For example, it is currently commonplace for profoundly deaf young people to be fitted either with high-powered digital hearing aids or to receive bilateral cochlear implants from 12 months old or even younger. The potential benefits of such devices need to be thoroughly understood by the therapist in order for him/her to be able to advise the family and young deaf person appropriately and to provide effective support. In addition, within educational contexts, knowledge of the role of assistive devices, which give children better access to their teachers in noisy classrooms and to recorded teaching material such as DVDs, is essential. Furthermore, many YDP like their hearing peers, choose to communicate through different media such as email, the internet, text and video phones and such technological advances can be incorporated into functional, meaningful assessment and therapy.

Developments in technology directly affect the achievements of YDP and service provision needs to be responsive to any subsequent changes in communication and educational needs (De Raeve 2010).

- What listening devices is the young deaf person using? Is it appropriate for his/her degree of hearing loss?
- Are they using it well/consistently? If not, why not?
- Would they benefit from the use of other assistive listening or visual devices such as radio aids, telephone amplification, text phone, loop/electro-magnetic field systems?
- How confident is the speech and language therapist in using technological aids? How easy is it to get support with managing such aids?

The communication process and therapy planning

Once it has been decided that speech and language therapy should be provided, further decisions need to be made about the type of support that might be given.

Figure 13.2 shows the issues for consideration when assessing communication with YDP which will influence therapy planning and which can also be applied to young people of all ages from pre-school to secondary. The focus is likely to differ depending upon the age group. For example with babies, attention will largely be on the input being provided and on establishing consistent hearing status. With a teenager, the focus may be more on comprehension and output, using strategies based upon their own understanding of deafness.

During the assessment process there is a need to examine barriers and enablers to communication, rather than being deficit based. It is important to remember that most formal assessments used by therapists are not standardised on deaf children (Halden and Beazley 2010). Most are English based and not transferable to another language such as BSL, or to a different modality, such as signing. Where YDP are using more than one language, such as sign and spoken language, all the languages in the repertoire may need to be assessed separately, although overall communicative competence also needs to be considered (Herman and Mann 2010).

Poor acoustic conditions or distracting visual backgrounds may influence YDP's communicative success and such factors must be taken into account. Overall speech intelligibility assessment needs to consider such contextual aspects but also listener experience and non-segmental and segmental features (Parker 1999).

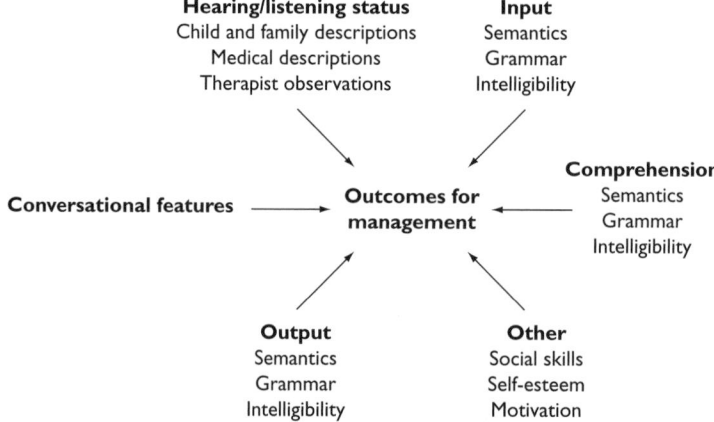

Figure 13.2 The influence on management planning for YDP of potential enabling/disabling factors in the communication process.

An exploration of the strategies that YDP and their families are already using is also essential in planning as these can perhaps be built upon or adapted to good effect. Careful initial and ongoing visual and auditory recordings of such aspects of communication, as well as subsequent setting of clear targets, continuous monitoring and follow-on assessments are key to allowing precise measures of efficacy and effectiveness to be made.

Hearing/listening status

Child and family description

It is important to establish what the family feel that the child can hear and the possible implications of this. For example, a profoundly deaf 6 year old child with digital aids may be able to respond when called loudly or to describe awareness of some environmental sounds that may help to warn of dangers. A child with a conductive loss might find it most difficult to hear speech when there is considerable background noise, such as in the classroom or at home when the television is on. A family might notice that a child with a unilateral cochlear implant sometimes finds it difficult to localise sounds, or to understand speech in noise.

It is also helpful for the speech and language therapist to determine YDP's views of their own hearing and listening, and how these match the comments of family and others.

- Under what circumstances do YDP feel it is easy/difficult to hear?
- Is there any family history or experience of deafness?
- Do the family and/or YDP notice that listening and attention skills fluctuate?
- What do YDP and their families understand about the nature of the hearing loss?
- What do YDP and their families feel can be heard?

Medical descriptions

Most therapists will be familiar with the types and degrees of hearing loss (Madell and Flexer 2008) but it is important to remember some significant factors that will influence management choices.

- Conductive losses affect the middle ear and reduce the overall volume of input with no distortion to the speech signal.
- Sensori-neural losses distort the speech signal and some speech sounds may be inaccessible. Increasingly audiometry is able to diagnose where exactly on the auditory pathway difficulties lie and hence these losses can now be defined as either sensory or nerve or mixed in origin.
- Auditory neuropathy spectrum disorder (ANSD) has been described as the auditory characteristics of people with normal outer hair cell function, shown by the presence of otoacoustic emissions or cochlear microphonic, but with aberrant neural activity in the peripheral and central auditory pathways. These individuals may experience difficulty hearing in noise, have fluctuating hearing sensitivity and have speech perception performance that does not match their residual hearing thresholds. Audiological management of these children needs close monitoring (Rance and Barker 2009). Specialist therapists need to ensure that YDP with this additional difficulty, and their families, receive a careful multi-disciplinary approach to their management. The prevalence of ANSD is difficult to define but appears to be increased in children with a hearing loss.
- YDP with similar audiograms may have different listening and communication skills, relating to both the internal and external resources, which may be developed into functional strategies.

- Age of onset of the hearing loss, of diagnosis and of receiving hearing aids will have a bearing on the prognosis for the development of spoken language.
- Audiological records need to be accessed, noted and carefully monitored by the therapist, including audiograms and information about amplification provision.

Thus, in order to support the decision-making process, the speech and language therapist needs to establish the young deaf person's medical history, the degree, nature and onset of hearing loss, and how it is currently being dealt with by the audiological services, and what bearing each of these factors may have on a young person's day-to-day functioning.

Therapist's observations

Observation of YDP in a range of natural contexts is essential for assessing functional communication, including listening skills. This will help the therapist decide:

- how communication and hearing are influencing each other;
- what acoustic considerations there are for any listening work;
- the way that current amplification might be working;
- the consistency of the young person's responses, especially for those with ANSD;
- the level of dependency upon speech reading;
- how and when the young deaf person responds to sounds/speech;
- whether this varies in different acoustic, social and/or linguistic conditions.

Such information will help to grade the listening environment. For example, by progressively adding noise, the speech and language therapist can enable YDP to build on strategies already used to distinguish speech patterns in quiet settings or, by varying the level of visual support given, the therapist can build a young person's confidence in his/her own listening.

Conversational features

Success in one-to-one and group conversations for YDP may vary considerably depending upon a range of factors such as the acoustic environment, whether conversational partners are hearing or deaf and whether or not they are using the same modality (Spencer and Harris 2006). Such information allows the speech and language therapist to determine whether support is needed in this area and, if so, how to help conversational partners and YDP extend approaches to recognising and dealing with breakdown. For example, conversation may be helped by improving environmental aspects such as lighting or reverberation, or the therapist may help the teacher to monitor conversational opportunities in the classroom, or find strategies for working with peers (Ibertsson *et al.* 2009).

- Do familiar people alter their conversational style with YDP?
- If there are changes in style what are they? What effect are they having on conversations?
- Are conversational partners aware of their own modifications?
- What strategies are being used in communication between YDP and others? If they are not understood what can the other conversational partner do to change this?

Input

The speech and language therapist needs to consider the nature of language input being used by others to YDP at home and at school. With the advent of neonatal hearing screening and early diagnosis, opportunities for improving the quality of early interaction have increased significantly as well as the advice that is being given to families as a result of these. They also need to be aware that it is not uncommon for people to reduce the overall amount of talk to deaf children, to restrict their vocabulary and limit their use of complex structures, including input around emotional talk (Moeller and Schick 2006).

- What is the nature of the input in the environment in general and does this differ from that given to YDP? If so, how? Why?
- How much are YDP spoken to? Signed to?
- Is the vocabulary used limited and/or context-bound to avoid communication breakdown?
- Are sentences kept short and simple to prevent loss of understanding?
- Is volume increased? Are lip patterns overemphasised in an attempt to help speech perception?
- How can the therapist change the nature of input from family, teachers and peers?

Comprehension and speech perception

When making decisions for working with YDP, therapists must be clear whether they are commenting on perception or comprehension difficulties. For example, it might be background noise, dim lighting, a speaker with a higher pitched voice or a cochlear implant with reduced functioning that prevents YDP from understanding an utterance, rather than a lack of comprehension.

- If there is more than one language in the environment, does the young person understand more in one language than in another?
- Are there some speakers that YDP find easier to understand? If so, why?
- What are the young person's receptive skills like (a) in quiet/noisy conditions, (b) with/ without visual cues?
- What are the young person's listening skills like in relation to the perception of speech cues, such as vowel, consonant or intonations contrasts?

Output

Some of the speech and language therapy assessments available for looking at aspects of output, for example PETAL (Parker 1999), may be appropriate for YDP. Where spoken English is not the preferred language, the speech and language therapist needs to decide whether tools designed for monolingual speakers are relevant to bilingual users, including those using different modalities such as sign language (Herman and Mann 2010).

Many YDP develop a variety of strategies over time to aid their intelligibility, such as pointing, gesturing, writing and drawing. The effectiveness of these techniques also needs to be explored.

- Is the young person able to make him/herself understood to familiar listeners? To strangers? To deaf people? To hearing people?
- Do they use a strategy or a hierarchy of strategies to make themselves understood?
- How are their lexical and structural semantic systems developing in spoken language? In signed language?
- Is grammatical development immature or exhibiting unusual patterns?
- Is phonology immature or is it showing 'non-English' type patterns?

Other influences

The speech and language therapist may need to explore other areas that are influencing the communication process. For example, theory of mind development (Chilton and Beazley 2010) and self-identity (Wheeler et al. 2007) as these may affect decisions about the focus and style of therapy.

Evidence-based practice

As with other complex interventions, speech and language therapy with YDP is built from a number of different components which may act both independently and inter-dependently and the effectiveness of some aspects of therapy might be easier to demonstrate than others. Also, the population of YDP is heterogeneous and of low incidence, which makes it difficult to iden-tify defined or broad enough groups for measuring the direct impact of any speech and lan-guage therapy intervention. However, since the advent of early neonatal screening, early cochlear implantation, bilateral implantation and improved hearing aid technology there has been an increased amount of larger scale research into the effects both of technology and of early intervention upon speech and language development in YDP. For example, in the report by Bamford et al. (2009) initial outcomes from the longitudinal study have shown that the use of sign support in the early months/years did not impede the development of spoken language and that parents showed a preference for professional support that is aimed at enabling them to work with their child directly rather than with the professional. Ertmer et al. (2002) demon-strated that shorter more frequent daily therapy sessions produced best results with cochlear implanted children. Geers and Brenner (2003) give evidence that supports speech and language therapists in providing early intervention. It is essential that specialist therapists consider the increasing flow of research about the full range of approaches and contexts and about how that also impacts on their own intervention practices with individual young people and their fami-lies. In addition, therapists must ensure that they reflect on their own intervention approaches and evaluations (Round and Beazley 2010), keeping in mind that formal assessments are not standardised on YDP and thus taking care in the interpretation of the results. It is critical to measure the outcomes for any therapy and to highlight the value it adds. For example, the use of detailed charting of parental input matching the developments in vocal play of deaf babies. There is less evidence for the use of specific interventions for older children therefore the speech and language therapist still needs to be vigilant and carry out careful evaluation through case studies and clear outcome measures, for example, the use of error analysis of grammar to show small changes that have improved classroom communication, or the use of qualitative and quantitative recording of repair strategies and their success rates for individual YDP in conver-sation with familiar hearing peers. They need to monitor progress and to compare this across different contexts, such as when talking to unfamiliar hearing people. Due to the low incidence of this population it can be difficult to build local expertise or specialist services. Therefore it is essential that therapists working in this field use the knowledge and expertise within regional and national RCSLT Special Interest Groups as well as local research and development struc-tures to ensure that their knowledge is continually updated through CPD opportunities (Round and Beazley 2010).

Summary

Decision-making for a speech and language therapist working with YDP involves understand-ing of a range of complex factors surrounding their families. The models described in this chapter are set in the context of the social model of disability and can be used to guide the therapist through some of the questions to be considered when working with this group of young people. It is important to think about the disabling and enabling processes which may face YDP and their families, and aiming for successful development of communication is crucial in supporting their right to equal access to information and education.

Chapter 14

Multicultural issues in assessment and management

Carolyn Letts

Learning outcomes

By the end of this chapter the reader should be aware of:

- the importance of cultural awareness when working with children;
- normal language acquisition in the context of more than one language;
- the limitations of standardised assessments when assessing a child from a multilingual background;
- strategies for assessing children from bilingual backgrounds or who are learning English as an additional language;
- how to adapt management procedures to the cultural and linguistic background of the children and their families;
- issues related to working with interpreters and bilingual co-workers.

Why are multicultural issues important?

Many areas of the world have populations that are diverse in terms of culture and language and who may be bi- or multilingual. In the UK, all major cities have sizeable multi-ethnic populations, many now into third or fourth generations. Different groups will originally have arrived at different times and for differing reasons, for example as refugees or as the result of seeking employment and other opportunities. There has moreover been a shift, especially over the last century, from a population in England that could be described as culturally homogeneous and monolingual to a much more diverse picture which is constantly changing. There are also indigenous bilingual communities in Wales, Scotland and Ireland. The extent to which the distinct languages and cultures of these populations has been preserved will vary from group to group and of course from individual to individual, but there now exists a considerable proportion of UK citizens and shorter term visitors to the UK (e.g. students and people who stay for a few years because of their work) with distinct and unique cultural mixes in their background. All have the same rights of access to services as other UK citizens, including of course speech and language therapy services.

Most speech and language therapists will, therefore, encounter clients at some point in their career who speak languages other than English, and whose social, religious and family lives reflect their wider cultural origins. Stow and Dodd (2003) estimate that there are '177,600 ethnic minority children under the age of 15 likely to have speech and language disorders in the UK' (p. 354), basing this calculation on incidence figures in the Middlesbrough area collected for publication in Broomfield and Dodd (2004), and estimates of minority population numbers (Scott *et al.* 2001). As will become clear, clients coming from such diverse linguistic and cultural backgrounds pose unique and highly complex challenges to the therapist. In addition, the privileged position of speech and language therapists in terms of understanding of language and language processing leaves them with the responsibility of helping other professionals to work with such clients in an optimal way.

Cultural attitudes

Before thinking about how to assess and manage children from differing cultural backgrounds, it is worth giving some consideration to how speech and language therapy services might be viewed and interpreted by potential clients and their families. Groups more recently arrived in the UK may be unfamiliar with such a service and somewhat baffled as to its purpose. Linked to this are attitudes to speech and language development and the importance that is attached to such development in the child: this is something given high priority by most typically Western communities. Families fleeing war and poverty will be primarily concerned with the mental and physical well-being of their children. Educational achievement is also likely to be valued, but this may be viewed in terms of developing good literacy and numeracy skills, without the link being apparent between these skills and adequate language development (see Chapter 16).

Attitudes to communication disability, child rearing and perceptions of how children learn and develop will also be different. The extent to which parents play and interact with their children will vary across cultures, and also the value they place on these activities in terms of promoting learning or good behaviour. The therapist also needs to deal sensitively with family structures and roles which may differ from those encountered in monolingual English-speaking families. In some communities, for example, it may be predominantly male members of a family who communicate with speech and language therapy services and bring children to initial assessment visits.

The practicalities of accessing services may also pose differences and possible problems. Obvious factors are the language in which items such as appointment letters and information sheets are written and communication with family members about the child's needs and management. Therapists should be aware that they may need to make modifications to usual practice, for example, by ensuring that written information is translated into the appropriate language. It is important also to avoid stereotyping: each group will be different, and may well differ in attitude from that of the original 'home' country, as each generation is influenced by local (in this case British) culture. Individuals from within the same cultural group will also differ from each other in terms of attitudes and beliefs and in proficiency with English. It will be important to take advice from bilingual co-workers on service delivery issues and for practice to be adapted accordingly. Isaac (2002) provides an excellent overview of factors related to culture that therapists should bear in mind when working with children from diverse backgrounds.

Language acquisition in a multilingual context

One of the immediate problems facing professionals wishing to assess children who come from different ethnic backgrounds from their own, is likely to be that of language. Many such children will have a language or languages other than English, and one of these other languages may well be the more dominant; in other words they will not respond well to any English-based assessment procedure because English is their weaker language. For the speech and language therapist a common and basic aim of assessment at this point is to establish whether any speech or language disorder in fact exists, or whether the children's apparent communication difficulties are the direct result of being in an environment where they are unable to make use of the language skills they have. This means that a primary requirement is that some assessment is carried out in all the child's languages. The sections in this chapter about assessment and about the use of bilingual co-workers will suggest how this daunting task might be achieved. The information given here focuses on language rather than speech, and readers are referred to Zhu Hua and Dodd (2005) for relevant information about speech development and impairment in a multilingual context.

With monolingual children, the established method for ascertaining the presence and severity of a speech and language disorder is to make a comparison between the child's performance and the norms for speech and language development for a child of that age. This is done through formal tests, and/or by sampling spontaneous speech and comparing this with what is known to be expected of children of different ages. If a formal test is used that is also standardised, comparison with the norm is explicit and robust, providing the standardisation sample is large and representative. Conveniently for UK therapists, there is a large pool of literature on English first language acquisition and many English-based test materials. In contrast, resources available for other languages are often severely limited, and the therapist must rely on general principles of language acquisition to make assessment judgements.

Research on acquisition in a variety of first languages suggests that, in broad terms, language acquisition proceeds in stages of development that are consistent across languages and also apply when the child is acquiring more than one language at the same time. It is most likely that children first of all show understanding of and produce single words (albeit sometimes embedded in strings of jargon) and then move on to multi-word utterances and simple sentences containing a verb plus one or more arguments. Then, at a later point still, they can understand and produce complex sentences that involve embedding one sentence within another and/or moving sentence components from their usual position in the word order of the sentence, as happens for example in English when passive constructions are formed. Comprehension of particular structures usually precedes production. This sequence may be found reflected in standardised tests such as the *Reynell Developmental Language Scales-III* (Edwards *et al.* 1997) where test items proceed from simple to more complex. The same sequence was found in the development of the *New Reynell Developmental Language Scales* (NRDLS, Edwards *et al.* 2011) and is reflected in the test.

Beyond this basic sequence though, particular structures may develop at different rates for different languages, reflecting factors such as the structural characteristics of the language and/ or features associated with the input directed at the child. For example, in many languages, possibly most, there is a 'noun bias' in early vocabulary: nouns make up a majority of early words, and are certainly higher in number than verbs. Research on Korean children, however, has suggested that the balance between nouns and verbs is much more even in early acquisition of Korean, or at least that young Korean speakers have a higher proportion of verbs than speakers of European languages (see for example Kim *et al.* 2000). To give a more complex example, there appears to be considerable variation in acquisition of verb inflections, depending on the language. In English, inflections are considered to be relatively 'sparse', so for present tense there is only the inflection '*s*' on the third person singular ('he runs'). Where verb morphology is richer, for example where verbs always have an ending of some sort, paradoxically this seems easier to acquire, especially if verb endings are very regular. It is thought that it takes the child longer to become aware of the rules governing use of inflections that only appear sporadically. For more examples of factors that affect acquisition in different languages, the reader is referred to the *Multilingual Toolkit* (Letts and Sinka 2011) which is provided as part of *NRDLS*.

A further issue is that children encountered by therapists will be likely to be living in dual- or multilingual environments, and thus be acquiring more than one language at the same time. Although the term 'bilingual' (or multilingual) is used to cover all instances of this kind, it obscures the fact that there is enormous variation in bilingual populations regarding the balance of their languages and time of initial exposure to each. The term 'balanced bilingual' can be used for the individuals who use their languages more or less equally, and are more or less equally competent in both. However, native-like competence in two or more languages is likely to be rare. More often the adult who is bilingual uses different languages competently for different purposes, rather like the monolingual speaker who uses different sociolinguistic varieties of their one language in different circumstances. For further discussion and critique of the term 'balanced bilingual', see Romaine (1995).

There is some evidence that children who are acquiring two languages from an early age may show a developmental lag in each when directly compared with typical monolingual speakers of each language. Gathercole and Thomas (2009), for example, report on vocabulary and morpho-syntactic development in young bilingual speakers in Wales and in Miami (acquiring English with Welsh or Spanish respectively). When each language was looked at individually, performance was found to relate to overall input that the child received in each language. Any bilingual child inevitably receives input that is split between their languages. However, there is evidence that the bilingual children quickly catch up, at least with the most dominant language (English in this case) and there is no detrimental educational or social impact on the child. In fact, given that the child is working with two language systems from an early stage, they have a total system that is age appropriate (but different from the monolingual). This means that young bilingual children cannot be expected to show the same degree of development in all of their languages as native speaker monolingual peers would show; rather there should be an overall degree of competence which allows the children to communicate adequately in all situations.

Another feature that is important for some children who acquire language in a bilingual context is that of code switching. This refers to the mixing of elements from each language within an utterance, either across different sentences (inter-sentential code switching) or within the same sentence (intra-sentential). In many communities code switching is the norm among adults and where intra-sentential code switching occurs this has been shown to conform to grammatical rules rather than random 'mixing' (Myers-Scotton 2002). Children living in such communities will also develop code switching in their language. Pert and Letts (2006) found evidence of systematic intra-sentential code switching among Mirpuri-English speaking pre-school children in Rochdale in the UK.

Assessment of children from diverse cultural and linguistic backgrounds

Assessment is essentially the same as for all children, with two important additions. First, aspects of the child's cultural background must be taken into account, especially when interacting and liaising with members of the child's family. Second, the child's individual linguistic background must also be considered when making diagnostic decisions, and when making decisions about management based on diagnosis.

Minimally, assessment should include a case history, a picture of the child's exposure to and use of the languages within his/her environment, measures of the child's ability in all relevant languages and an assessment of how the child's communication problems may be affecting him/her in different environments.

Case history

A full case history should be taken so that all the usual factors that are important in diagnosis are considered. These include hearing loss, developmental history and potential genetic and medical factors. This ensures that all possible aetiological factors have been taken into consideration. It is important not to miss any factors that may be masked by the child's presentation as a bilingual child or a child for whom English is a second language. For example, problems should not be attributed entirely to poor English, when in fact the child has a hearing loss.

Exposure to language

A picture needs to be built of the child's exposure to languages and the child's use of languages within his/her environment. This should include information about who uses which language, for how long and in what setting. It is also important to consider the child's exposure to TV and video/DVD. In summary, every attempt needs to be made to establish a child's pattern of language use and exposure in order to decide whether there is a general language disorder present. This will give an idea of what level of competence might be expected of the child in each language, and what linguistic demands are made on the child. Where children's skills do not match up to what might be expected in all of their languages, there is good reason to suspect a language disorder.

Measures of the child's ability in all languages

Measures need to be taken of the child's ability in all languages. These measures need to be both informal and formal wherever possible. This will give an indication of how the child compares with norms, as well as enabling a differential diagnosis to be made between an underlying language problem or lack of exposure and opportunity to learn one of the required languages.

Effects of the communication problem

The impact of the child's communication problems at home, at play and at school needs to be assessed. This can be done through discussion with the child and their family and through visits to nursery, school or home. As well as gaining information verbally through others, it is very useful to observe the child in a variety of situations.

Assessment methods

The issues around language acquisition discussed above mean that professionals must be extremely cautious in applying monolingual norms to bilingual children or to children acquiring English as an additional language. There are few normative speech/language tests that have been standardised on bilingual children. These include the *Sandwell Bilingual Screening Assessment Scales for Expressive Panjabi and English* (Duncan *et al.* 1988) which have been standardised on bilingual Panjabi- and English-speaking children in the UK; *Prawf Geirfa Cymraeg*, a test of bilingual vocabulary standardised on Welsh–English children (Gathercole and Thomas 2007); *Rochdale Assessment of Mirpuri Phonology with Punjabi, Urdu and English* (Stow and Pert 1998); *Clinical Evaluation of Language Fundamentals (CELF-4) (Spanish)* (Semel *et al.* 2005), normed on bilingual Spanish–English speakers in the USA.

In particular, the normative sample for any standardised monolingual test is not valid for a bilingual child. So, age norms and standardised scores must not be used to help with diagnosis. This is not to say that such tests may not be used for somewhat different purposes, for example, identifying areas of weakness in one language, or estimating how a child might be able to cope in certain language contexts. The *Multilingual Toolkit* (Letts and Sinka 2011) mentioned above, gives guidelines on adapting tests (in particular, *NRDLS*) to other languages, taking into account possible ways in which languages will differ structurally from English and what the implications of these differences might be for assessment. The toolkit is designed for use informally with individual children speaking languages for which there are no assessment tools, as a help to designing language measures that could be used in research projects and/or as a starting point for a full-scale development of a standardised assessment procedure for another language or for a bilingual situation. Minimally a native speaker 'informant' who speaks the language(s) concerned is needed to advise on assessment instructions and items. This could be a bilingual facilitator or co-worker.

There are, however, further issues to consider if attempting to assess in a formal context. Carter *et al.* (2005) identify the following factors as influencing a child's performance on tests, in addition to those related to language; culture, familiarity with the testing situation, the effect of formal education and picture recognition. Most of the tests commonly used by therapists have been developed in a context where the sorts of activities carried out by testers and the whole concept of being tested is familiar to children, where all children receive education from the nursery stage and where children have plenty of experience of pictures. Care must be taken in situations where these factors might not apply.

Given the problems associated with formal tests, informal observation is often a good way of commencing the assessment process, and helps the therapist to decide whether a communication problem is present or not. Indeed, observational techniques may be the only ones available to the therapist if the language is unknown and the child new to an educational environment. Some of the techniques from conversational analysis are useful here, and it may be possible to apply these with only minimal knowledge of the language being used. Further information on using conversation analysis in assessment can be found in Leinonen *et al.* (2000).

The following are some of the questions that could be asked while observing the child in a variety of settings.

- Does the child participate in the ongoing interaction?
- Is the child able to respond to initiations from others and are his/her responses listened to and accepted? If responses are ignored or rejected this may suggest either a less than optimal interactive approach from those around the child, or that the child's responses pose real difficulties of interpretation for fellow communicators.
- Does the child attempt to gain the attention of other participants?
- Does the child initiate interactions, and how successful is this?

Lack of appropriate interaction skills may give the therapist some idea of whether the child has problems of a pragmatic nature. Such a hypothesis would need to be followed up where possible with more systematic linguistic testing in order to exclude the possibility of a severe but specific speech or language impairment. Observation needs to take place in situations where each of the child's languages is used. More interaction with one language than the other may be an indication of limited second language ability. Limited verbal interaction in all languages, perhaps replaced by attempts to communicate non-verbally, would indicate a possible speech and/or language delay or disorder.

A development in evaluation of children's language is the use of dynamic assessment. This focuses on the learning process for the child, rather than presenting a static picture of performance at one point in time. Typically a skill is tested (e.g. vocabulary), some learning in that area is facilitated, and then the skill is re-tested. The amount of change gives a measure of the child's ability to learn. Peña and colleagues have found that this measure of change is useful in differentiating language-impaired from typically developing children with diverse cultural and linguistic backgrounds, when working on vocabulary (Peña *et al.* 2001) and on narrative (Peña *et al.* 2006). In each case, degree of change following a short intervention and measures of the child's response to the learning situation differentiated between typically developing children and those with low overall language ability. The advantage of this approach is that it does not matter what language the learning tasks are presented in, provided the child understands what they have to do. This suggests that dynamic assessment has good potential as a tool for differentiating children with underlying speech or language impairment from children with limited exposure to English or who for reasons associated with culture and experience do not perform well on formal assessment.

Bilingual co-workers

The need to assess in languages other than English poses obvious problems for most therapists, who will rarely feel competent to carry out assessments even if they have some knowledge of the relevant languages. The use of interpreters or bilingual co-workers is, therefore, largely unavoidable. When working in this context, interpreters need to have some awareness of what the speech and language therapist is trying to find out and what are the important variables to look for in any assessment situation. If interpreters are asked to provide translations of test material, they must be aware of how the linguistic demands of the material may be changed by the translation. When commenting on a child's communication, interpreters need some knowledge about aspects of language such as grammatical complexity, or phonological characteristics. It is helpful if therapists can offer training to co-workers that will help to get the best out of any assessment situation.

Management

Essentially, the decision-making process for children from multilingual environments should be no different from that for other children. Decisions regarding whether to intervene and how to deliver intervention should be made according to the same principles. However, one aspect that is different concerns the management of the two, or more, languages that the child is using or to which the child may be exposed.

Currently there is no research evidence to suggest that it is helpful to restrict the child to one language, for example, the language through which the child will be educated (usually English), although this is a common misapprehension among many professionals. There are, however, indications that such a restriction may work against the child's interests in many instances. Children's home language is their means of accessing the home culture, including, for example, being able to communicate and learn from older members of the family who may not have learned English. It enables them to participate in family celebrations and religious festivals. The psychological damage caused by restricting such access may be great.

Of equal concern is whether the artificial restriction to one language is in the child's best interests developmentally and educationally. If parents are encouraged to communicate with their child in a language they do not feel wholly comfortable with, and in which they may have limited proficiency, the natural flow of parent–child interaction is likely to be hampered, thus depriving the child of the social and communication benefits of this interaction (see Chapter 4).

At school level, it has been pointed out that some children may be at risk because they are required to develop academic skills, especially literacy, through a language in which they are not competent. At the same time they cannot rely on the competence they do have in their home language, because this is not used in school. This is sometimes called 'subtractive bilingualism' (see Cummins and Swain 1986). This is the rationale behind mother-tongue teaching, which is offered in some schools. If the child has the opportunity to learn school skills in a language in which they have a firm grounding, then these skills will transfer at a later date to the new language.

The conclusion to be drawn here is that not only is it not helpful for the child to be restricted to input from one language, but also that ideally, speech and language therapy intervention should address both languages. Without bilingual co-workers, this may be difficult. However, the therapist should try, wherever possible, to enlist the support and understanding of appropriate members of the child's family, so that they are able to carry out activities in the home language that mirror those carried out by the therapist or classroom assistant in the clinical or school setting. Ideally, an activity can be modelled in English, followed by discussion as to whether this would be appropriate in the home language. For example, with a specific grammatical structure, or set of vocabulary items, the questions need to be asked:

- is there relatively straightforward translation between the two?
- are they a problem for the child in both languages?

The family member can then experiment with the activity with the therapist present before trying it out at home.

For more detailed suggestions, Harten (2011) gives useful advice both on assessment and on management of children from diverse backgrounds.

Evaluating intervention

Measurement of effectiveness of intervention should also follow the same principles as with monolingual children. However, as with other children with communication needs, finding clear ways of measuring change is challenging. Peña *et al.* (2001) demonstrate that teaching naming strategies through mediated learning experience is effective for typically developing children, but that the child's response to this is limited in children with low language ability. A useful approach may be to explore how the child with speech, language and communication needs responds when this intervention is extended or modified in other ways.

It is unclear whether progress in one language results in carryover to the other language. However, where a child has, for example, a language delay, and benefits from general stimulation and rewarding communication in one language, it would seem likely that s/he would then feel confident to start experimenting with greater communication in the other language.

In summary, there are several procedures which therapists need to follow when a child from a multicultural background is referred for speech and language therapy.

1   Collect information on cultural factors that may influence management of this case and on relevant features of the child's environment and experiences.
2   Find out whether the child is exposed to languages other than English, and what these are.
3   Locate suitable help in the form of bilingual co-workers or interpreters.
4   Brief untrained interpreters fully, and discuss any difficulties that are likely to arise.
5   Take a full case history, including aspects of language use and exposure.
6   Conduct observations of the child in a variety of linguistic and social environments.
7   Carry out more formal assessments in order to pinpoint the nature of the difficulty and formulate targets for intervention. A dynamic assessment protocol may also be useful at this point.
8   Decide the mode of intervention delivery.
9   Formulate plans for carrying over intervention into the other language(s).

Summary

Working with bilingual children tends to take at least twice the amount of time when compared to similar work with monolingual children. Nevertheless, if services to such children are going to begin to approach the level of those offered to the monolingual population, these resources must be found and implemented. Due consideration must be given to the child's cultural background and experiences and to the linguistic contexts which permeate all aspects of their day-to-day life.

Chapter 15

Children with communication problems and additional emotional/behavioural problems

Alison Wintgens

Learning outcomes

By the end of this chapter the reader should understand:

- current terminology and classification of emotional/behavioural difficulties and their relationship with disorders of communication;
- how to engage with young people with emotional/behavioural difficulties and their parents;
- how to overcome difficulties in assessment;
- how to access additional resources, skills and training.

Introduction

Communication problems and emotional/behavioural problems are closely linked. When anyone has difficulty understanding what others say, or difficulty in expressing themselves, it often affects their behaviour, confidence and social interactions. This is more likely to occur if a person has a significant speech, language and/or communication impairment. It can also go the other way: emotions such as anxiety, depression and excessive anger or significant emotional events may affect communication. When the two areas co-exist they become closely interrelated. Consequently, a speech and language therapist needs to expect, recognise and manage emotional/behavioural problems effectively.

Many therapists working with children and adolescents with emotional and behavioural problems say they do nothing particularly different from working with any other client group. It is true that the speech and language therapist still has to assess the full range of communication skills, and advise on or carry out intervention strategies. What may be different is more a matter of approach or style, based on understanding, and holding in mind the nature of emotional and behavioural problems. There is no doubt that this area of work raises a number of dilemmas which therapists need to make decisions about. The therapist has to:

- consider how to engage possibly reluctant participants and their parents;
- assess withdrawn children or those who are challenging;
- decide on the best way to deliver therapy;
- have skills and resources to address the emotional aspects;
- manage any challenging behaviour and look out for clients who may need more support for their mental health needs;
- know how to discuss this with the young people and their parents.

The therapist will also need to consider how to get additional training for work in this area.

Understanding emotional and behavioural problems

Therapists need to be familiar with diagnostic labels that are used about a child who is referred for therapy, to know the features of the diagnosis and how these may affect or relate to the speech and language function, and to understand the implications of these features in relation to speech and language therapy management, assessment and treatment. They also need to understand how Child and Adolescent Mental Health Services (CAMHS) are organised.

Unpicking the terminology

The expression 'emotional/behavioural difficulties' may be used to cover both the educational term 'emotional/behavioural disorders' (EBD) and the medical term 'child mental health disorders'. It is estimated that 10–15 per cent of all children have a diagnosable mental health problem, and around four times that percentage in 'looked after' children or those with learning disabilities (DH/DfES 2007). These difficulties are recognised by their severity and by their characteristics.

Severity

Some displays of emotions and certain behaviours, such as moodiness, shyness, liveliness or difficulties in relationships are a normal part of life. But when they are more severe or extensive than might be expected for the child or young person's age or stage of development they become significant. Extra or specialised help may be needed, especially when these reactions interfere with the children's development and everyday lives, or cause them or their families considerable suffering.

Classification by characteristics

In order to provide a more uniform use of terminology across different centres and different countries two main classification systems are currently in use which give clinical descriptions and diagnostic guidelines for different conditions. The tenth revision of the *International Classification of Diseases (ICD-10)* covers adult and child mental and behavioural disorders and is produced by the World Health Organisation (WHO 1994). A different system, the *Diagnostic and Statistical Manual* which is now in its fourth version (DSM-IV), has been devised by the American Psychiatric Association (1994).

Historical and geographical factors dictate which classification is used within any one country or centre. However, while there may be agreement about the value of using ICD or DSM to make a diagnosis of specific conditions such as autism spectrum disorder (ASD) or attention deficit hyperactivity disorder (ADHD), some professionals are less keen to use such a system for behavioural problems.

Main diagnostic groupings

For descriptive purposes, there is a tendency to divide child mental health disorders into two broad diagnostic groupings: emotional disorders and disruptive behaviour disorders.

Emotional disorders

These are sometimes described as internalised, resulting from stresses that are turned inwards. This group includes anxiety disorders, depression, phobias and obsessive-compulsive disorder. Children may present as tearful or clingy, tense, self-conscious or withdrawn, or tired or unable to concentrate.

Disruptive behaviour disorders

These are said to be externalised, with the stresses turned outwards into behaviours that impinge on others. These include conduct disorder and oppositional defiant disorder. In its mildest form children may argue, lose their temper, blame and/or annoy others. The more severe features include aggression, destruction of property, deceitfulness and severe violation of social rules.

Hyperactivity also comes into this second group – to describe children with attention deficit disorder or ADHD who are inattentive, restless and impulsive.

However, this division is not entirely helpful since behind most behavioural problems lies an emotional problem, usually anxiety. Child mental health professionals are also concerned with conditions with symptoms which fall outside these two main groups. These include children with developmental disorders such as autistic disorder, eneuresis and encopresis, general learning disabilities and specific learning difficulties involving speech, language or reading problems. Some children or adolescents may also have feeding and eating disorders, or disorders more commonly associated with adults, such as schizophrenia or emerging personality disorder.

For further information about specific child mental health disorders, treatment and services, readers are advised to have access to an introductory book such as Goodman and Scott (2005). Rogers-Adkinson and Griffith (1999) give helpful information on communication disorders and children with psychiatric and behavioural disorders.

Multi-axial classification

A multi-axial approach to classification gives a fuller picture of the child's diagnoses and difficulties, and underlines their complexity.

Case example

Jane is 10 years old. She has mild learning disabilities and severely impaired language, Tourette's syndrome (a tic disorder) and hyperkinetic disorder (hyperactivity). There is a history of emotional abuse within the family, and parental separation, divorce and remarriage. In addition, there are psychosocial factors as within the family the girl is scapegoated and blamed for all the family's problems. Shown below is how significant information would be recorded using the ICD-10 multi-axial classification system

Axis 1: Psychiatric:	Tourette's syndrome
	Hyperkinetic disorder
Axis 2: Developmental:	Language disorder
Axis 3: Intellectual:	Mild learning disability
Axis 4: Medical:	None
Axis 5: Social:	Problems related to upbringing
	Problems related to primary
	support group
Axis 6: Psychosocial disability:	(Rated as level 3)

Making a formulation

No matter how information is recorded, the diagnostic process in child mental health should involve the gathering of a wide range of information about the child, and the putting together of a formulation – a summary based on all the data from the assessment. This includes incorporation of all the significant diagnostic features and possible explanations of the relevance of any predisposing, precipitating and perpetuating factors which may be contributing to how the child presents, as well as affecting the choice and effectiveness of interventions (see Wintgens 2002).

The organisation of CAMHS

The current trend is to recognise that 'mental health is everybody's business', a catchphrase used by a number of agencies. It fits with the view of mental health services as delivered across four tiers by people with varying levels of specialist knowledge and skills, having either a few or all of their clients with emotional/behavioural problems:

- Tier 1: general settings, such as in mainstream schools or health clinics.
- Tier 2: community settings, such as Children's Centres, special schools or Youth Offender Teams, where emotional/behavioural problems are more common than in Tier 1.
- Tier 3: now known as 'specialist CAMHS' – multi-disciplinary teams of mental health professionals, usually psychiatrists, clinical psychologists, psychoanalytic and systemic psychotherapists and specialist nurses seeing children and young people with significant emotional/behavioural problems.
- Tier 4: highly specialised in-patient mental health teams.

The relationship between emotional/behavioural problems and communication problems

Evidence of co-existence

There is evidence of a strong link between significant emotional/behavioural problems and communication disorders (Beitchman 2006; Law and Plunkett 2009). Most figures indicate co-occurrence rates of 40 per cent to 71 per cent (Giddan et al. 1996). Cross (2004) discusses children with emotional and behavioural difficulties and communication problems, and attention has been drawn to young offenders, with significant speech, language and communication problems reported in 60 per cent of those in custody (Bryan et al. 2007).

The author's experience in an inner-city London borough bears out several of the findings above. An informal study within a local child psychiatric day unit revealed that at any one time 40–60 per cent of under-fives in that unit had speech/language delay, and many were known to the community speech and language therapy service. The author also found that 19 out of 20 children in the local primary EBD school had moderate to severe problems with speech, language and communication skills, requiring the attention of a speech and language therapist.

In children where attention is focused on extreme emotional/behavioural problems there is a risk that disorders of communication may be overlooked. In addition, there is evidence (Cohen and Lipsett 1991) that children with previously undiagnosed language impairment show more delinquent behaviour when compared with children with known language impairment or normal language development. The implication is that behaviour problems may become less severe if the children's communication disorders are recognised and handled appropriately.

The data collected from the caseload of the speech and language therapists in the author's specialist CAMHS revealed that in practice the children seen by the therapists have one or more of the following problems: anxiety, including selective mutism, behavioural problems of all degrees of severity, including ADHD; ASD and learning disabilities.

The communication disorders usually involve some form of language impairment affecting syntax, semantics and pragmatics. A few children have problems with speech, fluency or dysphonia.

Understanding and engaging with parents and young people

Parents of children in this client group may be particularly apprehensive when attending an appointment, knowing that their child has not only communication but also emotional/behavioural problems and may 'not perform' or 'show them up'. It can be more difficult to establish good rapport with parents who may be feeling more than usually stressed, guilty, vulnerable, anxious or embarrassed.

The parents may have had bad experiences with authority figures – people in health, education, social services or with police or prison staff. They may see the therapist as another authority figure and may transfer their negative feelings to the therapist. They may come across as angry or uncooperative, making it more difficult for the therapist to work in partnership with them. They may have mental health problems themselves. They may have a lot of stress in their lives and meeting with the therapist may be one of the least of their priorities, or the final straw.

When working with this client group, therapists need to be particularly empathic and to adopt a direct, honest approach. The therapist needs to have an awareness and understanding of the underlying issues with children and their parents, and to avoid taking sides or apportioning blame.

Setting up the initial meeting

It is important to look carefully at a referral letter to plan how best to engage with both the child and the parent. For example, if it is known that the child is anxious or particularly disruptive it may be an advantage for the therapist to meet the parent first without the child. The letter should also indicate who the main carer is. In this client group it is not so unusual for the child to live with someone other than a parent; or for the parent to have a different surname to the child. Getting names and relationships correct from the start is good for rapport.

Whenever possible it is helpful to make a phone call to arrange the first appointment. It is a chance for initial introductions and rapport building, for ensuring as far as possible that the most convenient time is offered and for deciding who should attend the appointment. In a school it is worth discussing with whoever knows the child well how best to approach him or her.

Assessing withdrawn or challenging children

Deciding how best to assess children with communication problems and emotional/behavioural problems is one of the first and most difficult decisions for the therapist. The children are more likely to be erratic in their performance in an assessment situation, so calling into question the reliability of the results. They may not cope with formal assessments, for example if their anxiety leads to mutism or non-compliance. The therapist may also be required to contribute to a wider diagnostic opinion, such as whether the child presents with features of ASD or ADHD during the session, and will have to note and evaluate aspects of the child's behaviour. There are several areas which need to be considered in order that assessment may be carried out effectively.

Gathering information from others

Information needs to be gathered from a range of sources to provide the fullest picture of the child's communication skills across different settings. School information should be obtained either through a school visit or through telephone contact with the class teacher or SENCO. A school report may describe not only the child's speech and language in school but also social interaction skills, play and cognitive skills, and any concerns the teachers may have. Sometimes a report form can be sent to the SENCO or class teacher, such as the one available for children with selective mutism (Johnson and Wintgens 2001). Details of whether there are problems with language form, content, use or understanding could be gathered using an indicators list for identifying communication problems (Cross 2004).

Rather than a simple case history discussion there may be a need for a more detailed parental interview (see Johnson and Wintgens 2001), either at the initial stage of contact or later, if the child is not making progress. It is also important for the parents' and the child's views of the communication difficulty to be taken into account. This will help to provide a more holistic profile of the child and may also indicate the level of awareness of the child's difficulties, which in turn will suggest approaches for remediation, such as the need to educate or work with the parents or the child.

Questionnaires or checklists may also be used to gather information. With children and young people who are possibly on the autistic spectrum the *Children's Communication Checklist*, second edition (Bishop 2003a) may be helpful in evaluating the quality and pattern of the child's interactions.

Formal assessment

No child should be assessed more than is absolutely necessary; but often sufficient evidence of competence or impairment cannot be gained indirectly. Children with emotional/behavioural problems may find standardised assessments particularly difficult and therapists may be tempted to avoid them. However, since they can offer the most objective measurement of the child's skills, and some children and young people can manage them surprisingly well, it is often worth persisting. Therapists should focus on counteracting children's suspicions and fears which may arise from feeling a lack of control and a dread of failure. A reassuring, open and matter-of-fact approach is recommended. The therapist needs to help the child to understand the usefulness of the assessments and to negotiate an agreement that they will give it their best effort. They need to ask the child to say if they want a break, are tired or are finding it too hard. It is helpful to explain that assessments are meant to range from easy to hard, and the assessment will stop when the questions get too hard.

Breaks and variety can be built into the assessment process, as appropriate, and rewards for maintaining attention may be offered. If the child is lacking in confidence or is mute, receptive assessments requiring minimal and non-verbal responses should be used before assessments of expressive abilities. If children are erratic in their responses, perhaps because they are easily distracted, sense failure or lack persistence, it is permissible to 'test to the limits'. For example, it may be useful to continue testing beyond the ceiling item on a test, or to repeat a stimulus to see if this evokes the desired response. Adaptations to standardised assessments are permissible provided any deviation from the instructions given in the manual is clearly described in the assessment report. For example in Word Classes on the CELF (Wiig and Semel 2006) the therapist can point to four different coloured bricks as the four stimulus words are said, so that a mute child can point to two bricks when indicating which two are related. It may also be possible to train a parent of a quiet child to carry out a simple assessment such as the Renfrew Action Picture Test (Renfrew 2011a) or the Renfrew Word Finding Vocabulary Test (Renfrew 2011b). It is important to obtain as much information about how the children behave during the assessment. Information about their approach to the test, what they do, how they do it and what they do not do is as important in deciding on remediation as the raw or standardised scores.

When assessing a child who is said to be 'hyperactive' it is important to establish whether this is an observation, a suspicion or whether the condition has been diagnosed and treated. If diagnosed with ADHD and medication has been prescribed it is essential to note whether the medication was taken, and when. Ideally their language potential should be assessed after they have taken their medication, but this is not always in the hands of the therapist. If the pre-scribed medication has not been taken prior to the assessment, useful information can still be gained; but it may be wise to reassess the child on a different occasion when medication has been taken, using other assessment tools. In preparing the room it is helpful if it is as free as possible from distractions, with only one piece of equipment visible at a time and tasks should be of short duration.

Observation and informal assessment

From the moment the therapist meets the newly referred child, observations about the child's language, social interaction skills and behaviour at the various stages of the encounter will con-tribute to the assessment and evaluation. With this client group such details are particularly important, and should be included in a report. Structured observation is different and should be considered carefully. Since a child with selective mutism will be hyper-sensitive to anyone trying to observe them or trick them into talking, it is not advised. If there are concerns about language or communication skills in a young selective mute child some parents might agree to play with their child in a room with a one-way viewing screen. Otherwise a home DVD may be available. On the other hand, a well-planned and executed classroom observation of a child with social interaction problems can be a crucial part of an assessment. Observation of parent–child interaction is also important, giving indications both of contributing and remediation factors. It may point to the need, for example, for parent training or parent–child work.

If formal assessments cannot be carried out, the therapist will need to explore the different aspects of the child's language and communication skills through a variety of informal tasks, conversation and play. Some older children and adolescents may be prepared to fill in question-naires, checklists or worksheets (Kelly 2004; Johnson and Wintgens 2001) to supplement the information.

Deciding on service delivery

Usually the results of a full assessment indicate the best way to approach therapy with a child. However, additional decisions need to be made with children with emotional/behavioural prob-lems as well as communication difficulties. Therapists may need to evaluate the effectiveness of the therapy more frequently. They need to be flexible enough to switch to another style of delivery in order to be more effective, although it is not helpful if too many changes are made too quickly.

Individual therapy

Children who are very disruptive, anxious or vulnerable will often do better in individual rather than group therapy sessions. Those with complex anti-social behaviour problems, for example young offenders, do not do well grouped together with similar peers. In an individual setting they do not have to compete with other children, and they may respond well to one-to-one attention.

Some children struggle with individual therapy for several reasons. First, sessions may prove difficult if the tasks and activities are not at the right level. It may also prove difficult if they are not broken into small, structured, achievable targets, with a choice of activities, and heavy use of praise and rewards. Second, there may be something which has occurred outside the session that is worrying or upsetting the child. It is important to check this with the child and/or family. Finally, it may be that the style of therapy is too direct and seems threatening. A block of sessions that are more child centred and based around play or art may be more suita-ble. These sessions might still include specific targets for aspects of syntax or phonology, or social communication or more general language enrichment activities. A speech and language therapy assistant could carry out language enrichment sessions, under supervision, with the aim of enabling the child to have fun while talking and playing. The assistant would follow the child's lead within clearly set boundaries.

Group therapy

Small group sessions may be appropriate for some children with emotional/behavioural problems. They may need to practise social interaction skills with other children, even if they have mastered these skills with adults. If their attention span is short they may benefit from turn-taking activities with 'rest' periods while others are having their turns. Some children may be able to learn from others when working in a small group. The rest of the group may provide good role models, or it may be that it is easier to accept constructive criticism from peers rather than adults.

However, group therapy for children with behaviour problems can be very demanding for the therapist. Attention must be paid to these children's emotional/behavioural needs, and therapy must incorporate behaviour management as well as including ways to improve self-esteem. Clear rules and consequences need to be set for acceptable behaviour while at the same time giving the young people some degree of control through choice. Close attention must be paid to the content, style and relevance of the therapy, with the focus more on functional communication than speech and language targets. In addition, the importance of a high and consistent staff ratio is emphasised by Sivyer (1999) who gives a helpful account of effective group therapy with children excluded from schools.

Parent–child work

In some work settings, especially with younger children or those with learning disabilities, parent–child work will be indicated. Parents may need help to spend time with their children, to learn how best to play or stimulate their language, possibly using methods from Hanen (Pepper and Weitzman 2004) or Webster-Stratton (2005). If the child's behaviour is challenging the therapist may help parents understand that this challenging behaviour is a form of communication that can be shaped into a more acceptable type of expression.

Extra ways to address emotional/behavioural issues

Developing a young person's self-esteem is a vital part of therapy with this client group given the frequent experience of disappointment, frustration or failure. They need a high level of reinforcement, genuine and specific praise, acknowledgement of their feelings and encouragement of their dreams. They need reminders of their achievements and ways in which they may mark them. It also helps to enable the young people and their parents to see any mistakes or crises as opportunities to learn and grow. Learning how to solve problems and put things right is a valuable lesson for these young people.

Using a scale from zero to ten to evaluate how confident they felt talking in a certain setting may help to put things in perspective and to measure progress. Scaling can also be used to discuss change, as in Brief Solution-Focused Therapy originally developed by de Shazer and Berg.

Hierarchies or ladders can be used effectively to plan generalisation of fluent or confident speaking. Lists of likes and dislikes, hopes and wishes help the child to feel understood. Certain games and activities will be especially useful, and 'social and emotional' or 'mental health and well-being' sections are now common in resource catalogues. Worksheets are to be recommended such as Kelly (2004) as well as the use of art, music or drama.

Additional resources, skills and training

Speech and language therapists specialising in working with this client group will need to decide what other skills beyond their original training are necessary to work effectively. They are likely to make good use of behavioural treatment methods, social skills work, parent training and counselling skills. Depending on the workplace, it may be necessary to develop knowledge and skills in the cognitive, behavioural, psycho-dynamic or systemic fields. This may be through training in cognitive behavioural therapy, behavioural analysis, a therapeutic teaching course, brief solution-focused therapy or an introduction to family therapy. The RCSLT Special Interest Group in emotional/behavioural problems is an excellent resource for peer support from colleagues working in this area, and for relevant workshops and short training events.

Additional help in difficult situations

A therapist may experience a situation with a client that is difficult to handle or have significant concerns about emotional, behavioural or family issues. It is wise to act on intuition. It may be helpful to discuss the problem in supervision or with a trusted colleague, to review what is known and what has been done with the client and to consider whether a different approach should be tried with the child. It may be that more information is needed from the parents, school, social services or doctors. A referral for more help with assessment or management may be indicated for example to CAMHS. Safeguarding may be an issue, and risk and safe practice guidelines may need to be reviewed, with possible training in challenging behaviour.

Discussing and making a referral to CAMHS

The best way to make an effective referral for more specialised mental health support for a young person is to know about the local services. This may be, for example, through discussion with relevant colleagues or looking on the internet. Making a telephone enquiry to the intended service is useful to establish whether the concerns meet their current referral criteria and to learn about the waiting list time and procedure. In some services a Common Assessment Framework is requested. Others request a referral letter which should contain core information including a description of the emotional and behavioural concerns, the reason for the referral and whether anything specific, such as an ASD or ADHD assessment, is being requested. It is also helpful to include what interventions have been tried and a summary of significant factors regarding the family and the child's history.

Evaluating effectiveness

Speech and language therapists looking for ways of measuring effectiveness in their own work with children with additional emotional/behavioural problems can use the same evaluation methods as are used with other children. However, aims for this client group may more often reflect the importance of functional communication or social interaction skills than core language skills. Questionnaires and rating scales such as from Talkabout (Kelly 2004) are frequently used for measuring outcome in CAMHS. The Health of the Nation Outcome Scales for Children and Adolescents (Gower et al. 1998) are popular in mental health teams to assess the behaviours, impairments, symptoms and social functioning of children and adolescents with mental health problems, although their sensitivity has been questioned.

The literature for studies of effectiveness of speech and language therapy is limited. This may be because this area of work does not lend itself to traditional research. The Mental Health section of the RCSLT's *Manual for Commissioning and Planning Services for Speech, Language and Communication Needs* (RCSLT 2010) states that studies are too small or of a preliminary nature; although it commends useful and descriptive studies reviewed by Law and Plunkett (2009).

Summary

All therapists will come across children who have emotional/behavioural problems to varying degrees, and some will choose to specialise in this work. Information about mental health disorders, presenting features and knowledge about psychological therapies will help therapists to make appropriate decisions for such children. An understanding of the psychosocial issues and the use of certain strategies will help engagement with children and their families.

Chapter 16

Working with children with written language difficulties

Sarah Simpson

Learning outcomes

By the end of this chapter the reader should:

- be able to demonstrate understanding of current theories of literacy development;
- be able to discuss how spoken language relates to written language;
- be able to identify which children are at-risk for written language difficulties;
- have a working knowledge of a range of assessments of phonological skills;
- be able to discuss the role of the speech and language therapist in the management of children with written language difficulties.

Introduction

Learning to read and write in English requires an understanding of the ways symbols can be translated into speech sounds, and speech sounds can be represented by symbols. Byrne (1998) refers to this as 'acquiring the alphabetic principle'. When children begin to learn to read and write their spoken language is typically sufficiently robust to support the acquisition of the alphabetic principle. The speed with which they learn the names and sounds of letters of the alphabet, and the ease with which they learn to blend sounds into words and segment words into sounds, can be related to the integrity of their speech processing skills and phonological awareness. That is, to their ability to transform linguistic information into lexical representations and plan and execute the oral movements to produce these representations as speech, and to be aware that words have a sound structure that is separate from their meaning.

Children must also be able to understand what they read and convey their ideas in writing. It is the level of their semantic, syntactic and pragmatic language skills that will determine how readily and well they learn to do this (see Carroll *et al.* 2011). It follows, therefore, that a child whose spoken language is failing to develop normally will be disadvantaged when learning and using written language (Cain 2010).

In this chapter, the management of children with written language difficulties associated with spoken language difficulties will be discussed, but attention will be focused on children who are struggling to acquire an understanding of the alphabetic principle.

Overview of the normal development of written language

Before a child can be considered literate a number of skills must be acquired and integrated. First, children need language skills and print experience to prepare them for literacy learning. That is, for learning how letters (graphemes) relate to sounds (phonemes), and letter strings (orthographic units) to units of meaning (morphemes); and how sounds can be blended into words and words segmented into sounds. Children also need to develop the skills to allow them to read for meaning and to express themselves in writing. There is no one theory that can adequately explain the process by which, in a relatively short time, children learn these skills and become literate.

Word reading and spelling

Some frameworks detail the knowledge and skills which children characteristically develop as precursors to literacy. They outline an emergent literacy stage (see Rhyner *et al.* 2009), drawing attention to the place of behaviours such as awareness that print is meaningful and that books tell stories. Likewise, stage models of word reading and spelling view learning as a continuum and describe how a series of qualitatively different skills develop and merge with old skills (see Ehri 2005). Such models variously describe how, initially, young children apply visually based strategies. These enable them to recognise a limited number of words by making a connection between their dominant visual features or context and their meaning. They also allow children to write words by reproducing their obvious features, or whole words in the case of well-practised words such as familiar names.

However, recognising words by sight and writing them from memory has limitations. With print experience and explicit teaching, children acquire the sound-based, alphabetic strategies needed for mapping between symbols and sounds and decoding (reading) and encoding (writing) unfamiliar words. At first, words are decoded letter by letter and encoded sound by sound; however, as alphabetic knowledge is consolidated children make orthographic connections between familiar strings of letters and either 'chunks' of sound or morphemes. At this stage, orthographic strategies can be deployed to allow sound and meaning to be accessed simultaneously. With further experience of print and teaching these strategies become better specified and useful for spelling. Children at this stage continue to make errors but have the skills needed for reading and spelling words.

Stage models do not account for the skills that children bring to the process of learning to read and spell words. Nor do they explain how they acquire the strategies to move from one stage to the next. Goswami and Bryant (1990) have drawn particular attention to the interaction between children's developing phonological skills and early literacy development. Phonological skills are not a unitary entity; awareness of the phonological structure of words, storage and retrieval of phonological representations, and verbal short term memory all involve phonological skills. In essence, Goswami and Bryant's theory suggests that children who are able to appreciate rhyme will be able to use the strategy of reading and spelling by analogy. That is, children with phonological awareness at the level of onset and rime will be in a position to use a known word as a basis for reading or spelling an unfamiliar word. The onset is the consonant/s before the vowel and the rime the vowel plus any following consonant/s.

It has been counter-argued that reading by analogy is a strategy unlikely to be available to children who have yet to develop phoneme awareness and basic decoding skills. These arguments claim that phoneme awareness is more critical for the development of reading and spelling than onset and rime awareness (Muter *et al.* 2004). Whatever the reality, acquiring phoneme awareness is a complex process; it has a reciprocal relationship with word reading with gains in one promoting gains in the other (see Hester and Hodson 2009), making the direction of the influences between phonological awareness and literacy difficult to determine.

It may be that the central role afforded to phonological skills in learning to read and spell has to some extent been over-stressed, leading to other factors being overlooked. Connectionist or computational models have been used to inform theories of how children learn to read (see Coltheart 2005). These models suggest learning be viewed as a continuous process rather than one happening in discrete stages, and draw attention to the role of accessing word meanings in reading. In connectionist models, phonological, orthographic and semantic representations are conceptualised as interacting with one another, with the rate of learning dependent on learning opportunities. Real-life learning is acknowledged in so far as they recognise the interaction between the skills a child brings to the task and those acquired through experience. These models are also able to accommodate the suggestion that literacy acquisition is not determined by linguistic factors and learning experiences alone. They allow for the fact that a child's individual profile of cognitive strengths and weaknesses, emotional well-being and motivation will have an impact on the development of written language.

Although the precise nature of the relationship between language skills and learning to read and write has yet to be determined, there is robust evidence of a causal link between phonological skills and written language development. It can therefore be hypothesised that at the root of the difficulty some children face in the development of word reading and spelling lies a problem with phonological processing. Phonological processing is underpinned by speech processing, and children who experience problems with speech processing may have difficulty in building, storing and retrieving accurate phonological representations. Children who do not have access to good quality phonological representations will in turn have difficulty with tasks involving phonological awareness and those involving the processing, storage and retrieval of phonological information (Sutherland and Gillon 2005). There is consensus that such children are most appropriately described as dyslexic, with the severity of their phonological deficit being related to the severity of their literacy difficulties (Hulme and Snowling 2009).

Reading comprehension and expressive writing

Being able to read and spell words accurately and fluently is only one aspect of literacy. To be fully literate, children must also be able to read with understanding and to express themselves in writing. Inevitably, children's reading and writing will be constrained by their ability to decode and encode words, but there is a dynamic system of interactions between a range of linguistic skills and the development of skilled reading and writing. Specifically, a child's semantic and syntactic knowledge, morphological awareness, narrative ability and pragmatic skills will interact to influence its development in different ways at different points. Pragmatic skills are particularly important in later stages of literacy development for appreciating stylistic differences, looking beyond literal meaning, drawing inferences, making deductions and predictions, and monitoring comprehension (see Cain and Oakhill 2007).

These linguistic skills are themselves influenced by within-child factors such as ability, memory and motivation, and by environmental factors such as learning opportunities and socio-economic status. A framework which encapsulates the concept of the relationship between spoken and written language is the Simple View of Reading (Hoover and Gough 1990). This framework suggests reading comprehension is a product of word decoding and oral language comprehension, and is a guiding principle in the National Primary Framework for Literacy (DCSF 2008c) which informs literacy teaching in UK state schools.

Relationships between spoken and written language difficulties

Children with poorly specified representations are at-risk for speech and language difficulties and problems with word reading and spelling. Children who have difficulty with any aspect of their broader language skills may experience associated problems with reading comprehension and written expression.

Although there are significant stylistic differences between spoken and written language, the Simple View of Reading (Gough and Hoover 1990) highlights what can go wrong in the development of literacy (see Rose 2006). Children with good decoding and oral language comprehension can be expected to be accurate readers who read with understanding. Conversely, children with poor decoding and oral language comprehension can be expected to be inaccurate readers who read without understanding. Children with imbalances in their decoding and oral language comprehension will present with more complex profiles. Their literacy strengths and weaknesses will reflect the actual levels of their underlying language skills.

Those children with good decoding in the presence of poor oral language comprehension will be accurate readers with limitations in reading comprehension. Children at the extreme end of these variables are described as hyperlexic. Children with the opposite profile – poor decoders with good oral language comprehension – can to some extent use language comprehension to compensate for decoding difficulties and so become relatively competent, but inaccurate, readers. However, oral language comprehension is more relevant for reading than spelling and intractable spelling difficulties will invariably be a feature of the writing of a child with this profile. Inaccurate reading and persisting spelling difficulties, in the context of an underlying phonological deficit, are now generally viewed as important diagnostic indicators for dyslexia. Dyslexia, like hyperlexia, is best understood as a disorder without clear cut-off points but with difficulties evident on a continuum from mild to severe (Rose 2009).

Not all children who have difficulty in the development of spoken language have associated difficulties in the development of literacy. Methodological differences in the research have led to inconsistent findings. In relation to pre-school children, it appears that, together with a family history of literacy difficulties, the most significant risk factors are the severity, pervasiveness and persistence of any speech and language difficulties. A number of longitudinal studies have suggested that children who have problems with speech and language are at greater risk for later literacy difficulties than children with isolated speech or language difficulties (see Pennington and Bishop 2009). Similarly, it has been shown that children whose speech difficulties persist beyond school entry are at heightened risk for dyslexia (Nathan *et al.* 2004) and that children whose language difficulties are still evident at 11 years are at risk for concurrent word reading and comprehension difficulties (Simkin and Conti-Ramsden 2006). The prognosis for children whose early speech and language difficulties appear to have resolved, remains unclear. Finally, some studies have suggested that speech and language difficulties alone may not be enough to put a child at risk, and have drawn attention to the interaction between risk and protective factors in literacy outcomes (see Peterson *et al.* 2009).

Not all children with written language difficulties will have a history of spoken language difficulties. Some children may show little or no overt sign of spoken language impairment, and it is only through well-targeted assessment that a subtle deficit may be uncovered. Such a deficit may have no apparent impact on spoken language but a significant effect on the fluency or accuracy of single word, context-free, reading and spelling or on reading comprehension and narrative writing.

The role of the speech and language therapist

As understanding of the links between language and literacy grow so do expectations about the contribution speech and language therapists can make to the management of children with literacy difficulties. However, responsibility for assessing and meeting the needs of children at-risk for or experiencing written language difficulties does not rest with speech and language therapy services alone. Collaboration between a number of statutory and voluntary services is required (see RCSLT 2010). The therapist's contribution will be determined by factors related to the individual child and service delivery policies. A distinction may need to be made between the management of pre-school children at-risk for literacy difficulties and school age children experiencing them; between school age children with literacy difficulties in the context of spoken language impairment and those whose spoken language falls within the average range. Furthermore, responsibilities for assessment may differ from responsibilities for intervention.

In relation to pre-school children, the argument has been made that well-specified and distinct phonological representations serve as a basis for performance on a range of phonologically demanding tasks, including word reading and spelling. This has relevance for clinical decisions related both to assessment and intervention. However, the balance between a direct approach and a consultative approach involving parents and pre-school providers will be dictated by the extent and severity of a child's spoken language difficulties. Once children are in school, responsibility for meeting their learning needs rests primarily with their Local Authority. Nevertheless, an in-depth investigation into the nature of any underlying spoken language difficulties will usefully complement information from a school-based assessment. A collaborative approach both to assessment and to intervention can lead to well-founded targets for a child's education plan and appropriate suggestions for differentiation of the National Curriculum. Whatever the child's age, factors that may affect the process of change will also influence clinical decision-making (Bray and Todd 2005).

In the management of children with written language difficulties, it is the changing manifestation of their difficulties and their evolving needs, together with considerations about effective use of resources and delivery of an equitable service that will guide the therapist's decision about whether and how to be involved.

Decision-making in assessment

A speech and language therapist must consider how specific a child's difficulties are. A number of children have co-morbid difficulties or multiple barriers to learning, and any language or literacy difficulties must be viewed within the context of these. Careful attention to case history and school liaison will provide information about a child's learning experiences and any contributory or compensatory factors. Information from assessments in the early years and teacher and key stage assessments may be available, or schools can be asked to provide information about progress across the curriculum. Non-verbal ability and literacy skills should only be tested by an appropriately trained professional, but where literacy test results are available these can be analysed quantitatively and qualitatively by the speech and language therapist (Goulandris 2006). Psychosocial factors which will affect case management must also be considered (Nash 2006).

Children at-risk for or experiencing literacy difficulties will present with their own individual profiles of speech and language strengths and weaknesses. To provide a holistic picture, some broad-based language assessment will be needed together with focused assessment of phonological skills (see Gardner 2006a).

An initial assessment will provide both a baseline and insight into the nature of a child's difficulties; ongoing assessment will monitor progress and evaluate the effectiveness of intervention. Stackhouse and Wells (1997) advocate taking a psycholinguistic approach to assessment. This involves cross-comparing performance on a range of phonologically demanding tests or tasks and building a profile of a child's linguistic strengths and needs. Such an approach will allow the therapist to test hypotheses about the nature of a child's difficulties and will provide converging evidence about their phonological skills, leading to accurately targeted intervention.

Selecting appropriate tests and interpreting test performance are important steps in the decision-making process. Age is only one factor to consider. Differences in the speech processing, linguistic and cognitive demands of tests must also be taken into account. For example, some tests involve input processing, others output; some require implicit skills, others explicit; some use real words, others non-words; some require verbal responses, others picture pointing; some rely on modelling and demonstration, others on remembering and following verbal instructions. A further consideration in test interpretation is that children differ in how they approach and complete tests. Some trade speed for accuracy, others accuracy for speed; some draw on orthographic knowledge, others on semantic.

School age children with written language difficulties may have resolved any speech output problems, or their difficulties may be so subtle as to pass unnoticed. For some, an assessment of their phonological skills and their speech may be advisable. For others it will be enough to observe whether they use a full range of speech sounds (especially th, r, w, l, y), and to note any difficulty they may have with complex sound and syllable combinations and less familiar vocabulary. Attention should also be paid to connected speech where unstressed syllables may be omitted or difficulties at word boundaries may be evident.

Phonological skills are multi-faceted. They can be investigated using formal tests or informal tasks; but to build a complete picture a battery of tests or tasks will be needed. A full assessment will investigate phonological awareness at different levels of linguistic analysis (syllable, onset/rime, phoneme), together with the processing, storage and retrieval of phonological information. Non-standardised tests can be used for screening or for testing broad preliminary hypotheses. Interpretation of results of such tests is not always easy though, and a child's performance must be related to developmental norms. Standardised screening tests are also available, but their place is in the identification of children at-risk for literacy difficulties rather than as part of a diagnostic assessment. Formal assessments used in conjunction with informal tasks (see Stackhouse *et al.* 2007) will provide information about a child's skills in relation to their peers, together with information about the nature of their difficulties.

A number of formal assessments of phonological skills are available (see Table 16.1 for a selection). There is considerable overlap amongst these formal assessments, but they cannot be compared directly as they investigate different aspects of phonological skills, make different demands and are standardised for use with different age groups.

Formal assessment

Phonological awareness, letter knowledge, non-word reading, rapid serial naming

Popular and useful formal assessments of phonological skills are the Pre-school and Primary Inventory of Phonological Awareness (PIPA) (Dodd *et al.* 2000), the Phonological Abilities Test (PAT) (Muter *et al.* 1997) and the Phonological Assessment Battery (PhAB) (Frederickson *et al.* 1997). Each explores a range of phonological skills and makes demands on input and output processing and explicit and implicit awareness.

One consideration when deciding which assessment or subtests of an assessment to select is research that highlights specific predictors or markers for dyslexia. In the pre-school child, letter-name knowledge and phoneme awareness have been shown to be associated with later success in literacy acquisition. The PIPA, and the PAT offer useful subtests of both.

A further consideration is areas of difficulty that have been identified as markers for dyslexia such as persisting difficulty in fluent and accurate single word reading. In real word reading, semantic knowledge can be an important source of support. In non-word reading, more demands are made on phonological skills. The PhAB contains a non-word reading test that is suitable once a child has acquired some literacy skills; although the Graded Non-word Reading Test (GNWRT) (Snowling *et al.* 1996) may be preferred as the non-words are presented separately and acceptable pronunciations for responses are provided.

There are mixed findings about the association between difficulties in rapid serial naming and literacy difficulties. Rapid naming requires retrieval of phonological information at speed and some children with dyslexia demonstrate a 'double-deficit' in both phonological awareness and rapid serial naming (Wolf and Bowers 1999). The PhAB has subtests which measure rapid naming and the CELF-4[uk] (Wiig and Semel 2006) offers a series of subtests designed to measure 'Automaticity of speech'. For the younger child, the PAT provides a measure of speech rate; speech rate is important for naming speed as well as decoding and working memory.

A further consideration in test selection is the fact that literacy acquisition promotes phonological awareness. Therefore, older or more literate children may rely on orthographic knowledge to support test performance, making it difficult to assess the real level of their phonological awareness. For such children, the PhAB includes a demanding spoonerism subtest. Orthographic knowledge can be called upon to complete this, but this will slow the process down. Time is therefore an important consideration in interpreting test performance.

Table 16.1 A selection of assessments of phonological skills

Assessment	Age range	Details	Comments
Preschool and Primary Inventory of Phonological Awareness (PIPA)	3–6;11 years	Syllable segmentation; rhyme awareness; alliteration awareness; phoneme isolation; letter knowledge.	Standard scores; percentile ranks UK norms
Phonological Abilities Test (PAT)	4–7;11 years	Rhyme detection and production; word completion; phoneme deletion; speech rate; letter knowledge.	Percentile ranks Standardised in UK
Phonological Assessment Battery (PhAB)	6–14;11 years	Rhyme and alliteration detection; rhyme, alliteration and semantic fluency; naming speed; spoonerisms; non-word reading.	Standard scores; percentile ranks Standardised in UK
Early Repetition Battery (ERB)	2–6 years	Two expressive tasks: the Preschool Repetition Test (PSRep) involving repetition of real and non-words; Sentence Imitation Test (SIT) comprising sentences controlled for length and syntactic complexity.	Standard scores; percentile ranks Standardised in UK
Children's Test of Non-word Repetition (CN Rep)	4–8 years	Described as a test of short term auditory memory; involves repetition of non-words of increasing syllable length.	Standard scores; percentile ranks Standardised in UK
Graded Non-word Reading Test (GNWRT)	5–11 years	20 non-words of increasing difficulty; 10 single syllable words with consonant clusters, 10 two syllable words.	Percentile ranks Standardised in UK
Clinical Evaluation of Language Fundamentals-4uk (CELF)	5–16;11 years	Different combinations of subtests produce scores for: automaticity of speech; phonological awareness; working memory; language memory.	Standard scores; percentile ranks Standardised in USA; UK norms
Word Finding Vocabulary Test (WFVT) Renfrew (2011b)	3–9 years	Picture naming tasks.	Norm referenced; raw score related to an age range UK norms
Test of Word Finding – 2nd edition (TWF-2)	4–12;11 years	Picture naming, nouns; sentence completion naming; picture naming, verbs; picture naming, categories.	Separate measures for speed and accuracy. Standardised in USA
Working Memory Test Battery for Children (WMTB-C)	5–15 years	3 measures of central executive function; 4 measures of phonological loop function; 2 measures of visuo-spatial sketchpad function.	Standard scores; percentile ranks Standardised in UK
Assessment of Comprehension and Expression (ACE)	6–11;11 years	Naming: picture naming subtest	Standard scores; percentile ranks Standardised in UK

Working memory and word finding

School age children with dyslexia are also often reported to experience difficulties with working memory, word learning and word finding. This is hardly surprising given that, to varying degrees, all involve processing, storing and retrieving phonological information (Fowler and Swainson 2004). Assessment of these aspects of cognitive and linguistic skills contributes useful information about the integrity of a child's phonological skills.

A word level test of working memory is provided by a digit span test such as that in the CELF-4[uk]. Instructions for the rate of delivery need to be followed exactly otherwise the results will be invalidated. The forward recall condition requires storage and retrieval; the reverse condition requires storage, processing and retrieval and children with dyslexia may have particular difficulty with this additional demand. The Working Memory Test Battery for Children (WMTB-C) (Pickering and Gathercole 2001) is for use when more comprehensive assessment is required.

Non-word repetition tests can also provide useful diagnostic information about a child's working memory as the use of non-words separates phonological processing from semantic processing. The Early Repetition Battery (ERB) (Seeff-Gabriel *et al.* 2008) and the Children's Test of Non-word Repetition (CN-Rep) (Gathercole and Baddeley 1996) require the child to process and store phonological information in order to repeat a series of non-words of increasing syllable length. However, such tests make demands on more than working memory. All levels of speech processing are involved in such tasks, and cross-task comparisons will be necessary to determine whether difficulties are due to a breakdown in input processing, output processing or working memory.

At sentence level, the 'Recalling Sentences', 'Concepts and Following Directions' and 'Formulated Sentences' subtests from the CELF-4[uk] provide a composite 'Language Memory' score. These subtests also make demands on expressive language however, making error interpretation more difficult. Children with dyslexia may recall the meaning or gist of sentences without the exact detail, while children with broader language difficulties may focus on details and fail to grasp the meaning of the sentence as a whole.

When concerns are expressed about word learning and finding, receptive and expressive vocabulary should be compared and results from tests of naming or word finding should be analysed qualitatively as well as quantitatively. At word and sentence level, use of strategies such as circumlocution, substitutions, false starts and non-specific vocabulary will provide important diagnostic information. A confrontation naming task such as the Word Finding Vocabulary Test (WFVT) (Renfrew 2011b) or the 'Naming' subtest from the Assessment of Comprehension and Expression of Language (ACE) (Adams *et al.* 2001) are quick to administer and errors can be analysed qualitatively. The Test of Word Finding, second edition (TWF-2) (German 2000) offers a similar picture-naming test. Its advantage lies in its scope for comparing a child's performance on tasks making different demands, and speed of responses can also be measured and self-cueing strategies recorded.

To inform hypotheses about the source of a child's word-finding difficulties, errors in single word tests need to be analysed and compared with errors in discourse. If a number of responses bear a phonological relationship to the target (e.g. 'ankle' for ANCHOR), are not real words or are produced after some groping, hypotheses could be formulated about the quality of the information stored in the child's phonological representation and motor programme. Or hypotheses could be formed about the links between semantic representations and motor programmes. Alternatively, if many of the errors are semantically related to the target (e.g. 'nail' for SCREW), hypotheses about the child's vocabulary and semantic knowledge might be better founded.

Decision-making in intervention

Evidence for the efficacy of intervention with children with written language difficulties has important implications for the speech and language therapist. For some children, appropriate intervention and advice can minimise the negative consequences of struggling and failing with literacy. However, a number of factors affect clinical decisions related to intervention.

In relation to evidence-based practice, it is well attested that phonological training can be effective. This may be in:

- pre-school and school age children;
- children at-risk for, or already experiencing literacy difficulties;
- children whose speech and language are developing normally;
- children with identified speech sound disorders.

(See Ehri *et al.* 2001; Phillips *et al.* 2008; Schuel and Boudreau 2008.)

In addition, there is evidence that for some children with speech sound disorders, training in phonological skills alone has an effect on speech output (Gillon 2002). Crucially, there is also strong evidence that when training in phonological awareness is combined with structured phonics teaching it has an effect on both reading and spelling (see Hulme and Snowling 2009). Equally, there is evidence that such training can be carried out effectively by a range of professionals if they are given the right training.

In relation to young children at risk for reading difficulties, in a series of randomised control trials Carroll *et al.* (2011) provide evidence for the effectiveness of two intervention programmes delivered by trained teaching assistants. These programmes draw on the principles outlined in the Simple Theory of Reading (Hoover and Gough 1990) and are comprehensively described in Carroll *et al.* (2011).

In a detailed report, Rose (2009) makes a number of recommendations for meeting the needs of school-aged children with dyslexia in the UK. He suggests they should have access to high quality intervention implemented by a teacher or support staff with specialist qualifications or training, and outlines some key features of a specialist dyslexia teaching programme. Likewise the National Early Literacy Project report (2008) in the USA outlines suggestions for 'code focused' and 'shared reading' interventions which a meta-analysis of relevant studies has shown to be effective in promoting both spoken and written language.

Although primary responsibility for supporting school-age children with written language difficulties may lie with education providers, the speech and language therapist has the knowledge and skills to work collaboratively with schools. For the child with a deficit in phonological skills and difficulties with the early stages of literacy, advice may be closely linked to the National Primary Framework for Literacy (DCSF 2008c). For the child with broader language difficulties and associated difficulties in reading comprehension and expressive writing, the therapist can be involved in decisions about differentiation and accessing subjects across the curriculum, together with the development of compensatory strategies and meta-cognitive skills (Snowling and Stackhouse 2006). A technique such as 'Paired Reading' (see Topping 1995) may also be useful in promoting confidence and fluency in reading and as a vehicle for promoting all aspects of language.

At all ages, however, it will be important that one set of language skills is not emphasised at the expense of another and that children are encouraged to appreciate the communicative value of written language.

Summary

In this chapter, theories of literacy development have been summarised, and the complex relationships between typically and atypically developing spoken and written language have been discussed. The role and responsibilities of the speech and language therapist in the management of children with written language difficulties has been considered, and the need for a collaborative approach emphasised. Assessments of phonological skills have been described and issues related to intervention have been highlighted.

Chapter 17

Cleft palate and velopharyngeal anomalies

Debbie Sell and Anne Harding-Bell

Learning outcomes

By the end of this chapter the reader should:

- understand different types of cleft palate presentation, incidence, causes and other velopharyngeal anomalies;
- have an awareness of multidisciplinary cleft care from birth to maturity;
- understand the effects of a cleft palate/velopharyngeal dysfunction on pre-speech, speech development and resonance;
- have an awareness of the assessment and management of velopharyngeal dysfunction;
- have an awareness of the decisions made by speech and language therapists working with multidisciplinary team members.

Introduction

Cleft lip +/– cleft palate is the most common, congenital craniofacial abnormality occurring in approximately one in 700 live births in the UK. It is pertinent to reflect that worldwide approximately 250,000 infants with cleft lip and/or palate are born annually, of which 93 per cent are in the developing world (Mars *et al.* 2008). There is typically very limited access to surgery and treatment, resulting in millions of under-treated and untreated individuals, many of whom have severe speech disorders.

In the UK, cleft care has undergone a major reorganisation following a national investigation which found a very high number of 'low volume operators' with results which compared unfavourably with European counterparts (*CSAG Report* 1998). Services have been redesigned so they are delivered from designated high volume regional centres operating managed clinical networks.

Cleft lip and/or palate is not a simple cosmetic problem solved by surgery, but its consequences and the need for clinical care extend from birth into adulthood. There are multiple aspects of care which need to be addressed by a specialist interdisciplinary team, including feeding, timing of surgery, speech and language, hearing/ENT, facial growth, dental development, cosmesis and psychosocial functioning. Interventions have to be carefully timed, mindful of the changing structures of the facial complex over the growing years. The Cleft Team is also responsible for managing speech disorders arising from palatal and velopharyngeal anomalies in non-cleft aetiologies.

Cleft lip/palate: prevalence and aetiology

There is considerable variation in the presentation of clefts of the lip and palate. Isolated cleft lip is not usually associated with speech impairment. When cleft lip and palate co-occur, this results in either a unilateral (UCLP; incidence 25 per cent) or bilateral (BCLP; incidence 10 per cent) cleft lip and palate. Cleft palate alone (CP; incidence 40 per cent) varies in extent from a soft palate cleft only, to varying degrees of involvement of the hard palate. Cleft palate alone is more often associated with other anomalies/syndromes and developmental delay, which has implications for speech and language therapists. One particularly relevant form of cleft palate for speech and language therapists is submucous cleft palate (SMCP), in which the oral mucosa is intact but the underlying muscles of the soft palate are abnormally inserted into the posterior margin of the hard palate with resulting impaired soft palate function. Classical SMCP is associated with a triad of anomalies: bifid uvula, translucent central zone due to muscle diastasis and notched hard palate. It is now recognised that SMCP presents as a spectrum from the classical abnormality to very subtle signs only, sometimes described as the occult variety. Speech characterised by hypernasal resonance, nasal emission and abnormal consonant production often prompts an initial referral to a community speech and language therapist. There is usually a history of nasal regurgitation in infancy, recurrent ear infections and possible grommet insertion.

Cleft lip and palate, in the absence of other anomalies or associated syndrome, has a multifactorial aetiology often involving environmental and genetic factors. Current thinking suggests that there are multiple genes involved which may interact, not only with each other, but also with environmental factors such as certain maternal drugs, alcohol, pesticides and maternal smoking. In the majority of cases the cleft will be the only anomaly, but clefts also occur in association with other congenital anomalies, or as part of a syndrome. More than 400 syndromes include cleft lip and/or palate (Winter and Baraitser 1998), the most common of which is 22q11.2 deletion syndrome (see below).

Velopharyngeal anomalies

Cleft Teams manage the speech difficulties which arise from incomplete closure of the velopharyngeal sphincter during speech following palate repair known as velopharyngeal insufficiency. They are also responsible for the management of velopharyngeal anomalies where there is no history of overt cleft palate. Around 50 per cent of children assessed for nasal speech in cleft centres fall into this group. The non-cleft UK Velopharyngeal Dysfunction (VPD) annual workload consists of more than 1000 referrals annually, mirroring the birth rate of cleft lip and palate (Sell and Pereira 2011).

Aetiologies that account for non-cleft VPD include post-adenoidectomy (leading to, in about one-third of cases, the uncovering of a previously undiagnosed SMCP), congenital overroomy or capacious velopharynx, post-tumour resection and neurologically based disorders, such as dyspraxia or dysarthria. One particularly important syndrome for speech and language therapists is 22q11.2 deletion syndrome. This syndrome has a very distinctive communication profile, often with severe expressive language delay, severe speech problems which may be related to a submucous cleft palate and/or velopharyngeal dysfunction, and dyspraxic features (Kummer et al. 2007). The characteristic prevalent use of glottal stops or pharyngeal fricatives and severe hypernasality (Mills et al. 2006) may raise the index of suspicion for this syndrome, particularly in the context of cardiac history, facial dysmorphism, immuno-deficiency, hypocalcaemia, mild learning disabilities, feeding problems in infancy and behavioural and psychiatric problems; the latter particularly in adolescence. In the school years, language skills may lag, and social communication problems are not uncommon.

However, not all cases of suspected VPD are associated with a physical condition. Speech disorders may arise from a structural or neurological velopharyngeal dysfunction and 'velopharyngeal mislearning', all of which may be characterised by similar speech presentations.

The multidisciplinary team

Team members include the cleft surgeon, orthodontist, specialist speech and language therapist, specialist nurse, paediatrician, cleft team coordinator, ENT surgeon, audiologist, oral maxillo-facial surgeon, clinical psychologist, geneticist, paediatric dentist and restorative dentist. The paediatrician is the team member who takes a holistic view of the child (Habel 2001). Team working is interdisciplinary and at times transdisciplinary, when clinicians may offer advice on behalf of a discipline not represented in a consultation. The optimum timing and technique of primary palate surgery remains highly controversial (Lohmander 2011). In most UK centres, lip repair is undertaken at three months of age and palate repair between six and 12 months of age. The success of primary palate surgery largely determines the extent to which further surgery, orthodontic treatment and speech therapy become necessary.

All cleft centres have agreed protocols of care, and include multidisciplinary reviews, unidisciplinary speech and language therapy reviews and mandatory audit, all offered at specific ages, usually until the late teens. Table 17.1 is an example of a typical care pathway with a description of the key interventions at the different ages.

Specialist speech and language therapy

Centre-based therapists advise and give information about speech development, specialist assessment, differential diagnosis and investigations of velopharyngeal function. They also undertake therapy, audit and network with the community speech and language therapy services. Management of speech is a collaboration between the Cleft Team and local therapists. Regular therapy is usually provided locally either in a health centre or within an educational setting, ideally by a therapist with some training in cleft speech, and/or in close liaison with the centre therapist. Specialist training provided by the centre for the managed clinical network can be complemented by a post-graduate qualification, such as a Masters' certificate.

Although each centre's speech and language therapy protocol varies, the following overview broadly describes current UK practice.

Infant vocalisations and babble development

Newborn infants with cleft palate initially vocalise with the same glottal and pharyngeal sounds as non-cleft infants. By 4–6 months of age, normal infants produce anterior articulatory gestures with an oral airstream, resulting in [b d] sounds. In contrast, infants with cleft palate are unable to produce these sounds until after palate repair. The phonetic repertoire for babble and speech development associated with an infant's unrepaired cleft palate is restricted to vowels and consonants such as approximants [w l j], nasals [m n ŋ] and glottal stops which are not dependent on intra-oral pressure.

Active involvement of the parents in their child's speech development begins in early infancy. Explanations are given about the function of the palate in normal speech, the effects of a cleft palate on speech development and participative babble techniques are introduced (Russell and Albery 2005) in order to minimise the risk of language delay and maximise the child's emerging consonants (Harding and Grunwell 1996). Parents are also advised about the impact of fluctuating conductive hearing loss on speech development, which is very common in cleft palate. In order that communication and listening skills are maximised, collaborative working between speech and language therapists with audiologists/ENT specialists is crucial.

The use of the oral pressure consonants [p b t d] around 18 months of age implies probable velopharyngeal closure. In contrast, a phonetic inventory which is restricted to /g h m n/ is strongly indicative of a structural problem. Such a repertoire limits the development of phonological contrasts and hence may adversely affect language development and vocabulary size at 3 years of age.

Early speech development

Any signs of abnormal and unusual consonant production in early words during the second year of life may indicate the need for intervention aimed at modifying emerging, atypical phonological processes before they become fully established (Russell and Harding 2001).

Harding and Grunwell (1998) also reported atypical patterns of phonological development such as oral fricatives appearing before plosives, voiceless consonants appearing in the absence of voiced counterparts and weak word final consonants occurring with no word initial counterparts. These insights should guide clinicians to conceptualise cleft speech as an articulation disorder with phonological consequences (Harding-Bell and Howard 2011). They state that the analysis of patterns in consonant production data usually reveals phonological consistency.

Speech assessment

Services in the UK aim for normal or near normal speech progress by school entry (*CSAG Report* 1998). In a national review of three year speech audit data Britton (2011) reported a continuing need for therapy in 40 per cent of cases. More than 20 per cent of children with a cleft palate are reported to have persistent long term intransigent speech difficulties.

The recommended speech screening assessment for children with cleft palate in the UK is GOS.SP.ASS (98) (Sell *et al*. 1999). It provides a systematic framework in which to assess and document the particular speech parameters most affected by cleft palate/velopharyngeal anomalies. Descriptions and examples of cleft speech are available on the GOS.SP.ASS training DVD. One particularly important type of resonance is hypernasality and its presence/absence is viewed as an indicator of surgical success. This suprasegmental feature reflects any abnormal increase in nasal resonance perceived during speech production on vowels, and in more severe cases, voiced consonants. In contrast, a reduction or absence of expected nasal resonance during production of nasal consonant [m n ŋ] results in hyponasal resonance. Differential diagnosis between hypernasal resonance and hyponasality is critical. Ratings of hypernasality can be complicated by nasal congestion, dysphonia, prevalent glottal articulation and the nature of the speech sample. Unusual nasal airflow, in the form of nasal emission and nasal turbulence, also occurs in association with VPD or a fistula in the palate. This is the abnormal escape of air through the nasal cavity during the production of pressure consonants. Severity and consistency ratings are made for all aspects of nasality and note is made of any associated nasal or facial grimace during speech.

Consonant production is transcribed in word initial and word final position from a standardised list of sentences. Atypical realisations are categorised into ten possible cleft speech characteristics (Table 17.2), which are summarised into four broad categories: anterior, posterior, non-oral or passive patterns (Sell *et al*. 1999; John *et al*. 2006). Use of these categories facilitates differential diagnosis, guiding the clinician towards possible aetiological explanations for the speech pattern. For example, anterior characteristics usually relate primarily to occlusal and dental irregularities. Non-oral characteristics, produced in the pharynx, glottis or nasopharynx, may be the consequence of VPD or may be mislearnt patterns associated with an unrepaired palate. Passive patterns are nearly always associated with velopharyngeal dysfunction. Nasal realisations of plosives [b d] is an example of a typical passive process, well established as a stigmata of cleft palate speech, which prevents the speaker from achieving the critically important phonological contrast between oral and nasal sounds (Harding and Grunwell 1998).

Whilst all ten cleft-type characteristics, now referred to as cleft speech characteristics, are strongly associated with cleft palate they may also occur in non-cleft speech patterns. The process of differential diagnosis involves distinguishing between cleft-related/VPD and non-cleft patterns of consonant production. For example, interdentalisation of /s z/ is usually considered a normal developmental immaturity in pre-school children, but can also be associated with a 'cleft-related' class III malocclusion. Lateral and palatal articulation may occur in non-cleft speech patterns but are often found in cleft palate associated with abnormal dentition,

Table 17.1 An example of a UK cleft lip and palate care pathway

Age	Surgeries	Nature of interventions
Antenatal		Antenatal diagnosis: counselling with cleft surgeon and/or nurse + foetal medicine team
After birth		Meet team. Cleft care protocol explained Decision re +/– pre-surgical orthopaedics Feeding support +/– dysphagia specialist advice Audiology assessment and advice Information about CLAPA: parent support group +/– paediatrics and genetics
3 months	Lip repair	
6 months	Cleft palate repair +/– insertion of grommets (sometimes later repeated)	Post-operative SLT advice and monitoring ENT/audiology monitoring
18 months	Fistula repair (exact timing related to speech symptoms +/– nasal regurgitation)	ENT/audiology SLT assessment Sometimes SLT intervention
2 years	Cleft clinic review	Speech therapy intervention if indicated
3 years		SLT assessment/intervention ENT/audiology
3–6 years	Management of VPD Lip and/or nose revision	Speech therapy intervention if indicated

Age	
4 years	Cleft clinic review
5 years	Mandatory national audit recording with clinical review
7;5 years	Cleft clinic review
9–12 years	Alveolar bone grafting with alveolar fistula repair
10 years	Pre- and post-operative orthodontic treatment
12;5 years	Mandatory national audit recording with clinical review
15 years	Cleft clinic review
	Mandatory national audit recording with clinical review
16–20 years	Maxillary osteotomy
	Pre- and post-operative orthodontic treatment
	Psychology
	SLT assessment and treatment
18 years	Cleft clinic review
18 years onwards	Rhinoplasty
	Final lip revision
	Restorative dentistry (prosthetic replacement of teeth, permanent bridges, dentures)
	Genetic counselling
20 years	Mandatory national audit recording with clinical review

malocclusion and collapsed maxillary arches. 'Backing', nasal fricatives and gliding of fricatives/affricates may all occur without any history of VPD or cleft palate. Nasal realisation of vowels and vowel distortions are atypical characteristics sometimes observed.

Active and passive nasal fricatives

The differential diagnosis of active and passive nasal fricatives is crucial in order that appropriate management is undertaken. In active nasal fricatives (reflecting velopharyngeal mislearning) there is an incorrect use of an articulatory gesture inhibiting oral airflow, so that all airflow is directed through the nasal cavity. The consonant production is transcribed as a devoiced nasal stop reflecting the relevant place of articulation, e.g. bilabial [m̥], alveolar [n̥], velar [ŋ̊]. In contrast, passive nasal fricatives, as a consequence of VPD, have the articulatory oral posture for the intended oral target, but the lack of intraoral air pressure results in a nasal fricative /f /=> [m̥̃ m̃], /s/=> [ñ̊] or backed to velar [ŋ̊̃]. The nasal fricative transcription is modified to demonstrate that the oral fricative target was intended but not perceptibly produced [(s͡)n̥]. A simple but crude technique to help make the distinction between active and passive is to gently close the nares during the production of the sounds in isolation. The passive condition results in a strengthening of the oral friction; in contrast, the active condition is associated with no oral release. Active nasal fricatives require therapy and do not require surgical intervention. Passive nasal fricatives require physical management.

Speech aetiological factors

Apart from the many structurally related factors detailed in GOS.SP.ASS which may contribute to cleft speech, children born with cleft palate/velopharyngeal anomalies are also subject to the same influences on speech and language development as the non-cleft population. Assessment of cleft speech should not ignore neurological, cognitive, developmental, environmental and emotional factors and the impact of a syndromic diagnosis. In addition, social and psychological factors, the nature and timing of primary palate surgery and speech and language therapy support all contribute to the speech profile. The importance of ongoing monitoring of middle ear problems and intermittent conductive hearing loss has already been emphasised.

Differential diagnosis

Irrespective of the medical diagnosis, a speech diagnosis is necessary. When making decisions about differential diagnosis, the speech data, aetiological factors and documented observations are all taken into consideration. A period of diagnostic therapy may be necessary, testing the hypothesis of symptom-based differential diagnosis and the impact of therapy.

Table 17.2 Cleft speech characteristics and their categories

Anterior	*Non-oral*
Dentalisation	Pharyngeal articulation
Lateralisation/lateral articulation	Glottal articulation
Palatalisation/palatal	Active nasal fricatives
Double articulation	
Posterior	*Passive*
Backing to velar	Weak/nasalised consonants
Backing to uvular	Nasal realisations of fricatives
	Nasal realisations of plosives
	Absent pressure consonants
	Gliding of fricatives/affricates

Assessment and management of velopharyngeal dysfunction

In addition to the specialist perceptual assessment, instrumentation may be used to provide information on acoustic and aerodynamic measures of nasal tone and nasal airflow (Sweeney 2011). The preferred instrument for measuring nasal tone is the nasometer. Direct visualisation of the velopharyngeal mechanism is undertaken using videofluoroscopy and nasendoscopy. These investigations provide information about the structure, and also movement, its extent and some indication of the timing of velopharyngeal closure. The historical focus has been on velar elevation and lateral wall movements.

Sell and Pereira (2011) describe how videofluoroscopy and nasendoscopy are used to determine the nature of management, most usually the need for surgery and the type of surgery, but also the other interventions of speech therapy or speech prostheses. These investigations are used to counsel families, for predicting the success of an intervention, for visual biofeedback therapy, to accurately fit speech prostheses and in the evaluation of excessive nasal airflow during the playing of wind/brass instruments. They are also used importantly to document both the successful and failed outcomes of intervention, which is essential in order for teams and surgeons to have information on their surgical protocols. There has been a move in the UK and Sweden towards speech and language therapists undertaking nasendoscopy in the Cleft Teams. This has been endorsed by the RCSLT and is an appropriate practice of Consultant Allied Health Practitioners.

Treatment of VPD

When a consistent velopharyngeal gap is visualised during videofluoroscopy and nasendoscopy, treatment is often surgical. Palate re-repair and palate lengthening procedures have become popular surgical approaches to VPD. The previous frequent option of more obstructive procedures such as pharyngeal flaps or pharynogoplasties, may have to be the procedure of choice in some cases. Other treatment options include prosthetic appliances such as a palatal lift or speech bulb obturator. The palatal lift aims to lift the soft palate in a posterior and superior direction through the use of acrylic additions on the back of a dental appliance. It has been advocated for patients with a long soft palate which is immobile on phonation, and particularly in neurological conditions. The speech bulb obturator consists of a custom-made dental appliance with an extension, which courses behind the palate and terminates in an acrylic bulb or elliptical structure positioned in the velopharynx. This is effective for cases where there is severe pathology and surgery is contraindicated (Sell *et al.* 2006). These appliances can be a permanent alternative if there is no other treatment option, but can also be a useful temporary solution.

There is some evidence that hypernasality, nasal emission and/or nasal turbulence, co-occurring with abnormal consonant production may be reduced by therapy. Inconsistent closure related to consonant production can be confirmed on nasendoscopy and videofluoroscopy. In other words the mechanism is capable of closure but does not achieve this due to abnormal habitual articulatory patterns. Therefore therapy focusing on articulation can sometimes improve the functioning of the velopharyngeal mechanism. There is no evidence, however, that blowing and sucking techniques, or therapy directed at oral motor movements, improve velopharyngeal movements in speech and should not be undertaken for this purpose.

Past literature has often recommended that abnormal articulation should be corrected in the presence of velopharyngeal dysfunction in order to permit a valid assessment of velopharyngeal function. Current thinking is that one or two oral consonants should ideally be possible to elicit during the investigations. This should be as a minimum even if the oral consonants are weak and with accompanying nasal emission. After secondary surgery, it should not be assumed that the patient has an adequate velopharyngeal mechanism and/or that they will automatically learn to use this effectively. Surgery may or may not have been successful. Therapy may or may not be indicated. The specialist therapist will determine this in conjunction with the Cleft Team.

Some examples of interdisciplinary decision-making involving the speech and language therapist

Feeding: nurses and dysphagia speech and language therapist

Since the timing of surgery dictates that all infants have to establish feeding with an unrepaired palate, feeding difficulties are not uncommon and specialist nurses are responsible for managing this. Controversies exist as to breast feeding policies and the use of feeding plates although Masarei *et al.* (2007) reported one of the few randomised controlled trials in this area, in which pre-surgical orthopaedics did not improve feeding efficiency or general body growth within infants' first year of life. Where oral feeding is not established, and there are concerns regarding swallowing and aspiration consultation with a specialist dysphagia speech and language therapist is advisable.

Impact of fistula: surgeon and speech and language therapist

Sometimes, following surgery, a hole or fistula may remain or develop in the palate. Further surgery may be considered if there is persistent nasal regurgitation and/or speech problems directly attributable to the fistula. Specialist speech and language therapists make a differential speech diagnosis as to the source of the air leak, be it velopharyngeal and/or through the fistula, and make recommendations as to the need for surgery.

Hearing issues: ENT/audiologist and speech and language therapist

The abnormal attachments of the levator palati muscle around the entrance to the eustachian tube may adversely affect aeration and drainage of the middle ear. Therefore the ENT surgeon and audiologist regularly monitor children's hearing and ear status in order to prevent the adverse consequences of Otitis Media, particularly intermittent conductive hearing loss and chronic ear disease. Close liaison between all the professionals, together with the family, is paramount particularly in the pre-school and early school years as therapists strive for normal speech, and hearing loss and ENT status fluctuate. Current management options include watchful waiting, grommet insertion, temporary hearing aid(s) and/or advice to optimise the listening environment and development of auditory skills. It is noteworthy that Otitis Media with Effusion (OME) without cleft palate can be associated with the same nasal and glottal patterns as cleft palate (Miccio *et al.* 2001).

Velopharyngeal investigations and management: speech and language therapist and surgeon

Specialist therapists make decisions about the need for investigations of velopharyngeal function based on the speech assessment, followed by joint interpretation and decision-making by the surgeon/therapist and sometimes other team members. The therapist's views, based upon assessment and their expert knowledge, together with the patient/family, are central to the decision-making, whether this is the need for surgery, more rarely speech prostheses, or therapy. The timing of VPD surgery is highly controversial (Sell and Pereira 2011). Often a series of interventions is required. Sometimes a decision about surgery is postponed until after a further period of therapy, growth, speech/hearing maturation or in the knowledge of other interventions that may be required in the future. For example, when a maxillary advancement is likely, the management of nasal speech may be deferred until after this has taken place.

Therapy decision-making and delivery: specialist and local speech and language therapists

It is the role of the specialist therapist to determine when speech therapy is appropriate.

The detailed perceptual assessment underpins the therapist's management plan, and this is often further informed by instrumentation. Knowledge of the changes which can be achieved in therapy is crucial in decision-making. A trial of diagnostic therapy is often recommended. In some cases electropalatography may be indicated. Specialist therapists have a repertoire of techniques which they share with community colleagues usually on a case by case basis, although many of the skills therapists use in child speech impairments can be applied to this patient group. The challenge is often the elicitation of consonants and their integration into connected speech.

Maxillary advancement: speech and language therapist, orthodontist, oralmaxillofacial surgeon and psychologist

Mid-face retrusion, as a result of impaired facial growth, is commonly found in cleft patients. Once facial growth is complete at the end of the adolescent period, surgical advancement of the maxilla is undertaken in order to align the maxilla and mandible and improve facial appearance. Since maxillary advancement can result in speech deterioration, the therapist is involved in the decision-making and management both pre- and post-operatively.

Research and evaluation

Reilly *et al.* (2004) described how clinical practice has largely been informed by expert opinion, past practice and past teaching. It is now recognised, however, that clinical decision-making by health professionals should be fully embedded in the principles of evidence-based practice, integrating the best available external evidence from systematic research with the clinician's expertise and the patient's/family's views and expectations (Sackett *et al.* 1996). Interestingly, this shift in emphasis has paralleled a move away from the expert medical model with changes in the terminology and language used, a more equal relationship between the health professional and patients, and the appreciation of the service user's perspectives.

Whilst there has been much research on the nature and evaluation of speech disorders and speech outcomes of different surgeries, most studies are quantitative, with small numbers of subjects and cross-sectional in nature, focusing narrowly on speech impairment. Furthermore, in the area of intervention no evidence has been found to support the effectiveness of any one particular speech therapy approach. It is now recognised that due to the heterogeneity of cleft lip/palate that research needs to be undertaken on a multi-centre basis. One example of this is the Scandcleft Project, a randomised controlled trial of the impact of surgical technique and timing of primary palate repair. Research in this area has also largely been focused on 'body functions and structures' in the WHO's *International Classification of Functioning, Disability and Health* (2001), to the neglect of studies into the relationship of speech impairment to activity, participation, environmental and personal factors (Havstam 2010). Barr *et al.* (2007) concluded that impaired velopharyngeal function can have a major impact on speech intelligibility limiting quality of life such as activity and participation.

In the UK, efforts have been made to address the issue of mandatory audit (CSAG 1998) in order that regular monitoring of outcomes can be undertaken. Clinical audit, involving the defining of process and outcome standards against which care is measured and compared, has become fully integrated into cleft services. With regard to speech, a valid, reliable and applicable outcome tool has been developed which can be used in outcome studies (John *et al.* 2006). A training programme has been designed and implemented (Sell *et al.* 2009), not just nationally but internationally. There are many examples of the tool's application by trained therapists within centres, across centres and on a national basis.

Summary

This chapter provides an overview of cleft palate/velopharyngeal anomalies with emphasis given to emerging speech and typical speech disorders. It has drawn out the frequent interdisciplinary nature of the work, not only with the multidisciplinary team but also with local therapists. The mandatory clinical audit requirements and current thinking in research have been described.

Chapter 18

Children who stammer

Louise Wright

Learning outcomes

By the end of this chapter the reader should know how to:

- carry out appropriate assessment;
- identify children who are at risk of persistent stammering;
- plan therapy to suit individual needs;
- recognise when discharge is appropriate.

Introduction

Stammering (which may also be called stuttering, disfluency or dysfluency) is the abnormal disruption of speech fluency. Although not addressed in this chapter, therapists should also be aware of the disorder of fluency 'cluttering' (which may or may not include stammering) which is characterised by rapid unintelligible speech and associated writing and other difficulties (Ward 2006).

All young children developing language show some hesitancies that are normal, referred to as disfluency. These include pausing, repeating whole words or phrases, and saying 'er' or 'um' and usually occur if the speaker is tired, rushed or uncertain. The fluency breaks in young children who stammer are different from those who are fluent and these have been described by Yairi and Ambrose (2005) as Stuttering-Like Disfluencies. These are the most common speech disfluencies observed in children who stammer and also the most likely to be perceived as stammering. They are characterised by part-word repetitions, single word repetitions, prolongations and blocks.

Severe stammering can be tense and effortful and children may feel embarrassed and anxious about their speech. Children may try to cope with the physical and emotional experience of stammering in many ways, such as changing words, avoiding situations or trying different ways of speaking, for example, whispering.

Stammering is a developmental disorder that can begin as young as 18 months, but most commonly between two and four years of age. Onset is associated with rapid growth in language development. Children who have mismatches in speech and language skills, or advanced language abilities, may be more at risk of stammering. As with other speech and language difficulties, more boys stammer than girls, but the boy:girl ratio increases with age as more girls recover than boys. Incidence in pre-school children has been found to be as high as 8.5 per cent (Reilly *et al.* 2009) as compared to an estimated 1 per cent in the adult population. At least 75 per cent of young children experience spontaneous recovery (Yairi and Ambrose 2005), most doing so between 12 and 18 months following onset.

Speech and language therapists in the UK generally agree that the development of stammering involves a complex interaction between a number of factors (Kelman and Nicholas

2008). These factors include a possible neurophysiological and linguistic predisposition to stammer, which may be inherited, particularly if there is a history of persistent stammering in the family. The stammer may then be precipitated or maintained by a variety of environmental and psychological factors.

The Demand Capacity Model (DCM) can be useful in helping parents and teachers to understand the complexities of stammering in children (Stewart and Turnbull 2007). The DCM (Starkweather and Gottwald 1990) describes how fluency breaks down when environmental demands, and/or demands imposed by the children themselves, exceed their cognitive, linguistic, motoric (physical) or emotional capacities. For example, a child may:

- have low linguistic capacities while facing average demands;
- have average, or even high capacities, but face higher demands;
- be unable to cope with the balance of demands and capacities at a particular time in his/ her development.

Clinical implications

- The case history should gather information on time since onset and family history of stammering – particularly whether recovery occurred or not.
- Assessment of the child should not only include their stammering behaviours, awareness of their stammer and any coping mechanisms, but also their speech and language development.
- Children may be at higher risk of persistent stammering if the following indicators are present:
  - family history of persistent stammering;
  - child is male;
  - stable or increasing stammering (however, parents can be reassured that severity of stammering at onset appears to be unrelated to likelihood of recovery);
  - stammering for over 12 months since onset;
  - advanced or mismatched speech and language skills;
  - child or parents show strong reactions to stammering.
- Therapists may use a screening assessment to identify those children at higher risk of persistence. This approach should release more time for the therapist to undertake detailed assessment and early intervention for those children at higher risk.

Stammering at different ages

In this chapter the assessment and management of children from 18 months to the teenage years will be considered. Stammering may present differently at different ages. Below are descriptions of three boys of different ages who all stammer.

Case examples

Alex is 3 years old. He was using short sentences aged 2 years and now has above average vocabulary and sentence length. His parents say, 'He never stops talking.' He started to repeat and prolong sounds three months ago. The amount of stammering varies but, when frequent, he sometimes gives up on what he is saying. His mother stammers. She is very worried that Alex may not grow out of it, but his father is less concerned.

Ben is 8 years old and has stammered for four years. He talks freely, despite stammering in most situations. Mostly he repeats and prolongs sounds but he sometimes blocks and blinks when stammering. He is good at football and has many friends. There is no family history of stammering and his parents are not overly concerned. Ben has never expressed worry about his stammer but his teacher has made the referral.

Carl is 14 years old and has experienced some teasing about his stammer while at secondary school. He mostly blocks when he stammers and he avoids answering questions in class. He enjoys acting in plays and has some close friends who say they do not notice his stammer. He is unsure about what subjects he should choose at school in the future and what kind of job he might like to do.

Now read the above descriptions again as if they describe the *same boy* at different ages.

This exercise illustrates not only the individual nature of stammering and how it may develop over time but also the wide range of stammering problems that may be encountered by the therapist.

Referral

Speech and language therapists recommend referral as soon as possible after onset of stammering. However, health visitors and GPs often delay referral in the belief that the child will grow out of it (Christie 2000) and schools vary in their awareness of stammering and possible therapy. A child as described above may therefore be referred at any age.

The child may, or may not, be concerned about their stammering and it is important to find out why and how referral was made and to gather information about any previous therapy as this will affect the decision-making process in the management of the case.

For example, Ben, at eight years, and Carl, at 14 years, may both have had therapy before and previous therapy may have ended for a variety of reasons. Initial therapy may have been helpful but stammering later recurred due to changing demands; they may have been discharged because they were comfortable with their level of stammering, or they may have failed to attend because their speech was not a priority at that time.

Initial screening

With the pre-school child, an initial screening tool can be used to establish the risk of a child's stammer persisting and thereby select an appropriate therapy pathway (Kelman and Nicholas 2008). The therapist observes the parents and child playing to assess the child's fluency, language levels and parental interaction. The parents can then be asked about the child's stammer, date of onset, awareness and whether it is changing. Their level of concern can be established, as can any strategies they are currently using.

Low risk of persistence

A child with low risk of persistence should follow an 'advice and monitoring pathway' (Kelman and Nicholas 2008). The therapist provides the parents with information and some advice, followed by a period of monitoring which may be by telephone or face to face. This may be all that is needed to support the parents while the stammer recovers spontaneously.

High risk of persistence

If the child has a high risk of persistence, the child should proceed to a full assessment and intervention as described below.

Assessment

It cannot be stressed enough that insufficient time spent on assessment will lead to difficulties planning appropriate therapy and waste valuable therapy time later (Conture and Melnick 1999).

Carrying out the following assessment components can take two to three hours, longer if formal language assessments are needed. The therapist can choose whether to carry out all the assessments in one session or spread over two or three shorter sessions to facilitate meeting with the parents without the child.

Observation of parent–child interaction

The aim of the first assessment is to determine family interaction. In order to avoid parents modifying their usual behaviour it is suggested that the family are observed prior to any discussion with the therapist. The therapist observes the interaction (verbal and non-verbal) between parents and child, parental reactions to stammering and any effects on the child's fluency. Observations can be undertaken formally or informally, and ideally video-recorded as in the Palin Parent–Child Interaction (Palin PCI) programme (Kelman and Nicholas 2008).

Parental interview

It is strongly recommended that both parents attend assessment and that the parental interview takes place without the child being present (Rustin *et al.* 1996). Different appointments may be arranged for separated parents, depending on their wishes. See Guitar (2006) and Kelman and Nicholas (2008) for the content of the interview.

The initial interview serves a number of purposes. Primarily it is used to gather information about the child, his/her family and the stammer. Cultural and linguistic factors will be explored for children from linguistic minority communities (see Chapter 14). In addition, the therapist will demonstrate her/his understanding of the issues, provide the parents with information on stammering and speech and language therapy, and will begin to build a collaborative working relationship (see Chapter 8). It is hoped that this exchange of information will also help to alleviate any parental guilt about causing the stammer and reassure them that they have been helping their child in many ways (Manning 2010).

Assessment of the child

The aim of this part of the assessment is to collect samples of stammering, to investigate the child's awareness of stammering and to consider their language and general development.

Behavioural characteristics of stammering

Roberta Lees (2005) addresses the possible methods and pitfalls of assessing the behavioural aspects of stammering, in terms of quantity and quality, any secondary coping behaviours and the speaking rate. As stammering usually varies in different situations, a representative sample can be obtained by creating a variety of conditions during assessment.

Initially, the therapist may interact in a relaxed manner that facilitates fluency. S/he can then increase demands, for example, by increasing the rate of speech, asking questions and interrupting in order to assess the effects of such demands. This may be particularly useful if the child is fluent in clinic. Parents can also supplement the clinic sample with taped samples from home or by keeping a daily severity rating of stammering.

The therapist can also assess whether the stammering is modifiable. For example, the therapist can model slower speech without any reference to what she is doing, or explain and demonstrate to the child how to slow their speech. The therapist observes any effects on the child's fluency, and the results will inform her/his choice of modification approach.

Awareness, feelings and attitudes to stammering

Once rapport has been established, the therapist can talk to the child about their stammer. This is recommended with all children, however young (Rustin *et al.* 1996). It is important to establish how aware they are of their stammer, whether they are distressed, to reassure them that it can be talked about openly and that help is available.

The therapist should ask the parents beforehand if they think the child is aware and will gather evidence during observations of the child as to the possible level of the child's awareness. Opening questions such as, 'Do you know why you have come to see me today?' are used to initiate the topic and can be followed by more exploratory questions depending on the child's level of awareness. The therapist should take care to use language that is appropriate to the cognitive and linguistic level of the child, and use the child's words for stammering for example, 'getting stuck' or 'trouble talking'.

Children's attitudes towards their stammering can also be explored using drawing, or with older children, written descriptions or questionnaires such as the Communication Attitude Test (Brutten and Vanryckeghem 2007).

Co-existing speech and language problems

Bernstein-Ratner (2005) describes the high incidence of co-existing communication disorders in children who stammer and discusses issues of differential diagnosis. She confirms the need to carry out assessment of the child's speech, language and motor skills and this is done in the usual manner using initial observations followed by more detailed formal assessment as necessary.

Liaison with pre-school or school

If the child attends school or nursery it is important to gather information from teachers either by telephone, using a questionnaire or classroom observation (Rustin *et al.* 2001; Stewart and Turnbull 2007).

Management

The pathway of 'advice and monitoring' for children at low risk of persistent stammering has already been addressed. Following the detailed assessment of those children judged to be at higher risk of persistence, the therapist will be in a better position to select the appropriate pathway and individual management plan.

Working with the parents

Whatever the age of the child, therapy will involve some work with the family or carers. This will vary from being the only intervention required with the child in the very early stages of stammering to more limited involvement with an independent teenager. For those young children for whom work with the family is the main focus of therapy, parent participation is a key factor in the success of relatively short therapy programmes (Yaruss *et al.* 2006). By working closely with parents the therapist aims to empower them to support their child effectively long term, and this in turn helps to reduce the anxiety commonly felt by parents about their child's stammer. By listening to parents' fears, providing them with information and challenging negative stereotypes about stammering, most parents can be supported effectively whilst their child is in therapy.

Some children who are particularly at risk of persistent stammering have a parent who stammers. This issue should be addressed directly but sensitively and time may be required alone with the parent who stammers. The needs of such parents must be considered if their child is to be helped effectively in therapy. Referral to, or support from, a therapist who specialises in adult stammering therapy may be helpful.

Some parents welcome material to understand stammering in greater detail using books or audiobooks such as *Stammering: advice for all ages* (Byrne and Wright 2008), or reputable websites such as the British Stammering Association.

Parent-focused therapy programmes

For the pre-school child at higher risk of persistent stammering, the therapist initially has a choice of two parent-administered pathways. Parent–child interaction therapy or the Lidcombe Program are commonly used, and there is evidence that both can reduce stammering in young children (Millard *et al.* 2008; Jones *et al.* 2008).

The Lidcombe Program is usually used six to 12 months post onset to account for possible spontaneous recovery. Parent–child interaction can be used earlier if a child is judged to be at significant risk of persistent stammering and the parents would benefit from addressing their interaction with their child. Other possible factors to take into account when choosing which approach would best suit the child and family may include the parents' ability to commit sufficient time to the therapy programmes, their parenting styles and the child's reaction to direct verbal comments on their speech.

Parent–child interaction therapy

Parent–child interaction therapy aimed at decreasing demands in the environment may be the only intervention that is needed to return the child's fluency to normal levels. Alternatively, reducing demands can also complement direct therapy, the aim being to create an environment in which the child has the best chance of using his/her new fluency skills.

There are many descriptions of such approaches (Yaruss *et al.* 2006; Guitar 2006; Stewart and Turnbull 2007) and the Palin PCI programme (Kelman and Nicholas 2008) is commonly used in the UK. Palin PCI differs from other programmes in that rather than advise parents on standard ways to alter their interaction to enhance fluency, it helps parents select their own intervention strategies from video-recordings of their interaction with their child. Interaction targets may include following the child's lead in play, using more comments than questions, matching the parents' rate to the child's rate of speech and using pausing before and between utterances.

If the parents also identify family issues that they feel have an impact on their child's fluency such as openness about stammering, turn taking, behaviour management, sleep routines and pace of life, these issues can be addressed in the Palin PCI Family Strategies part of the programme, which follows the Interaction component.

The Lidcombe Program

The Lidcombe Program (Onslow *et al.* 2003) originated in Australia and is now widely used in the UK with pre-school children. Stammering is viewed as a neural processing deficit which children can learn to compensate for, before their neural networks for speech have become established, thus achieving stammer-free speech. It is described as a direct treatment approach which is delivered by the parent, who comments directly on the child's speech. The therapist teaches the parent how to deliver the 'verbal response contingent stimulation' in weekly visits in Stage 1 of therapy, and less frequently in Stage 2 maintenance therapy.

Measurement of the child's stammering plays a significant role in the therapist problem-solving the delivery of the programme and includes a parental perceptual severity rating (using a one-to-ten scale), a count of the child's stammering frequency and stammers per minute of speaking time.

In contrast to PCI, parents are not asked to change their language, rate of speech or interactions with their child. However, Ratner and Guitar (2006) propose a list of factors in the Lidcombe Program which may increase fluency. These include providing an active role for parents which helps to decrease their anxiety about stammering, improving bonding through daily practice activities and making stammering an acceptable topic for discussion. In addition, by disproportionately rewarding the use of shorter fluent utterances, children may decrease their expressive language demands to more age-appropriate levels which may also contribute to fluency.

Child-focused therapy

For a small percentage of children, stammering may persist following either PCI therapy or the Lidcombe Program. Alternatively the child may be referred late to speech and language therapy, with clear awareness of their stammer, having already developed negative attitudes towards communication and avoidance strategies.

Awareness will commonly have occurred by school age, and for some children is evident at pre-school age. Asking the child directly if they would like some help with their speech usually provides a reliable response, particularly if asked without the parent being present.

Therapy with the child will address all aspects of the child's stammer: the speech behaviours, emotional and cognitive reactions, and coping strategies such as avoidance. Children can also be empowered by understanding their individual stammer and wider aspects of good communication, as well as strengthening their social and problem-solving skills. Therapists will work with the child, their family, friends and school staff, and group therapy can provide invaluable support from their peers.

Overt stammering behaviours

There are a number of different ways to enhance a child's ability to change their stammering behaviours. Depending on the type and frequency of stammering and also the child's wishes regarding their preferred goal in therapy, the therapist can select from the options outlined below.

- If the child has little awareness of their stammer, the therapist can model slower easier ways of talking, to see if the child simply copies the slower rate, and becomes more fluent as a result. If this approach does not increase fluency, it may then be helpful to increase the child's awareness of their stammer in a supportive manner, helping them to identify and 'catch' stammers, first in the therapist's speech and then in their own. This can also help to increase the child's understanding of their stammer, is desensitising and helps self-monitoring during the following approaches.
- For children who have frequent or severe stammering, rapid speech and little natural fluency, a fluency technique can be taught where the overall speech rate is reduced and words flow smoothly together with gentle articulation. Teaching pausing may also be a powerful fluency tool in this case. This is always established first at a single word level, gradually increasing the length of utterance, content and use with different listeners, before transferring the technique to everyday speaking situations arranged in a hierarchy.
- Children who experience greater natural fluency, interspersed with occasional tense stammers, can be taught how to stammer more easily. The young person is taught to monitor the stammers and relax the articulators before or during the stammer, 'sliding' into or out of the stammer. This helps to say the difficult word more smoothly or even say the word

fluently. Modifying stammers can also be taught in combination with a fluency technique. Learning how to stammer in a relaxed manner is useful for older children and teenagers who are less likely to regain complete fluency and, therefore, benefit from a way of managing their stammer in the long term.

The aim in all of these approaches is to provide the young person with choice as to how they speak and is always delivered within an atmosphere of understanding, reassurance and encouragement by the therapist.

Detailed descriptions of therapy approaches and techniques can be found in many publications (Manning 2010; Guitar and McCauley 2010; Kelman and Nicholas 2008; Stewart and Turnbull 2007; McNeil *et al.* 2003). Some include worksheets and cartoon character representations of the techniques. Guitar and McCauley (2010) provide online video clips of client interactions and the Stuttering Foundation of America produces DVDs demonstrating a variety of therapy techniques by leading American clinicians. The provision of an evidence base for the interventions varies in the literature. Guitar and McCauley (2010), however, address this issue explicitly throughout their overview of established and emerging interventions.

It may seem confusing to less experienced therapists that so many therapy approaches and programmes have been published. Initially they may find it useful to select one approach and follow it in its entirety. However, as their experience grows and they become familiar with different therapy techniques they will be able to select elements from different programmes to suit individual clients and their own preferred therapy style.

Covert aspects of stammering

Direct therapy approaches will also address the covert non-speech elements of stammering, namely the cognitive and emotional aspects, which are as vital to successful outcomes as work on the speech itself.

Children can react to their stammering with such emotions as embarrassment, frustration, anger or helplessness. Some stammering therapy programmes and other materials created for children who do not stammer, can be helpful. Guitar (2006), amongst others, provides therapy information aimed at addressing emotional reactions to stammering and reducing sensitivity and avoidance. Thoughts about stammering can be addressed using forms of cognitive therapy such as that provided by McNeil *et al.* (2003) in the Swindon Packs.

Wider communication issues will be addressed in the older child, improving social skills, such as good listening and eye contact. Developing effective problem-solving skills also enables the young client to manage social issues and their stammer directly.

In the teenage years, therapy will need to help the client come to terms with the increased likelihood of a persistent stammer. Teaching easier ways of stammering contributes to this, but work on positive attitudes towards communication, good social skills and the ability to make life choices, independent of the stammer, all minimise the restrictions that may result from persistent stammering. Many of these issues can be addressed most effectively through therapy delivered in a group setting (see Chapter 7). Should group therapy not be available within the therapist's area, s/he can consider referral to one of the specialist centres offering intensive group stammering therapy in the UK, some of which is on a residential basis.

Working on co-existing communication difficulties

General assessment of the younger child may reveal deficits in the child's speech and language development that lower their capacity for fluency or which create demands, for example, delayed language, disordered phonology, poor oral motor performance or word finding difficulties.

When using the Lidcombe Program it is recommended that only stammering should be treated during Stage 1. Therapists using other therapy approaches, however, should not be afraid to address other communication disorders in therapy, although it is recommended that phonology is approached initially through listening and discrimination activities.

If felt to be primary contributory factors, speech and language may be addressed before attempting direct therapy on the stammering, as increasing capacity may improve fluency. Alternatively, they may be worked on concurrently with direct therapy on fluency, spending part of each therapy session on each component. Some language therapy can be blended into fluency exercises and for the younger child with delayed language, the Palin PCI approach may promote language development. A cyclic approach is also possible which may allow for spontaneous gains while one target is temporarily dropped from therapy to work on an alternative.

Therapists need to use their judgement as to whether and how working on other issues may increase or decrease demands for the child. If it is not possible to make such a judgement with available information, trial therapy may be needed.

School or pre-school liaison

Whatever the age of the child, the therapist will aim to increase the understanding of stammering in pre-school or school staff and pupils. They can help staff to create a supportive environment, and, if necessary, deal with teasing and bullying. There are excellent written resources (Rustin et al. 2001), and online video materials by the British Stammering Association. The Stammering Information Programme DVD 'Wait, wait I'm not finished yet' can be used by therapists for training purposes.

Successful outcomes and discharge

Therapy may be judged to be successful by different criteria depending on the age of the child, type of stammer, circumstances of therapy and resources available. Many of the assessment tools described previously can be employed as outcome measures or alternatively there are a small number of specifically designed outcome measures. Manning (2010) provides a comprehensive list and description of assessments and outcome measures. For example, the Yairi and Ambrose (2005) severity rating scale gives a numerical rating (from zero to seven), based on percentage of stammered syllables, duration of stammers and degree of tension and secondary behaviours observed. Covert features can be measured using the Communication Attitude Test (Brutten and Vanryckeghem 2007). More holistic outcome measures such as OASES (Yaruss and Quesal 2011) are in the process of development. These are for school age children and adolescents and measure change in overt, covert and other aspects of stammering, including quality of life.

Discharge following successful therapy will not be judged on fluency alone, but also on the reduction of negative thoughts and feelings, avoidance strategies and an increase in the child's ability and enjoyment in communicating. In addition, therapy should facilitate change in the communication environment of the child, both at home and at school, in order that the child can achieve his/her fluency potential and also function fully in a supportive environment, free of the negative reactions of others.

For example, for a young child, referred early with low risk factors, therapy should end when the child achieves normal fluency for at least six months. The case example, Alex, was referred relatively early after onset of stammering. However, he is at high risk of persistent stammering as he is male, his mother has a persistent stammer and he has delayed phonology. His recovery may, therefore, be slow and therapy must allow for this. It is possible that, despite early intervention, his stammer will persist and therapy aims will need to be revised accordingly.

Ben, is less likely to recover spontaneously as he is older, male and has been stammering for four years. The aim of therapy, therefore, could be successful use of a fluency technique.

Therapy should aim to build a positive attitude to communication in Ben, and his parents should be equipped with skills to manage variations in fluency. He may require a number of blocks of therapy until he reaches a comfortable level of fluency, he is communicating effectively and freely, and his parents and teachers feel equipped to help Ben manage his stammer. Although he is at high risk of persistent stammering, the possibility of recovery cannot be ruled out.

By the teenage years, it is unlikely that Carl will achieve complete fluency, and he will benefit most from group therapy with peers. A positive outcome of therapy would be the successful use of a combination of fluency techniques and easy stammering. He could be discharged when his confidence, communication and social skills were sufficiently good to enable him to manage speaking situations without avoidance. His attitude to himself and his stammer should also be sufficiently positive to enable him to make decisions about education and employment based on factors other than his stammer. He may return to therapy a number of times as life challenges change and he can benefit from learning new strategies as he matures.

Summary

The highly individual nature of stammering, and changing needs as children develop into teenagers, demand flexibility and perseverance from the therapist. Appropriate assessment and familiarity with a range of therapy approaches will enable selection of an appropriate pathway for each individual. Less experienced therapists may initially follow a therapy programme in its entirety, later using their clinical judgement to combine elements from different programmes. Successful outcomes will range from some young children achieving normal fluency, to others developing into well-adjusted young adults, for whom stammering is not the problem that it may have been without therapy.

Chapter 19

Children with severe learning disabilities

Celia Harding

Learning outcomes

By the end of this chapter, the reader will have:

- an understanding of pre-verbal communication development;
- knowledge about the tools to assess children with severe and profound learning disabilities;
- knowledge of strategies to consider for intervention to support children with severe and profound learning disabilities.

Introduction

This chapter focuses on working with children who have severe and profound learning disabilities. They are likely to require significant levels of support to enable them to understand and participate in their daily lives. Within the UK the term 'learning disabilities' (LD), is used to describe people who have learning needs. Children with more severe and profound needs are also described as having 'complex needs'.

Definition

The World Health Organisation (2006) ICD-10 defines learning disability as 'a condition of arrested or incomplete development of the mind'. In addition to this, it is recognised that there is also likely to be a reduced level of intellectual functioning and difficulties with adaptive behaviour as well as deficits in psychological and emotional functioning.

Epidemiology/prevalence

Within the UK, the Department of Health estimates that there are approximately 210,000 people of all ages with severe learning disabilities, and that potentially there are around 1.2 million people with mild/moderate learning disabilities (DH 2009). The National Statistics Office suggests that about 2 per cent of the UK population have some level of learning disability. It is recognised that there is no official statistic which accurately reflects this population.

The children referred to in this chapter are those who have severe learning disabilities (SLD) and profound and multiple learning disabilities (PMLD). Across the range of learning disabilities there are some core aspects that are central to disability as a whole. People with LD have difficulties with academic achievement and progress. Discrepancies may exist between a person's potential for learning and what s/he actually learns. So, for example, a child may have a certain level of cognition and receptive language skills, but may be using language and communication skills of a lower competence in relation to cognition and receptive function (Grove and Dockrell 2000; Harding *et al.* 2010).

Range of difficulties

Because of their learning disabilities, these children are at high risk of displaying an uneven pattern of development in the areas of language, physical development, academic achievement and/or perceptual development. Due to attention difficulties there may be problems with selecting information, filtering distractions, sustaining attention, habituation, transfer and general language processing skills. Children with learning difficulties have reduced joint attention behaviours and are therefore at risk of not developing communication skills that are representative of their potential (Cress and Marvin 2004). The development of joint attention and attention skills during social interaction are important for social competence, language learning and the development of receptive skills (Striano *et al.* 2006).

Verbal memory is also an area of difficulty in many individuals with LD (Merrill *et al.* 2003). This is a skill necessary for rehearsal of information, and is well developed by the time a child reaches seven years of age. Children with LD do not easily show spontaneous rehearsal skills.

Metacognitive skills include recall, self-monitoring, reality testing, generalisation, coordinating and controlling learning, inventiveness and flexibility of thinking. Children with LD tend to have difficulties in this area and with information adaptation and may also find generalisation of newly learnt language skills hard (Merrill *et al.* 2003). This is going to be even more of a challenge for children with SLD and PMLD where the level of support required to facilitate communication opportunities will be greater.

Children with SLD frequently show in their history some evidence of brain pathology, and it is likely that they may have other physical impairments (Emerson and Hatton 2004). Children with SLD are less likely to lead independent lives compared with children who have more moderate learning disabilities. They are also more likely to have significant receptive and expressive communication difficulties. About 80 per cent of people with SLD fail to develop effective speech and/or language skills and are highly likely to require access to augmentative and alternative communication (AAC) to promote communication opportunities; 20 per cent have no verbal skills, but demonstrate some level of communicative intent; around 20 per cent have no intentional communication skills (DH 2009).

Other sensory and health issues could significantly impact on the potential to develop competent speech, language, communication and social skills. Hearing, vision and epilepsy are more likely to be evident within this population (Kerr *et al.* 2003). Mental health difficulties tend to have a higher prevalence rate and after excluding challenging behaviours, prevalence rates are between 25 and 40 per cent compared with 25 per cent within the normal population. For further discussion see Emerson (2003). These issues need to be evaluated carefully during case history taking as they will impact on any intervention plan.

The importance of pre-verbal communication

It is important as a practitioner to be aware of the early sequence of pre-verbal development as this will provide information on how to make a clear distinction between pre-intentional and intentional interaction with children who have complex needs. The following section is a summary of pre-verbal development and should provide a framework for considering the level of the child with whom the therapist is working.

Pre-intentional stage (0–9 months)

At the beginning of the pre-intentional stage, an infant is likely to react to events rather than initiate contact with others. This is known as being reflexive. This is followed by the infant learning how to react to events, things and people. These reactions become more differentiated, as they perceive consistencies and develop specific preferences. Once the infant begins to establish some consistent patterns within the routine, then anticipatory skills develop. At this time, individuals learn about consistent sequences of events, and are able to anticipate or predict. So, for example, they will open their mouths when they hear a spoon in a cup, or quieten when they hear a familiar person coming upstairs. Alongside this development, awareness and sensitivity to person-specific voices and to prosodic and affective aspects of language and their association with particular contexts develops (Bloom 1993; Bruner 1978).

An awareness of the feelings of others is evident at one month, in that infants will cry in response to hearing other babies cry. At four months, infants respond to melodic and pitch cues, and by five months there is a developing ability to express interest, pleasure, fear, anger, sadness and distress in interactive contexts. This expression becomes more refined at six months to include joy, interest, anger, sadness and surprise. Infants will also respond differently to facial expressions and vocalisations of others.

From early on, infants vocalise in 'conversations' with caregivers. At first, carers fit their vocalisations around those of infants, but gradually infants take a more active role. True smiles emerge at around six weeks. Smiling is socially regulated from the beginning. Three month old infants take an active part in social interaction, altering gaze behaviour according to where mothers are gazing. They appear to prefer to gaze at the mother when she is looking at them. Mutual gaze is critical to the development of joint attention. Basic imitation is evident early on, usually restricted to opening mouths and protruding tongues (Bruner 1978).

Towards the end of the pre-intentional stage, at 6–9 months, babies begin to develop goal-directed interactions with the world. They form intentions to achieve certain ends and are persistent in realising these intentions. For example, they may reach for something that they wish to explore, persist in attempting to gain an outcome, alter their behaviour if a strategy does not work and express satisfaction when a goal is achieved.

From around six months, babies typically demonstrate that they have acquired goal-oriented behaviours. From this time, the mother's behaviour changes; she attributes both meaning and intent to her baby's behaviour, but not to all behaviours. Significant behaviours that cue mothers at this stage were vocalisations, looking and hand/arm gestures. Mothers seem to try to ensure that their infants achieved their presumed intention (Bloom 1993).

Intentional stage (9–12 months)

At this stage infants start to overtly signal their communicative intentions to others and their behaviour is both purposeful and social. They may use gaze to check an adult's response, or they will actively seek out someone for social interaction or comfort. If an adult does not respond immediately, or fails to respond, a child will make another attempt to gain that adult's attention.

Key skills that are emerging include an awareness of specific phrases and key words. There will also be an awareness of gestures and facial expressions during interactions. The most obvious gestures in development include reaching, pointing, waving and clapping that are incorporated into social routines.

At about this time, infants begin to produce utterances that are used in social contexts. Immediately prior to the emergence of first words, therefore, normally developing infants can express a variety of communicative intentions that include: expression of feelings, requesting, protesting, rejecting, commenting and some social responses.

How parents and carers respond to infants

Parents and carers actively scaffold interactions with infants using vocalisations, gestures and facial expression so that it appears like a conversation. They observe the infant, and then alter their communication to respond by encouraging what the infant does and feeding back an interpretation of the vocalisation heard. Parents often interpret the vocalisations as meaningful and this creates early interactive routines.

Early communication and learning disability

The infant with a learning disability will be developing more slowly than normally developing infants of the same chronological age. They are also likely to have some associated motor or sensory impairments that will have an impact on the ability to signal affect, engage in gaze and joint attention, and develop request behaviours. The ability to interpret the behaviour of children functioning at the earliest stages of communicative development may be compromised because they do not communicate in conventional ways; or their expressions may be the result of physical rather than communicative factors. In children with complex needs, behavioural state is likely to be variable, with levels of alertness and activity changing within short periods (Guess *et al.* 1993).

Children with disabilities have very specific needs. Babbling interactions are a much slower process, with children requiring longer periods of time to process information. The development of gaze behaviours, in particular mutual gaze and shared attention may develop later, or in a more inconsistent way. Intentional behaviours may exist, but be initiated in an idiosyncratic way, and, therefore, only be known to familiar people involved in that child's care. Developing request behaviours through pointing, touching and showing, together with natural gestures may be used less spontaneously and require greater prompting.

Assessment

When assessing, given the complexity of the caseload, it is important for therapists to focus on the purpose of their assessment. They will need to consider the nature and severity of the language/communication impairment as well as the background information (Abudarham and Hurd 2002). If it is known that the child has a diagnosis of Down syndrome, for example, it is possible to anticipate that they will have language and vocabulary needs. However, pragmatic skills may be a strength. Receptive language with such children is often well supported by visual information in the environment including signing, and expressive skills are often supported and facilitated by the use of signs. Using checklists and relevant assessments can highlight strengths as well as needs, and can also contribute to goal planning and outcome measurement (Enderby *et al.* 2006). Such approaches can be used again later to measure progress, re-appraise skills and for future planning.

Pre-assessment preparation and information gathering may provide important information. This could be done by relying on parents to fill in a detailed questionnaire before the therapist meets the child, or it could involve sending a photograph and some information for a parent to discuss with a child to prepare them. Therapists may work in a team where there are informal groups to meet clients and carers before beginning an episode of care. This allows them to discuss expectations, and plan an assessment.

Deciding what to assess

When assessing children with SLD and PMLD, observation within familiar routines will be essential. It is important to explore how a child engages with others and with a variety of activities. Important information will be gained by observing how a child responds to day-to-day routines, compared to less frequent experiences. The therapist will assess a child's ability to socially engage with others in order to see if the child can seek attention, make someone stop an activity, give information, share attention and/or maintain an interaction. The therapist will also want to know if the child can engage with a stimulus that is non-social and maintain their attention. If they can, can they be distracted from it to pursue another task? If not, is the behaviour stereotypic? Are there other behaviours that the child is showing that indicate challenging behaviour such as self-injury, or other non-purposeful behaviours such as spitting or tugging at someone? If these are observed, then what are the triggers for these, if any? In contrast, it may be useful to observe any disengagement states – what happens when the child chooses to opt out of an activity.

The following checklists offer a range of information that can provide frameworks on which to base observations with this particular group of children. None of these are norm-referenced, but give clear and comprehensive detail in relation to pre-verbal skills, both at the receptive and expressive level. For example, the Pre-Verbal Communication Schedule (Kiernan *et al.* 1987) provides areas to explore with children such as needs and preferences, communication mode, i.e. whole body movement or signs, and what sort of strategies support a child to enable them to understand and express themselves. As this checklist moves from pre-verbal to verbal skills it is useful for practitioners who work with primary school aged children who may be considered to have the ability to make some changes in their communication profile with intervention.

The Triple C: the Checklist of Communication Competencies (Bloomberg *et al.* 2009) is usually recommended for older children and teenagers, and can also be used with adults, therefore being useful as a tool for transition work, as can the Inventory of Potential Communicative Acts (Sigafoos *et al.* 2000). The Pragmatics Profile (Dewart and Summers 1995) is differentiated across the age range and can provide useful structure for observing children in different social settings. For more severe difficulties, the Affective Communication Assessment (Coupe and Goldbart 1998) can be used to explore how a child responds to different stimuli, thereby allowing people to gain a clearer profile of needs, likes and dislikes. Using these checklists can provide information on how to support children further as well as providing data that can contribute towards outcome measures.

Other aspects to consider

Parents of children with learning disabilities seem to have more difficulties adjusting to their child's communication and interaction style, especially if AAC is used. AAC can slow the rate of a communication interaction, and parents often find implementing some of the AAC strategies challenging. Research has shown that interactions between carers and children with LD generally tend to be more directive. A study by Dahlgren and Liliedhal (2008) identified mothers as using a much higher level of initiations compared to norm-matched pairs. They were not as responsive to their children's less-definite communication attempts. They used more words and rarely paused to allow for processing.

Decisions about intervention

How to support early communication

Speech and language therapists will be actively involved in modelling and training of various strategies, for children and their carers, that can promote and support communication. People with PMLD are likely to function at a pre-linguistic level throughout their lives, but they may still benefit from speech and language therapy support and make progress. Some of the decisions about the type of intervention can be seen in the following case example.

Case example

Abdi is 14 years of age. He has cerebral palsy and is hypotonic so he requires supportive seating. He is described as having severe hearing impairment and visual difficulties.

Attention and listening. Abdi appears to be passive to environmental stimuli, such as voices and sounds. However, he smiles or appears to focus intently on faces and smiles when brightly coloured objects are presented to him.

Understanding. Abdi interacts with his environment when prompted by touch and by movement. Abdi appears to show consistent responses, i.e. smiling and/or focusing when people sit close to him so he can see their facial expression, or when brightly coloured objects are presented to him.

Expressive skills. Abdi can indicate response to his environment by crying, smiling, frowning, body movement and by closing his eyes. He does not use vocalisations to initiate or respond.

Abdi's strengths. Abdi appears to show that he likes something by changes in his facial expression. He seems to relax when held in rocking games. When Abdi closes his eyes it seems to indicate that a task has finished. None of these strengths are consistent, and significant others in his life interact in different ways to the same responses.

Abdi's intervention. Video material was used in training for parents, staff and carers. This was essential when discussing his communication style and responsiveness. Video was also used to help chart his progress and the development of his skills, in discussion with the team.

Intervention also involved looking at Abdi's responses and providing facilitation through touch, repetition and use of praise. Video was used to record Abdi's non-verbal communication during these activities.

Objects of Reference

The most useful starting point is to explore how well the environment and caregivers' interactions are adapted to a child's needs. The therapist should make decisions about how the environment can be utilised to support a child's communication skills. Structure may be achieved, for example, through the use of Objects of Reference (Park 2002), and multi-sensory experiences such as taste, smell and voice recognition are important as receptive language markers. Originally developed for people with sensory impairments, Objects of Reference are tools that can support children functioning at a pre-symbolic level of development, and can enable them to maximise their communicative effectiveness (Harding *et al.* 2010).

Objects are used to inform children what is going to happen. Once they are familiar with them the objects may be used as a way of offering choices. It is important to start at the right level and not make too many demands on the child. The best starting point is an index, i.e. an object which the person actually uses in the activity. The next level is an icon, an object which represents something typically used in the activity. The most demanding is a symbol, an object which has no necessary connection with the activity, but the association is learned through a specific core feature.

Case example

Paul is 6 years of age. He is independently mobile. He has a visual impairment though his hearing is within normal limits.

Attention and listening. Paul needs to be guided by touch. Repetition and simplified language are needed to gain his attention, particularly in a group context.

Understanding. Paul uses smiling, vocalisation and whole body movement to indicate his responses to people. He turns to sounds and appears to comprehend sounds within routines. He stops crying when he hears a familiar voice and attempts to localise the source. He responds to basic phrases by attempting to turn towards the target person/item, e.g. 'Here's mummy', 'Where's your cup?' He seems to like feeling objects in order to understand what is happening. Informal assessment indicates a receptive level of language of about 15–18 months.

Expressive skills. Paul vocalises with intent. He can imitate some sounds and words. He waves spontaneously when people leave and he points if he is near an activity where there is an item of interest. He likes to hold up an object and vocalise, e.g. a ball if he wishes to engage in an activity with an adult. He uses approximately seven words, usually after an adult has provided a verbal and signed/gestured model. The words are: yes, no, more, hiya, bye, Mum, up, his sister's name, his LSA's name, Papa. Spontaneous initiation of his own specific vocabulary is rare, although he will spontaneously vocalise with intent to gain attention from others. Informal assessment indicates an expressive performance of 12–15 months.

Paul's strengths. He is responsive to strategies to gain his attention such as touch, repetition and simplified language. There is some intent to use vocalisations and gestures, plus some word approximations when he is motivated to have another turn, or if he wishes to gain someone's attention.

Intervention for Paul. Objects were chosen to be presented within his field of vision and near enough for him to touch them. Their principle use with Paul was to promote expressive opportunities.

A range of objects was selected on the basis of needs and motivation to facilitate choice and help him to express his needs The objects were to be used mainly through the medium of touch due to his visual impairment. They included bubbles, balloon, paper, cup, spoon, plate, drum, tambourine, whistle, shaker and bells. Paul's hands were moulded into the sign/gesture shapes and he received physical prompting for more, hello and bye. Implementation involved use of verbal prompts and helping Paul to feel two items/objects pre-specifying a choice. Giving him time to respond was part of the strategy.

Individualised Sensory Environments

For children who have more profound needs, Individualised Sensory Environments (Bunning 1997) may provide interaction opportunities. The aim is to influence the interactive behaviours of the child in the natural environment. In particular, the aim is to reduce non-purposeful engagement, characterised either by stereotypic behaviour and self-injury, or extreme passivity, and to increase purposeful interaction with people and objects. Other environments such as sensory rooms can be used to focus on developing and consolidating communication skills using various media.

Intensive Interaction

Intensive Interaction (Nind and Hewett 1994) is another approach that uses techniques from early interaction to foster awareness of other people and creative interaction opportunities as well as understanding how a child communicates pre-verbally. Intensive Interaction is often successful in increasing initiation of interaction. It may also lead to a decrease in stereotypic behaviours. This approach is also used as a precursor to implementing an AAC system as it can provide valuable information about a child's communication potential.

'Milieu' approach

Most therapists working with children will want to engage with their familiar environment and routine, and are likely to work in these contexts. One approach is the 'milieu' approach (Yoder and Warren 2001), where the environment is modified to provide naturalistic reinforcers and systematic procedures to develop, sustain and generalise behaviour. This focuses specifically on utilising natural visual and tactile props, facial expression, intonation and natural gesture, the premise being that these are essential foundations to support and maximise communicative opportunities.

AAC

The main types of AAC support for children and young people with SLD and PMLD include use of Objects of Reference, tactile and visual support, intonation, and basic switch use such as a Big Mack switch. This is a communication device which allows simple sound recording of a short message. Use of a simple switch like this can create some basic environmental control and communication opportunities.

Tactile and verbal cues as well as visual feedback can be used as support when teaching a child to use an AAC system and will help the child use it as independently as possible (Blairs *et al.* 2007). Signing can support receptive and expressive skills as auditory processing skills and memory may be impaired in this population, whereas visual-spatial skills are often a strength (Iverson and Goldin-Meadow 2005). Zampini and D'Odorico (2009) stress that use of gesture can support the comprehension of vocabulary and may lead to competent expressive use later. Some children with SLD may have the potential to learn some signs, and the speech and language therapist will be involved in the decision-making process about the use of signs. Simple eye-pointing frames, cause and effect switches and touch screens on the computer offer additional ways of helping children with SLD and PMLD to control their environment and communicate basic information (Schlosser 2003).

Purposeful listening can be improved by taking care with noise levels, using sound to cue activities and trying to avoid conversation that does not involve the children. Interactive opportunities will help provide a matrix for establishing the basic principles of early language development. This format provides an important foundation for building on increasing language skills.

Parents, carers, significant others and educators involved in the child's care need to be supported by the speech and language therapist to think about how they can promote communication opportunities on a daily basis. One important method can be to use video and/or observation to recognise the range of ways in which the child communicates. Modelling may need to take place to demonstrate how to respond contingently to communication initiations. It is also important to highlight communication strengths and indicate where communication needs to be developed or supported.

Communication Passport

All children and young people, particularly if they are changing environments, e.g. from nursery to school provision, or from a school to adult services, benefit from some form of visually presented information that they can share with significant others. A Communication Passport provides collated information about the child and how they communicate. It can be in a book or chart and needs to be made available to all who work with the child. A multi-media profile (Ladle 2004), is a computer version of a Communication Passport. This has the added bonus that the child can access dynamic images relevant to their life with sound through video clips and photographs stored on file. It can be opened via a touch screen or switch. An important part of the process is that the child or young person needs to be an active participant in the creation of the multi-media profile.

Summary

This chapter has summarised the essential aspects of pre-verbal communication and its importance in the lives with children who have complex needs. Support to enable children with SLD and PMLD needs to be both extensive and pervasive to their daily lives to make a meaningful impact on them and those around them.

Chapter 20

Children with acquired speech and language problems

Janet Lees

Learning outcomes

By the end of this chapter the reader should have improved their knowledge and understanding of:

- the distinction between developmental and acquired speech and language problems (ASLP) in childhood;
- the main causes of ASLP in childhood;
- some of the models relevant to managing children with ASLP;
- the selection of assessment tools appropriate for children with ASLP;
- the best available external evidence for the management of ASLP and the role of the speech and language therapist.

Introduction

This chapter is about speech and language problems which are secondary to cerebral dysfunction, arising in childhood after a period of normal development. They are called acquired speech and language problems (ASLP). Normal development proceeds as a result of cerebral maturation, and developmental disorders are a result of a delay or disorder in that maturation, the causes of which have been shown to be environmental and/or biological in origin. Acquired speech and language disorders, most commonly encountered when working with adult clients, are typically the result of an interruption to normal cerebral functioning. Thus, children, irrespective of age will be said to have an acquired disorder if normal cerebral functioning is interrupted, after it has been established, however briefly. Developmental disorders may persist throughout the lifespan, or acquired disorders may occur at any stage. It is important to understand how and why developmental and acquired disorders differ, particularly for different age groups.

The development of evidence-based practice has been of increasing importance in speech and language therapy. It has three basic principles: the best available external evidence, the therapist's clinical knowledge and expertise and the informed preference of the client/patient/user or their parents if this is a child (Stringer 2010). The management of ASLP in children that is advocated in this chapter will be based on the best external evidence. However, this area still attracts little research interest so that building knowledge and expertise may take more time than with more commonly presenting conditions. Furthermore, supporting the development of informed preference in service users and their parents can be more difficult in rare conditions.

Epidemiology

Developmental problems dominate the speech and language therapist's work with children. Each child is born with a certain developmental potential. It is the development of this potential that is the focus of attention during childhood. Acquired problems are rare in the first 20 years of life. Risk factors are likely to differ according to aetiology and they may also differ from the same aetiology in adults. They are frequently numerous and often complex (Roach 2000; Carter *et al.* 2003). However, more recently there has been a general increase in the chances of having an acquired basis for a communication problem during the second decade. This has been due to factors like the increased chance of survival from traumatic brain injury in those under 20 years of age and other progress in paediatric critical care. There are no epidemiological data concerning developmental versus acquired communication problems in childhood. The only UK figures, by Robinson (1991), suggested that acquired aphasias account for less than 10 per cent of the language problems presenting in childhood.

These figures also point to a 'grey area' somewhere between developmental and acquired problems. Clinically it can be difficult to answer the question, 'When is a problem an acquired problem?' For example, the origin of the language problem was uncertain for approximately 7 per cent of Robinson's (1991) sample. Included in the sample were children who had an incident within either the first or second year of life which was later thought to have contributed to their communication problem. It also included children who clearly had delayed development but who later lost some of their skills gradually or suddenly. This 'greyness' in diagnosis contributes to the complexity of managing children with ASLP.

Furthermore, epidemiology of ASLP is a changing field. There has been a fall in some types of cerebral infections, such as some types of meningitis, due to effective immunisation programmes in the UK which have led to changes in morbidity and mortality in some 'at risk' groups. In other parts of the world, a different pathogenesis occurs, such as the role of cerebral malaria as a cause of ASLP in countries like Kenya where severe malaria is a leading cause of childhood disability.

Models

There are a number of different models that can be used to understand the effects on a child of ASLP. When planning services for children who have ASLP and their families it is preferable to work in a way which draws on all of these models in order to get a holistic picture of the child. In this chapter these three models will be used interactively.

- A *Medical Model* emphasises the malfunctioning of a particular body system and the nature of the impairment that results from this. It enables the therapist to appreciate the causes of impairments and types of cerebral dysfunction which usually underlie these.
- A *Psycholinguistic Model* (Stackhouse and Wells 1997) emphasises what has gone wrong in the linguistic process and enables the development of working hypotheses which can be tested clinically. This model can be used to demonstrate ways in which these speech and language processing difficulties can be assessed and managed.
- In a *Social Model* children are viewed within context, in order to understand the effect of the communication impairment on their functioning. Each child's context is fundamental to the rehabilitation process and this model enables discussion of important contextual questions in the management of children with ASLP.

Causes of acquired aphasias in childhood

The brain is the vital organ in the processing of language, speech and communication. It is particularly vulnerable during childhood. There are a number of different disease processes which can affect the brain during childhood and lead to an acquired aphasia. These do not necessarily result in the same types of speech and language problems, or problems which have the same duration or prognosis. This is because the disease processes themselves affect the brain tissue in different ways and also because the brain will have reached a different level of maturation depending approximately on age.

It used to be thought that children were relatively resistant to long term speech and language difficulties after early brain injury. Reviews of more recent evidence have suggested different conclusions. Significant brain injury is likely to have long term consequences for the child at any age regardless of the mechanism of cerebral injury. Long term deficits have been reported subsequent to sub-cortical brain infarcts (Gout *et al.* 2005), focal brain lesions (Chilosi *et al.* 2008), focal epilepsies (Parkinson 2002) and cerebral infections like malaria (Carter *et al.* 2006) amongst others. The severity and duration of these deficits are dependent on several factors, which cannot yet be mapped precisely to outcome but the recovery from ASLP in children now appears to be less complete than previously thought (Paquier and Van Dongen 1995).

There is a distinction between a condition which has an acute onset and one that has a chronic onset. In the first the child presents with symptoms straight away, or very quickly, and in the second the symptoms are slower to emerge, perhaps being preceded by a period of developmental regression or loss of skills over several weeks or months. The main causes of acquired aphasias in childhood and some of the ensuing problems and prognoses have been summarised below (see also Lees 2005).

Other cases of ASLP in children have been described, for example subsequent to tapeworm parasite in the temporal lobe, or other disorders of developmental regression in childhood, the aetiologies of which may be hard to establish. In general the poorest prognosis is usually in those in which the greatest range of skills is lost or severe epilepsy occurs, and those which show little response to treatment in the first six months after onset.

Focal versus diffuse injury

The damage to brain tissue can be described as focal or diffuse and this will depend on the sort of injury the child received.

Focal injury is localised and usually lateralised, involving only one cerebral hemisphere. Diffuse injury is more widespread and can be bilateral. Subsequent injury might arise from:

- oedema (swelling);
- neurosurgery undertaken to help stabilise the condition;
- seizure activity secondary to the injury.

Focal brain injury is likely to have different consequences to diffuse injury. After focal injury, specific impairments are likely as a result of underlying damage. For example, a kick by a horse to the left side of the head above the ear led to non-fluent aphasia with severe word-finding difficulties in a 14 year old girl. A non-fluent aphasia is characterised by telegrammatic sentences, in which small function words and unstressed morphemes may be omitted and the style is hesitant.

In fluent aphasia there is a larger volume of words in the flow of speech although sentences may not be completely grammatical or semantically correct. Studies have suggested that the features of fluent and non-fluent aphasias are as likely to be found in the expressive language of aphasic children as they are in aphasic adults (Van Dongen *et al.* 2001).

Diffuse injury is more likely to result in non-specific difficulties in speech and the amount of information that can be processed and recalled. Or, it may lead to high level deficits of metalinguistic skills such as misunderstanding or misuse of prosodic features like stress to mark grammatical differences between sentences. For example, a 16 year old boy, three years after a severe head injury, seemed to have made a good recovery except for a continuing difficulty in distinguishing between question and exclamatory forms of similar sentences.

Table 20.1 Causes, problems and prognoses of acquired aphasia

Cause	Damage	Problems	Prognosis
Head injury open/closed	Diffuse and bilateral. May be combined with additional focal damage.	May include motor, cognitive, sensory deficits. Epilepsy may be a sequela.	Poor if initial aphasia very severe and persists for 6+ months. Acquisition of written language may be impaired.
Unilateral cerebrovascular lesions	Usually focal, may be subsequent to cortical or subcortical damage.	Visual field defects, hemiplegia may also occur. Epilepsy may be a sequela.	Good, if there is a return to within two standard deviations for verbal comprehension score within 6 months of onset.
Cerebral infections: meningitis, encephalitis, cerebral abscess	Ranges from diffuse to focal depending on aetiology and response to treatment.	Additional motor, cognitive, sensory deficits are common in severe cases.	Where damage is cortical the aphasia is usually moderate to mild.
Cerebral tumour	Usually focal; disruption of wider cerebral function possible if tumour extends or after the effects of some treatment.	An initial delayed period of mutism is common after surgery for some posterior fossa tumours. Epilepsy may be a sequela.	Additional treatments (radiotherapy / chemotherapy) can affect prognosis for speech and language abilities.
Epileptic aphasia	Aphasia may occur as a consequence of convulsive status.	Learning problems may occur, particularly after long and repeated convulsive status.	Language disturbance is variable.
Landau-Kleffner syndrome	May be preceded or followed by epilepsy.	Characterised by severe receptive aphasia, but other language problems can occur.	Variable.
Rett syndrome	Developmental disorder: motor and cognitive skills lost between 6 and 12 months.	Inappropriate social interaction, slowing of head growth, severe communication difficulties, abnormal oral movements.	No known recovery.

Prognosis

There are many factors which affect prognosis and consequently will affect the decisions made about management. These include:

- age at injury;
- extent/severity of injury;
- developmental level/status before injury;
- profile and severity of initial communication deficit;
- extent of initial recovery;
- access to services/resources for rehabilitation.

Children who sustain a brain injury when very young may appear to do better in some domains of function but lose out in others, such as the acquisition of more complex, highly integrated and flexible functioning. Not everyone working with children with brain injury will be aware of current research regarding age and susceptibility. The brain is most vulnerable during the first 16 years or so of development. The frontal lobes do not mature until adolescence. Thus both early and late injuries can have long term effects.

It is important to measure the extent or severity of injury and to try to establish the level of functioning prior to the injury. However, this may be difficult to establish although school records, family videos and discussion with appropriate relatives and friends may help.

Profiling the severity of initial communication difficulty can only be partial, and a comprehensive profile will need to be built up during the course of recovery. A multidimensional scoring system such as in the POSP (Brindley *et al.* 1996) will show how the child functions and where progress is occurring. Even so, most children with ASLP go through a short burst of initial recovery that, for some at least, will take them back to functioning within the normal range. When this happens it does not mean that the child's recovery will be trouble free or that later problems may not become apparent, especially where more complex learning is concerned.

However, the most contentious and under-researched aspect of recovery from ASLP is the contribution of rehabilitation or therapy. There are relatively few single case studies available. Access to specialist rehabilitation centres is often difficult to gain, and these are not spread uniformly across the country.

There are few published studies of rehabilitation of children with ASLP. The Paediatric Stroke Working Group (2004) found little evidence of the effectiveness of rehabilitation specifically for children affected by stroke. Few other comprehensive reviews have been carried out for other causes of ASLP in children. General rehabilitation advice includes the need to aim for 'relevant skills in all domains of activity and care appropriate to a child's home, school and community context' (Lees 2005, p. 53). Where a therapist is working with children with ASLP it is considered good professional practice to become a member of a Special Interest Group (SIG). A national network of these is promoted by the RCSLT.

A number of voluntary support networks have sprung up to provide information in what, for most families, prove to be difficult circumstances. The most well known are Afasic, CHIT (Children's Head Injury Trust) and FOLKS (Friends of Landau-Kleffner Syndrome). These can help families to become informed service users. Different Strokes seeks to do this for young stroke survivors.

When considering prognosis, it is important to remember that significant residual problems may persist for at least two years for children who are between 2 and 15 years of age at the time of onset of the aphasia. Even mild residual deficits may cause significant problems, often quite specific ones, particularly those affecting speed and amount of processing or recall. For example, a 13 year old girl made an excellent recovery in terms of formal language test scores but continued to have auditory processing difficulties three years after her stroke. This made classroom learning difficult for her (Lees 1997).

The extent to which a difficulty is of significance to the child, and therefore influences management decisions, depends on a variety of factors such as the presence of linked residual deficits. These include epilepsy, behaviour problems and other learning difficulties. In an unpublished study of 34 children surviving coma it was found that linked residual deficits were more commonly encountered in children who went on to have special educational needs. The coping characteristics of the individual and family and the rehabilitation resources available are also important factors. It is, therefore, important to describe in detail children's communication skills, their strengths and weaknesses, rather than using labels which may not adequately summarise the difficulties.

As children get older it is important that they play an informed part in the management of their condition, particularly as some studies have shown impairments persisting into adulthood (see Chilosi et al. 2008 for an example of a 20 year follow up of children with acquired aphasia).

Assessment and management

A systematic approach to assessment and management by the speech and language therapist can be based on:

- knowing what to do;
- knowing how to do it;
- knowing when to do it;
- knowing when to stop.

Knowing what to do

On referral all children need to be assessed in order to establish the areas of difficulties and the child's strengths from which intervention may be planned. Before beginning an assessment, the speech and language therapist needs to know about the nature and characteristics of acquired communication problems in children and the type of progress which may be expected. The therapist also needs to know about the strengths and weaknesses of different assessment approaches and a wide range of assessment materials relevant to culture and context (Carter et al. 2005).

Assessment is normally ongoing throughout the therapist's involvement with the child because it also includes information about:

- the child's progress with treatment;
- whether the child's problems have resolved;
- whether new problems can be identified.

Acquired communication difficulties arising from a disruption in cerebral function can be divided into three main groups:

- language disorders;
- speech disorders;
- social communication disorders.

Assessment approaches may be formal or informal. The strengths and weaknesses of these two approaches are reviewed by Lees (2005) and a wide range of issues related to assessment including scoring systems and useful assessment materials have also been reviewed there. It is important to assess all areas of communicative function and all stages of speech and language processing. These assessments should be carried out in depth and over time in step with treatment programmes. They should be culturally appropriate (see Chapter 14).

For example, multi-dimensional scoring makes it possible for the therapist to determine from the pattern of errors which sections of the assessment cause the child most difficulty and thereby which aspects of speech and language are most affected. This can help the assessor understand what other problems may be contributing to low performance; problems such as poor attention, motor difficulties or slow response time.

In some assessments, the importance of understanding what makes children fail the test is recognised. Bishop (2003b) provided a vocabulary checklist in the Test for Reception of Grammar (TROG) to ensure that children are not seen as having grammatical problems when it is the vocabulary content of the sentences which is causing the difficulty. Bishop also identified two other types of responses for which it is important not to penalise children: the slow response, and the child's need for an item to be repeated.

Furthermore, German (2000) includes information about patterns of response in her Test of Word Finding, recognising that patterns of cueing and delay are important in understanding children's lexical recall problems and developing a treatment hypothesis. Again, a correct or incorrect response will only provide so much information about a child's naming problems. Naming difficulties may include different kinds of paraphasia (naming errors) such as those related semantically or phonemically to the target item as well as unrelated strings of phonemes (neologisms). Naming may be helped with gestural self-cueing or, for example, when phonemic cues are provided. This can help to generate treatment hypotheses based on suggestions about how the child's lexicon is organised and accessed. Knowing how a response relates to the target response is, therefore, as important as knowing if the response is correct or not.

Language problems – or aphasias

Children with ASLP display a range of language difficulties:

- non-fluent and fluent aphasias;
- paraphasias, lexical organisation and naming problems which can be persistent;
- comprehension and auditory processing problems which can occur in the majority including impaired repetition and auditory memory problems;
- linguistic deficits in reading and writing.

For a more detailed review of the subtypes of language difficulty see Lees (2005) and Paquier and Van Dongen (1995).

Following the acute stage, during each of the stages of recovery, the clinician will need to decide which tests to use to establish a profile of language skills. Some may use a battery which covers many sub-skills, like the CELF 4[uk] (Wiig and Semel 2006) or the pre-school version (Wiig et al. 2000). Others may prefer individual tests which tap particular skills, as described by Lees (2005). Some may prefer the TROG (Bishop 2003b) and the Test of Word Finding (German 2000). Psycholinguistic profiling techniques (Stackhouse and Wells 1997) may also be used.

Speech problems or dysarthrias

It should be noted that:

- dysarthrias arise in some conditions more often than in others (for example, when injury or dysfunction of the cerebellum is indicated, after surgery to remove tumours in the fourth ventricle, or head injury at the base of the back of the skull);

- they can co-occur with aphasias or other cognitive deficits;
- they can co-occur with swallowing problems (dysphagia) (see Chapter 22).

Most approaches to motor speech problems in children are informal and a structured approach as outlined by POSP (Brindley *et al.* 1996) may be useful.

Objective assessment may be difficult with children who have acquired motor speech problems as compliance can be difficult. Nasendoscopy may be available for viewing palatal movement, and for those who have associated dysphagia difficulties, videofluoroscopy has become invaluable.

Social communication disorders or autism spectrum disorders

Acquired autistic symptoms have been reported as resulting from a range of neurological diseases after three years of age.

Knowing how to do it

Few specific intervention techniques have been reported for children with ASLP, although single case studies such as Vance (1991, 1997) provide useful information.

- The use of AAC. This involves sign and symbol languages, pictures, objects and communication aids (see Chapter 21).
- A psycholinguistic framework for speech, reading and spelling difficulties (Vance 1997).
- Structured grammatical training such as Language Through Reading (see Vance 1991 and Van Slyke 2002).

As with other client groups, parents and professionals need to work in partnership (see Chapter 8). Therapists working with children who have acquired problems must be prepared to listen, to explain their philosophy and modify their approach. Three issues which are commonly raised during the rehabilitation of a child with ASLP are:

- the use of non-verbal communication which may or may not lead to more formalised AAC therapy;
- the benefits of individual versus group therapy (see Chapter 7);
- the differences in methods used by different speech and language therapists.

There is evidence that children with ASLP are at increased risk of behavioural difficulties. But they may also be at risk of problems of social integration due to the attitudes of others; stigma and bullying have all been reported by children and young people with ASLP. Underlying issues of low self-esteem and low self-confidence may also need to be addressed and the support of a child's peers could be harnessed through peer mentoring.

Some families see the introduction of AAC as a sign that verbal language will not be regained or may not be seriously pursued as a therapy option. There is often a stigma attached to the use of such methods of communication. Therapists need to explain the benefits which children may derive from the use of such communicative methods.

Equally the different benefits to be gained from group or individual therapy need to be explained. Communication is a social activity and spending therapy time in groups of different sizes may be a more natural way of developing aspects of communication.

It can be confusing for child and family when changes in personnel mean that therapy also changes for no apparent reason. Different methods of managing particular speech and language difficulties should be acknowledged and discussed with everyone involved, so that informed decisions can be made. All of these things can help the child and parents to become more informed service users.

Knowing when to do it

Lees and Urwin (1997) recommend that for children with ASLP speech and language therapy should:

- begin early;
- be intensive;
- be specific to the child's needs;
- be structured rather than just involving general language stimulation principles;
- be consistent;
- be built on the child's success.

Some professionals advocate that the child does not need structured intervention until the period of rapid recovery is over and the situation has stabilised so that residual deficits are more apparent. Loss of communication skills can be catastrophic to the child and to the family. Reactions to this loss can vary and those observed have included selective mutism. Early intervention by a speech and language therapist should aim to support the child and the family in relation to the communication loss. The exploration of modes and methods of communication which are functional for the child and family are important in this phase, even if they are used as a temporary measure. Part of the therapist's role is to raise the awareness of communication skills and strategies of all those involved in working with the child.

Dysphagia

Where dysphagia presents as part of the initial problem, a specialist paediatric dysphagia therapist needs to be involved. Such a specialist would help in establishing the extent and severity of the problem and advising about management, for example type of feeding, type of food. Most specialist dysphagia therapists work as part of a dysphagia team which will also include other specialists such as a dietician and psychologist (see Chapter 22).

Knowing when to stop

A child's need for therapy will change and develop due to:

- the course of recovery;
- changes due to drug treatment or surgery;
- changes due to developmental progress;
- changes due to social situation.

There are three phases in recovery from an acquired aphasia in childhood; acute, steady progress and plateau (Lees 2005). The length of each phase will vary depending on the child, the cause of the aphasia and its severity, so it is not possible to say, therefore, how long each phase will last. The main variables are the speed at which the child's communication skills change and how quickly goals are reached. The main decision-making issues at each phase need to be based on comprehensive observation and discussion with parents and child.

There is no age limit regarding such children's need for therapy which may persist into the transition to adulthood and the problems specific to those whose communication problems began in childhood need to be understood by those who provide services to adult clients.

Summary

By now it will be clear that ASLP pose particular challenges to the child, the family and those professionals involved in their rehabilitation. Some progress has been made in managing this client group but as these are rare disorders and it is a rapidly changing field, the practitioner needs to keep abreast of current research. The less common nature of these problems for most therapists makes them challenging and means team work is particularly important as is the well-documented, reflexive approach to assessment and management that helps to build a corpus of knowledge and expertise that can be shared with colleagues and service users.

Chapter 21

Augmentative and alternative communication

Michael Clarke, Katie Price and Nicola Jolleff

Learning outcomes

By the end of this chapter the reader will:

- understand the value and role of augmentative and alternative communication equipment and techniques for children with severe speech and language needs as part of a total communication system;
- have a basic understanding of different types of augmentative and alternative communication systems;
- be able to identify factors to consider in assessment of the individual child and their environment.

Introduction

The range of communication methods needed by children with complex communication needs is often described as a total communication system, whereby all possible modalities are explored and developed to support communication. As part of this system, these children use augmentative and alternative communication (AAC) to support other communication skills: looking, pointing, some speech and vocalisation, and gesture. AAC is a generic term used to describe any mode or channel of communication that replaces or supports speech and/or writing. Traditionally, AAC to support speech is broadly categorised in terms of *signs* and *symbols*. Signs refer to a formal system of hand shapes, such as those used in sign languages by deaf speakers. The term symbol is usually used to refer to graphic representation of meaning, other than the written word. These symbols may be pictorial or iconic, such as the symbols used in everyday situations to show: 'No Smoking', 'One Way'.

This chapter is principally concerned with the introduction and use of symbols and pictures, rather than manual signs, objects, 'objects of reference' (Park 2002) or interventions for literacy support. In this chapter, issues will be addressed concerning selection and provision of AAC systems to support children's interaction goals. Current viewpoints on assessment are considered in the light of changing theoretical and evidence-based perspectives.

Symbols

Symbols tend to fall into two categories: symbol sets and symbol systems. A symbol set is a vocabulary, or dictionary, of symbols. Published symbol sets used commonly with children in England include the Picture Communication Symbols (PCS), published in various forms by Mayer-Johnson, Widgit Literacy Symbols (WLS), published in various forms by Widgit Software, and Makaton symbols, published by the Makaton Charity.

More complex symbol systems tend to be less transparent in meaning, but can go some way to offering a syntactic base, representing language. Symbol systems such as Blisssymbols, or the multi-meaning system Minspeak, have their own structural rules whereby symbol elements are repeated with consistent meaning in different combinations. In Minspeak systems, a single picture can, within the system, have multiple meanings. For example, the symbol for *bed* can not only be used to express the idea of a bed as a noun, but also be used, in conjunction with other symbols from the system, to convey 'sleeping, tired, furniture, saying goodnight', and 'underneath'.

Presenting symbols efficiently

Graphical symbols can be organised on specific communication devices, or as software on personal computers, including Smartphones and games consoles, or in paper form. Such organisation is conventionally categorised as a high-tech or lite-tech approach. High-tech systems are PC based, or electronic communication devices, also known as 'speech generating devices' or 'voice output communication aids' (VOCAs). They may use digitised voice, which has been recorded on to the device by an adult or friend, and stored digitally, or synthesised, artificially created, voice.

While the reliability of high-tech devices is reported to have improved in the last decade technology is not infallible, may not be the quickest method of message transfer and children will invariably also will need a lite-tech system, such as a book or charts of pictures, symbols or words.

How does AAC fit into a communication system?

Significant numbers of children with neurodevelopmental or acquired disabilities affecting oromotor musculature such as those with a clinical description of cerebral palsy, or severe dyspraxia, can experience difficulties developing functional intelligibility. This can often be true, even after positive changes to speech through therapy and development through maturation (Pennington *et al.* 2010). Consequently, the use of AAC has traditionally been most strongly associated with children with motor disorders and a poor prognosis for speech. However, AAC strategies and tools have been introduced to a range of clinical groups to support expressive communication, including, most significantly perhaps, children with autism spectrum disorder (see Van Der Meer and Rispoli 2010).

There is growing evidence also that AAC strategies have a place in supporting language development. This includes promoting verbal understanding (e.g. Soto and Zangari 2009) as well as the development of literacy skills (e.g. Dahlgren-Sandberg *et al.* 2010). When considering who may benefit from AAC it is also useful to consider the functional aims of AAC provision. Von Tetzchner and Martinsen (2000) propose that children who are likely to benefit from AAC fall within three groups which are distinguished by the type of functional communication support that AAC is intended to provide. In brief, children falling into the 'expressive language group' are those with profound difficulties producing speech, and experience a significant gap between their understanding of language and their ability to express themselves. Such children are likely to use AAC as part of a total communication system throughout their lives. A second group, termed the 'supportive language group', includes children for whom AAC is considered a temporary intervention to support language understanding and expressive development in the relatively short term. Included in this group are those for whom AAC tools can be used to support residual speech in certain situations such as when introducing a new or unfamiliar topic. The third, 'alternative language group', comprises those children who experience profound difficulties understanding and using language, for example, children with significant learning disabilities. For these children AAC options are intended to support and develop language learning and use across their lifespan.

Theoretical frameworks

Currently, therapists and researchers working with children using AAC lack theoretical models of language acquisition to support guidelines for decision-making (Von Tetzchner and Martinsen 2000). Rather, decision-making has tended to be informed by insights from typical language development; from the field of developmental psychology, and from research describing the course of communication skills development in children with little or no functional language.

Importantly, in the context of assessment of AAC options, decision-making has moved away from viewing the child's attainment of developmental criteria as prerequisites to AAC. Clinicians now typically employ a developmental perspective as a guideline for introducing AAC options at an appropriate level for the child's skills and interests at the time of assessment, rather than excluding discussion of AAC options if certain developmental criteria are not met.

Developments in assessment and intervention in the AAC field have also mirrored changes observed in the approach to assessment and management of communication difficulties in children generally. Essentially, perspectives on assessment have shifted from a reductionist approach to an approach based on an holistic view of the child and their environment. They have also moved away from considering the child as an impaired individual, to viewing the child as an active co-participant in interaction. In this respect the *International Classification of Function, Disability and Health* (WHO 2001, ICF) and a subsequent children and youth version (WHO 2007, ICF-CY) have had growing influence in framing management practice (Raghavendra *et al.* 2007).

The ICF and ICF-CY catalogue sociological, psychological and biological aspects of health and health-related functioning, and seeks to illustrate the complex nature of relations between body structure and functions, activity and participation, and contextual factors (environment and personal factors). Body structure and functions include, for example, description of 'mental functions' including temperament and personality functions, as well as sensory, voice and speech, and neuromusculoskeletal- and movement-related functions. Within the ICF and ICF-CY the distinction between activity and participation is not clear. Activity is characterised as 'the execution of a task', and could incorporate, for example, issues related to the operation of a communication aid (Raghavendra *et al.* 2007). Participation is defined as 'taking part, being included or engaged in a life area, being accepted' (p. 15), and is related to interactions in real-life everyday circumstances, such as interactions with family members. Environmental factors refer to products and technology, natural and human changes to the environment, support and relationships, and policies.

Assessment

Assessment objectives

Assessment may achieve several different objectives, including an appraisal of strengths/needs, finding out what the child might want to talk about, changing the way the child communicates, testing language comprehension, identifying goals, finding out what school staff need, establishing family priorities and choosing the right communication aid.

Assessment is a complex, diverse and continual process. In the next section consideration is given to this process in terms of gathering information; observation, testing and decision-making, speech and language assessment, and implications for decision-making.

The collation of information

For some children, particularly those with more severe physical involvement and complex needs, it is necessary to gather appropriate information from those with an interest in the child's communication strengths and needs. This may include the child, their friends and family, school staff, community medical teams and team members from specialist services. This information gathering is likely to involve both Education and Health services.

Body structures and functions

General health issues

Success in assessment and, ultimately, in communication will be influenced by the child's level of general health and physical well-being. It is not easy to study and work when you feel unwell. Children with a physical disability are vulnerable to a number of conditions which can give rise to discomfort and pain such as gastro-oesophageal reflux, a painful and often chronic condition whereby the acid contents of the stomach pass back up into the oesophagus.

It will be important to consider such general medical issues in partnership with the child's GP, community paediatrician or school doctor and, in particular, speech and language therapists will be aware of the significance of any feeding difficulties (Andrew and Sullivan 2010). Below are some observations which may be made by the speech and language therapist which may contribute to the identification of conditions that can restrict the child's progress with communication and learning.

Questions a therapist may wish to ask:

- Does this child look well nourished? What is their current nutritional status? Does the child have a history of aspiration – the passage of food and/or liquid into the lungs?
- Does the child have a history of gastro-oesophageal reflux? What is their current status? Difficulties might be indicated by crying without obvious cause, repeated periods of coughing, not necessarily at mealtimes, and poor sleeping patterns.
- Is the child constipated? Dehydration can be a serious problem for many children, particularly those with significant physical disabilities. Dehydration leads to many complications including constipation, and subsequent pain.
- Does the child have a history of epilepsy? What is their current status?
- Does the child appear comfortable in their positioning? Do they have any orthopaedic difficulties documented, and how are these being monitored?

It is important to be aware of the children's general health status and the potential significance of any difficulties they may have. Any concerns need to be discussed with the medical members of the child's team.

Sensory impairments and learning abilities

FUNCTIONAL GAZE BEHAVIOUR, VISION AND HEARING

Children with complex motor disorders are particularly dependent on the use of gaze to signal their interests and preferences. Gaze is best used as a communicative tool when a look towards an item such as an object, symbol or picture is combined with a look towards an adult in an act of joint attention. Maintaining and developing children's ability to use gaze for communication is a common goal of early intervention. Care should be taken to distinguish between gaze fixations, which may be inferred by an adult as the child's signal of preference, and unequivocal eye-pointing which will, where possible, include gaze shifts between items and adults by the child (Carter and Iacono 2002).

Careful appraisal of visual attention skills will also help to identify any additional descriptions co-occurring with existing diagnoses. Children with cerebral palsy, for example, may also show features of attention, play and behaviour which will make useful additional diagnoses such as autism or attention deficit difficulties.

It will, therefore, be important to assess the child's ability to orient to the appearance of items and fix gaze on them, transfer gaze between them and track them, and to systematically search and selectively attend to items from an array. Equally, insight into the child's development of social cognition is likely to inform reasonable expectations for the development of joint attention and use of eye pointing as a communicative resource. Information concerning the child's visual acuity, and particularly near vision in the use of AAC systems will also be essential. Again, this assessment is likely to involve input from several sources, and necessitate the collation of information by the speech and language therapist to ensure that a full picture of the child's visual skills is available to all team members.

The argument for the assessment of hearing is similarly important, as is the importance and value of an accurate understanding of the child's general learning or cognitive abilities.

LEARNING

A general sense of the child's level of intellectual ability can be gleaned through discussion with parent(s)/carer(s) and school staff. What are his or her interests? What do they enjoy playing with? What do they enjoy watching most on television? How is he or she coping with school work?

If the child is of school age, and has a Statement of Special Educational Needs, their education review document will prove an excellent source of this type of information. A copy of this report will most likely be held at the child's school. In addition, Educational Psychology Services may hold a record of the child's achievement in assessments of intellectual functioning.

Physical skills

Clearly, for AAC to be introduced, children need to be able to access their symbol systems to use them. For lite-tech, paper-based systems, this will mean establishing a way of pointing to the symbols needed, perhaps using hands, or eyes. For children using technology, the opinion of an occupational therapist, and/or *assistive* technologist, as part of the multi-disciplinary team, should be sought. These team members will be able to ensure the child is best-positioned, with suitable equipment to operate any channel of communication.

Questions a therapist may wish to ask:

- Does the child look comfortable in their chair?
- How well do they use their hands for other activities, for example, operating a remote control for TV, swiping a Smartphone for photos?
- Who is responsible within the school/local team for any adaptations to seating and positioning?

Temperament and personality factors

Features related to the child's personality may be influential in the assessment strategy. Clinical experience suggests that parents and professionals often account for observed profiles of behaviour in terms of child personality. For some children, factors of personality may be difficult to differentiate from features of behaviour that represent disability traits, particularly for children with profound difficulties in communicating (Clarke *et al.* 2011). Consequently, care is required not to over-represent or under-estimate the impact of child personality on decision-making, or as a factor accounting for outcomes of intervention.

Environmental factors

Environmental factors that are important to consider include those related to the family and school. Parents and carers vary in their response to bringing up a child with disabilities. Some experience increased levels of stress, while others do not. Equally, stress within the family may vary across time. Parents experiencing periods of heightened stress may be less receptive to assessment and intervention that can implicitly challenge their hopes and aspirations of their child, such as discussion concerning the introduction of AAC options.

The family's attitude, for example, towards assistive technology and others' attitudes are also understood to influence the outcome of assessment. The speech and language therapist will want to establish an understanding of how current attitudes may influence the direction of decision-making.

Similarly, assessment of the school environment will be useful in order to consider the essential support and training opportunities for staff working with children using AAC systems. Discussions and interviews may clarify the level and range of resources within the child's school team in terms of time, commitment, expertise and confidence.

Questions a therapist may wish to ask:

*   How does technology fit into this family's lifestyle?
*   Are there family members who would relish the challenge of supporting the child's use of technology?
*   Who would have responsibility for testing out/using a system at school?
*   Is/could there be a time allocation documented at school for work to support the use of a communication device?

Personal factors

Personal factors need to be taken into consideration in the assessment strategy. Perhaps most prominent of these is the child's age. In speech and language management a distinction is commonly drawn between the child's chronological age and the developmental age which typically represents the child's age-equivalent for language and cognitive functioning. Also, work within the sociology of childhood (James and James 2004) has promoted a viewpoint of children's competence that is relevant to speech and language therapists working to support total communication. Although children follow a maturational path, their actions, abilities, motivations and attitudes reflect their competence as children. Speech and language therapists need to be mindful of this in their support of current needs and future developments

Participation

The maintenance and enhancement of children's participation in their everyday lives is the ultimate aim of speech and language therapy management. Speech and language develops within participation in naturally occurring interactions. There is considerable debate about the ways in which participation can be conceptualised and measured (McConachie *et al.* 2006). For the speech and language therapist working with children who may benefit from AAC, establishing an understanding of children's profile of participation is likely to include developing insight into the frequency and diversity of activities engaged in, the people involved and level of enjoyment (King *et al.* 2004). An appraisal of such factors, relating to 'joining in' with home, school and community life, is likely to stimulate the generation of planning which will be more meaningful for the family and child.

The speech and language therapist will also want to explore participation from the perspective of the child itself. That is, their individual sense of participation which is related to self-concepts such as sense of self-efficacy (Granlund *et al.* 2011). For children with complex communication needs who are particularly reliant on the use of communication aids, conversations often proceed unlike those entirely based on speech (Clarke and Wilkinson 2007, 2008). Typically such conversations are characterised by asymmetry. The speaking partner tends to take more turns and more complex turns, fill the gaps in conversation, ask many questions that require yes/no response only and are often concerned with a particular conversational goal. Conversely, children with communication difficulties are commonly described as taking a more responsive role, providing shorter contributions and responding minimally to initiations. Clearly, then, difficulties can exist for children in articulating their views in everyday conversation and, for speech and language therapists, problems exist in identifying authentic views of importance to children. Nevertheless, time and effort spent in systematically supporting children in the exploration and expression of issues concerning their participation in school, home and community life, is likely to provide insights of significant importance to all (Clarke *et al.* 2011). The opinions of parents are well placed to provide their own additional, supplementary insights.

Questions a therapist may wish to ask:

- What are the child's interests? Are these available to them in their current communication system?
- How confident are the adults in their play and interaction with the child? Is additional support through training needed?

Speech and language

Assessment of the speech and language skills of children who may benefit from AAC is likely to take a considerable amount of time. The speech and language therapist will need to show imagination, flexibility and invention. There is a range of issues which will need to be considered in assessing children who combine a range of communicative modalities.

For some children, their physical difficulties may make it difficult to convey their responses clearly. It will be important to determine reliable and consistent access to assessment materials in discussion with the child's occupational therapist. For children with no speech and a restricted range of physical movements, it is essential to establish a consistent yes/no response before commencing with assessment. This might be a conventional nod and shake of the head or idiosyncratic use of gesture such as looking up for 'yes' and looking down for 'no'.

Children's performance can also be affected by other factors such as epilepsy control, general health and attention as these may all fluctuate. The child's parents will be anxious to be sure that s/he performs at his/her best level. It will be important to incorporate results from more formal testing with parental and school-staff interview data.

Comprehension of spoken language and symbolic understanding

In order to investigate the child's abilities with regard to language comprehension, speech and language therapists may use many of their familiar assessments. Any adaptations made need to be noted when reporting the results, as these will affect the standardised scoring. It must be emphasised that findings from norm-referenced assessments should be considered in the light of other formal assessment findings, informal assessment and observation.

Determining the level of symbolic representation most appropriate for the child's level of understanding is critical to successful decision-making. The following guide to assessment and decision-making provides a framework for addressing this important issue (adapted from Jones *et al.* 1990).

Table 21.1 Decisions on symbolic understanding

Comprehension/symbolic understanding	Decision-making
Appropriate comprehension level and good reading and spelling skills (to 8–9 year equivalent)	→ Consider the written word as an augmentative system, this would include opportunities for spelling (letter-based VOCA or alphabet chart)
Comprehension equating with a 5 year level and small sight vocabulary	→ The child is likely to be able to deal with a complex/abstract symbol system/set such as Bliss or Minspeak
Comprehension equating with a 3–4 year level	→ Consider the possibility of using a supported complex/abstract symbol system/set
Comprehension equating with a 2;5–3 year level	→ Consider using a more iconic symbol system such as Picture Communication Symbols, or Widgit Literacy Symbols
Comprehension 12–18 month level	→ Use of symbols such as pictures and photos on a chart or in a book
Comprehension below 12 months	→ Explore the use of tangible symbols/'objects of reference' (Park 2002) in familiar everyday routines

Expressive communication skills

Few published speech and language therapy assessments are designed to assess expressive skills for children using multiple modalities including communication aids. However, the Renfrew Action Picture Test (Renfrew 2011a) is one example of a standardised assessment which may provide repeatable measures. All aspects of the child's speech would need to be considered, including range of sounds and sound system use, the complexity of the child's utterances, the range of vocabulary available and the pragmatic deployment of the utterances. For children using multimodal strategies, including communication aids, detailed reporting on the ways in which modalities are deployed and combined in varying communicative contexts can provide a valuable expressive profile and resource for shared decision-making concerning potential areas for intervention.

Implications of assessment findings on decision-making

Decision-making following assessment may be influenced by multiple complementary or competing factors. The speech and language therapist will be active in guiding the integration of a range of information in the decision-making process concerning short and long term goals, recognising that goals will change with time.

The body of relevant published evidence to support decision-making remains relatively small or may not be readily accessible (Schlosser 2000). The profile of children in available studies may not correspond to, or align with, children on a current caseload, or children may not be adequately described (Pennington *et al.* 2007). Equally, intervention objectives may not match the therapist's or the key stakeholder's intervention preferences. For example, while intervention objectives may broadly be classified as relating to facilitating change in the child, the environment or both, there has been a tendency for intervention to target factors related to body structure and function, and activity domains rather than participation (Iacano 2003). In reviewing available evidence relevant to children provided with communication aids, the therapist may adopt a broad search to incorporate intervention strategies that are specific to multimodal communication and strategies that are common to a range of paediatric client groups, such as the use of scaffolding techniques (Granlund *et al.* 2008).

Given limitations in the research and clinical practice evidence base and paucity of relevant theoretical models of language and communication development available to clinicians, collaborative decision-making is commonly informed by the values held by stakeholders. Parents who do not have a voice in clinical decision-making are prone to view intervention that involves parent-led activities as an additional unwanted burden rather than work of value for their child and family. Arguably, then, for some families, therapists, in collaboration with other professionals, may focus their immediate energies most effectively on seeking to alleviate family stress before or in parallel with intervention focused on the child's communication (Granlund *et al.* 2008).

Case example

Bobby is 16; he takes a total communication approach to interactions with others. He mostly uses speech which he says is easy to understand if the listener knows him and understands the topic of conversation. He normally supports his speech with gestures when people don't understand. In class he tends to use symbols to ask questions to cue the listener in to what he is saying and to contribute to group discussions. Bobby is also learning to use a VOCA, and he enjoys using it to tell jokes. He says he does not need symbols or his VOCA to chat to his girlfriend: he says he does that best with speech and gestures. He also says he does not use symbols much at break time. He only really wants to play football then. At home, he uses his VOCA to play 'Battleships' with his father.

For Bobby, the context of his communication will involve decision-making related to his needs at home and at school, and an assimilation of the views of his friends, family, therapists and school staff. His teacher may want him to be able to access the National Curriculum more effectively by answering questions on the science topic for the term; batteries, axles and engines. His learning support assistant wants to know how to programme his VOCA. His speech and language therapist may feel that he would benefit from some training in combining more than two symbols. Bobby's mother does not use symbols at home, and his father might like him to be working on accessing the spelling facility on his VOCA. Bobby, however, wants to tell jokes and play football. The therapist may be aware of research evidence that could influence decision-making. For instance, interviews conducted with children and young people using communication aids identified that some children have a strong preference for one-to-one therapy (Clarke *et al.* 2001).

Since all these factors need to be brought together into a cohesive plan of action, the speech and language therapist is likely to have a coordinating role involving a strong collaborative ethos, to establish effective partnerships with the family and professionals to gain consensus in relation to intervention.

Summary

This chapter has been concerned with identifying the role for AAC in the support of children with complex communication needs. It has outlined the principles of assessment for children who may benefit from using graphic symbol-based communication equipment. The reader should have an awareness of the range of issues which need to be considered in assessment and, although there are no definitive guidelines to decision-making in planning therapy provision, the reader should be reassured: sensitivity to the needs of the child, and to those involved in communication support is likely to lead to decision-making that is functional and effective. Finally, the process of assessment is continuous and should be revisited with the changing demands of the child and their environment.

Chapter 22

Children with feeding difficulties

Carolyn Anderson

Learning outcomes

By the end of this chapter the reader should:

- recognise the factors which need to be taken into account when assessing a child with feeding difficulties;
- know the extent of the evidence base for intervention and management;
- be aware of the importance of a team approach in assessment and intervention;
- be aware of the importance of taking a holistic approach to a child's overall needs;
- understand some of the main aspects which need to be considered when making decisions about children with feeding difficulties.

Introduction

Eating and drinking are normally pleasurable experiences. But children with physical disability, chronic medical conditions or severe to complex learning disabilities are more likely to have eating problems which make mealtimes distressing or may compromise their health. Swallowing or deglutition involves coordinating muscle movements in the lips, tongue, palate, pharynx, larynx and oesophagus. There are three phases, oral, pharyngeal and oesophageal, and children may have difficulties in one or more of these areas.

Dysphagia is defined as eating and drinking difficulties that occur in the oral, pharyngeal or oesophageal phases of swallowing (RCSLT 2006). 'Feeding difficulties' is therefore a wider term including problems at mealtimes that are based on motivation or skills, such as food refusal, and developing self-feeding (Field *et al.* 2003). Problems with coordinating a swallow may result in aspiration where food or liquid passes into the trachea (Arvedson 2008). Children usually cough or choke when this happens but there may be no indication of problems in silent aspiration. Frequent chest infections may therefore be a sign of silent aspiration (Prasse and Kikano 2009). Gastro-oesophageal reflux (GOR) occurs when stomach contents are regurgitated into the oesophagus. For some children, GOR irritates the oesophagus resulting in pain and discomfort during and after feeding. There is a high incidence of GOR with more severe feeding difficulties (Field *et al.* 2003).

Signs and symptoms

Feeding difficulties are observable by such clinical signs as failure to thrive, delayed development of oral feeding skills, aspiration of food or liquid into the lungs often indicated by choking and coughing, or problems in moving from non-oral to oral feeding (Lefton-Greif and Arvedson 2007). Arvedson (2008) identified a number of indicators of feeding difficulties including the length of time for feeding (over 30 minutes), being dependent for feeding beyond the age when this would be expected in typical development, food refusal, failing to gain weight and difficulties with breathing when feeding. Parents may also report stressful mealtimes (Sullivan *et al.* 2002).

Causes of feeding difficulties

Feeding difficulties can arise from many congenital or acquired conditions (RCSLT 2006), which can be broadly grouped into behavioural, developmental, structural or respiratory causes. Behavioural causes can be due to a number of factors. Gastro-oesophageal reflux can cause food aversion when infants and children associate feeding with painful GOR. Critical periods of development may be missed if children are on non-oral feeding programmes during these times and their appetite and hunger responses may change in these regimes (Fischer and Silverman 2007). Behavioural causes also include food selectivity, for example, in autism where children refuse to eat different types of food or textures due to sensory disturbances (Field *et al.* 2003). Feeding difficulties due to developmental delay are usually associated with prematurity, learning disabilities or with neurological conditions, such as cerebral palsy. Children with severe motor involvement are more likely to have eating and drinking difficulties (Andrew and Sullivan 2010). Structural causes include cleft lip and palate, oesophageal and craniofacial abnormalities. Respiratory or cardiovascular problems can also affect feeding.

Working with paediatric dysphagia

Guidelines for paediatric dysphagia and the current position on pre-registration and post-graduate recommendations are available from RCSLT (2005). Risk management, including health and safety issues, is the responsibility of employers, and therapists should be aware of local policies and procedures. In the UK, therapists develop their experience and application of theory via post-graduate training, often by working under supervision (RCSLT 2006). An understanding of normal development is needed to identify differences, delay and difficulties in the sequence (Delaney and Arvedson 2008). The therapist should be aware of the aetiologies of dysphagia, and the physical and neurological implications of different conditions and syndromes (see Cichero and Murdoch 2006 for an overview). Therapists use knowledge of oral anatomy and physiology, neurophysiology and the neurology of swallowing in children as a reference point from which to evaluate structure and function (Arvedson 2006). An understanding of the coordination of breathing and swallowing is necessary in assessing the risks that may be involved in choking, aspirating and coughing (Delaney and Arvedson 2008).

The multi-disciplinary team

A multi-disciplinary team is essential in managing complex feeding problems in children (RCSLT 2005; Arvedson 2006; Andrew and Sullivan 2010). The composition of the team may include the child, depending on age, the parents, paediatricians, nurses, educational staff, dieticians, physiotherapists, occupational therapists, psychologists, social workers and radiologists (Andrew and Sullivan 2010). If a team does not exist, the speech and language therapist should liaise with relevant professionals as required during the course of assessment and intervention.

Assessment

Evidence-based decision-making will combine clinical judgement from assessment data with research evidence and the child and family's values and expectations (Arvedson and

Lefton-Greif 2007). The aim of observation and case history taking is to evaluate the function of the airway for safe swallowing, and to help the child reach their potential in feeding skills while achieving sufficient nutrition (RCSLT 2006). In addition to the child's health status, clinicians should consider issues for parents around mealtimes, including parent–child interaction (Arvedson 2008). The assessment process should enable the clinician to determine if a feeding problem exists and whether the difficulty is behavioural and/or functional in nature. For functional difficulties, assessment should identify which phase or phases of swallowing are affected and evaluate what techniques may help.

Joint assessment is preferable, but video evidence may be useful if the team cannot assess at the same time. Parental involvement is essential in the assessment, not only for case history taking but also for observations of eating routines at home.

Case history information

The aim of gathering background information is to identify the cause and nature of the eating difficulty in order to focus the assessment observations on factors that influence the problem and should include the following areas:

- The eating problem as indicated by the referring agent and by the child's parents.
- The child's medical history including any medical diagnosis. In addition, information about the child's birth and developmental history, including if possible the pattern of weight gain, medications, hospitalisation, surgical interventions or investigations such as videofluoroscopy, general health and history of chest infections, food allergies and bowel habits.
- Details of the child's feeding history, covering previous feeding experiences and methods of eating including oral or tube feeding, associated difficulties including gastro-oesophageal reflux, vomiting, dietary preferences, nutritional supplements and previous feeding interventions.
- Information about present eating patterns, outlining the time taken for meals, the child's and family's daily eating timetable, the quantity eaten, food preferences in texture, temperature and tastes, utensils used, variations in seating and positioning, people involved in feeding the child and factors which make child's eating more difficult, such as catarrh.

Arvedson (2006) recommends that therapists should ask four key questions during assessment. The length of time for meals is the first question as feeding sessions of longer than 30 minutes are of concern. The second question is about whether meals are stressful. The third question is whether the child has any respiratory difficulties including rapid breathing, 'gurgly' voice quality or increases in nasal congestion. The final question is about whether the child has gained weight in the last two to three months. Morris and Klein (2000) provide further suggestions for case history questions. Speech and language therapists also need to find out which other professionals are involved and identify any safety issues.

Feeding assessment

The child's eating and drinking should be observed following the case history taking and parental interview. RCSLT Clinical Guidelines (2005) list areas that should be considered in the clinical evaluation; some of these areas are outlined below. Feeding skills should be compared to the developmental stages for the child's chronological age. Assessment checklists such as Jays Observational Assessment of Paediatric Dysphagia (Hibberd and Taylor 2005), and the Schedule of Oral Motor Assessment (SOMA) (Reilly et al. 2000) provide structure for observations of eating in infants and older children. These observations can be used as a baseline measure for noting changes over time. Oral motor evaluation should include observation of eating and drinking movements in relation to muscle and cranial nerve involvement (Hibberd and Taylor 2005).

A detailed oral-motor assessment of the child is recommended. Assessment should include the appearance and function of the oral area in order to note facial symmetry, oral reflexes which may interfere with the development of any new eating skills, the movement of the jaw, lips and tongue during eating, palatal movement, the teeth and dental hygiene, and breathing patterns (Morris and Klein 2000). The aim of oral-motor assessment is to identify whether there are oral-sensory or oral-motor difficulties or a combination (Arvedson 2008).

Eating and drinking skills such as sucking, swallowing, biting and chewing need to be evaluated as part of the assessment process. The swallowing assessment will include how the child copes with different consistencies of food and liquid, different tastes, temperatures and food presentations such as amount and rate. It is also important to note the influence of reflexes on these patterns, any sensory aspects such as tolerance of touch, hypersensitivity and hyposensitivity as well as whether the child is able to self-feed and how he/she copes with different food textures. Morris and Klein (2000) and Winstock (2005) outline normal and abnormal patterns for these aspects of eating.

Assessment should include head control and the effect of head control and posture on eating skills, muscle tone, patterns of flexion and/or extension, the presence of primitive reflexes and their relation to the child's developmental level. Restraints and methods of release also need to be noted as well as the relative heights of the tables and chairs, and the position of the feeder. Collaboration with a physiotherapist and/or occupational therapist is essential if speech and language therapists do not have extensive experience in assessing physical development. Bower (2009) outlines physical development and handling skills used with children with physical disabilities, principally cerebral palsy.

Other factors that may affect management should also be considered including emotional, social and environmental factors. These factors include the interaction between the child and parent, methods of communication, environmental factors, behaviour and the organisation of the child's eating programme (Morris and Klein 2000). Eating should be evaluated in different settings if the child is fed at school as well as at home and the results from these settings should be compared for any differences in the process or feeding methods used. Assessment may also involve experimenting with different positions for eating or testing different textures to determine which consistencies facilitate the child's eating skills. Following these investigations, referral to other agencies may be necessary. For example, referral to a clinical psychologist may be appropriate if a child has behaviour problems which interfere with mealtimes but no mechanical eating difficulties (Fischer and Silverman 2007).

Instrumental assessment

Further investigations such as instrumental assessments may be required to check the child's feeding status. If the child is judged unable to eat or drink safely, they may be at risk of aspiration (da Silva *et al.* 2010). When aspiration is suspected, the assessment team will need to determine whether oral feeding presents a risk to the child and may request instrumental investigations. Guidelines on invasive procedures are available from RCSLT (2005); these outline the use in assessment of fibreoptic endoscopic evaluation of swallowing (FEES) and the vocal tract, and radiological imaging, commonly known as videofluoroscopy swallow study (VFSS) (Arvedson 2006). VFSS enables clinicians to view the pharyngeal phase of swallowing and is an accurate method of identifying aspiration, especially silent aspiration (De Matteo *et al.* 2005). The aim is to determine whether aspiration occurs before, during or after a swallow, and whether there is any difference with different consistencies (Arvedson 2008). If aspiration is confirmed, the decision may be taken by the team to opt for non-oral feeding as discussed below.

Management

For children with feeding difficulties, eating becomes an important part of their education and care. Not only is it vital for nutrition and health, but also it provides an opportunity to establish early bonding and develop social communication. Intervention aims are to treat the child taking their overall needs into account, to ensure safe nutrition, to develop eating skills, to improve the quality of mealtimes and to encourage social communication (Winstock 2005; RCSLT 2006). Intervention depends on a number of factors including the child's current medical condition, nutritional status, psychological state, level of development and prognosis (RCSLT 2005).

Deciding on management aims with multiple factors is often a complex process so team decisions are vital. Parents and carers have a key role in intervention and will be involved through goal setting, training and evaluation of home programmes (RCSLT 2006; Ayoob and Barresi 2007). Multi-disciplinary team working is good practice in feeding interventions and will require training parents, carers and other professionals to deliver the intervention consistently (RCSLT 2006).

Developing aims for intervention

Intervention is based on knowledge of normal development (Arvedson 2006) for oral-motor development and the acquisition of feeding skills. The assessed developmental level in eating is compared to the child's chronological age, and with parental expectations to identify goals. The child's medical condition, physical abilities, learning disabilities and behavioural influences may all have an effect on recommendations for intervention. The main aims addressed at this stage of management of the child are medical, nutritional, habilitative and social; these aims are outlined below. Any modifications should be recorded to enable their effect to be measured accurately (RCSLT 2005).

Medical aims relate to reducing aspiration risks and improving health for the child; where a child is assessed as having an unsafe swallow, non-oral feeding should be instigated. Changing posture and head position, texture modification and training carers to use techniques consistently may be effective in reducing the risk of aspiration. CQ3 (RCSLT 2006) recommends maximising development of motor skills including using the optimum posture to reduce the risk of aspiration and provide a stable background for voluntary movements. The optimum posture is aligned with a chin tuck to increase airway protection. There is consensus that the position of the child when eating is an important factor to consider in intervention (Bower 2009; Winstock 2005). However, a review of studies found that aspiration still occurred in children with cerebral palsy when they had optimum postural adjustments (West and Redstone 2004).

Nutrition is increasingly recognised as vital not only for health, development and growth but also for a child's daily state of alertness and well-being. For this reason nutritional and hydration aims are often a priority in planning intervention (Kirby and Noel 2007; Gisel 2008). Length of time taken for meals was highlighted as a priority indicator in assessment and would be considered in intervention. Winstock (2005) notes that the bulk of nutritional intake is consumed in the first 20–30 minutes of a meal. Where nutrition and hydration intake is too low for a child, non-oral feeding should be considered.

Habilitative aims may range from developing independence and reaching a child's developmental potential, to improving the quality of life. Management may include working towards parents' acceptance of their child's eating difficulties to adjusting to the changing effects of a degenerating condition. The child's developmental level of functioning will guide intervention planning (Arvedson 2008), with adaptation where appropriate for their chronological age. Morris and Klein (2000), Bower (2009) and Winstock (2005), provide comprehensive intervention advice based on developmental considerations.

Habilitative intervention strategies may include direct therapy for improving oral-motor skills which has been shown to be effective in children with cerebral palsy and moderate eating difficulties (Gisel 2008). Studies cited by Gisel show that gains were made in food retention, and the development of biting and chewing. However, in a review of the literature, Arvedson et al. (2010) found no conclusive evidence for efficacy of oral motor exercises in improving feeding.

Intervention to develop eating and drinking skills may include changes in positioning, texture modification and increasing tolerance for food textures and tastes, and altering feeding procedures such as adjusting volume and rate of presentation of food. There are critical periods in development when children are ready to move on to different food textures and intervention expectations should be sensitive to these periods (Arvedson 2006). Published material such as parent handouts are useful for general advice in working with children with special needs (Klein and Delany 1994); many of these resources are available online.

Social goals include, for example, creating communication opportunities during meals, signalling choices, reduction of drooling or enabling the child to cope with distractions. Arvedson (2006) cautions that careful management is needed to avoid children becoming stressed by altering feeding routines in intervention.

Non-oral feeding

Non-oral feeding may be the management choice for children where aspiration presents a serious health risk or for those with neurological impairments such as cerebral palsy who cannot meet their nutritional needs due to persistently inadequate oral intake (Rogers 2004). Short term intervention may involve naso-gastric tube feeding. Surgical options for longer term difficulties include percutaneous endoscopic gastrostomy (PEG); research has shown that this is a viable option for children with severe feeding difficulties and problems gaining weight (Rogers 2004; Davis et al. 2010). However, there are risks of overfeeding and excessive weight gain with gastrostomy and GOR can increase following the operation (Andrew and Sullivan 2010). The evidence remains inconclusive on the preferred intervention for GOR following gastrostomy (Vernon-Roberts and Sullivan 2007). Sullivan et al. (2004) also note that quality of life may improve for parents. However, clinicians should be aware of potential negative consequences of tube feeding in their decision-making with families (Davis et al. 2010).

Morris and Klein (2000) offer practical management for the transition from tube to oral feeding. There is limited evidence for behavioural interventions to help children make the transition from tube to oral feeding; see Davis et al. (2010) for a summary. Mason et al. (2005) reviewed the literature on tube feeding and transition to oral feeding. They identified factors affecting the development of oral skills including age of transition and ensuring that children have taste/texture experiences during critical developmental periods. There is some research support for oral-motor interventions, specifically non-nutritive sucking (NNS) to maintain skills during non-oral feeding and oral stimulation in producing positive outcomes for eating/drinking skill development (Arvedson et al. 2010). However, further studies are required to address methodological issues. The decision between oral and non-oral feeding options must be accepted as the joint responsibility of the team. Team involvement in the decision-making process is illustrated by the following case example.

Case example

Ben is a 10 year old boy who has always been orally fed. He has severe athetoid cerebral palsy and epilepsy. He has a history of slow eating and poor weight gain. His paediatrician is concerned because his weight has been falling for the last 6–12 months. She raises the possibility of PEG with Ben's speech and language therapist and his parents. The therapist reports that Ben has made minimal progress in his feeding programme. He has been able to take pureed food without regurgitation for some time, but attempts to change textures have been unsuccessful. Ben's parents are positive in their attitude to PEG as some of the other children in Ben's school have had the operation with good results. However, they are concerned that Ben continues to have some oral feeding so he can join the family mealtimes. The therapist is aware that research has found that oral feeding is important to families. She is also aware of the types of support that families find helpful (Sleigh 2005). The options for support and the mixed oral/non-oral feeding programme are discussed with the parents, dietician and the school before the operation.

Implementing the intervention plan

Following formulation of an intervention plan, the speech and language therapist is responsible for ensuring that personnel involved in implementing the plan understand their role and use the recommended strategies. Depending on the therapist's role within this plan, s/he may be providing a consultation service or may be involved in direct training and supervision (RCSLT 2006). Ayoob and Barresi (2007) support regular training for carers on implementing home programmes as an effective method of promoting maximum progress in intervention. Harding and Halai (2009) found that experienced teachers had difficulty judging how to modify textures and thicken liquids until they had specific training. They recommended that speech and language therapists demonstrate feeding goals along with training to support feeding programmes in educational settings. Training could include opportunities for communication at mealtimes, increasing understanding about the risks of aspiration and the importance of positioning, to increase adherence to programmes (Ayoob and Barresi 2007).

Awareness of different attitudes to food and eating practices must be considered in recommending changes to feeding patterns. Increasing cultural diversity in the UK means that clinicians must be aware of how to overcome potential barriers to including parents in the decision-making process. There may be different beliefs about disability, nutrition, children's health needs and feeding practices, for example, at what age solids should be introduced (Davis-McFarland 2008). Communication is a key part of the process of agreeing shared goals while respecting cultural values, dietary preferences or religious differences.

Recognition of a wider training role and the need for liaison with different services will require extra time allocated for these responsibilities. It may be possible to extend the service to provide a preventative role that may prove effective in early intervention, possibly reducing some dysphagia problems, although further research is required to establish the efficacy of such an approach.

Balancing needs

A holistic approach to any child with eating problems is essential as these are often part of a larger picture of needs which include educational, social and emotional needs. Within this wider context, a feeding programme may not necessarily be the primary focus of intervention. Flexibility is also required in planning in order to be able to respond to a child's changing abilities and needs. The implementation of planned aims may need modification depending on factors such as available resources, parental attitudes or school policies. Intervention may not always be a preferred course of action, for example, in safe feeding where there is little prospect of change, where there is limited support from carers or when the child uses good compensatory techniques with no risks to their health.

Ethical issues

Decision-making is defined as the process which 'results in the therapist determining the best course of action at the time given the particular set of circumstances' (RCSLT 2006, p. 33).

Therapists are advised to consider ethical principles along with any applicable legal principles, clinical evidence, options in relation to risks/benefits and to involve the client and parents/carers in decision-making.

When faced with ethical decisions, Arvedson and Lefton-Greif (2007) advise that the team consider options from the child's best interests. They review some of the literature relating to ethical decisions for premature babies, children with complex needs and in palliative care. They highlight the need for clinicians to consider children holistically and to be sensitive to stress on families, especially where children have long term disabilities.

Summary

The main considerations in assessing and managing eating and drinking difficulties in children have been outlined in this chapter. Feeding has been considered in relation to causes and signs of difficulty. The impact of feeding difficulty also needs to be assessed in relation to lengthy, stressful mealtimes, respiration and weight gain.

A holistic approach is essential in management of eating and drinking difficulties in children. Feeding difficulties may be of short duration or long term, requiring consideration of changes due to maturation and the growing child's needs. There is increasing evidence from research to help clinicians reach evidence-based decisions on management. However, as feeding difficulties are usually linked with physical, cognitive or behaviour difficulties, the influence of multiple factors continue to make decision-making a complex process.

References

Abudarham, S. and Hurd, A. (2002) *Management of Communication Needs in People with Learning Disability*, London: Whurr Publishers Ltd.

Adams, C., Baxendale, J., Lloyd, J. and Aldred, C. (2005) 'Pragmatic language impairment: case studies of social and pragmatic language therapy', *Child Language Teaching and Therapy*, 21 (3): 227–50.

Adams, C., Coke, R., Crutchle, A., Hesketh, A. and Reeves, D. (2001) *Assessment of Comprehension and Expression 6–11 (ACE)*, London: G.L. Assessment.

Adams, C., Lloyd, J., Aldred, C. and Baxendale, J. (2006) 'Exploring the effects of communication intervention for developmental pragmatic language impairments: a signal generation study', *International Journal of Language and Communication Disorders*, 41 (1): 41–65.

Allen, G. (2011) *Early Intervention: the next steps*, Crown Copyright: Cabinet Office.

American Psychiatric Association (1994) *Diagnostic and Statistical Manual of Mental Disorders DSM IV*, 4th edn, Washington, DC: American Psychiatric Association.

Andersen-Wood, L. and Smith, B. (1997) *Working with Pragmatics*, Bicester: Winslow Press.

Andrew, M.J. and Sullivan, P.B. (2010) 'Feeding difficulties in disabled children', *Paediatrics and Child Health*, 20 (7): 321–6.

Armstrong, S. and Ainley, M. (2007) *South Tyneside Assessment of Phonology (STAP)*, St Mabyn, Cornwall: STASS Publications Ltd.

Arvedson, J. (2006) 'Swallowing and feeding in infants and young children', *GI Motility online*, doi:10.1038/gimo17.

Arvedson, J. (2008) 'Assessment of pediatric dysphagia and feeding disorders: clinical and instrumental approaches', *Developmental Disabilities Research Reviews*, 14 (2): 118–27.

Arvedson, J. and Lefton-Greif, M. (2007) 'Ethical and legal challenges in feeding and swallowing interventions for infants and children', *Seminars in Speech and Language*, 28 (3): 232–8.

Arvedson, J., Clark, K., Lazarus, C., Schooling, T. and Frymark, T. (2010) 'The effects of oral-motor exercises on swallowing in children: an evidence-based systematic review', *Developmental Medicine and Child Neurology*, 52 (11): 1000–13.

Ayoob, K. and Barresi, I. (2007) 'Feeding disorders in children: taking an interdisciplinary approach', *Pediatric Annals*, 36 (8): 478–83.

Bailey, A., Le Couteur, A., Gottesman, I., Bolton, P., Simonoff, E., Yuzda, E. and Rutter, M. (1995) 'Autism as a strongly genetic disorder: evidence from a British twin study', *Psychological Medicine*, 25 (1): 63–77.

Bailey, A., Palferman, S., Heavey, L. and Le Couteur, A. (1998) 'Autism: the phenotype in relatives', *Journal of Autism and Developmental Disorders*, 28 (5): 369–92.

Baird, G., Charman, T., Cox, A., Baron-Cohen, S., Swettenham, J., Wheelwright, S. and Drew, A. (2001) 'Screening and surveillance for autism and pervasive developmental disorders', *Archives of Disease in Childhood*, 84 (6): 468–75.

Baird, G., Charman, T., Pickles, A., Chandler, S., Loucas, T., Meldrum, D., Carcani-Rathwell, I., Serkana, D. and Simonoff, E. (2008) 'Regression, developmental trajectory and associated problems in disorders in the autism spectrum: the SNAP study', *Journal of Autism and Developmental Disorders*, 38 (10): 1827–36.

Baird, G., Simonoff, E., Pickles, A., Chandler, S., Loucas, T., Meldrum, D. and Charman, T. (2006) 'Prevalence of disorders of the autism spectrum in a population cohort of children in South Thames: the special needs and autism project (SNAP)', *Lancet*, 368 (9531): 210–15.

Baker, E. (2010) 'Minimal pair intervention', in A.L. Williams, S. McLeod and R.J. McCauley (eds) *Interventions for Speech Sound Disorders in Children*, Baltimore, MD: Paul H. Brookes Publishing Co.

Bamford, J., Carr, G., Davis, A., Gascon-Ramos, Lea R., McCracken, W., Pattison, E., Woll, B., Woolfe, T. and Young, A. (2009) *Positive support in the lives of deaf children and their families: summary report for professionals and services*, University of Manchester and University College London.

Barker, P. (2007) *Basic Family Therapy*, 5th edn, Chichester: Wiley-Blackwell.

Baron-Cohen, S., Wheelwright, S., Cox, A., Baird, G., Charman, T., Swettenham, J., Drew, A. and Doehring, P. (2000) 'Early identification of autism by the CHecklist for Autism in Toddlers (CHAT)', *Journal of the Royal Society of Medicine*, 93 (10): 521–5.

Barr, L., Thibeault, S.L., Muntz, H. and De Serres, L. (2007) 'Quality of life in children with velopharyngeal insufficiency', *Archives of Otolaryngology – Head and Neck Surgery*, 133 (3): 224–9.

BATOD/RCSLT (2007) *Position Paper: collaborative working between speech and language therapists and teachers of the deaf*, BATOD. Online, available at: www.batod.org.uk/content/articles/guidelines/Pospaper1207.pdf and www.rcslt.org/members/publications/RCSLTBATOD_collab_pdf.

Baxendale, J. and Hesketh, A. (2003) 'Comparison of the effectiveness of the Hanen Parent Programme and traditional clinic therapy', *International Journal of Language and Communication Disorders*, 38 (4): 397–415.

Beitchman, J. (2006) 'Language development and its impact on children's psychosocial and emotional development', *Encyclopaedia of Language and Literacy Development*, 1–7.

Bercow, J. (2008) *The Bercow Report: a review of services for children and young people (0–19) with speech, language and communication needs*, Nottingham: DCSF.

Bernstein-Ratner, N. (2005) 'Stuttering and concomitant problems', in R. Lees, and C. Stark (eds) *The Treatment of Stuttering in the Young School-Aged Child*, London: Whurr Publishers Ltd.

Bishop, D.V.M. (1997) *Uncommon Understanding*, Hove: Psychology Press.

Bishop, D.V.M. (2003a) *The Children's Communication Checklist*, 2nd edn, Oxford: Pearson Assessment.

Bishop, D.V.M. (2003b) *Test for Reception of Grammar*, 2nd edn, Oxford: Pearson Assessment.

Bishop, D.V.M. (2004) 'Specific language impairment: diagnostic dilemmas', in L. Verhoeven and H. van Balkom (eds) *Classification of Developmental Language Disorders: theoretical issues and clinical implications*, Hove: Lawrence Erlbaum Associates Inc.

Bishop, D.V.M., North, T. and Donlan, C. (1995) 'Genetic basis of specific language impairment: evidence from a twin study', *Developmental Medicine and Child Neurology*, 37 (1): 56–71.

Blairs, S., Slater, S. and Hare, D.J. (2007) 'The clinical application of deep touch pressure with a man with autism presenting with severe anxiety and challenging behaviour', *British Journal of Learning Disabilities*, 35 (4): 214–20.

Bloom, L. (1993) *The Transition to Language: acquiring the power of expression*, Cambridge: Cambridge University Press.

Bloomberg, K., West, D., Johnson, H. and Iacono, T. (2009) *Triple C: checklist of communication competencies*, revd edn, Melbourne: SCOPE.

Bondy, A.S. and Frost, L.A. (1994) 'The picture exchange communication system', *Focus on Autism and Other Developmental Disabilities*, 9 (3): 1–19.

Botting, N. (2005) 'Non-verbal cognitive development and language impairment', *Journal of Child Psychology and Psychiatry*, 46 (3): 317–26.

Boud, D. and Feletti, G. (eds) (1997) *The Challenge of Problem-based Learning*, London: Kogan Page.

Bowen, C. (2009) *Children's Speech Sound Disorders*, Chichester: John Wiley and Sons.

Bower, E. (ed.) (2009) *Finnie's Handling the Young Child with Cerebral Palsy at Home*, 4th edn, Burlington, MA: Butterworth-Heinemann Elsevier.

Boyle, J., McCartney, E., Forbes, J. and O'Hare, A. (2007) 'A randomised controlled trial and economic evaluation of direct versus indirect and individual versus group modes of speech-and-language therapy for children with primary language impairment', *Health Technology Assessment*, 11 (25): 1–158.

Boyle, J., McCartney, E., O'Hare, A. and Forbes, J. (2009) 'Direct versus indirect and individual versus group modes of language therapy for children with primary language impairment: principle outcomes from a randomised controlled trial and economic evaluation', *International Journal of Language and Communication Disorders*, 44 (6): 826–46.

Bray, M. and Todd, C. (2005) *Speech and Language: clinical process and practice*, 2nd edn, Chichester: John Wiley and Sons.

Bridie, C., Riemsma, R., Pattenden, J., Sowden, A., Mather, L., Watt, I. and Walker, A. (2005) 'A systematic review of the effectiveness of health behaviour interventions based on the transtheoretical model', *Psychological Health*, 20 (3): 283–301.

Brindley, C., Cave, D., Crane, S., Lees, J. and Moffat, V. (1996) *Paediatric Oral Skills Package (POSP)*, London: Whurr Publishers Ltd.

Britton, L. (2011) *Auditing against Standards for Speech-Closing the Audit Loop: 3 years data*, London: Craniofacial Society of GB and Ireland.

Broomfield, J. and Dodd, B. (2004) 'Children with speech and language disability: caseload characteristics', *International Journal of Language and Communication Disorders*, 39 (3): 303–24.

Brumfitt, S.M., Enderby, P.M. and Hoben, K. (2005) 'The transition to work of newly qualified speech and language therapists: implications for the curriculum', *Learning in Health and Social Care*, 4 (3): 142–55.

Bruner, J. (1978) 'On prelinguistic prerequisites of speech', in R.N. Campbell and P.T. Smith (eds) *Recent Advances in the Psychology of Language*, New York: Plenum Press.

Brutten, G. and Vanryckeghem, M. (2007) *Behaviour Assessment Battery for Children Who Stutter*, San Diego, CA: Plural Publishing, Inc.

Bryan, A. (1997) 'Colourful semantics: thematic role therapy', in S. Chiat, J. Law and J. Marshall (eds) *Language Disorders in Children and Adults: a psycholinguistic approach to therapy*, London: Whurr Publishers Ltd.

Bryan, K., Freer, J. and Furlong, C. (2007) 'Language and communication difficulties in juvenile offenders', *International Journal of Language and Communication Disorders*, 42 (5): 505–20.

Bunning, K. (1997) 'The role of sensory reinforcement in developing interactions', in M. Fawcus (ed.) *Children with Learning Difficulties: a collaborative approach*, London: Whurr Publishers Ltd.

Burnard, P. (1997) *Effective Communication Skills for Health Professionals*, 2nd edn, Cheltenham: Stanley Thornes Ltd.

Burns, K. (2005) *Focus on Solutions: a health professional's guide*, London: Whurr Publishers Ltd.

Byrne, B. (1998) *The Foundation of Literacy: the child's acquisition of the alphabetic principle*, Hove: Psychology Press.

Byrne, R. and Wright, L. (2008) *Stammering: advice for all ages*, London: Sheldon Press.

Cain, K. (2010) *Reading Development and Difficulties*, Oxford: BPS Blackwell.

Cain, K. and Oakhill, J. (2007) 'Reading comprehension difficulties: correlates, causes, and consequences', in K. Cain and J. Oakhill (eds) *Children's Comprehension Problems in Oral and Written Language: a cognitive perspective*, New York: Guilford Press.

Camarata, S. and Nelson, K. (2006) 'Conversational recast intervention with preschool and older children', in R. McCauley and M. Fey (eds) *Treatment of Language Disorders in Children*, Baltimore, MD: Paul H. Brookes Publishing Co.

Carroll, J.M., Bowyer-Crane, C., Duff, F.J., Hulme, C. and Snowling, M.J. (2011) *Developing Language and Literacy: effective intervention in the early years*, Chichester: John Wiley and Sons.

Carter, J.A., Lees, J.A., Murira, G.M., Gona, J., Neville, B.G.R. and Newton, C.R.J.C. (2005) 'Issues in the development of cross-cultural assessments of speech and language for children', *International Journal of Language and Communication Disorders*, 40 (4): 385–401.

Carter, J.A., Lees, J.A., Gona, J., Murira, G., Rimba, K., Neville, B.G.R. and Newton, C.R.J.C. (2006) 'Severe falciparum malaria: a common cause of acquired childhood language disorder', *Developmental Medicine and Child Neurology*, 48 (1): 51–7.

Carter, J.A., Neville, B.G.R. and Newton, C.R.J.C. (2003) 'Neuro-cognitive impairment following acquired central nervous system infections in childhood: a systematic review', *Brain Research Reviews*, 43 (1): 57–69.

Carter, M. and Iacono, T. (2002) 'Professional judgments of the intentionality of communicative acts', *AAC: Augmentative and Alternative Communication*, 18 (3): 177–91.

Catts, H.W., Adolf, S.M. and Weismer, S.E. (2006) 'Language deficits in poor comprehenders: a case for the simple view of reading', *Journal of Speech, Language, and Hearing Research*, 49 (2): 278–93.

Chandler, S., Charman, T., Baird, G., Simonoff, E., Loucas, T., Meldrum, D., Scott, M. and Pickles, A. (2007) 'Validation of the social communication questionnaire in a population cohort of children with autism spectrum disorders', *Journal of the American Academy of Child and Adolescent Psychiatry*, 46 (10): 1324–32.

Charman, T., Pickles, A., Simonoff, E., Chandler, S., Loucas, T. and Baird, G. (2011) 'IQ in children with autism spectrum disorders: data from the Special Needs and Autism Project (SNAP)', *Psychological Medicine*, 41 (3): 619–27.

Children Act (2004) London: HMSO.

Chilosi, A.M., Cipriani, P., Pecini, C., Brizzolara, D., Biagi, L., Monatanaro, D., Tosetti, M. and Cioni, G. (2008) 'Acquired focal brain lesions in childhood: affects on development and reorganisation of language', *Brain and Language*, 106 (3): 211–25.

Chilton, H. and Beazley, S. (2010) 'Theory of mind development', British Association of the Deaf (BATOD) magazine, *Communicating Clearly Together*.

Christie, E. (2000) *The Primary Healthcare Workers Project: a four year investigation into changing referral patterns to ensure the early identification and referral of dysfluent pre-schoolers in the UK*, London: British Stammering Association.

Cichero, J. and Murdoch, B. (2006) *Dysphagia: foundation, theory and practice*, Chichester: John Wiley and Sons.

Cirrin, F.M., Schooling, T.L., Nelson, N.W., Diehl, S.F., Flynn, P.F., Staskowski, M., Torrey, T.Z. and Adamczyk, D. (2010) 'Evidence-based systematic review: effects of different service delivery models on communication outcomes for elementary school-age children', *Language, Speech, and Hearing Services in Schools*, 41 (3): 233–64.

Clarke, M.T. and Wilkinson, R. (2007) 'Interaction between children with cerebral palsy and their peers 1: organizing and understanding VOCA use', *AAC: Augmentative and Alternative Communication*, 23 (4): 336–48.

Clarke, M.T. and Wilkinson, R. (2008) 'Interaction between children with cerebral palsy and their peers 2: understanding initiated VOCA-mediated turns', *AAC: Augmentative and Alternative Communication*, 24 (1): 3–15.

Clarke, M.T., McConachie, H.R., Price, K. and Wood, P. (2001) 'Views of young people using augmentative and alternative communication systems', *International Journal of Language and Communication Disorders*, 36 (1): 107–15.

Clarke, M.T., Newton, C., Cherguit, J., Donlan, C. and Wright, J.A. (2011) 'Short-term outcomes of communication aid provision', *Journal of Assistive Technologies*, 5 (4): 169–80.

Clouston, T., Westcott, L., Whitcombe, S.W., Riley, J. and Matheson, R. (eds) (2010) *Problem-based Learning in Health and Social Care*, Chichester: Wiley-Blackwell.

Cohen, N.J. and Lipsett, L. (1991) 'Recognised and unrecognised language impairment in psychologically disturbed children: prevalence and language and behavioural characteristics', *Canadian Journal of Behavioural Science*, 23 (3): 376–89.

Coltheart, M. (2005) 'Modelling reading: the dual-route approach', in M. Snowling and C. Hulme (eds) *The Science of Reading: a handbook*, Oxford: Blackwell Publishers.

Conti-Ramsden, G., Botting, N., Simkin, Z. and Knox, E. (2001) 'Follow-up of children attending language units: outcomes at 11 years of age', *International Journal of Language and Communication Disorders*, 36 (2): 207–19.

Conture, E. and Melnick, K. (1999) 'Parent–child group approach to stuttering in preschool children', in M. Onslow and A. Packman (eds) *The Handbook of Early Stuttering Intervention*, London: Singular Publishing Ltd.

Corey, G. (2004) *Theory and Practice of Counseling and Psychotherapy*, 7th edn, Pacific Grove, CA: Brooks/Cole Publishing Co.

Coupe, J. and Goldbart, J. (1998) *Communication before Speech*, London: David Fulton Publishers.

Cress, C.J. and Marvin, C.A. (2004) 'Common questions about early AAC services in early intervention', *AAC: Augmentative and Alternative Communication*, 19 (4): 254–72.

Cross, M. (2004) *Children with Emotional and Behavioural Difficulties and Communication Problems*, London: Jessica Kingsley.

Cross, M. (2007) 'Language and social exclusion', *I CAN Talk* Series, Issue 4.

Crosskey, L. and Vance, M. (2011) 'Training teachers to support pupils' listening in class: an evaluation using pupil questionnaires', *Child Language Teaching and Therapy*, 27 (2): 165–82.

CSAG (Clinical Standards Advisory Group) (1998) *CSAG Report*, London: HMSO.

CSP (Commissioning Support Programme) (2011) *Tools to Support the Commissioning of Services for SLCN*, London: CSP.

Cummins, J. and Swain, M. (1986) *Bilingualism in Education: aspects of theory, research and practice*, London: Longman.

Cummins, K. and Hulme, S. (1997) 'Video a reflective tool', *Speech and Language Therapy in Practice*, Autumn: 4–7.

CWDC (2009) *The Common Assessment Framework for Children and Young People: a guide for practitioners*, London: Children's Workforce Development Council.

da Silva, A., Lubianca-Neto, J. and Santoro, P. (2010) 'Comparison between videofluoroscopy and endoscopic evaluation of swallowing for the diagnosis of dysphagia in children', *Otolaryngology-Head and Neck Surgery*, 143 (2): 204–9.

Dahlgren, A. and Liliedhal, M. (2008) 'Patterns of early interaction between young pre-school children with severe speech and physical impairments and their parents', *Child Language Teaching and Therapy*, 24 (1): 9–30.

Dahlgren-Sandberg, A., Smith, M. and Larsson, M. (2010) 'An analysis of reading and spelling abilities of children using AAC: understanding a continuum of competence', *AAC: Augmentative and Alternative Communication*, 26 (3): 191–202.

Data Protection Act (1998) London: HMSO.

Davies, K., Lewis, J., Byatt, J., Purvis, E. and Cole, B. (2004) 'An evaluation of the literacy demands of general offending behaviour programmes', *Findings*, 233, 1–4. London: Home Office.

Davis, A., Bruce, A., Cocjin, J., Mousa, H. and Hyman, P. (2010) 'Empirically supported treatments for feeding difficulties in young children', *Current Gastroenterology Reports*, 12 (3): 189–94.

Davis-McFarland, E. (2008) 'Family and cultural issues in a school swallowing and feeding program', *Language, Speech and Hearing Services in Schools*, 39 (2): 199–213.

Dawson, G., Rogers, S., Munson, J., Smith, M., Winter, J., Greenson, J., Donaldson, A. and Varley, J. (2010) 'Randomized, controlled trial of an intervention for toddlers with autism: the Early Start Denver Model', *Pediatrics*, 125 (1): e17–23.

DCSF (Department for Children, Schools and Families) (2008a) *Aiming High for Disabled Children: transforming services for disabled children and their families*, Norwich: The Stationery Office.

DCSF (Department for Children, Schools and Families) (2008b) *Better Communication: an action plan to improve services for children and young people with speech, language and communication needs*, London: DCSF.

DCSF (Department for Children, Schools and Families) (2008c) *National Primary Framework for Literacy*, London: DCSF.

DCSF (Department for Children, Schools and Families) (2009) *Every Child a Talker: guidance for consultants and early years practitioners* (Third instalment), London: Crown Copyright.

DCSF (Department for Children, Schools and Families) (2010) *Working Together to Safeguard Children: a guide to inter-agency working to safeguard and promote the welfare of children*, London: The Stationary Office.

De Matteo, C., Matovich, D. and Hjartarson, A. (2005) 'Comparison of clinical and videofluoroscopic evaluation of children with feeding and swallowing difficulties', *Developmental Medicine and Child Neurology*, 47 (3): 249–57.

De Raeve, L. (2010) 'Education and rehabilitation of deaf children with cochlear implants: a multidisciplinary task', *Cochlear Implants International*, 11 (Supplement 1): 7–14.

De Shazer, S. (1985) *Keys to Solution in Brief Therapy*, London: Norton.

Delaney, A. and Arvedson, J. (2008) 'Development of swallowing and feeding: prenatal through 1st year of life', *Developmental Disabilities Research Reviews*, 14 (2): 105–17.

Dewart, H. and Summers, S. (1995) *The Pragmatics Profile of Everyday Communication Skills in Pre-school and School-aged Children*, Windsor: NFER-Nelson.

DfE (Department for Education) (2011a) *The Education Bill*, London: HMSO.

DfE (Department for Education) (2011b) *The SEN Green Paper Support and Aspiration: a new approach to educational needs and disability*, London: HMSO.

DfES (Department for Education and Skills) (2001) *The SEN Code of Practice*, London: HMSO.

DfES (Department for Education and Skills) (2003) *Every Child Matters*, Norwich: The Stationary Office.

DfES (Department for Education and Skills) (2004) *Removing Barriers to Achievement: the government's strategy for SEN*, Nottingham: DfES.

DfES (Department for Education and Skills) (2006) *Helping you Choose: making informed choices for you and your child ES47. Family file and monitoring protocol*, London: HMSO.

DH (Department of Health) (1997) *The New NHS: modern, dependable*, London: Crown Copyright.

DH (Department of Health) (2004) *The NHS Knowledge and Skills Framework and the Development Review Process*, London: Crown Copyright.

DH (Department of Health) (2005) *Agenda for Change: NHS terms and conditions of service handbook*, London: HMSO.

DH (Department of Health) (2006) *Our Health, Our Care, Our Say: a new direction for community services*, London: Crown Copyright.

DH (Department of Health) (2009) *Valuing People Now: making it happen for everyone*, London: Department of Health Publications.

DH (Department of Health) (2010a) *Equity and Excellence: liberating the NHS*, Crown Copyright, London: HMSO.

DH (Department of Health) (2010b) *Preceptorship Framework for newly registered nurses, midwives and allied health professionals*, Crown Copyright. Online available at: www.dh.gov.uk.

DH (Department of Health) (2011) *Health and Social Care Bill*, London: HMSO.

DH/DfES (2007) *National Service Framework for Children, Young People and Maternity Services: the mental health and psychological well being of children and young people: standard 9*, London: Crown Copyright.

Dickson, K., Marshall, M., Boyle, J., McCartney, E., O'Hare, A. and Forbes, J. (2009) 'Cost analysis of direct versus indirect and individual versus group modes of manual-based speech-and-language therapy for primary school-age children with primary language impairment', *International Journal of Language and Communication Disorders*, 44 (3): 369–81.

Dodd, B., Crosbie, S., MacIntosh, B., Teitzel, T. and Ozanne, A. (2000) *Preschool and Primary Inventory of Phonological Awareness (PIPA)*, Oxford: Pearson Assessment.

Dodd, B., Holm, A., Crosbie, S. and McIntosh, B. (2010) 'Core vocabulary intervention', in L. Williams, S. McLeod and R. McCauley (eds) *Interventions for Speech Sound Disorders in Children*, Baltimore, MD: Paul H. Brookes Publishing Co.

Dodd, B., Hua, Z., Crosbie, S., Holm, A. and Ozanne, A. (2003) *Diagnostic Evaluation of Articulation and Phonology*, Oxford: Pearson Assessment.

Duncan, D., Gibbs, D., Noor, N. and Whittaker, H. (1988) *Sandwell Bilingual Screening Assessment Scales for Expressive Panjabi and English*, Windsor: NFER-Nelson.

Dunsmuir, S., Clifford, V. and Took, S. (2006) 'Collaboration between educational psychologists and speech and language therapists: barriers and opportunities', *Educational Psychology in Practice*, 22 (2): 125–40.

Ebbels, S. (2007) 'Teaching grammar to children with specific language impairment using shape coding', *Child Language Teaching and Therapy*, 23 (1): 67–93.

Ebbels, S. (2008) 'Improving grammatical skill in children with specific language impairment', in C.F. Norbury, J.B. Tomblin and D.V.M. Bishop (eds) *Understanding Developmental Language Disorders: from theory to practice*, Hove: Psychology Press.

Edwards, S., Fletcher, P., Garman, M., Hughes, A., Letts, C. and Sinka, I. (1997) *Reynell Developmental Language Scales III*, London: GL-Assessment.

Edwards, S., Letts, C. and Sinka, I. (2011) *New Reynell Developmental Language Scales*, London: GL-Assessment.

Ehri, L.E. (2005) 'Learning to read words: theory, findings and issues', *Scientific Studies of Reading*, 19 (2): 167–88.

Ehri, L., Nunes, S., Willows, D., Schuster, B.V., Yaghoub-Zadeh, Z. and Shanahan, T. (2001) 'Phonemic awareness instruction helps children learn to read: evidence from the National Reading Panel's meta-analysis', *Reading Research Quarterly*, 36 (3): 250–87.

Emerson, E. (2003) 'The prevalence of psychiatric disorders in children and adolescents with and without intellectual disability', *Journal of Intellectual Disability Research*, 47 (Pt 1): 51–8.

Emerson, E. and Hatton, C. (2004) *Estimating Future Need/Demand for Supports for Adults with Learning Disabilities in England*, Lancaster: Lancaster University, Institute for Health Research.

Enderby, P., John, A. and Petherham, B. (2006) *Therapy Outcome Measures for Rehabilitation Professionals*, 2nd edn, Chichester: John Wiley and Sons.

Eraut, M. (1994) *Developing Professional Knowledge and Competence*, London: Falmer Press.

Ertmer, D.J., Leonard, J.S. and Pachuilo, M.L. (2002) 'Communication intervention for children with cochlear implants: two case studies', *Language, Speech, and Hearing Services in Schools*, 33: 205–17.

Fawcus, M. (1992) *Group Encounters in Speech and Language Therapy*, Kibworth: Far Communications Ltd.

Fenson, L., Dale, P., Reznick, J., Thal, D., Bates, E., Hartung, J., Pethick, S. and Reilly, J. (2003) *MacArthur Communicative Development Inventories: user's guide and technical manual*, Baltimore, MD: Paul H. Brookes Publishing Co.

Field, D., Garland, M. and Williams, K. (2003) 'Correlates of specific childhood feeding problems', *Journal of Paediatric Child Health*, 39 (4): 299–304.

Field, F. (2010) 'The foundation years: preventing poor children becoming poor adults', *Report of the Independent Review on Poverty and Life Chances*, London: HM Government.

Fischer, E. and Silverman, A. (2007) 'Behavioral conceptualization, assessment, and treatment of pediatric feeding disorders', *Seminars in Speech and Language*, 28 (3): 223–31.

Flahive, L. (2009) 'Symptomatic management of SSD', in C. Bowen (ed.) *Developmental Speech Sound Disorders*, Chichester: Wiley-Blackwell.

Fombonne, E. (2003) 'Epidemiological surveys of autism and other pervasive developmental disorders: an update', *Journal of Autism and Developmental Disorders*, 33 (4): 365–82.

Fowler, A. and Swainson, B. (2004) 'Relationships of naming skills to reading, memory, and receptive vocabulary: evidence for imprecise phonological representations of words by poor readers', *Annals of Dyslexia*, 54 (2): 247–80.

Frederickson, N., Frith, U. and Reason, R. (1997) *Phonological Assessment Battery (PhAB)*, Windsor: NFER-Nelson.

Freedom of Information Act (2000) London: HMSO.

Freeman, J., Epston, D. and Lobovits, D. (1997) *Playful Approaches to Serious Problems*, New York: Norton.

Fry, H., Ketteridge, S. and Marshall, S. (2009a) 'Understanding student learning', in H. Fry, S. Ketteridge and S. Marshall (eds) *A Handbook for Teaching and Learning in Higher Education: enhancing academic practice*, 3rd edn, London: Routledge.

Fry, J.P., Botterill, W.M. and Pring, T.R. (2009b) 'The effect of an intensive group therapy program for young adults who stutter: a single subject study', *International Journal of Speech-Language Pathology*, 11 (1): 12–19.

Fuller, A. (2010) 'Speech and language therapy in Sure Start Local Programmes: a survey-based analysis of practice and innovation', *International Journal of Language and Communication Disorders*, 45 (2): 182–203.

Furnham, A. (1997) *The Psychology of Behaviour at Work*, Hove: Psychology Press.

Gallagher, A. and Chiat, S. (2009) 'Evaluation of speech and language therapy interventions for pre-school children with specific language impairment: a comparison of outcomes following specialist intensive, nursery-based and no intervention', *International Journal of Language and Communication Disorders*, 44 (5): 616–38.

Gardner, H. (2006a) 'Training others in the art of therapy for speech sound disorders: an interactional approach', *Child Language, Teaching and Therapy*, 22 (1): 27–46.

Gardner, H. (2006b) 'Assessing speech and language skills in the school-age child', in M. Snowling and J. Stackhouse (eds) *Dyslexia Speech and Language: a practitioner's handbook*, 2nd edn, Chichester: John Wiley and Sons.

Gascoigne, M. (2006) *Supporting Children with Speech, Language and Communication Needs within Integrated Children's Services*, London: RCSLT.

Gathercole, S.E. and Baddeley, A.D. (1996) *Children's Test of Nonword Repetitions*, Oxford: Pearson Assessment.

Gathercole, V.C.M. and Thomas, E.M. (2007) *Prawf Geirfa Cymraeg, Fersiwn 7–11*. Bangor, Gwynedd: Bangor University.

Gathercole, V.C.M. and Thomas, E.M. (2009) Bilingual first-language development: dominant language takeover, threatened minority language take-up. *Bilingualism: Language and Cognition*, 12 (2): 213–37.

Geers, A. and Brenner, C. (2003) 'Background and educational characteristics of pre-lingually deaf children implanted by five years of age,' *Ear and Hear*, 24 (1): 2S–14S.

German, D.J. (2000) *Test of Word Finding*, 2nd edn (TWF-2) Texas: PRO-Ed Inc.

Gibbard, D., Coglan, L. and Macdonald, J. (2004) 'Cost-effectiveness analysis of current practice and parent intervention for children under 3 years presenting with expressive language delay', *International Journal of Language and Communication Disorders*, 39 (2): 229–44.

Giddan, J.J., Milling, L. and Campbell, N.B. (1996) 'Unrecognized language and speech deficits in pre-adolescent psychiatric inpatients', *American Journal of Orthopsychiatry*, 66 (1): 85–92.

Gierut, J.A. (1998) 'Treatment efficacy: functional phonological disorders in children', *Journal of Speech, Language and Hearing Research*, 41 (1): S85–S100.

Gierut, J.A. (2008) 'Fundamentals of experimental design and treatment', in D.A. Dinnsen and J.A. Gierut (eds) *Optimality Theory, Phonological Acquisition and Disorders*, London: Equinox.

Gillon, G.T. (2002) 'Follow-up study investigating the benefits of phonological awareness intervention for children with spoken language impairment', *International Journal of Disorders of Communication*, 37 (4): 381–400.

Gillon, G.T. (2004) *Phonological Awareness: from research to practice*, New York: Guilford Press.

Girolametto, L., Pearce, P.S. and Weitzman, E. (1996) 'Interactive focused stimulation for toddlers with expressive vocabulary delays', *Journal of Speech and Hearing Research*, 39 (6): 1274–83.

Girolametto, L., Weitzman, E., Wiig, E.H. and Steig-Pearce, P. (1999) 'The relationship between maternal language measures and language development in toddlers with expressive vocabulary delays', *American Journal of Speech-language Pathology*, 8: 364–74.

Gisel, E. (2008) 'Interventions and outcomes for children with dysphagia', *Developmental Disabilities Research Reviews*, 14 (2): 165–73.

Glogowska, M. and Campbell, R. (2000) 'Getting in, getting on and getting there: investigating parental views of involvement in pre-school speech and language therapy', *International Journal of Language and Communication Disorders*, 35 (3): 391–405.

Goldberg, S. (1997) *Clinical Skills for Speech and Language Pathologists*, San Diego, CA: Singular Publishing Ltd.

Goodman, R. and Scott, S. (2005) *Child Psychiatry*, 2nd edn, Oxford: Blackwell Science.

Goswami, U. and Bryant, P. (1990) *Phonological Skills and Learning to Read*, Hove: Laurence Erlbaum Associates Inc.

Goulandris, N. (2006) 'Assessing reading and spelling skills', in M. Snowling and J. Stackhouse (eds) *Dyslexia, Speech and Language: a practitioner's handbook*, 2nd edn, Chichester: John Wiley and Sons.

Gout, A., Seibel, N., Rouviere, C., Husson, B., Hermans, B., Laporte, N., Kadhim, H., Grandin, C., Landrieu, P. and Sebire, G. (2005) 'Aphasia owing to subcortical brain infarcts in childhood', *Journal of Child Neurology*, 20 (12): 1003–8.

Gower, S.G., Harrington, R.C., Whitton, A., Veebor, A.S., Lelliott, P., Wing, J.K. and Jezzard, R. (1998) *The Health of the Nation Outcome Scales: child and adolescent mental health*, Liverpool: University of Liverpool.

Granlund, M., Bjorck-Akesson, E., Eriksson-Augustine, L., Pless, M., Simeonsson, R., Maxwell, G., Adlofsson, M., Arvidsson, P. and Niia, A. (2011) 'Differentiating activity and participation of children and youth with disability in Sweden: the need for a third qualifier in ICF-CY', *American Journal of Physical Medicine and Rehabilitation* (forthcoming).

Granlund, M., Bjorck-Akesson, E., Wilder, J. and Ylven, R. (2008) 'AAC interventions for children in a family environment: implementing evidence in practice', *AAC: Augmentative and Alternative Communication*, 24 (3): 207–19.

Green, J., Charman, T., McConachie, H., Aldred, C., Slonims, V., Howlin, P., Le Couteur, A., Leadbitter, K., Hudry, K., Byford, S., Barrett, B., Temple, K. and Macdonald, W. (PACT Consortium) (2010) 'Parent-mediated communication-focused treatment in children with autism (PACT): a randomised controlled trial', *Lancet*, 375 (9732): 2152–60.

Grove, N. and Dockrell, J. (2000) 'The analysis of multi-sign combinations in children with intellectual impairments', *Journal of Speech, Language and Hearing Research*, 43: 309–23.

Grunwell, P. (1987) *Clinical Phonology*, 2nd edn, Baltimore, MD: Williams and Wilkins.

Guess, D., Roberts, S., Siegel-Causey, E., Ault, M., Guy, B., Thompson, B. and Rues, J. (1993) 'Analysis of behavior state conditions and associated environmental variables among students with profound handicaps', *American Journal of Mental Retardation*, 97 (6): 634–53.

Guitar, B. (2006) *Stuttering: an integrated approach to its nature and treatment*, 3rd edn, London: Lippincott Williams and Wilkins.

Guitar, B. and McCauley, R. (eds) (2010) *Treatment of Stuttering: established and emerging interventions*, Baltimore, MD: Lippincott Williams and Wilkins.

Habel, A. (2001) 'The role of the paediatrician' in A.C.H. Watson, P. Grunwell and D. Sell (eds) *Management of Cleft Lip and Palate*, London: Whurr Publishers Ltd.

Halden, J. and Beazley, S. (2010) 'Test questions' British Association of the Deaf (BATOD) magazine, *Assessment*.

Harding, A. and Grunwell, P. (1996) 'Cleft palate speech characteristics: a literature review', *European Journal of Disorders of Communication*, 31 (4): 331–58.

Harding, A. and Grunwell, P. (1998) 'Active versus passive cleft-type speech characteristics: implications for surgery and therapy', *International Journal of Language and Communication Disorders*, 33 (3): 329–52.

Harding, C. and Halai, V. (2009) 'Providing dysphagia training for carers of children who have profound and multiple learning disabilities', *British Journal of Developmental Disabilities*, 55 (1): 33–47.

Harding, C., Lindsay, G., O'Brien, A., Dipper, L. and Wright, J. (2010) 'The challenges of implementing AAC to children with profound and multiple learning disabilities: a study in rationale underpinning intervention', *Journal of Research in Special Educational Needs*, 11 (2): 1–10.

Harding-Bell, A. and Howard, S.J. (2011) 'Phonological approaches to speech difficulties associated with cleft palate', in S. Howard and A. Lohmander (eds) *Cleft Lip and Palate: speech assessment, analysis and intervention*, Chichester: John Wiley and Sons.

Hargie, O. and Dickson, D. (2004) *Social Skills in Interpersonal Communication*, 4th edn, London: Routledge.

Hartas, D. (2004) 'Teacher and speech-language therapist collaboration: being equal and achieving a common goal', *Child Language Teaching and Therapy*, 20 (1): 33–54.

Harten, A.C. (2011) 'Multicultural issues in assessment and intervention', in R.B. Hoodin (ed.) *Intervention in Child Language Disorder*, London: Jones and Bartlett.

Hartshorne, M. (2006) 'The cost to the nation of children's poor communication', *I CAN Talk* Series, Issue 2.

Hasson, N. and Joffe, V. (2007) 'The case for dynamic assessment in speech and language therapy', *Child Language Teaching and Therapy*, 23 (1): 9–25.

Havstam, C. (2010) 'Attitude to speech and communication in individuals born with cleft lip and palate', unpublished thesis, University of Gothenburg.

Herman, R. and Mann, W. (2010) 'Where are we now?' British Association of the Deaf (BATOD) magazine, *Assessment*.

Hesketh, A. (2010) 'Metaphonological intervention: phonological awareness therapy', in A.L. Williams, S. McLeod and R.J. McCauley (eds) *Interventions for Speech Sound Disorders in Children*, Baltimore, MD: Paul H. Brookes Publishing Co.

Hester, E. and Hodson, B. (2009) 'Metaphonological awareness: enhancing literacy skills', in P. Rhyner (ed.) *Emergent Literacy and Early Language Acquisition: making the connection*, New York: Guilford Press.

Hibberd, J. and Taylor, J. (2005) *Jays Observational Assessment of Paediatric Dysphagia*, Birmingham: Quest Training.

Hoover, W.A. and Gough, P.B. (1990) 'The simple view of reading', *Reading and Writing: an interdisciplinary journal*, 2 (2): 127–60.

Howlin, P., Goode, S., Hutton, J. and Rutter, M. (2004) 'Adult outcome for children with autism', *Journal of Child Psychology and Psychiatry*, 45 (2): 212–29.

HPC (Health Professions Council) (2006) *Your Guide to our Standards for Continuing Professional Development*, London: HPC.

HPC (Health Professions Council) (2007) *Standards of Proficiency. Speech and Language Therapy*, London: HPC.

HPC (Health Professions Council) (2008) *Standards of Conduct, Performance and Ethics*, London: HPC.

Hulme, C. and Snowling, M.J. (2009) *Developmental Disorders of Language, Learning and Cognition*, Chichester: Wiley-Blackwell.

Hulme, S. (2005) 'ACT! Innovative training for child care staff', *RCSLT Bulletin*, 644: 12–13.

Hus, V., Pickles, A., Cook Jr, E., Risi, S. and Lord, C. (2007) 'Using the Autism Diagnostic Interview: revised to increase phenotypic homogeneity in genetic studies of autism', *Biological Psychiatry*, 61 (4): 438–48.

Iacono, T. (2003) 'The evidence base for augmentative and alternative communication', in S. Reilly and J. Oates (eds) *Evidence-based Practice in Speech Pathology*, Chichester: John Wiley and Sons.

Ibertsson, T., Hansson, K., Maki-Torkko, E., Willstedt-Svensson, U. and Sahlen, B. (2009) 'Deaf teenagers with cochlear implants in conversation with hearing peers', *International Journal of Language and Communication Disorders*, 44 (3): 319–37.

Irons, A. (2007) *Enhancing Learning Through Formative Assessment and Feedback: key guides for effective teaching in higher education*, London: Routledge.

Isaac, K. (2002) *Speech Pathology in Cultural and Linguistic Diversity*, Chichester: John Wiley and Sons.

Iverson, J.M. and Goldin-Meadow, S. (2005) 'Gesture paves the way for language development', *American Psychological Society*, 16 (5): 367–471.

James, A. and James, A.L. (2004) *Constructing Childhood: theory, policy and social practice*, Basingstoke: Palgrave Macmillan.

Joffe, V. (2006) 'Enhancing language and communication in secondary school-aged children', in J. Clegg and J. Ginsborg (eds) *Language and Social Disadvantage*, Chichester: John Wiley and Sons.

John, A.K., Sell, D., Harding-Bell, A., Sweeney, T. and Williams, A. (2006) 'CAPS-A: a validated and reliable measure for auditing cleft speech', *Cleft Palate-Craniofacial Journal*, 43 (3): 272–88.

Johnson, M. and Elias, A. (2010) *East Kent Outcome System for Speech and Language Therapy*, Whitstable: East Kent Coastal Primary Care Trust.

Johnson, M. and Wintgens, A. (2001) *The Selective Mutism Resource Manual*, Milton Keynes: Speechmark Publishing Ltd.

Jones, M., Onslow, M., Packman, A., O'Brian, S., Hearne, A., Williams, S., Ormond, T. and Schwartz, I. (2008) 'Extended follow-up of a randomised controlled trial of the Lidcombe Program of early stuttering intervention', *International Journal of Language and Communication Disorders*, 43 (6): 649–61.

Jones, S., Jolleff, N., McConachie, H. and Wisbeach, A. (1990) 'A model for assessment of children for augmentative communication systems', *Child Language Teaching and Therapy*, 6 (3): 305–21.

Kelly, A. (2004) *Talkabout Relationships*, Milton Keynes: Speechmark Publishing Ltd.

Kelman, E. and Nicholas, A. (2008) *Practical Intervention for Early Childhood Stammering: Palin PCI approach*, Milton Keynes: Speechmark Publishing Ltd.

Kelman, E. and Schneider, C. (1994) 'Parent–child interaction: an alternative to the management of children's language difficulties', *Child Language Teaching and Therapy*, 10 (1): 81–95.

Kerr, A., McCulloch, D., Oliver, K., McClean, B., Coleman, E., Law, T., Beaton, P., Wallace, S., Newell, E., Eccles, T. and Prescott, J. (2003) 'Medical needs of people with intellectual disability require regular reassessment and the provision of client and carer-held reports', *Journal of Intellectual Disability Research*, 47 (2): 134–45.

Kersner, M. and Parker, A. (2004) 'Change: an educational experience', *Speech and Language Therapy in Practice*, Summer: 8–10.

Kersner, M. and Wright, J.A. (2002) 'Getting comfortable with collaboration', *Speech and Language Therapy in Practice*, Autumn: 21–3.

Kiernan, C., Reid, B. and Jones, L. (1987) *The Pre-verbal Communication Schedule*, Windsor: NFER-Nelson.

Kim, M., McGregor, K.K. and Thompson, C.K. (2000) 'Early lexical development in English- and Korean-speaking children: language-general and language-specific patterns', *Journal of Child Language*, 27 (2): 225–54.

King, G., Law, M., King, S., Hurley, P., Rosenbaum, P., Kertoy, M. and Young, N. (2004) *Children's Assessment of Participation and Enjoyment*, San Antonio, TX: Harcourt Press.

Kirby, M. and Noel, R. (2007) 'Nutrition and gastrointestinal tract assessment and management of children with dysphagia', *Seminars in Speech and Language*, 28 (3): 180–9.

Kiresuk, T.J., Smith, A. and Cardillo, J.E. (eds) (1994) *Kiresuk Goal Attainment Scaling: applications, theory, and measurement*, Mahwah, NJ: Lawrence Erlbaum Associates Inc.

Klein, M. and Delaney, T. (1994) *Feeding and Nutrition for the Child with Special Needs: handouts for parents*, London: Psychological Corporation.

Knowles, W. and Masidlover, M. (1985) *The Derbyshire Language Scheme*, Ripley: Derbyshire Education Office.

Kolb, D.A. (1984) *Experiential Learning*, Englewood Cliffs, NJ: Prentice Hall.

Kovas, Y., Hayiou-Thomas, M.E., Oliver, B., Dale, P.S., Bishop, D.V.M. and Plomin, R. (2005) 'Genetic influences in different aspects of language development: the etiology of language skills in 4;5 year-old twins', *Child Development*, 76 (3): 632–51.

Kubler-Ross, E. (1997) *On Death and Dying*, London: Collier Books.

Kummer, A.W., Lee, L., Stutz, L.S., Maroney, A. and Brandt, J.W. (2007) 'The prevalence of apraxia characteristics in patients with velocardiofacial syndrome as compared with other cleft populations', *Cleft Palate-Craniofacial Journal*, 44 (2): 175–81.

Ladle, J. (2004) 'Multimedia profiling: a tool for inclusion', *Living Well*, 4 (1): 13–15.

Lancaster, G. (2009) 'Implementing auditory input therapy', in C. Bowen (ed.) *Developmental Speech Sound Disorders*, Chichester: Wiley-Blackwell.

Law, J. and Harris, F. (2006) 'The effects of intervention on the communication skills of socially disadvantaged children', in J. Clegg and J. Ginsborg (eds) *Language and Social Disadvantage*, Chichester: John Wiley and Sons.

Law, J. and Plunkett, C. (2009) 'The Interaction between Behaviour and Speech and Language Difficulties: does intervention for one affect outcomes in the other?' Technical Report, Nuffield Speech and Language Review Group.

Law, J., Boyle, J., Harris, F., Harkness, A. and Nye, C. (1998) 'Screening for speech and language delay: a systematic review of the literature', *Health Technology Assessment*, 2 (9): 1–184.

Law, J., Boyle, J., Harris, F., Harkness, A. and Nye, C. (2000) 'Prevalence and natural history of primary speech and language delay: findings from a systematic review of the literature', *International Journal of Language and Communication Disorders*, 35 (2): 165–88.

Law, J., Garrett, Z. and Nye, C. (2004) 'The efficacy of treatment of children with developmental speech and language delay/disorder: a meta-analysis', *Journal of Speech, Language and Hearing Research*, 47 (4): 924–43.

Lees, J. (1997) 'Long term effects of acquired language disorders in childhood,' *Pediatric Rehabilitation*, 1 (1): 45–9.

Lees, J. and Urwin, S. (1997) *Children with Language Disorders*, 2nd edn, London: Whurr Publishers Ltd.

Lees, J.A. (2005) *Children with Acquired Aphasias*, 2nd edn, London: Whurr Publishers Ltd.

Lees, R. (2005) 'The assessment of children who stutter', in R. Lees and C. Stark (eds) *The Treatment of Stuttering in the Young School-aged Child*, London: Whurr Publishers Ltd.

Lefton-Greif, M. and Arvedson, J. (2007) 'Pediatric feeding and swallowing disorders: state of health, population trends, and application of the International Classification of Functioning, Disability, and Health', *Seminars in Speech and Language*, 28 (3): 161–5.

Leinonen, E., Letts, C. and Smith, B.R. (2000) *Children's Pragmatic Communication Difficulties*, London: Whurr Publishers Ltd.

Leonard, L.B. (1998) *Children with Specific Language Impairment*, Cambridge, MA: MIT Press.

Letts, C. and Sinka, I. (2011) 'Multilingual toolkit', part of *New Reynell Developmental Language Scales*, London: GL-Assessment.

Lewis, V. and Boucher, J. (1997) *Test of Pretend Play (ToPP)*, London: Psychological Corporation.

Lindsay, G., Dockrell, J., Desforges, M., Law, J. and Peacey, N. (2010) 'Meeting the needs of children and young people with speech, language and communication difficulties', *International Journal of Language and Communication Disorders*, 45 (4): 448–60.

Lindsay, G., Dockrell, J., Letchford, B. and Mackie, C. (2002) 'Self esteem of children with specific speech and language difficulties', *Child Language Teaching and Therapy*, 18 (2): 125–43.

Locke, A., Ginsborg, J. and Peers, I. (2002) 'Development and disadvantage: implications for the early years and beyond', *International Journal of Language and Communication Disorders*, 37 (1): 3–16.

Lohmander, A. (2011) 'Surgical intervention and speech outcomes in cleft lip and palate', in A. Lohmander and S. Howard (eds) *Cleft Lip and Palate: speech assessment, analysis and intervention*, Chichester: John Wiley and Sons.

Lord, C., Rutter, M., DiLavore, P.C. and Risi, S. (2001) *Autism Diagnostic Observation Schedule (ADOS)*, Los Angeles, CA: Western Psychological Services.

Lord, C., Shulman, C. and DiLavore, P. (2004) 'Regression and word loss in autistic spectrum disorders', *Journal of Child Psychology and Psychiatry, and Allied Disciplines*, 45 (5): 936–55.

Loucas, T., Charman, T., Pickles, A., Simonoff, E., Chandler, S., Meldrum, D. and Baird, G. (2008) 'Autistic symptomatology and language ability in autism spectrum disorder and specific language impairment', *Journal of Child Psychology and Psychiatry*, 49 (11): 1184–92.

Lovaas, O.I. (1987) 'Behavioral treatment and normal educational and intellectual functioning in young autistic children', *Journal of Consulting and Clinical Psychology*, 55 (1): 3–9.

Luyster, R.J., Kadlec, M.B., Carter, A. and Tager-Flusberg, H. (2008) 'Language assessment and development in toddlers with autism spectrum disorders', *Journal of Autism and Developmental Disorders*, 38 (8): 1426–38.

McAllister, L. and Lincoln, M. (2004) *Clinical Education in Speech-Language Pathology*, London: Whurr Publishers Ltd.

McCartney, E., Boyle, J., Ellis, S. and Bannatyne, S.T. (2011) 'Indirect language therapy for children with persistent language impairment in mainstream primary schools: outcomes from a cohort intervention', *International Journal of Language and Communication Disorders*, 46 (1): 74–82.

McConachie, H., Colver, A.F., Forsyth, R.J., Jarvis, S.N. and Parkinson, K.N. (2006) 'Participation of disabled children: how should it be characterised and measured?' *Disability and Rehabilitation*, 28 (18): 1157–64.

McLeod, S. (ed.) (2007a) *The International Guide to Speech Acquisition*, Clifton Park, NY: Thomson Delmar Learning.

McLeod, S. (2007b) 'Speech acquisition and participation in society', in J.E. Bernthal, N.W. Bankson and P. Flipson Jr (eds) *Articulation and Phonological Disorders: speech sound disorders in children*, 6th edn, Boston, MA: Pearson Education.

McNeil, C., Thomas, C., Maggs, B. and Taylor, S. (2003) *The Swindon Fluency Packs*, Swindon: Swindon Primary Care Trust.

MacNeill, V. (2009) 'Forming partnerships with parents from a community development perspective: lessons learnt from Sure Start', *Health and Social Care in the Community*, 17 (6): 659–65.

Madell, J.R. and Flexer, C.A. (2008) *Pediatric Audiology: diagnosis, technology, and management*, New York: Thieme.

Malcomess, K. (2005) 'The care aims model', in C. Anderson and A. van der Gaag (eds) *Speech and Language Therapy: issues in professional practice*, London: Whurr Publishers Ltd.

Manning, W. (2010) *Clinical Decision Making in Fluency Disorders*, 3rd edn, New York: Delmar, Cengage Learning.

Mars, M., Sell, D. and Habel, A. (2008) 'Introduction', in M. Mars, D. Sell and A. Habel (eds) *Management of Cleft Lip and Palate in the Developing World*, Chichester: John Wiley and Sons.

Marschark, M. and Spencer, P. (eds) (2010) *Oxford Handbook in Deaf Studies Vol. 2*, Oxford: Oxford University Press.

Marsh, K., Bertranou, E., Suominen, H. and Venkatachalam, M. (2010) *An Economic Evaluation of Speech and Language Therapy: final report*, London: Matrix Evidence.

Marshall, J., Goldbart, J. and Phillips, J. (2007) 'Parents' and speech and language therapists' explanatory models of language development, language delay and intervention', *International Journal of Language and Communication Disorders*, 42 (5): 533–53.

Martin, D. (2008) 'A new paradigm to inform inter-professional learning for integrating speech and language provision into secondary schools: a socio-cultural activity theory approach', *Child Language Teaching and Therapy*, 24 (2): 173–92.

Masarei, A.G., Wade, A., Mars, M., Sommerlad, B.C. and Sell, D. (2007) 'A randomised control trial investigating the effect of pre-surgical orthopaedics on feeding in infants with cleft lip and/or palate', *Cleft Palate-Craniofacial Journal*, 44 (3): 321–8.

Mason, S., Harris, G. and Blissett, J. (2005) 'Tube feeding in infancy: implications for the development of normal eating and drinking skills', *Dysphagia*, 20 (1): 46–61.

Mawhood, L., Howlin, P. and Rutter, M. (2000) 'Autism and developmental receptive language disorder: a comparative follow up in early adult life 1: cognitive and language outcomes', *Journal of Child Psychology and Psychiatry*, 41 (5): 547–59.

Meadow-Orlans, K.P., Spencer, P.E. and Koester, L.S. (2004) *The World of Deaf Infants*, New York: Oxford University Press.

Merrill, E.C., Lookadoo, R., Rilea, S. and Abbeduto, L. (eds) (2003) 'Memory, language and comprehension, and mental retardation', in L. Abbeduto and L.M. Glidden (eds) *Language and Communication in Mental Retardation* (International Review of Research in Mental Retardation, Vol. 27), Kidlington: Elsevier Ltd.

Miccio, A.W., Gallagher, E., Grossman, C.B., Yont, K.M. and Vernon-Feagans, L. (2001) 'Influence of chronic otitis media on phonological acquisition', *Clinical Linguistics and Phonetics*, 15 (1): 47–51.

Millard, S., Edwards, S. and Cook, F. (2009) 'Parent–child interaction therapy: adding to the evidence', *International Journal of Speech-Language Pathology*, 11 (1): 61–76.

Millard, S., Nicholas, A. and Cook, F. (2008) 'Is parent–child interaction therapy effective in reducing stuttering?' *Journal of Speech, Language and Hearing Research*, 51 (3): 636–50.

Mills, L., Gosling, A. and Sell, D. (2006) 'Extending the communication phenotype associated with 22q11.2 microdeletion syndrome', *Advances in Speech-Language Pathology*, 8 (1): 17–27.

Moeller, M.P. and Schick, B.S. (2006) 'Relations between maternal input and theory of mind understanding in deaf children', *Child Development*, 77 (3): 751–66.

Moon, J.A. (2005) *Reflection in Learning and Professional Development*, Abingdon: RoutledgeFalmer.

Moorey, M. and Mahon, M. (2002) 'Recognising hearing problems', in M. Kersner and J.A. Wright (eds) *Managing Communication Problems in Young Children*, 3rd edn, London: David Fulton Publishers.

Morris, C. (2001) 'Student supervision: risky business?' *International Journal of Language and Communication Disorders*, 36 (Supplement): 156–61.

Morris, S. and Klein, M. (2000) *Pre-Feeding Skills*, 2nd edn, Tuscon, AZ: Therapy Skill Builders.

Muter, V., Hulme, C. and Snowling, M. (1997) *Phonological Abilities Test (PAT)*, Oxford: Pearson Assessment.

Muter, V., Hulme, C., Snowling, M.J. and Stevenson, J. (2004) 'Phonemes, rimes, vocabulary, and grammatical skills as foundations of early reading development: evidence from a longitudinal study', *Developmental Psychology*, 40 (5): 665–81.

Myers-Scotton, C. (2002) *Contact Linguistics: bilingual encounters and grammatical outcomes*, Oxford: Oxford University Press.

Nash, P. (2006) 'The assessment and management of psychosocial aspects of reading and language impairments', in M. Snowling and J. Stackhouse (eds) *Dyslexia, Speech and Language: a practitioner's handbook*, 2nd edn, Chichester: John Wiley and Sons.

Nathan, L., Stackhouse, J., Goulandris, N. and Snowling, M. (2004) 'The development of early literacy skills among children with speech difficulties: a test of the "critical age hypothesis"', *Journal of Speech, Language, and Hearing Research*, 47 (2): 377–91.

National Early Literacy Project (2008) *Developing Early Literacy: report of the National Early Literacy Panel*, Washington, DC: National Institute for Literacy.

NIASA (National Initiative for Autism: Screening and Assessment) (2003) *National Autism Plan for Children*, London: National Autistic Society.

Nicholas, J. and Geers, A. (2007) 'Will they catch up? The role of age at cochlear implantation in the spoken language development of children with severe to profound hearing loss', *Journal of Speech, Language and Hearing Research*, 50 (4): 1048–62.

Nind, M. and Hewitt, D. (1994) *Access to Communication: developing the basics of communication with people with severe learning difficulties through intensive interaction*, London: David Fulton Publishers.

Olswang, L.B., Rodriguez, B. and Timler, G. (1998) 'Recommending intervention for toddlers with specific language learning difficulties: we may not have all the answers but we know a lot', *American Journal of Speech-Language Pathology*, 7 (1): 23–32.

Onslow, M., Packman, A. and Harrison, E. (2003) *The Lidcombe Program of Early Stuttering Intervention: a clinician's guide*, Austin, TX: Pro-Ed Inc.

Ozanne, A. (2005) 'Childhood apraxia of speech', in B. Dodd (ed.) *Differential Diagnosis and Treatment of Children with Speech Disorder*, London: Whurr Publishers Ltd.

Paediatric Stroke Working Group (2004) *Stroke in Childhood: clinical guidelines for diagnosis, management and rehabilitation*, London: Royal College of Physicians.

Pappas, N., McLeod, S., McAllister, L. and McKinnon, D. (2008) 'Parental involvement in speech intervention: a national survey', *Clinical Linguistics and Phonetics*, 22 (4): 335–44.

Paquier, P. and Van Dongen, H. (1995) 'Review of research on the clinical presentation of acquired childhood aphasia', *Acta Neurologica Scandinavica*, 93 (6): 428–36.

Park, K. (2002) *Objects of Reference in Practice and Theory*, London: SENSE.

Parker, A. (1999) *PETAL: phonological evaluation and transcription of audio-visual language*, Bicester: Winslow Press.

Parker, A. and Cummins, K. (1998) 'Group placements in under fives centres', *Speech and Language Therapy in Practice* (Winter), 13–15.

Parker, A. and Kersner, M. (1998) 'New approaches to learning on clinical placement', *International Journal of Language and Communication Disorders*, 33 (Supplement): 255–60.

Parkinson, G.M. (2002) 'High incidence of language disorder in children with focal epilepsies', *Developmental Medicine and Child Neurology*, 44 (8): 533–7.

Parsons, S., Law, J. and Gascoigne, M. (2005) 'Teaching receptive vocabulary to children with specific language impairment: a curriculum based approach', *Child Language Teaching and Therapy*, 21 (1): 39–59.

Paul, R. (1996) 'Clinical implications of the natural history of slow expressive language development', *American Journal of Speech-Language Pathology*, 5 (2): 5–21.

Paul, R. and Wilson, K.P. (2008) 'Assessing speech, language and communication in autism spectrum disorders', in S. Goldstein, J.A. Naglieri and S. Ozonoff (eds) *Assessment of Autism Spectrum Disorders*, London: Guilford Press.

Peña, E., Iglesias, A. and Lidz, C.S. (2001) 'Reducing test bias through dynamic assessment of children's word learning ability', *American Journal of Speech-Language Pathology*, 10 (2): 138–54.

Peña, E.D., Gillam, R.B., Malek, M., Ruiz-Felter, R., Fiestas, C. and Sabel, T. (2006) 'Dynamic assessment of school-age children's narrative ability: an experimental investigation of classification accuracy', *Journal of Speech, Language and Hearing Research*, 49 (5): 1037–57.

Pennington, B.F. and Bishop, D.V.M. (2009) 'Relations among speech, language, and reading disorders', *Annual Review of Psychology*, 60: 283–306.

Pennington, L., Marshall, J. and Goldbart, J. (2007) 'Describing participants in AAC research and their communicative environments: guidelines for research and practice', *Disability and Rehabilitation*, 29 (7): 521–35.

Pennington, L., Miller, N., Robson, S. and Steen, N. (2010) 'Intensive speech and language therapy for older children with cerebral palsy: a systems approach', *Developmental Medicine and Child Neurology*, 52 (4): 337–44.

Pennington, L., Thomson, K., Lamers, P., Martin, L. and McNully, R. (2009) 'Effects of "it takes two to talk": the Hanen Program for parents of preschool children with cerebral palsy: findings from an exploratory study', *Journal of Speech, Language and Hearing Research*, 52 (5): 1121–38.

Pepper, J. and Weitzman, E. (2004) *It Takes Two to Talk: a practical guide for parents of children with language delays*, 4th edn, Toronto: Hanen Centre.

Pert, S. and Letts, C. (2006) 'Codeswitching in Mirpuri speaking Pakistani heritage preschool children: bilingual language acquisition', *International Journal of Bilingualism*, 10 (3): 349–74.

Peterson, R.L., Pennington, B.F., Shriberg, L.D. and Boada, R. (2009) 'What influences literacy outcome in children with speech sound disorder?' *Journal of Speech, Language and Hearing Research*, 52 (5): 1175–88.

Phillips, B.M., Clancy-Menchetti, J. and Lonigan, C.J. (2008) 'Successful phonological awareness instruction with preschool children: lessons from the classroom', *Topics in Early Childhood Special Education*, 28 (1): 3–17.

Pickering, S. and Gathercole, S. (2001) *Working Memory Test Battery for Children (WMTB-C)*, Oxford: Pearson Assessment.

Prasse, J. and Kikano, G. (2009) 'An overview of pediatric dysphagia', *Clinical Pediatrics*, 48 (3): 247–51.

Preston, D. and Carter, M. (2009) 'A review of the efficacy of the picture exchange communication system intervention', *Journal of Autism and Developmental Disorders*, 39 (10): 1471–86.

Prochaska, J. and Di Clemente, C. (1986) 'Towards a comprehensive model of change', in W. Miller and N. Heather (eds) *Treating Addictive Behaviors*, New York: Plenum Press.

Raghavendra, P., Bornman, J., Granlund, M. and Bjorck-Akesson, E. (2007) 'The World Health Organization's International Classification of Functioning, Disability and Health: implications for clinical and research practice in the field of augmentative and alternative communication', *AAC: Augmentative and Alternative Communication*, 23 (4): 349–61.

Rance, G. and Barker, E.J. (2009) 'Speech and language outcomes in children with auditory neuropathy/dys-synchrony managed with either cochlear implants or hearing aids', *International Journal of Audiology*, 48 (6): 313–20.

Ratner, N.B. and Guitar, B. (2006) 'Treatment of very early stuttering and parent-administered therapy: the state of the art', in N.B. Ratner and J. Tetnowski (eds) *Current Issues in Stuttering Research and Practice*, Mahwah, NJ: Lawrence Erlbaum Associates Inc.

RCSLT (Royal College of Speech and Language Therapists) (2005) *Clinical Guidelines*, Milton Keynes: Speechmark Publishing Ltd.

RCSLT (Royal College of Speech and Language Therapists) (2006) *Communicating Quality 3*, 3rd edn, London: RCSLT.

RCSLT (Royal College of Speech and Language Therapists) (2007) *Speech and Language Therapy Competency Framework to Guide Transition to certified RCSLT Membership*. London: RCSLT.

RCSLT (Royal College of Speech and Language Therapists) (2010) *Resource Manual for Commissioning and Planning Services for Speech, Language and Communication Needs*, London: RCSLT.

Reed, P., Osborne, L.A. and Corness, M. (2007) 'Brief report: relative effectiveness of different home-based behavioural approaches to early teaching intervention', *Journal of Autism and Developmental Disorders*, 37 (9): 1815–21.

Rees, R. (2002a) 'Principles of psycholinguistic intervention', in J. Stackhouse and B. Wells (eds) *Children's Speech and Literacy Difficulties 2: identification and intervention*, London: Whurr Publishers.

Rees, R. (2002b) 'What do tasks really tap?' in J. Stackhouse and B. Wells (eds) *Children's Speech and Literacy Difficulties 2: identification and intervention*, London: Whurr Publishers Ltd.

Reilly, S., Douglas, J. and Oates, J. (2004) *Evidence Based Practice in Speech Pathology*, London: Whurr Publishers Ltd.

Reilly, S., Onslow, M., Packman, A., Wake, M., Bavin, E., Prior, M., Eadie, P., Cini, E., Bolzonello, C. and Ukoumunne, O. (2009) 'Predicting stuttering onset by the age of 3 years: a prospective, community cohorts study', *Pediatrics*, 123 (1): 270–7.

Reilly, S., Skuse, D. and Wolke, D. (2000) *Schedule for Oral Motor Assessment*, London: Whurr Publishers Ltd.

Renfrew, C. (2011a) *Action Picture Test*, revd edn, Milton Keynes: Speechmark Publishing Ltd.

Renfrew, C. (2011b) *Word Finding Vocabulary Test*, revd edn, Milton Keynes: Speechmark Publishing Ltd.

Rhyner, P.M., Haebig, E.K. and West, K. (2009) 'Understanding frameworks for the emergent literacy stage', in P. Rhyner (ed.) *Emergent Literacy and Early Language Acquisition: making the connection*, New York: Guilford Press.

Riddall-Leech, S. (2003) *Managing Children's Behaviour*, Oxford: Heinemann.

Rinaldi, W. (1992) *Social Use of Language Programme*, Windsor: NFER-Nelson.

Roach, E.S. (2000) 'Etiology of stroke in children', *Seminars in Pediatric Neurology*, 7 (4): 244–80.

Robinson, R.J. (1991) 'Causes and associations of severe and persistent specific speech and language disorders in children', *Developmental Medicine and Child Neurology*, 33 (11): 943–62.

Rogers, B. (2004) 'Feeding methods and health outcomes of children with cerebral palsy', *Journal of Pediatrics*, 145 (2) Supplement: S28–32.

Rogers, S.J. (2006) 'Evidence-based interventions for language development in young children with autism', in T. Charman and W. Stone (eds) *Social and Communication Development in Autism Spectrum Disorders*, London: Guilford Press.

Rogers-Adkinson, D. and Griffith, P.L. (1999) *Communication Disorders and Children with Psychiatric and Behavioural Disorders*, London: Singular Publishing.

Romaine, S. (1995) *Bilingualism*, 2nd edn, Oxford: Blackwell.

Rose, J. (2006) *Independent Review of the Teaching of Early Reading: final report*, Nottingham: DCSF.

Rose, J. (2009) *Identifying and Teaching Children and Young People with Dyslexia and Literacy Difficulties*, Nottingham: DCSF.

Roulstone, S. (1997) 'What's driving you? A template which underpins the assessment of pre-school children by speech and language therapists', *European Journal of Disorders of Communication*, 32 (3): 299–315.

Roulstone, S., Peters, T.J., Glogowska, M. and Enderby, P. (2003) 'A 12-month follow-up of preschool children investigating the natural history of speech and language delay', *Child: Care, Health and Development*, 29 (4): 245–55.

Round, S. and Beazley, S. (2010) 'Launching and sustaining an evidence-based specialist service', in H. Roddam and J. Skeat (eds) *Implementing Research Evidence in Speech-Language Pathology Practice: clinical perspectives* Chichester: John Wiley and Sons.

Russell, J. and Harding, A. (2001) 'Speech development and early intervention', in A.C.H. Watson, D. Sell and P. Grunwell (eds) *Management of Cleft Lip and Palate*, Chichester: John Wiley and Sons.

Russell, V.J. and Albery, E. (2005) *Practical Intervention for Cleft Palate Speech*, Milton Keynes: Speechmark Publishing Ltd.

Rustin, L. and Kuhr, A. (1999) *Social Skills and the Speech Impaired*, 2nd edn, London: Whurr Publishers Ltd.

Rustin, L., Botterill, W. and Kelman, E. (1996) *Assessment and Therapy for Young Dysfluent Children*, London: Whurr Publishers Ltd.

Rustin, L., Cook, F., Botterill, W., Hughes, C. and Kelman, E. (2001) *Stammering: a practical guide for teachers and other professionals*, London: David Fulton Publishers.

Rutter, M., Bailey, A. and Lord, C. (2003) *Social Communication Questionnaire*, Los Angeles, CA: Western Psychological Services.

Rutter, M., LeCouteur, A. and Lord, C. (2003) *Autism Diagnostic Interview: revised*, Los Angeles, CA: Western Psychological Services.

Sackett, D.L., Rosenberg, W.M.C., Muir-Gray, J.A., Haynes, R.B. and Scott-Richardson, W. (1996) 'Evidence based medicine: what it is and what it isn't', *British Medical Journal*, 312 (7023): 71–2.

Safeguarding Vulnerable Groups Act (2006) London: HMSO.

Sanders, P. (2002) *First Steps in Counselling: a student's companion for basic introductory courses*, 3rd edn, Ross on Wye: PCCS Books.

Schlosser, R. (2000) *The Efficacy of Augmentative and Alternative Communication*, Boston, MA: Academic Press.

Schlosser, R. (2003) 'Roles of speech output in AAC: narrative review', *AAC: Augmentative and Alternative Communication*, 19 (1): 5–28.

Schon, D.A (1983) *The Reflective Practitioner: how professionals think in action*, London: Maurice Temple Smith.

Schuel, C.M. and Boudreau, D. (2008) 'Phonological awareness intervention: beyond the basics', *Language, Speech and Hearing Services in Schools*, 39 (1): 3–20.

Schwartz, R.G. (2009) *Handbook of Child Language Disorders*, New York: Psychology Press.

Scott, A., Pearce, D. and Goldblatt, P. (2001) *Population Trends: the sizes and characteristics of the minority: ethnic populations of Great Britain: latest estimates*, London: Office for National Statistics.

Secord, W., Semel, E. and Wiig, E.H. (2006) *Clinical Evaluation of Language Fundamentals: preschool 2 UK*, Oxford: Pearson Assessment.

Seeff-Gabriel, B., Chiat, S. and Roy, P. (2008) *Early Repetition Battery (ERB)*, Oxford: Pearson Assessment.

Sell, D. and Pereira, V. (2011) 'Instrumental/speech imaging to analyse structure and function', in S. Howard and A. Lohmander (eds) *Cleft Lip and Palate: speech assessment, analysis and intervention*, Chichester: John Wiley and Sons.

Sell, D., Harding, A. and Grunwell, P. (1999) 'Revised GOS.SP.ASS (98): speech assessment for children with cleft palate and/or velopharyngeal dysfunction', *International Journal of Disorders of Communication*, 34 (1): 17–33.

Sell, D., John, A., Harding-Bell, A., Sweeney, T., Hegarty, F. and Freeman, J. (2009) 'Cleft audit protocol for speech (CAPS-A): a comprehensive training package for speech analysis', *International Journal of Language and Communication Disorders*, 44 (4): 529–48.

Sell, D., Mars, M. and Worrell, E. (2006) 'A process and outcome study of prosthetic treatment for velopharyngeal dysfunction', *International Journal of Language and Communication Disorders*, 41 (5): 495–511.

Semel, E., Wiig, E.H. and Secord, W. (2005) *Clinical Evaluation of Language Fundamentals (CELF-4) (Spanish)*, San Antonio, TX: Psychological Corporation.

Shewell, C. (2009) *Voicework: art and science in changing voices*, Chichester: Wiley-Blackwell.

Shriberg, L.D. and Campbell, T.F. (eds) (2002) 'Proceedings of the 2002 childhood apraxia of speech research symposium', Hendrix Foundation, Carlsbad, CA.

Sigafoos, J., Woodyatt, G., Keen, D., Tait, K., Tucker, M., Roberta-Pennell, D. and Pittendreigh, N. (2000) 'Inventory of potential communicative acts: identification of potential communicative acts in children with developmental and physical disabilities', *Communication Disorders Quarterly*, 21 (2): 77–86.

Simkin, Z. and Conti-Ramsden, G.M. (2006) 'Evidence of reading difficulty in subgroups of children with specific language impairment', *Child Language Teaching and Therapy*, 22 (3): 315–31.

Simonoff, E., Pickles, A., Charman, T., Chandler, S., Loucas, T. and Baird, G. (2008) 'Psychiatric disorders in children with autism spectrum disorders: prevalence, co-morbidity, and associated factors in a population-derived sample', *Journal of the American Academy of Child and Adolescent Psychiatry*, 47 (8): 921–9.

Sivyer, S. (1999) 'Listening and quietness and making new friends', *RCSLT Bulletin*, 570: 13–15.

Skeat, J. and Roddam, H. (2010) 'The role of reflective practice in supporting EBP', in J. Skeat and H. Roddam (eds) *Embedding Evidence-based Practice in Speech and Language Therapy*, Chichester: Wiley-Blackwell.

Skuse, D., Warrington, R., Bishop, D., Chowdhury, U., Lau, J., Mandy, W. and Place, M. (2004) 'The developmental, dimensional and diagnostic interview (3di): a novel computerized assessment for autism spectrum disorders', *Journal of the American Academy of Child and Adolescent Psychiatry*, 43 (5): 548–58.

Sleigh, G. (2005) 'Mothers' voice: a qualitative study on feeding children with cerebral palsy', *Child: Care, Health and Development*, 31 (4): 373–83.

SLI consortium (2002) 'A genome wide scan identifies two novel loci involved in specific language impairment', *American Journal of Human Genetics*, 70 (2): 384–98.

SLI consortium (2004) 'Highly significant linkage to the SLI1 locus in an expanded sample of individuals affected by specific language impairment', *American Journal of Human Genetics*, 74 (6): 1225–38.

Smith, A. and Inder, P. (1993) 'Social interaction in same and cross gender pre-school peer groups: a participant observation study', *Educational Psychology*, 13 (1): 29–42.

Snowling, M., Stothard, S. and McClean, J. (1996) *Graded Non-word Reading Test*, Bury St Edmonds: Thames Valley Test Company.

Snowling, M.J. and Stackhouse, J. (eds) (2006) *Dyslexia, Speech and Language: a practitioner's handbook*, 2nd edn, Chichester: John Wiley and Sons.

Soto, G. and Zangari, C. (2009) *Practically Speaking: language, literacy, and academic development for students with AAC needs*, Baltimore, MD: Paul H. Brookes Publishing Co.

Spencer, P. and Harris, M. (2006) 'Patterns and effects of language input to deaf infants and toddlers from deaf and hearing mothers', in M. Marshark and P. Spencer (eds) *Advances in the Sign Language Development of Deaf Children*, New York: Oxford University Press.

Stackhouse, J. and Pascoe, M. (2010) 'Psycholinguistic intervention', in A.L. Williams, S. McLeod and R.J. McCauley (eds) *Interventions for Speech Sound Disorders in Children*, Baltimore, MD: Paul H. Brookes Publishing Co.

Stackhouse, J. and Wells, B. (1997) *Children's Speech and Literacy Difficulties 1: a psycholinguistic framework*, London: Whurr Publishers Ltd.

Stackhouse, J., Vance, M., Pascoe, M. and Wells, B. (2007) *Compendium of Auditory and Speech Tasks*, Chichester: John Wiley and Sons.

Starkweather, C.W. and Gottwald, S.R. (1990) 'The demands and capacities model: II clinical implications', *Journal of Fluency Disorders*, 15: 143–157.

Stewart, T. and Turnbull, J. (2007) *Working with Dysfluent Children: practical approaches to assessment and therapy*, revd edn, Milton Keynes: Speechmark Publishing Ltd.

Stoel-Gammon, C. and Vogel Sosa, A. (2010) 'Phonological development', in E. Hoff and M. Shatz (eds) *Blackwell Handbook of Language Development*, Chichester: Wiley-Blackwell.

Stothard, S.E., Snowling, M.J., Bishop, D.V.M., Chipchase, B.B. and Kaplan, C.A. (1998) 'Language impaired preschoolers: a follow up into adolescence', *Journal of Speech, Language and Hearing Research*, 41 (2): 407–18.

Stow, C. and Dodd, B. (2003) 'Providing an equitable service to bilingual children in the UK: a review', *International Journal of Language and Communication Disorders*, 38 (4): 351–77.

Stow, C. and Pert, S. (1998) *The Rochdale Assessment of Mirpuri Phonology with Punjabi, Urdu and English*, Rochdale: Pert.

Striano, T., Chen, X., Cleveland, A. and Bradshaw, S. (2006) 'Joint attention social cues influence infant learning', *European Journal of Developmental Psychology*, 3 (3): 289–99.

Stringer, H. (2010) 'What is evidence-based practice?' *Bulletin RCSLT*, 699: 22–3.

Stringer, H. and Clegg, J. (2006) 'Language, behaviour and social disadvantage', in J. Clegg and J. Ginsborg (eds) *Language and Social Disadvantage*, Chichester: John Wiley and Sons.

Sullivan, P., Lambert, B., Rose, M., Ford-Adams, M., Johnson, A. and Griffiths, P. (2002) 'Prevalence and severity of feeding and nutritional problems in children with neurological impairment: Oxford feeding study', *Developmental Medicine and Child Neurology*, 42 (10): 674–80.

Sullivan, P.B., Juszczak, E., Bachlet, A.M., Thomas, A.G., Lambert, B., Vernon-Roberts, A., Grant, H.W., Eltumi, M., Alder, N. and Jenkinson, C. (2004) 'Impact of gastrostomy tube feeding on the quality of life of carers of children with cerebral palsy', *Developmental Medicine and Child Neurology*, 46 (12): 796–800.

Sutherland, D. and Gillon, G.T. (2005) 'Assessment of phonological representations in children with speech impairment', *Language, Speech and Hearing Services in Schools*, 36 (4): 294–307.

Sweeney, T. (2011) 'Nasality: assessment and intervention', in S. Howard and A. Lohmander (eds) *Cleft Lip and Palate: speech assessment and intervention*, Chichester: John Wiley and Sons.

Tager-Flusberg, H., Rogers, S., Cooper, J., Landa, R., Lord, C., Paul, R., Rice, M., Stoel-Gammon, C., Wetherby, A. and Yoder, P. (2009) 'Defining spoken language benchmarks and selecting measures of expressive language development for young children with autism spectrum disorders', *Journal of Speech, Language, and Hearing Research*, 52 (3): 643–52.

Teoh, A.P. and Chin, S.B. (2009) 'Transcribing the speech of children with cochlear implants: clinical application of narrow transcriptions', *American Journal of Speech-Language Pathology*, 18 (4): 388–401.

Throneburg, R., Calvert, L., Sturm, J., Paramboukas, A. and Paul, P. (2000) 'A comparison of service delivery models: effects on curricular vocabulary skills in the school setting', *American Journal of Speech-Language Pathology*, 9 (1): 10–20.

Tollerfield, I. (2003) 'The process of collaboration within a special school setting: an exploration of the ways in which skills and knowledge are shared and barriers overcome when a teacher and speech and language therapist collaborate', *Child Language Teaching and Therapy*, 19 (1): 67–84.

Tomblin, J.B. (2008) 'Validating diagnostic standards for specific language impairment using adolescent outcomes', in C.F. Norbury, J.B. Tomblin and D.V.M. Bishop (eds) *Understanding Developmental Language Disorders: from theory to practice*, Hove: Psychology Press.

Tomblin, J.B. and Buckwalter, P.R. (1998) 'Heritability of poor language achievement among twins', *Journal of Speech and Hearing Disorders*, 54 (2): 287–95.

Tomblin, J.B., Records, N.L., Buckwalter, P., Zhang, X., Smith, E. and O'Brien, M. (1997) 'Prevalence of specific language impairment in kindergarten children', *Journal of Speech and Hearing Research*, 40 (6): 1245–60.

Topping, C., Gascoigne, M. and Cook, M. (1998) 'Excellence for all children: a redefinition of the role of the speech and language therapist', *International Journal of Language and Communication Disorders*, 33 (Supplement): 608–13.

Topping, K.J. (1995) *Paired Reading, Spelling and Writing: the handbook for teachers and parents*, London: Cassell Education.

Tuckman, B. (1965) 'Developmental sequence in small groups', *Psychological Bulletin*, 63 (6): 384–99.

Ullman, M.T. and Pierpont, E.I. (2005) 'SLI is not specific to language: the procedural deficit hypothesis', *Cortex*, 41 (3): 399–433.

van Balkom, H., Verhoeven, L. and van Weerdenburg, M. (2010) 'Conversational behaviour of children with developmental language delay and their caretakers', *International Journal of Language and Communication Disorders*, 45 (3): 295–319.

van Bysterveldt, A., Gillon, G. and Foster-Cohen, S. (2010) 'Integrated speech and phonological awareness intervention for pre-school children with Down syndrome', *International Journal of Language and Communication Disorders*, 45 (3): 320–35.

van der Gaag, A., McCartan, P., McDade, A., Reid, D. and Roulstone, S. (1999) *The Early Communication Audit Manual*, London: RCSLT.

Van Der Meer, L.A.J. and Rispoli, M. (2010) 'Communication interventions involving speech-generating devices for children with autism: a review of the literature', *Developmental Neurorehabilitation*, 13 (4): 294–306.

Van Dongen, H.R., Paquier, P.F., Creten, W.L., Borsel, J. and Catsman-Berrevoets, C.E. (2001) 'Clinical evaluation of conversational speech fluency in the acute phase of acquired childhood aphasia: does a fluency/nonfluency dichotomy exist?' *Journal of Child Neurology*, 16 (5): 345–51.

Van Slyke, P.A. (2002) 'Classroom instruction for children with Landau-Kleffner Syndrome', *Child Language Teaching and Therapy*, 18 (1): 23–42.

Vance, M. (1991) 'Educational and therapeutic approaches used with a child with acquired aphasia with convulsive disorder (Landau-Kleffner Syndrome)', *Child Language Teaching and Therapy*, 7 (1): 41–60.

Vance, M. (1997) 'Christopher Lumpship: developing phonological representations in a child with an auditory processing deficit', in S. Chiat, J. Law and J. Marshall (eds) *Language Disorders in Children and Adults*, London: Whurr Publishers Ltd.

Vernon-Roberts, A. and Sullivan, P. (2007) 'Fundoplication versus post-operative medication for gastro-oesophageal reflux in children with neurological impairment undergoing gastrostomy', *Cochrane Database of Systematic Reviews*. Online, available at: www.cochrane.org.

Virues-Ortega, J. (2010) 'Applied behaviour analytic intervention for autism in early childhood: meta-analysis, meta-regression and dose-response meta-analysis of multiple outcomes', *Clinical Psychology Review*, 30 (4): 387–99.

von Tetzchner, S. and Martinsen, H. (2000) *Introduction to Augmentative and Alternative Communication*, London: Whurr Publishers Ltd.

Ward, D. (2006) *Stuttering and Cluttering: frameworks for understanding and treatment*, Hove: Psychology Press.

Washington, K.N. (2007) 'Using the ICF within speech-language pathology: application to developmental language impairment', *International Journal of Speech-Language Pathology*, 9 (3): 242–55.

Webster-Stratton, C. (2005) *The Incredible Years: a trouble-shooting guide for parents of children aged 2–8 years*, Seattle, WA: Incredible Years.

West, J. and Redstone, F. (2004) 'Alignment in feeding and swallowing: does it matter? A review', *Perceptual Motor Skills*, 98 (1): 349–58.

Wetherby, A.M. and Prizant, B.M. (2002) *Communication and Symbolic Behavior Scales Developmental Profile*, Baltimore, MD: Paul H. Brookes Publishing Co.

Wheeler, A., Archbold, S., Gregory, S. and Skipp, A. (2007) 'Cochlear implants: the young people's perspective', *Journal of Deaf Studies and Deaf Education*, 12 (3): 303–16.

Whitehurst, G.J. and Fischel, J.E. (1994) 'Practitioner review, early developmental language delay: what, if anything, should the clinician do about it?' *Journal of Child Psychology and Psychiatry*, 35 (4): 613–48.

WHO (World Health Organisation) (1993a) *International Classification of Diseases-10 (ICF-10)*, Geneva: WHO.

WHO (World Health Organisation) (1993b) *The ICD-10 Classification for Mental and Behavioural Disorders: diagnostic criteria for research*, Geneva: WHO.

WHO (World Health Organisation) (1994) *The ICD-10 Classification of Mental and Behavioural Disorders: clinical descriptions and diagnostic guidelines*, Geneva: WHO.

WHO (World Health Organisation) (2001) *The International Classification of Functioning, Disability and Health (ICF)*, Geneva: WHO.

WHO (World Health Organisation) (2006) *ICF: International Classification of Functioning, Disability and Health*, Geneva: WHO.

WHO (World Health Organisation) (2007) *International Classification of Functioning, Disability and Health for Children and Youth (ICF-CY)*, Geneva: WHO.

Wiig, E.H. and Semel, E. (2006) *Clinical Evaluation of Language Fundamentals*, 4th edn, UK, Oxford: Pearson Assessment.

Wiig, E.H., Secord, W. and Semel, E. (2000) *CELF-Preschool UK*, London: Psychological Corporation.

Williams, A.L., McLeod, S. and McCauley, R.J. (eds) (2010) *Interventions for Speech Sound Disorders in Children*, Baltimore, MD: Paul H. Brookes Publishing Co.

Williams, K.R. (2006) 'The Son-Rise Program intervention for autism', *Sage Publications and The National Autistic Society*, 10 (1): 86–102.

Williams, P. and Stevens, H. (2010) 'The Nuffield Dyspraxia Programme', in L. Williams, S. McLeod and R. McCauley (eds) *Interventions for Speech Sound Disorders in Children*, Baltimore, MD: Paul H. Brookes Publishing Co.

Wing, L. and Gould, J. (2011) *Diagnostic Interview for Social and Communication Disorders*, London: National Autistic Society.

Winstock, A. (2005) *Eating and Drinking Difficulties in Children: a guide for practitioners*, 2nd edn, Milton Keynes: Speechmark Publishing Ltd.

Winter, R. and Baraitser, M. (1998) *London Dismorphology Database*, Oxford: Oxford University Press.

Wintgens, A. (2002) 'Links between emotional/behavioural problems and communication difficulties', in M. Kersner and J.A. Wright (eds) *How To Manage Communication Problems in Young Children*, 3rd edn, London: David Fulton Publishers.

Wolf, M. and Bowers, P. (1999) 'The double deficit hypothesis for the developmental dyslexias', *Journal of Educational Psychology*, 9 (3): 415–38.

Woll, B. (2010) 'The deaf brain', British Association of the Deaf (BATOD) magazine, *Communicating Clearly Together*.

Woodhouse, L., Hickson, L. and Dodd, B. (2009) 'Review of visual speech perception by hearing and hearing-impaired people: clinical implications', *International Journal of Language and Communication Disorders*, 44 (3): 253–70.

Wren, Y., Roulstone, S. and Williams, A.L. (2010) 'Computer-based interventions', in A.L. Williams, S. McLeod and R.J. McCauley (eds) *Interventions for Speech Sound Disorders in Children*, Baltimore, MD: Paul H. Brookes Publishing Co.

Wren, Y. (2003) 'Using scenarios to evaluate a professional development programme for teaching staff', *Child Language Teaching and Therapy*, 19 (2): 116–34.

Wright, J.A. (1996) 'Teachers and therapists: the evolution of a partnership', *Child Language Teaching and Therapy*, 12 (1): 3–16.

Wright, J.A. and Kersner, M. (2009) *A Career in Speech and Language Therapy*, 2nd edn, London: Metacom Education.

Wright, J.A., Newton, C., Clarke, M., Donlan, C., Lister, C. and Cherguit, J. (2006) 'Communication aids in the classroom: the views of education staff and speech and language therapists involved with the Communication Aids Project (CAP)', *British Journal of Special Education*, 33 (1): 25–32.

Wright, J.A., Stackhouse, J. and Wood, J. (2008) 'Promoting language and literacy skills in the early years: lessons from interdisciplinary teaching and reading', *Child Language Teaching and Therapy*, 24 (2): 155–71.

Yairi, E. and Ambrose, N. (2005) *Early Childhood Stuttering: for clinicians by clinicians*, Austin, TX: Pro-Ed.

Yalom, I.D. (2005) *The Theory and Practice of Group Psychotherapy*, 5th edn, New York: Basic Books.

Yaruss, J.S. and Quesal, R.W. (2011) *Overall Assessment of the Speaker's Experience of Stuttering (OASES)*, San Antonio, TX: Pearson.

Yaruss, J.S., Coleman, C. and Hammer, D. (2006) 'Treating pre-school children who stutter: description and preliminary evaluation of a family-focussed treatment approach', *Language, Speech and Hearing Services in Schools*, 37 (2): 118–36.

Yoder, P.J. and Warren, S.F. (2001) 'Relative treatment effects of two prelinguistic communication interventions on language development in toddlers with developmental delays vary by maternal characteristic', *Journal of Speech Language Hearing Research*, 44 (1): 224–37.

Young, A.M., Carr, G., Hunt, R., McCracken, W., Skipp, A. and Tattersall, H. (2006) 'Informed choice and deaf children: underpinning concepts and enduring challenges', *Journal of Deaf Studies and Deaf Education*, 11(3): 322–36.

Zampini, L. and D'Odorico, L. (2009) 'Communicative gestures and vocabulary in 36 month old children with Down's syndrome', *International Journal of Language and Communication Disorders*, 44 (6): 1063–74.

Zens, K., Gillon, G.T. and Moran, C. (2009) 'Effects of phonological awareness and semantic intervention on word-learning in children with SLI', *International Journal of Speech-Language Pathology*, 11 (6): 509–24.

Zhu Hua and Dodd, B. (eds) (2005) *Phonological Development and Disorders in Children: a cross-linguistic perspective*, Bristol: Multilingual Matters.

Zimmerman, I.L, Pond, R.E and Steiner, V.G. (2009) *Preschool Language Scale (PLS-4^{UK})*, 4th edn, Oxford: Pearson Assessment.

Zwaigenbaum, L., Bryson, S., Lord, C., Rogers, S., Carter, A., Carver, L., Chawarska, K., Contantino, J., Dawson, G., Dobkins, K., Fein, D., Iverson, J., Klin, A., Landa, R., Messinger, D., Ozonoff, S., Sigman, M., Stone, W., Tager-Flusberg, H. and Yirmiya, N. (2009) 'Clinical assessment and management of toddlers with suspected autism spectrum disorder: insights from studies of high-risk infants', *Pediatrics*, 123 (5): 1383–91.

Index